Richard Collier was born in London in 1924, and educated at Whitgift School, Croydon. By the age of twenty-two he had already served as a war correspondent in the Far East, where he was also employed on counter-espionage, and had gone on to become editor of *Town and Country* magazine. He has travelled through thirty-six countries gathering material for his books. His work includes *Ten Thousand Eyes*, *The Sands of Dunkirk*, *The General Next to God*, *Eagle Day* and *Duce!*

Richard Collier is married and lives in Surrey.

1940

The World in Flames

Richard Collier

Penguin Books

Penguin Books Ltd, Harmondsworth,
Middlesex, England
Penguin Books, 625 Madison Avenue,
New York, New York 10022, U.S.A.
Penguin Books Australia Ltd, Ringwood,
Victoria, Australia
Penguin Books Canada Ltd, 2801 John Street,
Markham, Ontario, Canada L3R 1B4
Penguin Books (N.Z.) Ltd, 182–190 Wairau Road,
Auckland 10, New Zealand

First published by Hamish Hamilton Ltd 1979
Published in Penguin Books 1980
Reprinted 1980

Set, printed and bound in Great Britain by
Cox & Wyman Ltd, Reading
Set in Intertype Times

Alas, yes! a whole world to remake ... For all is wrong, and gone out of joint; the inward spiritual and the outward economical; head or heart, there is no soundness in it. As indeed, evils of all sorts are more or less of kin and do usually go together: especially it is an old truth that wherever huge physical evil is there, as the parent and origin of it, has moral evil to a proportionate extent been.

Thomas Carlyle, *The French Revolution*

Contents

Illustrations

Sources of Illustrations

1a Paul Popper   1b Keystone

2a Erik Seidenfaden   2b Keystone

3a Mrs Drysdale   3b Theodor Broch   3c Keystone

4 Central Press

5a Camera Press   5b Central Press

6 Mirrorpic

7a Imperial War Museum   7b Central Press

8 Keystone

1

'A Shabby and Dangerous Place . . .'

1 January–16 February 1940

The Oval Office of the White House was silent. The President was writing intently; only the scratch of his pen broke the stillness. Smoke from a forgotten cigarette spiralled upwards in the desk light; the flags hung limp on the mahogany standards. In a bold vertical hand, the President was drafting his eighth State of the Union message. 'It becomes clearer and clearer,' he wrote, 'that the future world will be a shabby and dangerous place to live in – yes, even for Americans to live in – if it is ruled by force in the hands of a few . . .'

Thus, on 1 January 1940, in Washington, D.C., the thirty-second President of the United States, Franklin Delano Roosevelt, prepared himself for the arduous months stretching ahead: the burden of operating a vast peaceable democracy in a war-gripped world, the problem of holding together his 'New Deal', the now-sagging social welfare programme which he had inaugurated back in 1933, the vexed question of whether he should become the first President in American history to seek election for a Third Term.

They were challenges which Roosevelt would face as squarely as he had faced the polio attack which for the past nineteen years had confined him to a wheelchair. Already, on 23 December 1939, with the Second World War 120 days old and Germany's twenty-six day conquest of Poland an established fact, the President had written to Pope Pius XII in Rome to explore the prospects for world peace. Prompted by the Book of Isaiah, he had spoken of a time like the present, when 'nations walked dangerously in the light of the fires they had themselves kindled'.

11

For the first time since 1868, a personal presidential representative had been appointed to the Vatican: Myron Charles Taylor, 65-year-old retired head of the United States Steel Corporation. Along with him as Roosevelt's envoy extraordinary, would journey U.S. Under Secretary of State Sumner Welles, on a fact-finding mission to sound out the statesmen of Europe. 'If Welles' visit delays an offensive by the Germans, or even prevents it,' Roosevelt summed up to the State Department's Breckinridge Long, 'that will help Britain and France buy time.'

Time was now of the essence. On 3 January, Roosevelt was to warn a joint session of Congress of 'the vicious, ruthless, destructive' forces that were abroad in the world – and demand of them a mountainous $2,309,445,246 to maintain the greatest peacetime military force America had ever known. Not for the first time he made his stance crystal-clear: 'There is a vast difference between keeping out of war and pretending war is none of our business.'

It was an issue on which Roosevelt and countless million American isolationists were deeply at odds. Many shared the view of their idol, the aviator Colonel Charles A. Lindbergh: 'The wars in Europe are not wars in which our civilization is defending itself against some Asiatic intruder. There is no Genghis Khan or Xerxes marching against our Western nations.' Few of them had ever forgiven Britain and France, their one-time allies, for reneging on their debts after the First World War, while even committed New Dealers feared that any preparations for war would forfeit the social gains made by labour since Roosevelt took office. Others were deeply disillusioned with all things European. All through the 1930s Britain and France had shown little more than a rare talent for appeasement, standing tamely on the sidelines while Germany swallowed up Austria and Czechoslovakia and Italy ravaged first Ethiopia, then Albania. How staunch would such faint-hearts prove as allies when the chips were down?

'U.S. citizens,' noted the financier Bernard Baruch in his diary, 'seem to have washed their hands of all concern in Europe,' a phenomenon confirmed by the British Ambassador in Washington, Lord Lothian. 'Their moral preparedness is about that of England in the Baldwin* period,' he wrote to the Minister for the Coordination of Defence, Lord Chatfield. Responded Chatfield cynically: 'They will ... fight the battle for freedom and democracy to the last Briton ... Can we blame them?'

But for millions of Americans, fighting was the last thing they had in mind. Eight hundred miles south of Washington, Miami Beach, Florida, was in hothouse bloom, the giddiest, gaudiest season since the Wall Street crash of 1929. Lots on Lincoln Road, the plush shopping street, were fetching $50,000 apiece; the yachts and cruisers in harbour included the *Virago*, lately chartered by the millionaire J. P. Morgan. The actress Nancy Carroll was in town, along with fashionable hatter Lilly Daché and the couturier Hattie Carnegie. Columnists noted that a new arrival was Alfred Ilko Barton, a Philadelphia socialite who taught the new-rich how to be lavish with their money.

For the moment at least, Franklin Roosevelt, bound and gagged by laggard public opinion, must bide his time. Still unresolved was the question: if the 'vicious, ruthless, destructive forces' were to triumph, what would the United States be called upon to do?

More than 3,000 miles closer to the war front, the same indifference to war prevailed. 'The French nation,' one Frenchman wrote, 'has gone to war looking over its shoulder, its eyes searching for peace.' Opinion polls placed the Premier, Edouard Daladier, as more popular than either Joan of Arc or Napoleon: despite shortages, he still made gasoline available for spins in the Bois de Boulogne or to the racecourse at Longchamps. The phrase of the day was *Il faut en finir* (We've got to stop it), a resolute motto, embroidered on chiffon handkerchiefs or inscribed on gold charm bracelets, but the reality was a staggering unconcern. In this *drôle de guerre*, bored boulevardiers checked their watches by the air-raid sirens, tested punctually each Thursday at noon, and the most chic gift of the day reduced all war to mockery: terracotta dogs lifting their legs over terracotta copies of *Mein Kampf*.

In Berlin, the author of *Mein Kampf*, Adolf Hitler, Führer

---

* Stanley Baldwin (1st Earl Baldwin of Bewdley, 1867–1947), three times British Premier between 1923 and 1937, had been an early exponent of appeasement.

and Chancellor of the Third Reich, seemed the one man still determined to prosecute the war to the utmost. If Germany secured Holland and Belgium, he maintained, their airfields could be used to deal Great Britain a lethal blow – a projected offensive against the west which his generals had opposed strenuously and in vain for three months now. But although the coldest European winter in forty-six years had mired down both tanks and aircraft, Hitler would not be deflected. After 9 October, when the British had rejected his first peace offer, he declared angrily, 'They will be ready to talk only after a beating.'

Few Germans shared his enthusiasm. After twenty years in the economic wringer, including seven of building the world's most streamlined military machine, few civilians had reaped much personal benefit. The seventy million Germans outside the armed forces saw meat and butter no more than twice a week. Because of fuel shortages, they enjoyed hot water only at week-ends, and subsisted on a poorhouse diet of stuffed cabbage or boiled potatoes with onion sauce. Even diners-out were beset by loudspeakers barking, 'Achtung! This is the kitchen speaking. There is no more veal.'

Reflecting this disillusion, New Year's Day 1940 had seen more drunks on Berlin's fashionable Kurfürstendamm than at any time in living memory. Even Dr Josef Göbbels, Hitler's club-footed Minister for Propaganda and Enlightenment, confided to an American newsman: 'The average German feels [about the war] like a man with chronic toothache – the sooner it is out the better.'

In blacked-out England, where the cost of the conflict was running at $24 million a day, the American naval attaché in London noted the same 'undercurrent of distaste and apathy for the whole war'. Three million Londoners, among them 1,500,000 evacuee children and their mothers, had left the capital, but though the British would be rationed, from 8 January, to four ounces of bacon weekly, four of butter and twelve of sugar, they still chose to make light of it. Things, they joked, were 'so quiet you could hear a Ribbentrop'.* Forty-three

---

* Joachim von Ribbentrop, Germany's Foreign Minister, and Ambassador to Britain from 1936–8 had aroused ridicule for greeting King George VI with the Nazi salute.

theatres were open and doing land-office business, among them The Globe with the young John Gielgud in *The Importance of Being Earnest*, for above all Londoners sought to banish the war with a laugh. The lament of a Cockney evacuee in the revue *Lights Up!* caught the mood of the day:

I didn't really never ought 'ave went;
In London I was really quite content.
I wouldn't have been windy with the planes up overhead,
Talk of blinkin' aeroplanes, you should have heard what Father said
They couldn't hit the Forth Bridge, let alone small boys in bed.
No, I didn't really never ought 'ave went.

Most Britons were hoping, like their Tory Premier, Neville Chamberlain, not for a military victory but for 'a collapse of the German home front', though a surprising number went further than that. On 8 January, a memorandum to Chamberlain, drawn up by ten members of the House of Lords, urged the Premier: 'It is now widely felt that, on a long view, the weakening or dismemberment of Germany would destroy the natural barrier against the Western march of Bolshevism. We would suggest to you that this is a strong reason in favour of an early peace.' The same feeling was rife in less august circles: Ministry of Information poll-takers estimated that four million Britons would settle for peace at any price.

Did Chamberlain and the First Lord of the Admiralty, Winston Churchill, really own shares in the German armaments firm of Krupp, as the American columnist Drew Pearson alleged? Few Britons showed concern either way.

To be sure, the British had taken precautions – 'just in case'. The National Gallery's director, Kenneth (later Lord) Clark, had seen almost 3,000 pictures off to Penrhyn Castle, near Bangor, North Wales. (Later, for greater safety, they were transferred to a disused slate quarry at Manod, thirty-five miles north.) Most of the British Museum's treasures were also in Wales, in an underground air-conditioned tunnel in Aberystwyth. At London's Regent's Park Zoo, all poisonous snakes had been humanely killed off, to prevent them from getting loose in air raids – but would air raids ever come to pass?

Above all, the British felt an acute sense of anti-climax. For four long months they had been geared for Armageddon. Now, in a winter that had brought twenty-five degrees of frost, they faced only burst water pipes, a chronic coal shortage and a black-out that had plunged the United Kingdom into the pitch darkness of the seventeenth century. As January dawned, the black-out, with its thirty-three deaths a day, was taking more toll than the war, and Britons wanted it to stay that way.

The Secretary of State for Air, Sir Kingsley Wood, mirrored perfectly the mood of a war in which as yet neither ally was minded to strike a mortal blow. Urged to bomb the Black Forest and ravage Germany's timber supplies, the little man replied, outraged: 'Are you aware it is private property? Why, you will be asking me to bomb Essen next!'

On 24 August 1939, one week before the German panzer divisions lanced into Poland, the 90/20 Horse Company of the 2nd French North African Division took up stations in a suburb of Toul on the Moselle River, 300 miles from Paris. On that day, the unit's Captain Denis Barlone summed up in his diary what most men felt: 'We know that our land is safe from invasion, thanks to the Maginot Line; none of us has the least desire to fight for Czechoslovakia or Poland, of which ninety-five Frenchmen out of every hundred are completely ignorant.'

From French general to private, this belief in the Maginot Line's impregnability was central to Army thinking. Most men were mesmerized by the sheer statistics of a project that in the twelve years of its construction had come to rival the Great Wall of China. Running 400 miles from the Alps to the Belgian frontier at Sedan, the Line, named after its creator, former War Minister André Maginot, was a veritable honeycomb of fortresses and casemates, 'like row upon row of sunken earthbound battleships', some of them housing formidable 75-mm guns. Of the 1,800,000 *poilus*, who manned its ramparts, at least 200,000 were men living underground in perpetual artificial light.

The Line was the solid embodiment of the play-for-safety strategy of the ageing Commander-in-Chief, General Maurice Gustave Gamelin: 'Whoever is the first to leave his shell in this war is going to get badly hurt.' A future Minister of Propaganda, Louis Frossard, put it in terms that thrifty Frenchmen could understand: 'The gold stays in the bank – each Army in its fortress of ferro-cóncrete.'

Few of France's 6,500,000 *poilus* realized it, but this was a terrifying fallacy. Both to the north and to the south, France lay naked to her enemies. As far back as 1935, the then Minister for War, 78-year-old Marshal Henri Philippe Pétain, had stubbornly resisted extending the southern end of the Maginot Line. The wooded heights of the Ardennes Forest, Pétain maintained, which girdled either side of the Meuse River, were 'equal to the best fortifications'. Moreover, no man had ever propounded extending the Line northwards, to the sea. To do so would have meant transforming a rich area of mines and furnaces, yielding two-thirds of France's coal, into a potential battlefield.

In truth, the Line was a costly symbol of the arrogance, stupidity and inept leadership which had characterized the Third French Republic for almost seventy years – a Republic which both Right and Left, for diverse reasons, had long yearned to dissolve. As recently as 1934, Communists, Royalists (intent on restoring a monarchy) and Fascists had made common cause in storming the Chamber of Deputies, intent on bringing down the government. For all factions, self-interest, not patriotism, had been the guiding star; despite the need for sizeable new credits to strengthen the armed forces, French financiers had invested 4 per cent of the country's capital in profitable loans abroad. An unbridgeable gulf yawned between businessmen, often dependent on state concessions and corrupt politicians to feather their nests, and a workforce, stubbornly opposed to democracy, which saw the general strike as its ultimate weapon. Since 1875, such bitterly irreconcilable differences had seen the overthrow of 107 Cabinets.

The keynote of Republican feeling had all along been hatred of Germany. The bitterness engendered by the Franco-Prussian war of 1870, when France had been crushed in forty-two days, had, by 1918, hardened into an implacable resolve that 'the Boche will pay'; the harsh provisions of the Treaty of Versailles had been dominated by the memory that Paris, four times within a century, had been within range of German guns. Intent on securing a Germany permanently disarmed and paying war reparations to the hilt, the French had, in fact, achieved neither aim and had sown the seeds of the Second World War.

Given such dissent, all classes of society prized security above all. The bourgeoisie, six million strong, resisted social change as steadfastly as they resisted taxes; in 1937 they had rejoiced wholeheartedly when Léon Blum's Popular Front government, in an attempt to provide a Roosevelt-style New Deal for millions below the poverty line – including a 40-hour week and paid holidays – had fallen after a year in office. The spectre of Bolshevism, they felt, was now receding. The Army General Staff feared change equally. Composed of what one editor termed 'an odd assortment of Methuselahs', they clung to the time-worn methods of the past; even in 1937 they had urged the purchase of 50,000 saddle horses rather than invest their armament credits in tanks. Thus, by 1940, the Army – and all France – had come full circle; the Maginot Line was, in effect, the fortress cities of 1870 adapted to the twentieth century.

A few more prescient Frenchmen had doubts. At Bachy, in Lorraine, the headquarters of the 3rd British Infantry Brigade, only eight miles from the Line, Lieutenant René de Chambrun was wondering. Though currently serving as a liaison officer with the British, de Chambrun, a 34-year-old Parisian lawyer, had spent three months in the Maginot Line, time enough to qualify as what his fellow-officers termed a *gars du béton* (concrete guy). Enduring the clammy twilight, the aching claustrophobia, the eternal throbbing of the Diesels pumping in air and light, de Chambrun had felt from the first that this was a strange way to fight a war. And he alone had an advantage over his fellows: as a great-great-grandson of the Marquis de Lafayette, the French soldier and statesman who had embraced the cause of the colonists in the War of Independence, de Chambrun was an honorary American citizen and thus a veteran of Pullman upper berths. It had fallen to him to instruct his men how to pull their trousers off without getting out of their hammocks.

There had been other disquieting factors. Prominent among the orders issued to Maginot personnel was one with a disconcerting ring of peacetime: 'Officers must adhere approximately to the 40-hour week and must not order work at night, or on

Saturdays and on Sundays.' At a later stage, de Chambrun had taken the C.-in-C. of the British Expeditionary Force, General Viscount Gort, on a tour of the line, and Gort had been staggered. How much, he asked, had all this cost? The answer was an unheard of £58 million – which perhaps explained why French assembly lines had turned out 30,000 tourist cars since war began but not one tank.

Now, at Bachy, de Chambrun was pondering a New Year letter from an old friend in New York. It echoed a phrase coined by the isolationist Senator William Borah, of Idaho: 'Dear René, It looks like a phoney war to a lot of us over here.' Momentarily, de Chambrun wondered again, then shrugged his doubts aside. How, after all, could a certified civilian like himself presume to doubt the wisdom of veterans like Gamelin and Pétain?

But de Chambrun could hardly deny that the morale of many *poilus* was at rock-bottom. To them this was a futile and unsought war, and it was plain even to the rawest recruit that their equipment was pitiable. One reserve artillery regiment had only tractors unrepaired for twenty years to tow its guns into battle. The 21st Foreign Volunteers were outfitted both with 1891 rifles and iron rations date-stamped 1920. At Metz, a quarter of the 42nd Active Division's infantrymen, whose socks had rotted away, were reported to be marching barefoot.

The backlash, all too often, was sullen apathy – and blatant disobedience. At Merlebach in the Maginot Line, the dismayed Lieutenant Philippe de Bosmelet found that no man in his unit would advance into a wood unless an officer went fifty yards ahead to prove that there was no danger. Drunkenness was so rife that large railway terminals now set up drying-out rooms – *salles de déséthylisation* – to sober up stupefied *poilus*.

These unpalatable truths had long been known to Daladier, though Neville Chamberlain remained blissfully unaware of them. The sole British war correspondent to report them to the Foreign Office, Kenneth de Courcy, got short shrift. The Ministry of Information's Ivone Kirkpatrick had dismissed his warnings summarily: 'Mr de Courcy is a calamitous man.'

Lack of morale was nowhere apparent among the 390,000 men of Lord Gort's British Expeditionary Force who, following the tradition of the First World War, were again subordinate to the French High Command. In this long lull of the 'phoney war', most of them were having the time of their lives. By night, merry on ten francs' worth of white wine, they sang the songs their fathers had sung: *Pack Up Your Troubles In Your Old Kitbag*, *It's A Long Way to Tipperary*, and a new one which had pride of place, *We're Gonna Hang Out The Washing On The Siegfried Line*. By day they proposed to fight 'Jerry', if he came, in the same way that their fathers had fought him: from trenches dug on the First World War order, six foot deep and four foot six inches wide.

In Tourcoing, Northern France, the lot of Private Bill Hersey of the 1st Battalion East Surreys somehow embodied the British Tommies' cloud-cuckoo land. Within weeks he was to be the only private granted a permanent sleeping-out pass. Hersey, a handsome devil-may-care regular who had soldiered all over India and spent many a night in the guardhouse, had always secretly yearned for a wife and home. Now he was about to get married.

The wildly improbable romance had started when Bill entered the Café l'Épi d'Or one quiet day during the 'phoney war'. He had burned his hand on a camp petrol stove, and when Papa Six, the proprietor, saw the wound he insisted that his daughter attend to it. Was not Augusta learning first aid and in need of practice?

Augusta's methods had seemed a shade primitive, for the alcohol she splashed on the burn sent Hersey leaping for the ceiling. Yet somehow, after that first meeting, Bill found his wound needed dressing at least once a day. There was no better excuse for holding hands.

Augusta spoke no word of English, but Bill launched into a whirlwind courtship with the aid of a pocket dictionary. Soon he and Augusta were deeply in love. One night Bill went to Augusta's father, pointed to the word *mariage* in the dictionary and said simply, 'Your daughter.' Papa exploded. 'He is no good that fellow,' he roared at Augusta. 'He spends too much on cognac!' 'He'll change,' Augusta said confidently. The local clergy, too, had disapproved, but at length the Roman

Catholic padre from Bill's brigade had successfully interceded for the young lovers.

The wedding date was now set for 17 April. Neither Bill nor Augusta had any premonition.

At 10 a.m. on 10 January, one German officer unwittingly won the Allies a four-month reprieve from Hitler's long-delayed onslaught on the west.

At this hour, Major Helmut Reinberger of the Luftwaffe was crossing the tarmac at Loddenheide airfield, near Münster, Westphalia, along with the airfield's commander, his old friend Major Erich Hönmanns. The two men were bound for Cologne in Hönmanns' new plane, a Messerschmitt 108, on what for Reinberger was a strictly illicit flight.

The orders of the Luftwaffe's C.-in-C., *Feldmarschall* Hermann Göring, expressly forbade couriers like Reinberger to carry secret papers by air. The prospect of bad rail connections and the promise of a quick flight had persuaded Reinberger to ignore this injunction.

It was a rash impulse. Inside the yellow pigskin briefcase that rested on Reinberger's knees were the top-secret plans of a daring German offensive against Holland and Belgium. The strike, a paratroop drop by men of General Kurt Student's 7th Air Division, to which Reinberger was attached as commandant of the Paratroop School at Stendal, was timed for one week hence: 17 January.

Minutes after Hönmanns' ME 108 was airborne from Loddenheide, Reinberger was already regretting his decision. Abruptly the plane had flown into a bank of fog – 'flying blind as though in a Turkish bath'. Soon Hönmanns, too, became anxious; it was his first-ever flight in a ME 108 and he was uncertain of the controls. In an effort to navigate by the landmark of the Rhine River he took the plane down to 600 feet. Peering through the murk he at length spotted a river, but now his uncertainty increased. 'This is not the Rhine,' he told Reinberger, perplexed. 'It isn't wide enough.'

Now flying in an ever-widening circle, next fumbling with the instrument panel, Hönmanns somehow contrived to cut off his fuel. The engine coughed and spluttered, then abruptly gave out. The ME was going down fast now, racing virtually out of control towards the frozen ground. Next instant, in a terrifying swoop between two trees, both wings were torn bodily from the plane; the fuselage pitched clear to land in a high hedge. As the two men clambered shakily out, Reinberger's first thought was for his still-intact briefcase. 'If it ever comes out that I flew with what's in there, I shall be court-martialled,' he told Hönmanns.

As both men debated, an old peasant came lumbering up to them. Yet strangely he spoke no word of German, and Hönmanns knew a growing disquiet. 'Where are we?' he asked tentatively in French. 'The Maas,' the old man replied. 'My God,' said Reinberger, appalled. 'We've crashed in Holland or Belgium.'

Intent on destroying those incriminating documents, he began groping frantically for matches, but like Hönmanns, he was a non-smoker. It took time to convey their need to the old man, who grudgingly parted with a box. Snatching them, Reinberger quickly ducked behind a hedge, but not quickly enough.

At 11.30 a.m. the sound of the crash had alerted the Belgian guards at the Mechelen-sur-Meuse control point, and soldiers hastening towards the wreckage took in the scene at a glance. An officer in a long coat – Hönmanns – raised his hands at the first sight of their rifles. Behind the hedge Reinberger now had the first batch of papers well alight. The soldiers resourcefully stamped them out, disarmed both men, then brought them before the control-point chief, Captain Rodrique.

Sensing that an interrogation would prove fatal, Hönmanns tried to stage a diversion. He asked to visit the lavatory. As Rodrique stepped back to let him pass, Reinberger, huddled silently in a corner of the guardhouse, sprang forward. Seizing the papers he tried to bundle them into the guard-room stove, but Rodrique was quicker. Burning his hand badly, he tore the papers from the stove and once more stamped out the flames.

Now Reinberger vainly tried to snatch the Belgian's pistol from its holster, but Rodrique manhandled him roughly into a chair. 'Sit there and don't move again,' he ordered furiously. Reinberger buried his face in his hands. 'I wanted your pistol to use on myself, not you,' he explained wretchedly. 'There will be no pardon for me.'

By 7 p.m. the papers had been passed to the Belgian General Staff in Brussels but now a doubt arose. Were they genuine – or were they an elaborate ruse? Despite Reinberger's haste, the fragments from three documents, approximating ten pages of typescript, remained intact. These detailed Dutch and Belgian targets assigned to the Stuka dive-bombers of General the Baron von Richthofen's 8th Flying Corps, operating along the line of the Maas in conjunction with the German VIth Army. One document, signed by General Student, detailed five dropping areas for the paratroops of the 7th Division.

Despite Belgium's neutrality, King Leopold II, using the French military attaché as intermediary, did pass on this information to the Allies. But as Allied C.-in-C., Gamelin, timid and indecisive as always, shrank from any resolute action. Praying that this was a German trick, he at length persuaded himself that it was no more than that. Apart from placing the French First Army in a state of immediate preparedness, he did nothing.

'The Führer rebuked me frightfully as the C.-in-C. of the unfortunate courier,' Göring lamented to his intimates. 'What a ghastly burden on my nerves.' Later he relaxed, when word arrived from General Wenninger, the German air attaché in Brussels, that he had secured an *in camera* interview with the officers, who claimed to have burned the documents. But Göring was still not certain. At his wife's suggestion he first consulted a clairvoyant, who confirmed Wenninger's story, then, with inconclusive results, tried to burn a similar bundle in his own fireplace.

In any event, as the Luftwaffe's Inspector-General, General Erhard Milch, noted in his diary, the 'big event had been postponed for some days because of the weather (thaw)'. Three days later Hitler went further still: the offensive was deferred until the spring. Europe relapsed into its twilight sleep, poised on the threshold between life and death.

Despite the threat that hung like a thunderhead over Europe, many nations stayed obstinately neutral. To all intents and purposes they made common cause with America's isolationists: the Allies' quarrel with Hitler's Third Reich was no concern of theirs.

Some had little to fear. In Spain, the *Caudillo*, General Francisco Franco, pronounced a policy of *hábil prudencia* (skilful prudence) and with good reason: after thirty-two months of civil war between Franco's Nationalists and Communist-supported Loyalists, Madrid's ruined suburbs were a silent testimony to the suffering the country had endured. Switzerland held two trump cards: the mighty Simplon and Gothard railroad tunnels, vital links for a Germany dependent not only on transit traffic through Switzerland but on Swiss engineering skills. To some citizens, the whole vexed question of neutrality was a puzzle in itself. In Ireland, when the ailing leader, Eamon de Valera, forbade the use of Irish territorial waters and Irish air-space to any belligerent nation, one man's reaction was truly Irish: 'Who are we neutral against?'

Some nations, to keep the peace they had come to hold so dear, performed near-acrobatic feats of neutrality – particularly the five Balkan nations of Hungary, Yugoslavia, Bulgaria, Romania and Greece. Most strove for 'faithful collaboration' with Germany and 'greater friendship' with Italy, at the same time keeping the wires open to Paris and London.

Others were patently at risk, but still stayed aloof, disillusioned all through the 1930s by the League of Nations' failure to impose curbs both on Hitler and Benito Mussolini. Despite his timely warning to the Allies, Belgium's King Leopold had imposed a neutrality so strict that Britain had no knowledge whatsoever of Belgium's military dispositions or road system, indispensable in event of war. To all British queries as to their intentions if Holland was invaded, the Belgians maintained a stubborn silence.

In Denmark, the eleven-year-old Socialist Government had virtually reduced the Army to sentry duty. 'A Nordic defence alliance,' scoffed the Premier Thorvald Stauning, 'belongs to Utopia' – echoing the cry of the shaky old Dutch Prime Minister Dirk Jan De Geer: 'This totally wrong war was a self-born evil … no good can come of it.' And in Stockholm, former

Foreign Minister Rickard Sandler spoke for both Norway and Sweden, which had basked in 126 years of peace: 'No power should count us, or any one of us, among its allies. No power should count us, or any one of us, among its enemies. The North must be struck out of the calculations of General Staffs – for or against.'

Then, on 20 January, ten days after the Reinberger briefcase incident, Britain's First Lord of the Admiralty, Winston Churchill, took the neutrals soundly to task. From a studio in London's Broadcasting House, speaking with a back-throat lisp caused by a badly fitting upper plate, Churchill voiced thoughts that hitherto Great Britain had only uttered under her breath. What would happen, he speculated, if the neutral nations 'were with one spontaneous impulse to do their duty in accordance with the covenant of the League [of Nations] and were to stand together with the British and French Empires against aggression and wrong?'

Failing such a stand Churchill offered them scant comfort. 'At present their plight is lamentable and it will become worse. They bow humbly and in fear to German threats of violence, comforting themselves meanwhile with the thoughts that the Allies will win . . . Each one hopes that if he feeds the crocodile enough, the crocodile will eat him last. All of them hope that the storm will pass before their turn comes to be devoured.'

To one nation only did Churchill offer unstinting praise – a nation that ironically had clung to its neutrality to the last, only to suffer the ravages of Josef Stalin's Red Army: 'Only Finland, superb, nay, sublime, in the jaws of peril, Finland shows what free men can do . . .'

In Finland at that time of year, the trek from the towns began early. From Tammisaari and Hanko, from Viipuri and Turku, the old men, the mothers and the children, all those useless for fighting, moved out to the spruce and birch glades, a mile beyond the suburbs. There, in the four brief hours of daylight, they held picnics, gossiped, played games. When they heard the roar of bombers in the dead grey sky, they cowered until the droning had died away.

From Tammisaari alone, 3,000 out of 3,800 had gone to fight

the Red invader. Meanwhile the people reverted to the Middle Ages, when peasants hid in the forests while armies marched.

Few of the forest-dwellers knew precisely why the armies were marching. As yet scant details had been released of a top-secret two-day conference which had been convened in Moscow on 12 October 1939. To the dismay of the Finnish delegates, Josef Stalin and his Foreign Minister, Vyacheslav Molotov, had been quietly implacable in their demands for territory and base facilities. They sought not only a 30-year lease of the port of Hanko, at the mouth of the Gulf of Finland, with garrison facilities for 5,000 men, but the cession of all islands in the Gulf of Finland. This 'mutual assistance pact', as Molotov styled it, further demanded the shifting of the land frontier on the Karelian Isthmus, on the Russo-Finnish border, seventy kilometres further away from the nearest Russian city, Leningrad.

To the astonishment of Juho Kusti Paasikivi, Finland's Minister in Stockholm and the leader of the delegation, Stalin, who had only concluded a non-aggression pact with Germany in August 1939, made his reasons plain: 'We want to be able to shut off access to the Gulf of Finland ... if once a hostile fleet gets into the Gulf of Finland, it cannot be defended any longer. You ask what power would attack us? Britain or Germany. We have good relations with Germany now, but in this world anything can change ...'

Paasikivi's reply spoke for all those still clinging to neutrality: 'We wish to remain at peace and outside all conflicts.' Stalin's last word was on behalf of all aggressors: 'I understand that, but I assure you that it is impossible. The Great Powers will not permit it.'

On 30 November 1939, with Finland still stubbornly refusing all pacts, Russian bombs were showering on Finnish soil.

For 105 days thereafter, the Finns were to astonish the world. Their army, only nine divisions strong, lacked almost everything that an army could: not one anti-tank gun, little more than 2,000 Suomi machine-pistols. To defend her main cities, Helsinki and Viipuri, from air attack, Finland had barely 100 anti-aircraft guns. Her land defences were primitive. Across the 485-mile waist of the country the much-vaunted Mannerheim Line, named after Finland's C.-in-C., Field Marshal Carl Gustav Mannerheim, covered only eighty-eight miles. No impregnable Maginot, the Line was scarcely more than an ordinary trench system, dug by volunteers in the summer of 1939. At intervals, sixty-six concrete nests, two-thirds of them obsolete, stood in as tank barriers.

To smash it, the Russians claimed, would be 'a deed without parallel in the history of war' – but this was a comfortable fiction to hearten their troops. What held the line was what the Finns called *sisu* (guts), for in Finland, Mannerheim claimed with reason, 'a Thermopylae is fought out each day'.

In the strange false twilight of the forests, where temperatures dropped to minus forty-six degrees centigrade, *sisu* took many forms. Infighting with Russian tanks armed only with the wryly-christened 'Molotov Cocktails', bottles packed with potassium chloride, coal oil and sulphuric acid, took *sisu*. To man one of Finland's forty-eight fighter planes, when the Russians were deploying 3,000 planes, called for *sisu* and perhaps more. Each time Captain Eino Luukkanen and the pilots of Fighter Squadron 24 took off from Utti Airfield, 200 miles north-west of Helsinki, they drank an unvarying toast before boarding their Fokker DXXI single-seaters: *Tolkku Pois* (Good-bye to reason).

In Finland lay the shape of the war to come, for women were in the front line, too: 100,000 auxiliaries called Lottas, who worked as nurses, fire-wardens and cooks. Some, spotting for Russian planes, lay for hours astride water towers, then, too numb with cold to climb to safety, crashed to their deaths. It took *sisu* for a Finnish bride to put a torch to her new home with its hope chest and hand-embroidered linen rather than yield it to the Russians.

The Finns' stubborn resistance was prompted, in part, by bitter memories; until 1917, Finland had been an autonomous grand duchy of the Russian Empire for more than a hundred years, and the word *perivihollinen* (hereditary enemy) had always been synonymous with 'Russian'. Following the Bolshevik Revolution, a private army – the White Guards, under Mannerheim – had sprung up to eject the 40,000 Russian troops still on Finnish soil, an army savagely opposed by the socialist Red Guards, who supported the Russian presence. In the four months of civil war that followed, more than 1,500 Finns had died, a struggle that had prefigured the merciless combat of 1940.

Few men admired the Finnish stand more than Troop Commander Mikhail Soloviev of the Red Army. As the special emissary of Leo Zakharovich Mekhlis, Stalin's Finnish plenipotentiary, and *de facto* head of the Soviet Political Administration, Soloviev travelled everywhere along the front, and what he saw shocked him profoundly. Already, through no fault of its own, the Red Army was taking a beating that would go down to history. Few among them were competent skiers, and thus most were road-bound when the thick snows began. All lacked white camouflage clothing, and frost-proof weapons and equipment. Near Viborg, Soloviev chanced on one troop train where the soldiers had five times burnt their bunks in order to keep warm.

Their courage was never in doubt, but initiative was sorely lacking. No man thought to deploy through forest territory; they moved in dense masses, easy prey for keen-eyed snipers. Their fatalism was a byword with the Finns; as they advanced across the minefields, they came on hand in hand and singing, indifferent to the explosions that tore their ranks apart.

Their leaders had told them it would be a four-day campaign at most; after that, they would be 'eating Finnish cream and cuddling the Finnish girls'. Soloviev saw the reality. 'We were suffering from self-confidence passed on to us by our fathers,' he confessed later. 'We believed that Finland could not last for one more day of war, but day followed day . . .'

All through January, touring the front, Soloviev found his disillusions growing. The cold was unbelievable, and many men could not survive it. In one unit, the 45th Mountain Cavalry Division, posted from the burning wastes of Turkestan, 100 men had already frozen to death, despite three sets of warm underwear. The ice-cold metal of the gun-barrels seared the flesh; in the field-kitchens, soup had literally to be hacked from the cauldrons with axes. Often at night, the Russian artillery would open up without aim or direction, baffling the Finns. Soloviev knew why. When the guns had fired long enough the gunners huddled together, warming their hands on the barrels.

Many feared the Finnish snipers more than the cold; eerie white-clad figures, flitting like will o' the wisps, flexible, fast-moving, striking always at the flank and the rear. No matter how hard a man looked, the *Bielaja Smert* (The White Death) was always there, invisible in the silence of the forests.

Unversed in forest warfare, the Red Army used the *motti* (hedgehog) position, digging in behind rings of tanks, and the snipers were ingenious at chopping them into sectors and destroying them piece by piece. At Field-Marshal Mannerheim's headquarters at Mikkeli, in eastern Finland, the *motti* were shown as green circles on a large-scale map covered with mica shields. Each day a duster wiped more circles from the map. At other times the Finns concentrated their fire on the Russian field-kitchens, picking them off one by one. 'A hungry human,' wrote a Russian of the badly-mauled 18th Division, 'is an animal.'

To Troop Commander Soloviev it was the conduct of the 11th Perm Regiment, made up of homespun villagers from the foothills of the Urals, which somehow symbolized all that was wrong with the Finnish campaign. The men were mature by army standards, reservists in their thirties; at home their families were finding life hard on the collective farms and all of them were bitterly discontented. The day that Soloviev visited them, morale was low in any event, and on this day the *Bielaja Smert* caught up with them.

Three men had ventured into the forest to dig a primitive pit for a Russian bath, lighting a brushwood fire to heat pitchers of melted snow. At dawn the snipers found them, and there now began a game of cat-and-mouse. Each time a man raised his head from the pit, a bullet spurted a fountain of snow behind him. After two hours, one man's nerve broke. Crawling forth, he ran naked through the snow towards regimental headquarters, bullets spattering at his head. Hundreds saw him running so that now his panic infected those who had seen nothing at all. In the staff dug-out Soloviev heard shouting and the padding of hundreds of feet; dashing out he saw a floodtide of men pouring to the rear, some of them lashing madly at the flanks of sturdy transport horses. A man with frenzied eyes stumbled past, shouting, 'They're killing us off to the last man.'

For more than five kilometres, Soloviev and the regimental company commanders pursued the fugitives until at last they ran them to earth in a forest glade. Their rifles were flung down in a heap; they had been disarmed by a Red Army Military Police Force armed with sub-machine pistols, and now they huddled in a tight ring, grumbling and defiant. 'How can you behave like that, comrades?' a divisional commissar rebuked them. 'Here's the country in peril and you run away from your posts.' Unabashed, the men roared back: 'Half of us have been wiped out, that's a fact!'

Soloviev, watching them, thought that only narrowly had mutiny been averted.

Back at Viborg, he reported on this and similar incidents to Leo Zakharovich Mekhlis. Stalin's man heard him out in cynical silence before commenting: 'Another two or three Russian victories and nothing will remain of us.'

In the last week of January, Mannerheim reaffirmed the Finns' determination to the world. They were brave and bitter words, soon to hold a terrible significance for all nations still at peace. 'We shall fight to the last old man and child. We shall burn our forests and homes, destroy our cities and industries – and what we yield will be cursed by the scourge of God.'

Early in January, two widely disparate men reached the same conclusion: Adolf Hitler had picked the wrong adversary.

From Doorn, in the Netherlands, where he had completed twenty-one years in exile, ex-Kaiser Wilhelm II of Germany, pondering the front-line dispatches from Finland, set down his thoughts in a letter to his old friend, Poultney Bigelow, of Malden-on-Hudson, N.Y. The son of a former U.S. Minister to France, Bigelow, the Kaiser thought, might prove a sure pipe-line to channel those thoughts to President Roosevelt.

'The magnificent stand of the Finns has smashed the nimbus of Bolshevism,' the Kaiser opined, '... with the result that the wish for peace is gaining ground. The belligerents should stop fighting and join their forces to help the Finns. They should fight in one line to rid the world and civilization of Bolshevism.'

On 3 January, Benito Mussolini, who had thus far begged out of the war on the grounds of unpreparedness, despite the Axis Pact he had signed with Germany seven months earlier, plucked up courage to deliver an almost identical warning to his fellow dictator. From his lofty office on Rome's Piazza Venezia, a room as wide and empty as an abandoned temple, Mussolini had dispatched a letter urging the Führer to abandon all ideas of an offensive in the West. 'Military successes are possible,' he conceded, 'but all the greater then the danger that the war may spread to involve the U.S.A.'

The German–Russian Pact of 1939, he held, was a disaster of the first magnitude – 'you cannot abandon the anti-Semitic and anti-Bolshevist banner which you have been flying for twenty years, and for which so many of your comrades have died; you cannot renounce your gospel, in which the German people have so blindly believed. It is my definite duty to add that a further step in your relations with Moscow would have catastrophic repercussions in Italy . . .'

'Until four months ago,' the *Duce* wound up, 'Russia was World Enemy No. 1. She cannot become, and is not, Friend No. 1 . . . the solution of your *Lebensraum* problem is in Russia and nowhere else.'

The time when Hitler would share this conviction was not yet come. His sole response to the Italian's plea was an icy two-months' silence.

Saturday, 10 February, dawned raw and drizzly in Washington, D.C., but the weather was not bleak enough to damp the spirits of 4,446 cockily defiant members of the American Youth Congress as they surged up Constitution Avenue to seek a confrontation with the President of the United States. One day earlier the delegates, assembled in the capital for a four-day Citizenship Institute, had made their isolationist sympathies abundantly plain. Against a backdrop of banners reading 'SCHOLARSHIPS NOT BATTLESHIPS', the A.Y.C.s New York chapter had condemned any prospect of U.S. aid to Finland as 'an attempt to force America into an imperialistic war'.

As they marched they chanted a rebellious song:

No, Major no, Major, we will not go,
We'll wager, we'll wager, this ain't our show,
Remember that we're not so green
As the boys in seventeen.

The youngsters were due for a surprise. By mischance they had arrived an hour too early: the President was scheduled to broadcast to the United States at 12.30 p.m. and until that time the delegates huddled, miserable under the driving rain, on the White House lawn. More daunting yet, the President who was wheeled out on to the South Portico to address both them and the nation was no benign paternal figure but an angry tight-lipped man, blunt to the point of brutality.

He warned them sharply against passing resolutions on sub-jects 'which you have not thought through and on which you cannot possibly have complete knowledge'. In a scathing com-ment on their reference to 'an imperialistic war', he sneered, 'My friends, that reason was unadulterated twaddle.' If Roose-velt heard the resentful chorus of booing that now arose, he affected to ignore it. American sympathy, he told them, was 98 per cent with the Finns in their effort to stave off invasion. 'That the Soviet Union would, because of this, declare war on the United States is about the silliest thing that I have ever heard advanced in the fifty-eight years of my life.'

On this chill Saturday, it was not only a horde of deluded youngsters who had aroused Roosevelt's ire. If the future of civilization was involved, as he indeed believed it was, the United States was still determined to debate it by committee. Faced with the President's proposal for a modest loan to Finland, the Senate pondered the protocol: should the matter be referred to the Committee on Banking and Currency or the Committee on Foreign Relations? No matter that Secretary of the Treasury Henry Morgenthau urged, 'One battleship to Finland would be the best investment we could make.' The Senate needed time to deliberate – and finally played safe by sending the letter to both committees.

Angrily Roosevelt castigated the Senators as 'a bunch of Uriah Heeps'.

The Finns enjoyed no good friend in Cordell Hull, a courtly Tennesseean and Roosevelt's Secretary of State; in this election year Hull feared that any hint of aid to Finland would spark off isolationist charges of projected aid to Britain and France. On 22 January – and again on 8 February – Hull told the Finnish Minister bluntly that there was no chance of a direct loan to enable the Finns to purchase arms.

The outcome was much as Roosevelt had feared. On 13 February, by a vote of 49 to 27, the Senate approved a loan in principle, but two more weeks elapsed before Congress, by 168 to 51, passed the measure on 28 February. In accordance with the Neutrality Act of 1939, the Finns were belatedly granted $20 million – none of it to be used for 'arms, ammunition, or implements of war'.

'The sympathy of the United States,' commented Eljas Erkko, the Finnish chargé in Stockholm, later, 'was so great that it nearly suffocated us.'

The irony was fitting. On the day that the Senate had belatedly given Finland its blessing, the Red Army, now numbering more than one million men, broke through the Mannerheim Line.

At 5 p.m. on Friday, 16 February, Winston Churchill saw his chance. Pacing the floor of the dingy basement that served as the Admiralty's War Room in London, tugging at his coattails, chewing on an unlit cigar, the First Lord was as preoccupied as his staff had ever seen him.

Churchill's stern broadcast warning to the neutrals had been no random impulse. As far back as September 1939, he had urged the War Cabinet to mine Norwegian territorial waters; only thus, he argued, could the flow of Swedish iron ore shipped to Germany each year via the Norwegian ore port of Narvik be successfully checked. At the time, Britain's Dominions – South Africa, Australia, New Zealand – had strongly opposed this, fearing that a violation of neutrality would outrage public opinion, but in January, Churchill, undaunted, had raised the issue again. By now, both Dominions and Cabinet were reconciled – until a personal appeal from Norway's King Haakon VII to King George VI saw the project shelved once more.

Now, on 16 February, Scandinavia's 'absolute neutrality' was again at stake, and the decision facing Churchill threatened the onset of a major international incident.

All reports from the British Embassy in Oslo, Norway's capital, indicated that the 12,000-ton tanker *Altmark*, former supply ship of the German pocket battleship *Admiral Graf Spee*, was on the last lap of her homeward journey to Wilhelmshaven. Moreover, rumour suggested that 300 British seamen – the crews of nine merchantmen sunk in the South Atlantic by the *Graf Spee* – were held prisoner below *Altmark*'s decks, en route to P.O.W. camps.

Both report and rumour were true. On 19 December 1939, the *Graf Spee*, dogged hungrily by British cruisers, had scuttled herself in the River Plate estuary, outside Montevideo. Promptly, *Altmark*'s Captain Heinrich Dau, a 65-year-old goatee-bearded martinet, had set course for home. All had seemed set fair. At the height of a blizzard, *Altmark* – known always as 'Mother' to *Graf Spee*'s crew – had passed undetected between Iceland and the Faeroe Islands. By 14 February, she had reached Trondheim, on Norway's west coast.

Some 300 miles down that coast, beyond the seaport of Bergen, lay the Skagerrak, the 80-mile wide strait dividing Norway and Denmark – and 200 miles further on, Germany.

Below *Altmark*'s decks, in holds no more than ten feet high, 299 British merchant seamen had almost abandoned hope. Some had endured the dripping fetid darkness for four months now – sustained mostly by black bread and watery goulash, dragging on tea-leaf cigarettes, their only latrines the brimming 40-gallon oil drums which were almost never emptied. Few shared the heady optimism of Able Seaman Thomas Foley, of the *Doric Star*, who had offered a £400 to £1 bet on a naval rescue. So many more had reached breaking point that one bearded barefoot seaman confided to *Trevanion*'s second officer, Ronald Cudbertson: 'I wish I was a woman, and then I could have a good cry.'

Though few men suspected it, fortune was to favour them. Overtly a grey-painted merchantman, her 6-inch guns concealed, *Altmark*'s passage through neutral waters was closely watched by the Norwegians – alerted perhaps by her unmercantile custom of posting eleven look-outs. Thus, as she inched at eight knots along the coastline, barely twenty yards from the shore, the bearded Dau, whom the prisoners called 'Knitty Whiskers', was subjected to polite but non-stop harassment. First to board the *Altmark* was an officer from the torpedo-boat *Trygg*. In stolid silence, he heard out Dau's protest: *Altmark* was a tanker, unarmed, carrying no prisoners.

In the warm stinking darkness below decks, 299 men, sensing the Norwegian presence, now screamed and caterwauled like madmen, beating on the latrine drums with girders and wooden wedges – but the squealing of the ship's winches, which Dau had ordered must be kept turning, drowned out all sound.

Still the Norwegians kept up their gentle pressure. North of Bergen, the torpedo boat *Snoegg* moved in – the same boarding procedure, the same inquisition – and following her the destroyer *Garm*. For the fuming Dau these delays were crucial, for the waters of the Skagerrak lay barely 100 miles ahead.

Meanwhile, the Admiralty's first instructions had passed to Captain Philip Vian, commander of the 4th Flotilla Group, aboard the destroyer *Cossack*. Ordered to sail from Rosyth, Scotland, on 14 February, along with the cruiser *Arethusa* and four Fleet destroyers, Vian had at first engaged on an abortive sweep of the Skagerrak for German iron-ore ships. Then, at ten minutes past midnight on 16 February, the Commander-in-Chief, Home Fleet, Admiral Sir Charles Forbes, signalled a change of plan: 'ALTMARK YOUR OBJECTIVE ACT ACCORDINGLY.'

At first Vian was at a loss, for the one picture of the *Altmark* available, in that week's wardroom copy of the *Illustrated London News*, identified her, incorrectly, as a 4-masted freighter. Not until almost 1 p.m. on 16 February did a Hudson from R.A.F. Coastal Command signal an 'enemy first sighting': *Altmark* was now at 58° 17′ N, 06° 05′ E, steaming at eight knots. At once Vian ordered the flotilla to intercept at full speed.

It was now, in the Admiralty War Room, that the full implications of the dilemma came home to Churchill. If no prisoners were aboard *Altmark*, to authorize the use of force was a grave violation of neutrality while she remained within Norwegian territorial waters. Yet if *Altmark* was a prison ship, she, too, was in breach of neutrality, and to let her go was unthinkable.

At 5.20 p.m. Churchill's patience snapped. To Albert Victor Alexander, soon to succeed him as First Lord, he ground out: 'I can't wait any longer. Get me Halifax.' Hunched in a green leather armchair, it took him less than a minute to expound his problem to Edward, Lord Halifax, the Foreign Secretary.

Imperturbable as always, Halifax promised him: 'Give me ten minutes and I'll call you back.'

Within the time span, Churchill was dictating to the Duty Signal Officer a message embodying Halifax's verdict. In part it read: UNLESS NORWEGIAN TORPEDO BOAT (the *Kjell*, which had halted *Cossack*) UNDERTAKES TO CONVOY ALT-MARK TO BERGEN WITH A JOINT ANGLO-NORWEGIAN GUARD ON BOARD AND A JOINT ESCORT YOU SHOULD BOARD ALTMARK, LIBERATE THE PRISONERS, AND TAKE POSSESSION OF SHIP ... IF NORWEGIAN TORPEDO-BOAT INTERFERES, YOU SHOULD WARN HER TO STAND OFF ... SUGGEST TO NORWEGIAN DESTROYER THAT HONOUR IS SERVED BY SUBMITTING TO SUPERIOR FORCE.

As the Signal Officer hastened away, Britain's First Lord was moved to pay spontaneous tribute: 'That was *big* of Halifax.'

Eight hundred miles north-west, Captain Dau was now in desperate straits. Almost three hours before Churchill's signal he had sighted the menacing silhouettes of Vian's flotilla on his starboard, to the south-south-west. Now he ordered First Officer Paulsen: 'Signal to the Norwegians. The English warships are sailing in Norwegian territorial waters. It is their duty to stop them.'

It was too late. As the first destroyer, H.M.S. *Intrepid*, bore down on *Altmark*, the gunboat *Skarv* made a half-hearted attempt to check her, but with the destroyers to starboard Dau's escape to the open sea was cut off. Now he took the only evasive action left to him – ramming the *Altmark* through the splintering pack ice of Jossing Fjord, a 1½ mile-long arm of the sea hemmed in by mountains.

It was a self-defeating gambit, for Vian's flotilla could now seal off all hopes of escape as effectively as cats grouped round a mousehole. Dau had just one hope; the Norwegians would resist the British incursion so resolutely that Vian would back down.

But Churchill's fighting message had spurred Vian to action, though at 10 p.m. he made one last attempt to persuade the Norwegians to see reason. Hailing the gunboat *Kjell* through his megaphone, Vian urged: 'My orders are to ask you to join us and take the *Altmark* to Bergen for inspection. Come on in with me.' But again the Norwegians refused.

'Half-speed ahead,' Vian ordered then. 'We're boarding.'

As *Cossack* ground painfully into the ice of the fjord, men noted a scene of strange and eerie beauty: the destroyer's searchlight gliding among the fir trees and the snow-capped mountains, toy houses perched precariously above the dark-green water. On *Altmark*'s bridge, Dau alerted by a danger signal on his cabin's telephone, was peering ahead of him, almost blinded by the brilliant light. Abruptly, *Cossack*'s searchlight cut out.

'What ship?' the *Altmark*'s Morse lamp blinked again and again. 'What ship?' But no answer came: only the steady inexorable approach of a stranger through darkness.

Aboard *Cossack* Lieutenant-Commander Bradwell Turner, heading the 25-strong boarding party, checked over last-minute details: already the destroyer's rails had been let down, the hazelwood 'fenders' secured with wire to blunt the impact of the collision. Now a message flashed from *Cossack* to *Altmark*: 'Heave-to or we open fire.'

It was 11.12 p.m. Alarmed, Dau directed his searchlight on to *Cossack*'s bows. '*Es ist ein Engländer*,' he shouted, and in this moment *Altmark* swung astern towards *Cossack*. 'She's going to ram us,' an officer warned Vian.

Vian had anticipated the move. As *Altmark* closed in, he swung *Cossack* round, as lightly as a yacht, warding off the force of the blow. Now *Altmark* swung in again, to ram at a 30-degree angle, and Turner ordered the boarding party to double from starboard to port. *Cossack*'s port bow was now grinding alongside the tanker's starboard poop at little more than walking pace.

Then, in a manoeuvre which Churchill, to the delight of the waiters, would re-enact with crusts and cutlery in London's smart Mirabelle Restaurant, Turner sprang outwards over five clear feet, to grasp the tanker's rail. 'Come on,' he yelled, 'what the hell are you waiting for?' The others were swift to follow, rifles thudding on the deck.

At a porthole on *Altmark*'s 'E' Deck, Fourth Officer John Bammant, of *Doric Star*, kept up a blow-by-blow account like a sports commentator at a racetrack: 'An officer's jumping across, revolver in hand ... now a sailor ... Another! Good! Another ...'

Pandemonium broke loose. Gunfire crackled, ricocheting from the high mountains. All over the catwalks and the fo'c'sle, groups of Britons and Germans lunged and gouged and grappled. Suddenly there was a sharp impact, and the combatants staggered, cursing, caught off balance. *Altmark* had run aground on rocks at the far end of the fjord.

Plainly Vian could no longer follow his instructions to take *Altmark* in prize: what mattered now was the captives below. On *Altmark*'s bridge, Turner, revolver levelled, ordered Sub-Lieutenant Geoffrey Craven, whose German was faultless, 'Tell them to take us to the prisoners.'

By now the hatchway above the flats had been lifted; in the humid half-light the captives had listened enthralled to the shouting and the spatter of gunfire. Suddenly from far above a voice hailed them: 'Any Englishmen down there?'

The voices were a thunderous chorus from the darkness: 'We're *all* English down here.'

Turner recalls his own salutation as, 'We've come to rescue you', but at another hatchway an anonymous bluejacket coined a phrase for history, 'Come up – the Navy's here.'

The words were to echo throughout the world for this unrepentant act of piracy struck a chord among the free nations. Whooping and cheering, their faces radiant, 299 grimy bearded men stumbled up the trunkway, to pump the hands of their rescuers, to gulp in the icy air. Most were too euphoric even to bear a grudge against their captors; Second Engineer George King, of *Doric Star*, found himself shaking hands with Captain Dau. Able Seaman Thomas Foley, by contrast, besought a rifle from a *Cossack* sailor; he wanted to shoot 'Knitty Whiskers'. Patiently the bluejacket chided him, 'Don't be silly, old man, this is not for private use.'

At five minutes to midnight on 16 February, a petty officer shouting through cupped hands to Captain Vian marked the end of the *Altmark* affair: 'All prisoners and boarding party aboard, sir.' (Adjudging the situation 'already complex enough', Vian had decided to leave the Germans behind.) The gangplank went up, and a phalanx of wildly cheering men lined the decks as *Cossack* moved slowly out of Jossing Fjord.

The world was swift to react. In the *Storting*, the Norwegian Parliament, Foreign Minister Halvdan Koht protested bitterly at 'this grave violation of Norwegian neutrality', though from the sidelines the United States press comments more resembled rave reviews following a triumphant first night. 'Daringly conceived and brilliantly carried out,' was the verdict of the *New York Sun*. 'A boldness reminiscent ... of the seventeenth century,' enthused the *Baltimore Sun*. In Berlin, Dr Josef Göbbels was beside himself. 'All propaganda must be focused on this single incident,' he instructed editors at his press conference. 'Tonight the sea should boil.'

In the space of a night, by violating Norwegian neutrality, Churchill had ended 'the phoney war'. Already the first subterranean rumblings of a world-wide avalanche could be heard in the chancelleries of Europe.

2

'The Position of Small Nations . . . is Clarified'

At Utti airfield, 200 miles north-west of Helsinki, Captain Eino Luukkanen and the pilots of Fighter Squadron 24, were puzzled and angry. None of them could understand the bewildering reversal of fortune. For weeks, Luukkanen's men had been so sure of ultimate victory that Finnish bombers had even carried out a leaflet raid on Leningrad, offering deserting Russian soldiers specific prices for their arms: 150 roubles for a rifle, up to 1,500 for a machine-gun, 10,000 for a tank.

Then, inexplicably, everything had begun to go wrong. More and heavier Russian artillery was being moved up to the Mannerheim Line, including the formidable 'Little Berthas', with a 25-mile range. In their wake came fresh troops from Siberia and the Caucasus, trained for bitter-weather fighting. In the eighteen days since the Mannerheim Line had been breached, these men seemed irresistible. The thrust of their attack was in the Summa sector, aiming for Viipuri, Finland's Gulf port and second city, and often their advance was backed by 500 aircraft at a time. A new sophistication was apparent: infantrymen were brought into action in armoured sleds towed by tanks, while flame-thrower vehicles sprayed the Finns with burning naphtha. The phrase 'total war' was taking on a new and – up to now unthinkable – dimension.

By 3 March, the Red Army was closing on Viipuri, ten miles behind the Mannerheim Line. A great and ominous quiet lay over the capital, Helsinki, but the blood-soaked snow south of Viipuri had become Finland's Verdun. Block by burning block, the port was yielding, the Russian troops urged on by commissars bellowing through loud-hailers: 'Comrades, destroy the white Finnish snakes.' Their cries jarred incongruously with the voice of Radio Moscow, crooning through the gutted suburbs: 'The Red Army sends affectionate greetings to the people of Finland ... workers in every country love the Red Army.'

By now it was evident that no help would be coming in time from any foreign power. The reason was plain: a mooted Anglo–Finnish expeditionary force could only reach Finland by passing through neutral Norway and Sweden, uncomfortably close to the Swedish iron ore fields at Gallivare, on the Gulf of Bothnia. Fearing an allied plan to 'guard' and 'protect' both Gallivare and the Norwegian iron-ore port of Narvik, Norway and Sweden, insistent on their neutrality, would permit no access to Finland.

Meanwhile, by 4 March, Finland's Fighter Squadron 24 had moved closer to the battle zone. Now, oppressed by the news of Viipuri's plight, they were shuttling between Lemi airfield, south-west of Ruokolahti, and the solid ice of Lake Kivijärvi. On this overcast Monday, with ten-tenths cloud cover, and a ceiling nearing 600 feet, there seemed little chance of action: Luukkanen and his men, huddled in the alert shack, had settled to a game of cards. Then, soon after noon, the phone bell jangled. A coastal artillery battery reported an attempted Russian landing in force across the frozen gulf at Virolahti. The squadron was to strafe the advancing columns.

Luukkanen and his men exchanged glances. Their experience of ground strafing was almost nil – and close to the gulf was the Russian fighter base at Suursaari.

Assigning four pilots to act as top cover, Luukkanen took the squadron off in sections through broken cloud. As they flew, the weather deteriorated still further. Over Luumäki, wet spattering drifts of snow assailed them. At Miehikkälä, black snow-laden clouds forced them to treetop level. Mercifully, as they reached the Gulf, the ceiling lifted. The squadron climbed to an altitude of 1,000 feet.

As Luukkanen first sighted the Russian column, he sucked in his breath. As yet it was six miles away – but where, he thought, is Stalin finding these reinforcements? From the air the column was an unending line of men and horses, more than 500 strong,

41

a long black snake seeming motionless on the ice. And Suur-saari airfield was blanketed by fog; not a Russian fighter was in sight. Luukkanen signalled: 'Single file strafing run.'

The column was a perfect target. Not one among the Russians was wearing white camouflage clothing; they were black ant-men, sharply defined against the glittering ice. Strangely, as Luukkanen eased forward on the control column they made no attempt to break formation, even as the snarl of the Mercury engines ruptured the silence. At thirty feet Luukkanen levelled off; a bright stream of bullets from his four Browning M-36 machine guns sliced into the trudging men.

Panic seized the Russians. In fleeting seconds Luukkanen saw some men drop dead in their tracks; others were grabbing at the bridles of rearing plunging horses. Scores were scattering in all directions, slithering as ludicrously on the ice as drunken men. As Luukkanen began his pull-up, he was so low that his Fokker's undercarriage came close to scraping their heads.

Now the squadron's ace, Flight Master 'Illu' Juutlainen, took up the strafing, and the others were close behind him. Luukkanen had already reefed round, picking out a four-barrel organ gun mounted on a cart as target. At thirty feet, Fighter Squadron 24 moved up and down the column like tractors ploughing a field; eight planes, thirty-two machine guns, pumping 8,000 rounds into the squirming diving Russians. Luukkanen was surprised to feel a fierce atavistic joy, such as he had never felt when aerial combat was involved. Here was one Russian formation that would never attack Virolahti.

By early afternoon, the fighters were once again touching down on the ice of Lake Kivijärvi. Already the coastal artillery had signalled its congratulations. More than 200 Russians lay dead or dying in the snow. The rest were in full retreat, forced-marching painfully back across the ice.

On the evening of 10 March, Erik Seidenfaden, political editor of the Copenhagen daily *Politiken*, boarded the Copenhagen–Stockholm ferry, on his way to cover the Finnish war, along with United Press correspondent Webb Miller. From the saloon-deck the two men could hear the lusty sing-song of a dozen young Danish volunteers, en route to offer their services to Mannerheim. 'That's a pity,' Seidenfaden commented casually. 'There'll be peace long before they get there.'

Miller was curious. Did Seidenfaden have inside information? The Dane confessed that he hadn't. He had spoken unthinkingly, prompted by some inner hunch.

At thirty, Seidenfaden was already a veteran of the turmoil besetting Europe. In Germany, in 1932, he had so accurately charted Hitler's rise to power that the Nazis had warned him to stop filing stories or face arrest. Seidenfaden, a tall relaxed man who smiled a lot, had taken the hint – but he had gone on to cover Franco's civil war in Spain, and, later, in 1939, he watched the German columns roll into Prague as Hitler breached the Munich Agreement and annexed Czechoslovakia. In all this time Seidenfaden had seen himself as an anti-Nazi crusader, striving desperately to awake the apathetic Danes to the menace that Hitler posed.

Eight years' reporting had given Seidenfaden a profound faith in inner hunches. In Stockholm, he took pains to contact a Foreign Office source close to the Minister, Christian Günther. His man was unreserved. The first Finnish peace-feeler to Moscow had gone out on 6 March. An armistice would take effect from 12 March.

Seidenfaden knew some anxious moments. By 6 p.m. on 11 March he had cabled the story to Copenhagen, and Editor Nils Hasagdr, scenting a scoop, had ordered an emergency run of stop-press leaflets rushed on to the streets. Only at midnight, when the news became official, did Seidenfaden relax.

The world at large was less concerned with the when than the why. What indeed had induced the Finns to give up after 105 days of titanic struggle? In truth, the decision had rested with Mannerheim alone. As early as 2 March, he had asked himself: How long could his exhausted army hold Viipuri? By now the front had become dangerously extended, and the ice so thick and strong that it bore the weight of Russian tanks across Viipuri Bay. Trained manpower was now so short that even convicts serving light sentences were being rushed into uniform. To save his soldiers from annihilation, Mannerheim reluctantly opted for peace.

It was Stalin, as the U.S. ambassador to Moscow, Lawrence

43

A. Steinhardt, reported to the State Department, who in this last hour overruled the Red Army's leaders and the Politburo, both of whom had favoured a war to the death. But Stalin was adamant. If the war continued his troops might become embroiled with that Anglo–French Expeditionary Force – which had never ever taken physical shape.

The average Finn was stunned. Towards noon on 13 March, scores of them crowded into Helsinki's large cooperative restaurants, to listen in numb proud solitude to the broadcast voice of Foreign Minister Väinö Tanner, enumerating the conditions of surrender. A band played Luther's hymn, *Ein feste Burg*, and slowly in the too-bright sun, the white and blue flags slipped to half mast.

The Russians were exacting a harsh price: 25,000 square miles of land, including all the islands in the Gulf of Finland, the ports of Viipuri and Hanko, most of the Karelian Isthmus. Captain Eino Luukkanen saw it, above all, in terms of people. Over 500,000 people in the areas ceded to the Soviet must now quit their homes; along the roads of Karelia, he watched 1940's first refugees, men young and old, trudging beside their cattle, women, young children, the aged and sick, riding atop piled carts.

Some Russians had mixed feelings. Troop Commander Mikhail Soloviev heard the news in a field hospital, following a pile-up on a motor cycle and found himself thinking long and deeply about the Finns. 'Had they weakly laid down their arms,' he thought, 'all of us would have despised them. We wanted simply to maintain our self-respect as a people.' The Finns' bravery, he thought, had helped the Russians to do that.

'Did we defeat them?' Soloviev wondered. But that was a harder question to answer. 'Our victory seemed very much like a defeat – and their defeat like a victory.'

North of Viipuri, now, the land lay littered with the aftermath of battle. For mile upon mile, the snow was polka-dotted with black and yellow craters, trees gashed by shells and machine-gun fire. The surreal debris of war was everywhere: empty vodka bottles, torn copies of *Pravda*, mounds of frozen dung, gutted tanks, the grinning heads of horses with wide-open frozen eyes, festoons of field telephone wire.

In the forests, snow was falling very fast upon the dead.

The bitter inquests began within the week – the first of many such to be held throughout 1940. Finland blamed Sweden for not permitting Allied aid. Sweden accused Britain and France of spoiling to turn Scandinavia into a battlefield. The French blamed the British for not pressing aid to Finland. The British blamed the Swedes.

In Sweden, the sense of shame went deep. The Premier, pudgy little Per Albin Hansson, excused his stubborn stand by saying: 'I have to deal with a nation that is selfish about peace.' Yet the majority of the Swedish General Staff had favoured armed intervention before Russia reached Sweden's borders and many Swedes were bitter that, in the last resort, Sweden had saved her own skin by leaving Finland to perish. 'Sweden ... failed democracy's case,' a Göteborg newspaper charged roundly. 'She failed a brother in the hour of distress. She failed her historic obligations and failed her future.'

There was soul-searching in Britain, too: only thirty field-guns had been sent out of 166 promised, no more than twenty-five howitzers out of 150 pledged. Even these, like the United States loan, the 11,500 foreign volunteers spoiling to fight for Finland, had arrived too late, for the Chamberlain Government's heart had never resolutely embraced the Finnish cause. All along their intention had been to improve relations with the Soviets and wean Russia away from her unholy German alliance. No one had seriously encouraged Finland to resist Russian demands for bases and military facilities.

'The position of small nations in the world as it is at present is clarified,' summed up the columnist Dorothy Thompson, in the *New York Herald Tribune*, 'They have no position.'

But what rankled most bitterly for the free world was that a dream had died. After a decade in which brute force had ruled, it had seemed, for 105 days, that right could triumph over might against insuperable odds. Now this illusion had perished.

Davids could in no way worst the Goliaths. The gods of war marched with the big battalions.

In his office at 10 Downing Street, London, overlooking the Horse Guards Parade, Neville Chamberlain had visitors in the late afternoon of 11 March. Watched by his Foreign Secretary, Lord Halifax, and Joseph P. Kennedy, the isolationist American ambassador, Chamberlain was studying a sheet of blue notepaper, die-stamped in red, 'The White House', handed to him by a tall aloof man in full morning dress.

'My dear Chamberlain,' the Prime Minister read, 'Sumner Welles, my Under Secretary of State and old boyhood friend, will give you this. What you tell him will be maintained in the strictest confidence – and will be told solely to myself and to Cordell Hull. At this grave moment, I deeply hope this exchange of views may be of real value towards a peace which is neither "inconclusive nor precarious" – Enough said. My warm regards, Faithfully, Franklin D. Roosevelt.'

Welles was unaware that Chamberlain, inherently anti-American, had dubbed his fact-finding mission 'a sensational intervention', certain that it would 'cause embarrassment to the democracies from which Germany, still unconvinced of the failure of the policy of force, will reap advantage'. Most of the Prime Minister's talk, Welles noted, was of German treachery: how Hitler had lied to him, how Hitler had deceived him. His dark eyes piercing, his voice low and incisive, Chamberlain made no effort to contain his 'white-hot anger'.

Welles did not attempt to stem the flow. In any event, as Roosevelt had told the State Department's Breckinridge Long, Welles' visit to Chamberlain and to the French Premier, Daladier, was no more than 'window-dressing'. The real purpose of his European mission, Roosevelt explained, was 'to get the lowdown on Hitler and get Mussolini's point of view . . .'

As he left No. 10, Welles was unaware that Chamberlain had just cause for agitation. Pressed by the forceful Churchill, the Premier was now unwillingly involved in a military manoeuvre of which he had grave moral doubts: an unprovoked invasion of both Norway and Sweden.

At next day's War Cabinet Meeting, on 12 May, all Chamberlain's revulsion against war, which had prompted his long appeasement of the dictators, was readily apparent. The burly Chief of the Imperial General Staff, General Sir Edmund Ironside, faced a Premier who at first appeared 'tired and lugubrious', then 'more and more horrified' as he grappled with the implications of the coup. Peering at a chart of Narvik, he first asked Ironside what scale it represented, then pondered what effect an 8-inch shell would have on shipping. Told that it could be devastating, Chamberlain promptly opted for 4-inch shells. Faced with such vacillation, the Chief of the Air Staff, Air Chief Marshal Sir Cyril Newall, pronounced the whole scheme as 'hare-brained'. 'I came away disgusted with them all,' Ironside noted in his diary.

The essence of Churchill's project, Operation Wilfred, was the mining of Norwegian territorial waters, regardless of whether Norway agreed or not. But this operation, if need be, was to be supplemented by Plan R.4 – a counter-measure designed to thwart any German violation of Norwegian neutrality which might follow on the mining.

In this event, a force under General Pierse Mackesy, 20,000 strong, was to seize Narvik in three-division strength, with simultaneous landings along the Norwegian coastline at Trondheim, Bergen and Stavanger. Trekking on to Sweden, this force was then to seize and destroy the contested Gallivare ore fields at the mouth of the Gulf of Bothnia.

The crucial obstacle to this plan was the Swedes themselves, for no road connected Narvik with the Swedish frontier – hence Narvik's key-role as a port when the Gulf of Bothnia was frozen. The Swedes had only to cut off the railway's electric current to bring Mackesy's force to a standstill.

Pressed as to his views, Mackesy conceived the idea of somehow reaching the Swedish frontier then courteously demanding passage across. 'And if the way was barred?' Chamberlain asked. If he could not get through without fighting, Mackesy assured him, he would call it off. Lord Halifax agreed. 'If we can't get in except at the cost of Norwegian lives, I am not for it,' he decided, 'ore or no ore.'

On this same day, the news of the Finnish surrender robbed the British of all pretext for the foray, but in the weeks following Sumner Welles' visit, Churchill kept up the pressure. Even so, his Cabinet colleagues remained uncertain. The *Altmark* incident had had 'a good press' in the United States, Lord Lothian reported from Washington, D.C., 'but action such as we now proposed might be less well received. Anything which would be regarded as bullying a small neutral would be resented . . .' Chamberlain, too, added his warning: 'We entered the war on moral grounds and we must be careful not to undermine our position.' Now Halifax seemed to veer in Churchill's favour: could Britain feel bound to keep the rules of war 'and thereby allow the enemy the double advantage of disregarding those rules which suited him'? Churchill had no doubts at all. Such action was more than a naval foray; it might prove to be one of the turning points of the entire war.

But many still had misgivings – among them Premier Edouard Daladier of France, who wanted no part in the operation. It was, in his words, 'a dangerous toy', and one which might well bring serious German reprisals against French aircraft factories. Others, fighting men among them, had doubts on moral grounds. On 5 April, Captain Ralph Edwards, R.N., Director of Operations (Home) on duty in the Admiralty War Room, noted in his diary: 'We deliberately infringe international waters and therefore the law – I thought we were fighting for international law and order.'

At this hour, however, there was no turning back. With or without the French, the British were going ahead, and Mackesy's final operational order left wide scope to provoke an international incident: 'Subsequently [to the seizure of the Norwegian ports] an opportunity may arise to go on to Gallivare, and the role of the force would then become the denial of the Gallivare orefields to Germany . . . In this event you are to obtain instructions from the War Office before entering Sweden.'

Now the die was cast, Chamberlain seemed more confident. 'Hitler,' he told a meeting of the Conservative Central Association on 5 April, 'has missed the bus.'

Six weeks earlier, in Berlin's Reich Chancellery, Adolf Hitler, unusually for him, had yielded to rational argument.

Until mid-February Hitler had genuinely had no territorial plans for the Baltic. What the Führer wanted, in event of war, was to keep Norway, Sweden and Finland neutral, for, in this way, the Baltic would remain an open sea for Germany, with the area's resources and raw materials available for the German war economy.

As early as October 1939, *Grossadmiral* Erich Raeder had proposed the seizing of Norway's bases to increase Germany's power of attack against British sea-routes. His reasoning was impeccable. In November 1937, Hitler had alerted his Chiefs of Staffs to prepare for 'Case I', a period between 1943 and 1945, at which time his 'unalterable resolve to solve Germany's problem of space' might bring him into conflict with the British. Accordingly, Raeder had formulated Plan 'Z', which provided for the completion, by 1945, of a modern high-seas fleet built around eight huge battleships, five battle cruisers and two aircraft carriers.

Thus, in September 1939, the news of war with Britain and France had come to Raeder like a thunderclap. Moreover, Hitler had scrapped Plan 'Z', so that Germany's naval potential was less than half the size of the French and Italian fleets and was altogether eclipsed by the British. The two large battleships, *Bismarck* and *Tirpitz*, the aircraft carrier *Graf Zeppelin*, and the heavy cruisers *Prinz Eugen, Seydlitz* and *Lutzow* had been launched but not yet completed. Only the 32,000-ton battle cruisers *Gneisenau* and *Scharnhorst* were in commission. Thus the German Navy could never at any time venture into the Atlantic as a fleet, while the U-Boat arm had less than half the strength required to cripple Britain's supply line.

At first Hitler, preoccupied with his western offensive, had shown scant interest in Raeder's Norwegian proposition; as much as any German warlord, he suffered from the historical sense of inferiority that saw Britain as invincible at sea. Then the onset of the Finnish war gave him pause to think. If the Allies gained access to Norway, Germany's Swedish ore supply was threatened – and that supply totalled eleven and a half million out of Germany's total annual consumption of fifteen million tons.

Two factors now combined to galvanize Hitler into action. The incident of Major Reinberger's briefcase, which had temporarily stalled the western offensive, had for the time being freed his hands, and Churchill's impulsive *Altmark* signal to Captain Vian set the seal on it. Exercise *Weser*, which called for the invasion of Norway and a simultaneous seizure of Denmark to secure her air bases, was on with a vengeance.

On 20 February, General Nikolaus von Falkenhorst, 55-year-old commander of the XXIst Corps, stationed at Coblenz, was summarily hailed to Berlin and given command of the Norwegian invasion forces. Von Falkenhorst was bewildered, and with reason: although he had served in Finland in 1918, and thus had practical experience of northern warfare, his meeting with Hitler was no more than a matter of minutes before the Führer's midday conference. Since no one thought to provide him with a map, von Falkenhorst had to move fast; Hitler had given him five brief hours to finalize his plans. Hastening to the city centre, the General bought a Baedeker guide to Norway and returned to his hotel room. By 5 p.m. the invasion was charted, and von Falkenhorst returned to the Reich Chancellery. Allotted only five divisions, his choice seemed logical: one division apiece would be launched against the five large harbours of Oslo, Bergen, Stavanger, Trondheim and Narvik.

The target date, set for 5 April, marked Hitler's biggest gamble yet, for Raeder was staking virtually the whole German fleet to achieve success. And on 8 April, five cruisers and six destroyers of the British Navy would move out on their 'hare-brained' Operation Wilfred – with a sporting chance of occupying precisely those ports earmarked by the Germans.

It had been an exhausting trip, and he was glad to be done with it, but in forty-one days he had become the best-informed man on the Second World War. By special train, aeroplane and steamer he had covered 14,000 miles. He had conferred with one Pope, two Kings – Britain's George VI and Vittorio Emmanuele III of Italy – one Führer, one Duce and three Premiers (Neville Chamberlain, Daladier and the fiery little Paul Reynaud, who had succeeded Daladier on 20 March). Finally on 28 March, Sumner Welles returned to Washington.

No one, aside from Franklin Roosevelt, had ever had the slightest faith in his mission. Assistant Secretary of State Adolf A. Berle had viewed it as 'one of the most difficult and unhappy trips a man ever started on'. Secretary of State Hull had been less charitable; the mission was 'calculated to hold out false hopes'. Both the British and the Germans had been at one in distrusting Welles' motives. 'He can say what he wants to,' was

Ribbentrop's lofty comment. 'I have nothing to say to him.' Sir Alexander Cadogan, Permanent Under-Secretary to the Foreign Office, stigmatized the trip as 'an awful half-baked idea'.

Chamberlain, who could never raise his eyes above the squalid level of party politics, went further. 'President Roosevelt is ready to play a dirty trick on the world and risk the ultimate destruction of the Western Democracies in order to secure the re-election of a Democratic candidate in the United States,' was his considered verdict. 'I feel strongly that we should exert the greatest and most immediate pressure on [him] to prevent him selling the world for his own particular mess of pottage.' His cynical appraisal mirrored that of General Franz Halder, Chief of Staff of the German High Command: 'Elections! Angel of Peace!'

Even so, in his search for peace, Welles had endured much. Aside from Chamberlain's querulous self-justification, he had heard Count Ciano, Mussolini's son-in-law and Foreign Minister, denounce Germany's perfidy for concluding her Soviet alliance without even informing Italy. He had twice met an 'elephantine' Mussolini, 'his close-cropped hair snow-white', predicting lugubriously: 'The minute hand is pointing to one minute before midnight.' He had been harangued for two hours non-stop by von Ribbentrop, who sat with eyes almost continually closed as he delivered a hissing monologue denouncing England's 'craft and guile'. 'The man,' Welles noted later, 'is saturated with hate for England.'

From Hitler he had received a raucous tirade: 'I did not want this war. It has been forced upon me against my will . . . My life should have been spent in constructing, not destroying.' From Deputy Führer Rudolf Hess he had learned of the necessity for a 'a total and crushing German military victory'. Hermann Göring, garbed in a white tunic, his diamond-studded hands 'like the digging paws of a badger', had told Welles that the German Luftwaffe was supreme 'and would remain supreme'.

In Paris, the President of the French Republic, Albert Lebrun, had contributed a potted history of his own life and a conducted tour of the portraits in the Elysée Palace. Premier Edouard Daladier saw no hope for Europe without an airborne international police force to maintain peace. His successor, Paul

Reynaud, proudly proclaimed himself 'the hardest man in the French Government with regard to our relations with Germany'.

Out of all these parleys, Welles himself saw one probably vain hope – that some promise of economic assistance, conceivably coal, might yet induce Mussolini to stay out of the conflict.

On 29 March, at a White House press conference, Roosevelt digested these tortuous deliberations into a bleak sentence: 'There may be scant immediate prospects' – a phrase he twice read and emphasized – 'for the establishment of any just, stable and lasting peace in Europe.'

A sense that Western civilization was now irrevocably at risk prompted the *New York Times* to headline with involuntary humour:

WAR SEEN ENTERING
PHASE OF VIOLENCE

As Britain courted trouble in Scandinavia, her enemies in other parts of the world were alerted to step up the pressure. Millions of Indians, Burmese and Malays now looked to Hitler as their liberator from the hated yoke of imperialism, for the Axis looked set to create the new world order which was the Far East's dream.

On 19 March, at Ramgarh, India, one such body-blow to British prestige was narrowly averted. At this, the fifty-third session of the All-Indian National Congress, held in the jungles of Bihar, the party leadership of the tiny ascetic Mahatma Gandhi, whose white cotton loin-cloth was almost a trade-mark, was being challenged by a six-foot lawyer and *bon viveur* who had sedulously courted the Axis powers all through the 1930s: Subhas Chandra Bose.

From the moment that Hitler secured power in 1933, Bose had been a familiar figure in Berlin's Reich Chancellery. Although he hated the Nazis and all that they stood for, he hated the British who had enslaved his country for three centuries even more. 'It must be done, even if it means the collapse of Europe,' he told all who looked askance at the company he kept. 'British Imperialism in India is as intolerable as Nazism is in Berlin.'

To Bose's chagrin, Gandhi, in September 1939, when India stood at 'the crossroads of history', had approached the Viceroy, Lord Linlithgow, to pledge the Congress Party's unconditional help in prosecuting the war. As Bose saw it, 'an unique opportunity for winning freedom' had been cast away.

Bose promptly seized his own opportunity. He founded the Forward Bloc of the Congress Party, a splinter group pressing for a campaign of civil disobedience – both sit-down strikes and mass demonstrations designed to paralyse British India's shaky economy. By March 1940, he had harangued a thousand meetings, overt subversion which the British tolerated, lest repression led to a nation-wide passive resistance campaign.

To outsiders, it seemed likely that Bose would carry the day. On 28 February, the American Consul-General in Calcutta, J. C. White, reported the air 'thick with rumours of anti-Gandhi demonstrations at Ramgarh'. At railway terminals, Bose supporters had lately greeted the Mahatma with a silent phalanx of black flags – an Indian symbol of rebuke for his devious dalliance with the British Raj. The demand for instant Home Rule was now so clamorous that on 5 March, White reported further: 'The principal danger of these subversive activities at present is sabotage in industrial plants ...' Bose declared, '... that if the Government did not retrace its steps, he and his friends would again consider that British gaols were places of pilgrimage for them.'

Gandhi, a master of political timing, adjudged that the moment was not yet ripe. Civil disobedience at the height of a war, which the British were waging for their lives, would be 'suicidal', the Mahatma argued. It could lead only to 'anarchy and red ruin', and he would not unleash it.

Thus, on 19 March, as 100,000 Congress Party delegates met in a specially constructed city of bamboo huts at Ramgarh village, the battle for leadership was joined. From the outset, though, the British were in luck, for it was Gandhi who made the running. He urged the Congress guiding committee to pass a resolution in favour of delaying civil disobedience, while yet pressing for independence by negotiation. The Mahatma –

whom Consul-General White summed up as 'very shrewd and quite unscrupulous ... loves the limelight' – next flattered and won his supporters anew by a speech bristling with humility. 'I am called Mahatma (one with supernatural powers) but I am an ordinary man,' he told them. 'I am perhaps the poorest general any army ever had.'

As a result, the Punjab leader Gopal Singh Himh's attack on the Mahatma's behind-the-scenes tactics – 'Everyone is ready for action except Gandhi' – was swiftly rebutted by other top Punjabis. 'Gandhi and Congress,' asserted Sardar Kartar Singh, 'are identical.'

The next day, under blazing sunlight, Bose staged his counter-challenge. In a field across the Damodar River, within shouting distance of the Gandhi camp, he harangued 5,000 of his followers. Damning Gandhi's dilatory tactics, he cited Mussolini's exemplary march on Rome in 1922, when the Fascists stormed the capital and seized power. Then, mounting a farmer's cart drawn by two white bullocks, Bose rode in noisy triumph through the Gandhi lines.

Gandhi's final supporter clinched his victory, for now the Congress President Abul Kalam Azad rose on the dais. Although Gandhi was a Hindu, Azad, himself a Moslem, still hailed the Mahatma as the Congress Party's natural leader – a man who sought India's independence as purposefully as Bose but who would attain it more shrewdly.

The next day, 21 March, the delegates, hit by a sudden cloudburst, stood bedraggled and up to their shins in water, and hastily and unanimously voted that their confidence still reposed in the Mahatma. It was, reported Consul-General White one week later, 'an overwhelming triumph' for Gandhi – and, he might have added, for the beleaguered British, too.

Restless spring had come to Europe, and with it, a chill wind of fear. Not since Napoleon Bonaparte's nineteenth-century rampage had the small nations, caught up by the relentless pressures of *Realpolitik*, felt so helpless.

There were small signs, but few were yet so sophisticated in war to interpret them correctly. On 6 April, as the Swedish liner *Drottningholm* edged into harbour at Bergen, Norway, the passengers abruptly learned of an unforeseen delay. Word had come that the liner must anchor in mid-harbour for two hours before the quays could be cleared for docking. At this moment a German depot-ship, the *Karl Peters*, was alongside, and, inexplicably, twenty German ore freighters, riding at anchor, with no sign of life aboard. From mid-harbour, they seemed like ghost ships, their bridges deserted, only faint wisps of blue smoke curling from their funnels.

No one aboard the *Drottningholm* viewed them more curiously than Polly Peabody, a 20-year-old socialite from New York. The descendant of George Peabody, the Massachusetts shipping magnate and philanthropist, Polly was one American of whom Franklin Roosevelt would have wholeheartedly approved; nine-tenths of her childhood had been passed in France and Germany and Polly felt passionately that Europe was her concern. Determined to give all the help she could, Polly had enlisted the aid of Baron Bror Blixen-Finecke, the King of Denmark's cousin, to raise $100,000 through charity appeals and found the American Scandinavian Field Hospital, a 28-strong team of doctors and nurses, equipped to furnish post-battle medication to the Finns. Now Polly's smart flat on East Fifty-Fourth Street, the fashionable life of first nights, hectic parties at the Stork Club and week-ends with the Vanderbilts on Long Island, were behind her. Ahead stretched the war's front line.

Stepping ashore in Bergen, en route for Oslo with forty-five tons of medical equipment, neither Polly nor any of her team suspected that the front line was even closer at hand. Crouching in the darkened holds of those freighters, German soldiers were awaiting H-Hour.

Two days later on 8 April, strange reports were coming out of Esbjerg, Denmark. Truck drivers heading for Hamburg with loads of North Sea fish reported an awesome column of German troops thirty-five miles long marching for the Danish frontier. Even now neutrality died hard; the Prime Minister, 66-year-old Thorvald Stauning, rejected all suggestions that he should mobilize the Army. To do so would be 'a hostile act which would entail consequences'.

Here, too, in four German colliers moored near Copenhagen's Langelinie, the favourite summer promenade dominated by the statue of Hans Andersen's 'Little Mermaid', 2,000 German troops lay in readiness.

On the afternoon of 8 April, Erik Seidenfaden, the Danish newsman, who a month before had scooped the world's press on the Finnish armistice, boarded the afternoon flight from Copenhagen to Oslo, a 16-seater Junkers JU 52. This time Seidenfaden thought himself fully briefed on the story he was to cover; the British had announced to the world their intention of mining Norwegian waters and Seidenfaden aimed to see them in action.

He was due for a surprise. Among the passengers was a man he knew well, Captain Riiser-Larsen, Chief of Staff of the Norwegian Air Force. Suddenly a white-jacketed steward came hastening down the aisle; Larsen was wanted in the cockpit.

Curious as to why, Seidenfaden craned from the window and beheld an astonishing sight. Six thousand feet below, the grey waters of the Kattegat separating Denmark from Sweden were black with German warships: the battle-cruisers *Scharnhorst* and *Gneisenau*, the cruisers *Blücher* and *Emden*, along with many torpedo boats, destroyers, E-boats and other craft. By pure chance, Seidenfaden had netted another scoop – yet such was the mental climate of 1940 that he failed to recognize it.

His first instinct was to rationalize the scene: the German Navy was reacting swiftly to Britain's defiant pronouncement. Thus there seemed every chance that the two Navies would do battle to the death in the Atlantic Ocean off the Norwegian coastline. The realization that he was witnessing a full-dress invasion of Norway never even occurred to him.

Thus when the plane touched down at Oslo's Fornebu airport, Seidenfaden hastened not to a phone booth but to the Press Gallery of the *Storting*, the rotunda-shaped Parliament building on Karl Johansgaten. The day's big story, he thought, would certainly be the formal protest that Foreign Minister Halvdan Koht would deliver to the British. But the debate dragged on so long and inconclusively that it was too late to file a cable for *Politiken*'s morning edition. By midnight, Seidenfaden was in bed and asleep at Oslo's Grand Hotel.

Soon after 4 a.m. on 9 April, a phone call brought him very wide awake. It was his colleague Sten Gudme, calling from

Copenhagen. German troops had crossed the Danish frontier.

It was an invasion with bizarre undertones. At 4.30 a.m. the German Minister, Count Cecil von Renthe-Fink, who had all along believed Ribbentrop's assurance that Denmark's neutrality would be honoured, tearfully awoke the Foreign Minister, Dr Peter Munch, to announce that they were now at war. Munch's first thought was to arouse King Christian X, but despite his efforts the phone at Amalienborg Palace rang on unanswered. In desperation Munch at last dispatched a taxi-driver to wake up the Court for the most fateful Cabinet meeting in Denmark's 1,000-year history.

As the lights of Copenhagen burned brightly in the night, Admiral Rechnitzer, the Naval C.-in-C., stubbornly refused to order his ships to open fire; one year earlier, Admiral Raeder had solemnly assured him that Germany would never attack Denmark. Few among the country's four million citizens ever realized that within a two-and-a-half hour time span, a bloodless occupation was taking place; as German troops poured ashore unopposed along the Langelinie, night shift workers cycling home thought that a movie was being shot. Sporadic rifle fire spattered through the streets, but no one, least of all the Danish Cabinet, knew for certain what was going on. At Amalienborg Palace, King Christian X, aware that his army was in no shape to fight, ordered an immediate ceasefire, but the C.-in-C., General W. W. Pryor, indignantly refused to pass on the order. At 6.25 a.m., the King's Adjutant did it for him, and all fighting ceased.

In the *Politiken* newsroom, near the City Hall, Seidenfaden's colleagues were bemused as the teletypes of the Ritzaus Bureau, the national news agency, clattered out its messages: 'Korsør, 9th April, R.B. – German troops landed here at 5 a.m.' Even as they debated, an aerial blizzard of green surrender leaflets, couched in a gibberish mixture of German, Danish and Norwegian was descending on the city. Near by, in the Palace Hotel, the German Commandant, General Leonhard Kaupisch, who had checked in as a tourist one day earlier, was placidly changing into uniform.

Despite the humiliation that had befallen his country, King Christian received the German Chief of Staff, General Kurt

57

Himer, in sporting spirit: 'General, may I tell you something? As soldier to soldier? You Germans have done the incredible again!'

Three hundred miles north, in Oslo, the Germans had achieved a surprise as total. At 11.30 p.m. on 8 April, the Prime Minister, Johan Nygaardsvold, was abruptly awoken by a call from his Minister of Defence, Colonel Birger Ljungberg. The ships that Erik Seidenfaden had sighted earlier were now entering Oslo Fjord.

'Have mines been laid?' Nygaardsvold asked, but Ljungberg's answer was negative.

'Why not?' the Premier wanted to know. 'It was too late,' Ljungberg replied lamely. 'They can't be laid in the dark.'

For the last time, the tired old man who controlled Scandinavia's destinies had hesitated too long.

Inexplicably, the lights in the city centre had been extinguished by a master switch; the 11-person Norwegian Cabinet, unable to find a taxi between them, had to grope their way in total darkness to the Foreign Office on Vika Terrassen. Inexplicably, too, for no aircraft were as yet overhead, the air-raid sirens kept up an eerie non-stop wail – 'like a bunch of trucks with their horns jammed', one man was to recall. In the Foreign Minister's office, the Cabinet could confer only by the wavering light of candles; when the German Minister to Norway, Dr Curt Bräuer, arrived to deliver his ultimatum, Foreign Minister Koht had to hold a candle above the text to enable the German to read it.

The news grew worse hourly. At intervals the telephone, a direct link with the Ministry of Defence, rang shrilly in the darkness. At 2 a.m. the Germans were pouring ashore in Bergen, from the freighters which Polly Peabody had noticed, then at Kristiansand, at Trondheim and at Narvik. At length, the Cabinet decided on mobilization, though incredibly no one among them thought of using the radio. Towards dawn on 9 April, mobilization notices were sent out by post.

But on one point the Cabinet was unanimous: neither they nor King Haakon VII and his Court or the 150 Members of Parliament must fall into German hands. Promptly they issued an Order in Council transferring their seat to Hamar, seventy miles north, along with twenty truck-loads of gold reserves. It was a decision taken so hastily that many citizens of Oslo still had not realized that the Germans were on their way. When the President of the *Storting*, Carl Hambro, told the Chief of Police, the man just stared at him sceptically.

'Surely you have the date wrong, Mr President?' he ventured. 'This is not the 1st of April, this is the 9th.'

In the iron-ore port of Narvik, 700 miles up the coast from Oslo, the Mayor, 36-year-old Theodor Broch, was asleep in his house on the Framnes Peninsula, fifteen minutes' walk from the main square. A dark, dedicated man, and a lifelong Socialist, Broch had hung up his lawyer's shingle in Narvik ten years earlier and for six of those years had officiated as Mayor. Although he and his wife Ellen were natives of Oslo, both found Narvik's small-town ambience curiously beguiling; the roast beef and tinned pineapple dinners that every family of substance took turns to give, the sedate 8 p.m. promenades along Street One each evening after supper, when a man might raise his hat fully thirty times in ceremonial greeting. 'Could anything ever happen in such a sleepy little town?' Broch had asked Ellen once.

At 4.45 a.m. on 9 April, Broch, belatedly, had his answer. The little yellow house with the green window frames was rocking as violently as if an earthquake had struck. As explosion followed explosion, Broch and Ellen tumbled from bed. 'It's probably dynamiting on the iron company's grounds,' was Broch's first explanation, but as he parted the window curtains he knew that he was wrong. The thick mist that blanketed the harbour was shot through with tongues of flame. 'That's not from the company, that's from the sea!' Ellen cried distraught.

Above the thunder of the bombardment, the Brochs now heard the patter of small bare feet. The noise had awakened their 3-year-old daughter, Siri, mindful of her father's promise that all ships in harbour would stage a firework display on Christmas Eve. 'Is it Christmas?' Siri asked anxiously.

Dressing hastily, Broch ran for Narvik's town centre. There he stopped short, stupefied. Huge flags with black swastikas were flying above the City Hall and the Telegraph Building.

German soldiers, loaded with hand grenades 'as though they were walking Christmas trees', swarmed everywhere in the cobbled square. Broch acted fast. In his City Hall offices, he buttonholed the first clerks arriving, speeding them to contact all members of the City Council and the railway and hospital authorities. Within the hour, as the first arrivals gathered round the green baize table, disquieting news was filtering through. Two Norwegian men-of-war, the *Eidsvold* and the *Norge*, had been torpedoed in the harbour, with appalling loss of life. Few among the council members could find words to express what they felt; all of them, as neutral Norwegians, were still groping in the dark. 'We understood, and yet could not understand,' Broch said later.

At dawn, an escort of German soldiers stomped into City Hall. Broch and the Chief of Police were summoned to the Grand Hotel to meet the commanding general, *Generalleutnant* Edouard 'The Bull' Dietl, a pre-war ski-ing champion. To Broch's astonishment, Dietl, a tall stooping man, was crimson with mortification; he lacked the necessary Norwegian kröner to pay off the cab which had brought him from the harbour. 'Only an oversight, Herr Mayor,' he apologized profusely.

Then, crisp and businesslike, Dietl made the German position clear. 'We have come as friends to protect your country against any further British breaches of your neutrality. Norway is now occupied peacefully in the name of *Der Führer*. Meanwhile,' Dietl added, 'the civil administration must continue as usual.'

Still bewildered, Broch and the Police Chiefs returned to the City Council. A long day stretched ahead, and with it many decisions. Their first was to evacuate as many civilians as possible, and within this time-span as many as 1,500 civilians left by boat for neighbouring islands. The Germans had fixed the currency rate at one *kröne* sixty *öre* to the *reichmark* and this fact had to be explained to countless shopkeepers. Ration cards must be printed; to avoid incipient trouble, liquor stores must close. The whole day was a nightmare of activitiy, and Broch, a devout man, thanked God for it. For the moment, at least, there was no time to think about what had gone wrong.

It was late when Broch arrived home. Soon, drugged with

exhaustion, he and Ellen had retired to bed. Next morning, Siri woke them early.

'Isn't it Christmas today either?'

'No, it is war,' her father told her.

'Is war nice?' Siri asked.

On this same eventful day, at 7.32 p.m., a legend was born. A tall fair-haired blue-eyed man, untidily dressed, with bulging eyes, accompanied by three henchmen, bluffed his way into Oslo's radio station and seized a microphone to tell almost three million Norwegians: 'The Nygaardsvold Government has withdrawn. The national government has assumed power with Vidkun Quisling as its head.'

In this way Vidkun Quisling passed into history as one of Dr Göbbels' greatest propaganda triumphs. Embodying as he did the myth of the Fifth Column, Quisling unwittingly helped to spread the clever innuendo that the Germans had previously recruited a large army of secret agents, 'the patriotic traitors' in every country they took over.

The truth was more prosaic. A stubborn, opinionated man, Quisling was an ineffectual dreamer, patterned on the lines of Ibsen's Peer Gynt. A one-time Minister of Defence, and founder of the ultra-right Nasjonal Samling (National Unity) Party, he had been for years in the political wilderness – never at any time polling more than 30,000 votes. Even so he saw himself as a political messiah, believing with many of his European ilk that Bolshevism was the 'unspeakably dangerous enemy' which Germany alone could quell.

To be sure, in December 1939, Quisling had had two meetings with Hitler in Berlin, an encounter stage-managed by Admiral Raeder, who was exploring the chances of a Norwegian coup from within. 'What were the chances?' Hitler asked them, but Quisling had thought very few. He had barely 80,000 supporters in all Norway.

Despite subsequent legend, there was little evidence that Quisling had any coup in mind. Although a Nasjonal Samling congress had assembled in Oslo days earlier, Quisling had dispersed the party caucus on the final day. The sudden arrival of the Germans had surprised him as much as anyone – and General von Falkenhorst had received no instructions to seek his cooperation. It was not treachery but the total passivity of the departed Government that abetted his take-over; Quisling saw the vacuum and moved swiftly to fill it.

The result was as vexed a chapter of misunderstandings as any in Norwegian history. 'When the Germans arrived,' Quisling was to complain bitterly, 'they did not even pay their respects.' The reason was simple: few of them even knew he existed. In his extempore broadcast, Quisling had grandiloquently named an eight-man Cabinet – but most of them were not Party members and had never met Quisling.

Thus, on 11 April, a stinging rebuke for Quisling came in a phone call from von Ribbentrop. Germany could not possibly recognize his pretensions, Ribbentrop raged, since Ambassador Bräuer was still trying to find the King and reach a settlement with him. As Quisling listened to this savage tongue-lashing, his secretary, Harald Franklin Knudsen, watched his face turn ashen.

Now, as so often, Hitler stepped in to complicate the situation anew. Overruling Ribbentrop's objections that Quisling had little value and that the King was the constitutional monarch, the Führer insisted that Germany must stand by Quisling. Heartened by this backing, Quisling, as *de facto* Premier, sent an emissary, Captain Kjeld Irgens, Commodore of the Norwegian–American line, to persuade King Haakon to return to the capital. He suggested that an arrangement could be reached similar to that of Denmark, where Haakon's brother, King Christian, continued to rule.

When the King, predictably, refused, Ribbentrop once again went to work on Hitler. Far from winning friends for Germany, he urged, Quisling's presence was making matters worse for the occupation forces. Hitler, reluctantly, then yielded to persuasion. At noon on 15 April, six days after appointing himself Premier, Quisling was forced to resign. The logic was inescapable: since none of his 'Cabinet' had answered the call, there was no Government for him to head. On 24 April, Josef Terboven, the *Gauleiter* of Essen, became Hitler's *Reichskommissar* for Norway.

Four months later, Hitler's further intercession put Quisling back into politics, despite the vehement opposition of von Ribbentrop, Terboven and General von Falkenhorst. But since the Government was now subservient to Terboven, Quisling refused to serve in it; as leader of the Nasjonal Samling Party, he merely exercised indirect influence on the eight Party members in the thirteen-strong Cabinet. Even so, his ultimate fate would be to take the blame for every error that they perpetrated thereafter.

Unwittingly, though, Quisling served Germany better than he knew. In the weeks and months that followed, his name, symbolizing treachery from within, was to cast a pall of fear and suspicion over all Europe.*

For thousands of Norwegians, Quisling's impulsive broadcast had just one effect: it stiffened their will to resist. At first, stunned by the impact, Oslo's 258,000 citizens had watched with awe as 1,500 goose-stepping troops of General von Falkenhorst's advance guard took over the capital unopposed. Dazzled by the bandoliers of bronzed bullets gleaming in the sunlight, they stared, as one man put it, 'like children seeing a new kind of animal'. Many flocked to hear the twelve-piece German band playing *Roll out the Barrel* in the park beside the *Storting*, and the Grand Hotel's doorman was quick to cultivate the Nazi salute. But with Quisling's broadcast, much of the passivity was changed. 'If the choice is between Quisling and war,' one man summed up, 'we'll take war.'

By 10 April, the greatest migration in modern Norwegian history was under way. The southern half of the country came quietly alive with moving men: young men in sports coats, toting rucksacks, armed with nothing more than sheath knives, trekking across Oslo's Nordmarka Park and slipping northwards into the forests. Some were college students, others were labourers and taxi-drivers, and few had ever fired a gun, but all of them were intent on fighting a desperate delaying action from

* On 19 April, *The Times* in London, pondering Quisling's name, had an alliterative field-day: 'Visually [the word Quisling] has the supreme merit of beginning with a Q, which has long seemed to the British mind to be a crooked, uncertain and slightly disreputable letter, suggestive of the questionable, the querulous, the quavering of quaking quagmires, and quivering quicksands, of quibbles and quarrels, of queasiness, quackery, qualms and quilp.'

village to village and farm to farm. To one American observer, recalling the War of Independence, these were Norway's Minute Men, militia who had pledged to enter the fray at a moment's notice, and for them each township would be as bitterly contested as Lexington, Massachusetts.

Even the 'regulars' like the men of the Alta Battalion, north of Narvik, who rallied to the Norwegian C.-in-C., General Otto Ruge, were fishermen and crofters, some with no more than forty-eight days' military training, who went into battle wearing ski-ing outfits made from old tablecloths.

The lot of a youngster like Eiliv Hauge, a clerk living in Asker, a small suburb of Oslo, was typical. Reaching the city by street-car around 9 a.m. on 9 April, Hauge found his office deserted. At the Norsk Telegrambyra (Norwegian News Agency) Bureau, near by, he heard that mobilization had been cancelled. But back in Asker, other rumours were current: mobilization day was Thursday 11 April, and the mobilization point was at Hönefoss, thirty miles away. Promptly Hauge and a friend hitched a ride there but not a soldier was to be seen. Another group of youngsters, chatting on a street corner, said they had been told to wait; the Army was not yet ready to take on recruits.

Soon a fresh rumour was current; the nearest military H.Q. was at near-by Helgelandsmoen, and recruits should report there. Hitching another ride, Hauge finally hit on a barracks, where soldiers were loading up trucks, preparatory to pulling out. A passing officer protested that he was too busy to talk; what did Hauge want? 'We thought of joining up to fight the Germans,' Hauge explained. The man brushed him aside: 'Then simply go into the depot and find a uniform that fits.' Almost before he realized it, Hauge was an infantryman.

Later that day, the unit, now 250 strong, moved out, crammed into trucks and buses, moving steadily northwards. Hauge thought he was part of the 6th Regiment, but nobody knew for certain. As they went, cheering storekeepers made up their deficiencies, pressing free sleeping bags on them, skis, even sets of plus-fours. By night they bedded down in barns and sheds and farm women cooked for them, feeding them on smoked lamb and potato cakes. By day, Hauge grappled for the first time with the mysteries of a Krag-Jörgensen service rifle.

Two days later, crouched in a mountain pass, Hauge and all of them got their first taste of action. A long column of German buses was stalled by the tree-trunk barrier the Norwegians had erected and, as the Germans descended, puzzled and angry, the unit opened fire. The surprise was complete: rifle and mortar-gun fire tore into the scattering Germans. Within minutes, four buses were blazing; the dead and wounded lay in heaps, groan-ing and crying aloud. White flags of truce were waved in vain; coming shamefully of age, Hauge and his comrades fired on these, too, until 200 Germans lay silent in the snow.

'Earlier wars were like boxing,' summed up the Columbia Broadcasting System's Ed Murrow, at this time, 'hitting only with the fists and above the belt. This one is rapidly reaching the point where nothing is barred – teeth, feet, heads, toes and fingers will be used by all belligerents; anything to get at a vulnerable part of the opponent's anatomy.'

Erik Seidenfaden, still in search of a story, was meanwhile dogging the Norwegian Cabinet on their journey north. Plans were formulated, then changed overnight: no sooner had they reached Hamar, seventy miles from Oslo, than it was decided to split the party in two. The Cabinet and 150 members of Par-liament moved on to Elverum, thirty miles north-east. King Haakon VII with Crown Prince Olav and their entourage went to Nybergsund, forty-five miles farther on and barely twenty miles from the Swedish frontier.

Seidenfaden was fascinated by his first-ever glimpse of government-on-the-run. When officials needed petty cash, Finance Minister Oscar Torp had to dig deep into the rucksack that he kept beneath his bed. Other Ministers toured the village, buying up its entire stock of paper and pencils to transact Cabi-net business. Already Elverum was filled to bursting point as more and more refugees poured in, and even staid Ministers were living a gipsy life. In one guest-house kitchen, twenty-seven people were attempting to boil eggs on one stove. Others clustered at the pump in the yard, breaking icicles to clean their teeth.

By sheer mischance, Seidenfaden had arrived one day too late for the most sensational aspect of the flight thus far. Angered that King Haakon had spurned entreaties to return to the capital from both the German Minister, Dr Bräuer, and Quisling's emissary, Captain Irgens, the German High Command made an illiberal attempt to wipe out the Royal party.

At 5.20 p.m. on 11 April, as the King was conferring with his Cabinet in the inn at Nybergsund, an urgent tooting of car horns from the road signalled enemy aircraft were approaching. Minutes later, as the King, still struggling with his topcoat, hastened towards the edge of the forest, followed by his Ministers, seven German bombers swooped low over the rooftops. As the King dived head first for a spruce grove, crawling on hands and knees, a whistling rain of high explosive bombs bracketed the forest. Machine-gun bullets whipped the snow into frantic flurries, and barns and outhouses took fire, the flames bright red against the white dead land. In a panic-stricken effort to make themselves invisible, some Ministers took off their dark topcoats, then, shivering and numb with cold, hastily put them on again. For more than one hour the bombers raked the forest, swooping low more than a dozen times: tall firs snapped like matchsticks and earth and snow cascaded skywards until every man's face and hair was plastered black with dirt.

At long last the bombers gave up, droning away in a straight line towards the west, and an eerie hush descended. The sun had gone down below the edge of the forest, leaving the sky a livid red. Stiff and frozen, the Government Party picked their way back towards the burning village. At their head marched the gaunt 68-year-old King Haakon, still clutching a spent machine-gun bullet.

'This is a personal present,' he proclaimed dryly, 'from Hitler to me.'

For Theodor Broch, in Narvik, there could be no thought of flight. As Mayor, it was his duty, for the time being, at least, to stay put.

News from the outside world filtered through with difficulty. All the townsfolk were shattered by the news of the bombing attack on their King, although they took fresh heart as they heard of the gallant resistance of the Minute Men. On 13 April, crouched in a cellar out of earshot of the Germans, Broch and his Council heard a secret broadcast by the King urging them all to stand fast. By now, the fury of the naval battle raging between the Germans and the Allies in Narvik Fjord decided Broch to move Ellen and Siri away from the house on the Framnes Peninsula. At night, all three bedded down on the floors of friends' houses in the city centre. In daylight hours, Broch worked from the City Hall basement, cohering the rationing system, regulating wages according to each man's family burden, planning the conversion of cellars into air-raid shelters with the City Engineer.

On Sunday, 14 April, Broch, sitting sombrely outside the office of General Edouard Dietl in Narvik's Royal Hotel, saw the end of all he had striven for. Under Section 36 of German Military Law the General had just condemned him to death for sabotage.

Broch reflected wryly that the sentence was just. Towards 4 p.m. on 13 April, the British naval bombardment had become so awe-inspiring that many German troops had withdrawn from the town. Fully nine destroyers – among them the flotilla leader, *Heidkamp*, *Roeder* and *Schmitt*, and the ammunition ship, *Ravenfels* – had been sunk or crippled in the harbour.

With only a few Germans remaining in Narvik, Broch saw this as the moment when the Allies had to land. Along with three of the town's volunteer firemen he hastened to the telephone exchange. Only one non-com remained on duty but, though Broch and his men were unarmed, the Mayor bluffed the German that the game was up. The British were already disembarking, and Narvik was once more Norwegian. The corporal, bowing to the inevitable, surrendered his pistol, but Broch's triumph was short-lived. As they prepared to leave the exchange, a squad of fifty Germans came marching down the street. Abandoning their prisoner, Broch and his volunteers fled precipitately, bullets whining in their wake. That evening he had been arrested and now, on the early morning of 14 April, he sat awaiting the firing squad.

Two hours later, the situation had changed again. An uncomprehending Broch heard from the German Army prosecutor that an urgent plea from the City Council, stressing that Broch spoke German and was indispensable to the civil administration, had decided General Dietl to pardon him. He must report to German Military H.Q. twice a day, but was otherwise free to go. 'They wanted to win the Norwegian war without fighting the Norwegians as well,' was Broch's later appraisal.

Nonetheless, in the Narvik area, the Norwegians alone were contesting Dietl's troops. Word had come through, on 17 April, of Anglo–French landings, but where, Broch and the townsfolk asked one another, and when?

As Broch stared out across the shell-torn piers and blackened wreckage of the harbour, a German lieutenant seemed to read his thoughts. 'I can assure you of one thing,' he told Broch scornfully. 'Your friends the British will never come.'

On Monday, 15 April, some 20,000 British troops, aboard warships at anchor along the Norwegian coast, were indeed preparing to go ashore. Their task, in Churchill's words, was to 'purge and cleanse the soil of the Vikings ... from the filthy pollution of Nazi tyranny'.

In the course of the next seventy-two hours they would find tentative toe-holds on Harstad island, forty miles from Narvik, at Bödo and Mo, towns below Narvik, at Namsos, 100 miles north of the vital port of Trondheim, at Molde and Andalsnes, 125 miles south-west of Trondheim and at Laerdal, 130 miles from Norway's biggest (and German-held) airbase, Stavanger.

Though their commander, General Mackesy, did not yet realize it, their chances of establishing any permanent bases were minimal. Mackesy, in any case, was at his wits' end: between 5 April and 12 April, when he sailed from Scapa Flow, he had received three separate sets of orders from the War Office, each cancelling the other. One instruction, however, remained finite: Mackesy was not to attempt any landing if the Norwegians opposed him. Yet the operation's naval commander, Admiral of the Fleet the Earl of Cork and Orrery, had been briefed by the Admiralty to prepare for a no-holds-barred assault.

Most of Mackesy's other instructions had been concerned with minutiae – 'There should be considerable numbers of ponies [in Narvik] ... let no question of paying trouble you ... don't allow any haggling over prices.' But what troops were at his disposal, where they were located, and how they were armed, as yet remained a mystery.

The answers to these questions finally appalled him. At Andalsnes, the total strength of the so-called 148 Brigade added up to two battalions – two companies of Sherwood Foresters, and one of Leicesters – raw conscripts, lacking entrenching tools, all of them armed with rifles but some of them lacking topcoats. These men, equipped with mortars but with only smoke bombs as ammunition, were expected to stand fast against the Germans in the freezing slush of Tretten Gorge, inland from Andalsnes.

At Harstad, the 1/4th King's Own Yorkshire Light Infantry, having landed on the island, found no boats to transport them ashore. They, too, lacked artillery and field-pieces, yet were so weighed down with kit they could scarcely walk; their lambskin Arctic coats alone weighed 15 lb. They had been victualled with just two days' supplies and, since ponies were nowhere to be seen, the sole communication between companies was a runner on a bicycle.

These troops were as ill-equipped to fight a campaign in barren mountainous land as the Russians had been in Finland, but with this difference: no irresistible flood-tide of men existed to reinforce them if they failed.

Predictably, within four days, the front had fallen apart.

At Steinkjer, north of Trondheim, on 20 April, the two British battalions comprising 146 Brigade, the King's Own Yorkshire Light Infantry, and the Hallamshires, lacking both anti-aircraft guns and air cover, were soon punch-drunk and reeling as the Luftwaffe enjoyed a field-day of strafing along the Namsos–Steinkjer road. 'It was just bloody slaughter,' one K.O.Y.L.I. officer raged impotently.

By 21 April, 146 were withdrawing by night, linking hands to maintain contact in the darkness, discarding their steel helmets to avoid recognition from the air when daylight came. After four days in Norway, they were in headlong retreat, a 58-mile flight, that lasted forty-two hours. 148 Brigade, pulling out from Tretten, were down to 300 men and nine officers. With no more concrete orders than 'Make for Andalsnes' they, too, had ceased to exist as a fighting unit.

Even as General Otto Ruge rallied his Norsemen, 'The time for retreating is past,' that time for the British had only just begun and the first of many bitter recriminations they would incur from their Allies was about to be voiced. On 30 April, as the Navy re-embarked the battered battalions from Andalsnes, a Norwegian, who had covered the withdrawal of 146 Brigade from Steinkjer, commented: 'It looks as if the British are going to fight to the last Norwegian.'

Within two weeks, the remnant of these bruised, bemused men would come under a new Commander, who on his own initiative supplanted Mackesy: Major-General Claude Auchinleck, a veteran of the Indian Army. His assessment of their calibre as soldiers was unremittingly stern, and presaged trouble for other British commanders if and when Hitler launched his offensive in the West.

'By comparison with the French, or the Germans for that matter,' Auchinleck growled, 'our men for the most part seemed distressingly young, not so much in years as in self-reliance and manliness generally.

'They give an impression of being callow and undeveloped, which is not reassuring for the future . . .'

'This War is Sheer Madness'

25 April–25 May 1940

In London, on Tuesday, 7 May, the atmosphere in the fine panelled Chamber of the House of Commons was electric with suspense. By 3 p.m. the Peers' Gallery was crowded, the Distinguished Strangers' Gallery packed out with the massed ambassadors and ministers of two dozen nations. One of the gravest debates in the history of Parliament, whose outcome might decide the fate of the British Empire, was about to begin. Its central issue was the ignominious flight of the British Expeditionary Force from Namsos, Norway.

As Neville Chamberlain rose from the Government Front Bench at 3.48 p.m. a volley of boos and catcalls from the Labour Opposition greeted him. 'He missed the bus! He missed the bus! Resign! Resign!' At first the Premier rocked slightly, as if receiving a physical blow, but there was otherwise no sign that he was affected. Although he had been challenged to address the House on the mounting disaster in Norway, Chamberlain's faith in his own judgement was still unwavering. 'I'm quite confident we shall get away with it,' he had told an aide earlier, as he left 10 Downing Street. On his own briefing he had noted in longhand: 'Extenuate nothing, but exaggerate nothing. Not a Gallipoli.'

But even a Chamberlain supporter as devout as Henry 'Chips' Channon, the Tory M.P. for Southend-on-Sea, was forced to admit that the Premier 'did not make a good case'. In the face of defeat, he could do little but praise the courage of the soldiers, sailors and airmen as they retreated from position to position. He angered the Labour Opposition by reminding them haughtily that the debate was a concession at most. Now the baying cries of 'He missed the bus!' echoed from Tory dissidents, too, but still, for fifty-seven minutes, Chamberlain rambled on, a querulous spate of self-exculpation such as Sumner Welles would have recognized. It was a speech so devoid of substance that the Egyptian Ambassador dropped off to sleep.

Try as Chamberlain might to juggle the book-keeping, the balance on Norway showed deep red. Even as the debate wore on, Hitler was in the process of snatching a neutral state from under the muzzles of British naval guns, and this was only one ironic aspect. At one moment on 9 April, the rumour that 800 British bombers were approaching Oslo had emptied the streets of the capital, yet all told the British only possessed 200 bombers and none of them was then approaching Norway. In the vital forty-eight hours when the Germans were taking over Oslo, no Allied bombers had struck at Fornebu Airport. 'If the British had struck then,' a German colonel told the *Christian Science Monitor*'s Edmund Stevens, 'our whole expedition would have ended in disaster. Fortunately, one can always count on the British to arrive too late.'

There were other disquieting factors – among them, Churchill's irrational obsession with Narvik. It was true that whoever controlled central and southern Norway would ultimately gain Narvik as a prize – but to single out Narvik as an operational base for the entire Norwegian campaign was never remotely on the cards. Yet even now, on 7 May, as the first contingent of raw and routed troops returned to Britain, 25,000 men were still involved in a vain attempt to capture the port. The prestige factor of Narvik now outweighed all other considerations.

The true prize of war, as Norway's General Ruge had urged Chamberlain, had been Trondheim, for whoever held Oslo and Trondheim would ultimately hold Norway, once the linking valleys had been secured. 'We are coming in great strength,' had been Chamberlain's reply to Ruge, meaning the diversion of three battalions of conscripts, all of whom had been badly mauled and then shipped out from Namsos.

Still convinced from his weekly postbag that Britons saw him as their saviour, the man whose 1938 Munich agreement had averted the onset of war by ceding much of Czechoslovakia to

Germany, Chamberlain's obstinacy and vanity permitted him no self-doubts. Burdened by 'a mind considered enlightened and advanced at the end of the nineteenth century', he barely recognized that not only the Opposition but the rebels of his own Tory Party, men whose phones he had not hesitated to tap, were out to topple him.

Few among the latter were more determined than tubby little Leo Amery, a former Secretary of State for the Colonies. But Amery, noted as a turgid orator, had emptied the Chamber more than once in the past; at 8.03 p.m., when he rose to speak, all but twelve among 500 M.P.s had left the House. It was the Liberal Party's Clement Davies, sensing Amery's wrath, who took it upon himself to act as an unofficial Whip, hustling through lobbies, the smoking room and the dining room, urging Members to return. And many, as they drifted back, sensed like Major-General Edward Spears, Tory M.P. for Carlisle, that Amery's 'small squat figure' was 'hurling stones as large as himself'.

Amery himself, though bitterly incensed against the Chamberlain régime, was uncertain as to how far he could decently go. The immortal words of Oliver Cromwell dismissing the Long Parliament in 1653 had earlier crossed his mind, but he at first shrank from using them. Then suddenly, catching the admiring glance of David Lloyd George, the Liberals' elder statesman and himself a former Prime Minister, Amery summoned up courage. 'You have sat here too long for any good you have been doing,' was his savage finale; 'Depart, I say – let us have done with you. In the name of God, go!'

'I hope the matter will not end with fine speeches in the Commons,' the South African Premier, Jan Smuts, noted in his diary, but his concern was premature. The next day, 8 May, saw fine speeches in plenty, but much more besides. At first light, Captain Martin Lindsay, the first Namsos staff officer to reach London, alighted from the night train from Scotland and called Clement Attlee, Leader of the Labour Opposition, at the House of Commons. Although a pre-war Tory candidate, Lindsay saw plainly where his duty lay. Over lunch at the Athenaeum, he gave Attlee a chapter-and-verse briefing on the scandal of the territorial battalions at Steinkjer and Tretten, evidence which

Attlee was quick to pass on to Labour's Herbert Morrison, the pugnacious one-eyed leader of the London County Council. Morrison was opening that afternoon's debate for the Opposition.

Although Morrison, no military man, blithely confused 'divisions' with 'battalions', the case he presented was overwhelming. He concluded it with a flat ultimatum: not only Chamberlain but his old cronies from the appeasement era, Secretary for Air Sir Samuel Hoare and Chancellor of the Exchequer Sir John Simon must also resign.

It was then, with three sentences, that Chamberlain destroyed himself. Although he had yawned all through Morrison's speech, he was on his feet in an instant – 'showing his teeth like a rat in a corner', as Labour's Hugh Dalton pictured him. 'I accept the challenge,' he cried petulantly, 'I welcome it, indeed! At least we shall see who is with and who is against us, and I will call on my friends to support me in the lobby tonight.'

Those words were a fatal blunder. By reducing so grave a debate to the level of personal loyalties, Chamberlain gave his opponents a club which they now wielded mercilessly. On the evening of this day, Churchill, who bore as much blame for Norway as anyone, did his best to support his leader, but Lloyd George, in one sharp sentence, demolished much of his effectiveness. 'The right honourable gentleman,' he countered, 'must not allow himself to be converted into an air-raid shelter to keep the splinters from hitting his colleagues!'

Churchill's speech, though no great oration, was at least an honest exposition of the Norwegian failure and an earnest plea for national unity. Moreover, in the fifty minutes that he spoke, he demonstrated that he was the one man present commanding the respect of a vast majority of the House. As Big Ben's chimes sounded 11 p.m., it was Churchill who called for a vote of confidence on the question of adjournment or further debate.

'Don't speak too convincingly,' the Tory M.P. for Stockton-on-Tees, Harold Macmillan, had warned him earlier in the smoking room. 'We must have a new Prime Minister and it must be you.'

Now an astonishing sight was seen. Despite the implacable resentment on the face of the Tory Chief Whip, Captain David

Margesson, almost every Tory in uniform was streaming into the Opposition lobby to vote against the Government. At least one officer had tears streaming down his face. One dissident was Captain Quintin Hogg (later Lord Hailsham), protesting 'the total failure of the War Office to provide for his battalion's equipment or training'. Another was the Tory M.P. for Smethwick, Captain Roy Wise, a Namsos veteran, who explained simply: 'I voted on behalf of my men.'

Ten minutes after the division, Margesson announced the result: for adjournment, 281 votes, against, 200. A split second later, Labourites, Liberals and dissident Tories reverted to the same steady barracking that had marked much of the debate: 'Resign! Go! Go!' In vain, Margesson signalled to the faithful to cheer their Leader; the scene of what Chamberlain's Minister of Information, Sir John (later Lord) Reith, termed 'disgusting jubilee', continued unabated. As Harold Macmillan struck up a tuneless chant of *Rule Britannia*, Chamberlain's loyal Transport Minister, Captain Euan Wallace, barely restrained himself from striking Macmillan across the face.

Pale and angry, smiling wanly, Chamberlain left then, picking his way with difficulty over the outstretched legs of his followers. The time was 11.10 p.m. on Wednesday, 8 May.

Few Prime Ministers, aside from Neville Chamberlain, would have tried to cling to office with a majority of 81, in a house traditionally Tory by a lead of 210. Even so, for two days thereafter, Chamberlain worked stubbornly to maintain himself in power. One Churchill crony, Brendan Bracken, commented disgustedly, 'It's as hard getting rid of him as getting a leech off a corpse.'

The accommodation that Chamberlain now sought was one that he had rejected in the past: a National Government, with seats in the Cabinet for Labourites Attlee and Arthur Greenwood, along with the Liberal leader, Sir Archibald Sinclair. But even initial parleys between intermediaries revealed this as a hollow hope. Labour would be prepared to discuss entering the Government, Hugh Dalton told the Tory Under-Secretary of State for Foreign Affairs, R. A. Butler, provided that Chamberlain, Sir John Simon and Sir Samuel Hoare resigned. Although

Butler objected – 'there is great loyalty to Neville among the Tories' – Dalton was inflexible. 'In our view, Chamberlain and Simon have failed so often, both in peace and war, and have such long crime sheets that they must go.'

Ironically, the last man that Labour sought as Prime Minister was Winston Churchill, whom they viewed as a diehard reactionary. Their unanimous choice was Lord Halifax, known to some for his air of pious sincerity as 'Lord Holy Fox'. But Halifax all along demurred; he could not sit in the House of Lords and at the same time serve as Prime Minister. On the morning of 10 May, Chamberlain, who had once stigmatized Attlee as 'a cowardly cur', made one last effort to wheedle the Labour Party to accept seats in his Cabinet. Attlee's reply left little room for doubt: 'Mr Prime Minister ... our party won't have you, and I think I am right in saying that the country won't have you either.'

King George VI had as little enthusiasm for Churchill, but Halifax's refusal to assume power left him no choice. It was left only for Attlee and Greenwood to hasten to Bournemouth and obtain approval for their negotiations from the Labour Party Congress. 'Not very impressive,' commented the Labour pundit, Harold Laski. 'I feel as though the cook and the kitchenmaid were telling us how they sacked the butler.'

The next day, one silent confrontation said it all. Back in 1937, Chamberlain had installed his *éminence grise*, Sir Horace Wilson, in an office adjoining his Cabinet Room, overlooking the Horse Guards Parade. As Permanent Head of the Civil Service, seconded to the Treasury for service with the Prime Minister, Wilson somehow symbolized the whole shabby process of appeasing the dictators that had brought Britain low.

On 11 May, Sir Horace opened his office door and received a shock. There on his sofa sat Randolph Churchill, Winston's son, together with Brendan Bracken. In hostile silence they stared at him, not smiling, not speaking. Sir Horace hesitated, then withdrew. A door closed softly. An era died.

After forty years of political frustration and vacillation, Winston Churchill had come into his own. Known primarily to a generation of parliamentarians as a brilliant but somewhat untrustworthy political chameleon, who had been by turns Tory Democrat, Liberal, Anti-Socialist, Constitutionalist and Conservative, he now faced the task of welding a people that had never wanted war into a nation of willing warriors. Despite his outward buoyancy, Churchill had few illusions as to the task ahead. To Chamberlain, whom he loyally retained as his Lord President of the Council, he wrote on 10 May of 'the long dangerous defile through which we must march for many months'. When his bodyguard, Detective-Inspector Walter Thompson, congratulated him on taking office, Churchill answered with tears in his eyes, 'I only pray it is not too late.' He told his new Minister for Economic Warfare, Hugh Dalton, soberly: 'The public will stand everything except optimism.'

This was the Churchill seen by his intimates. The public Churchill, by contrast, was a dynamic hustler, moving so fast to transform the laggard war economy that he left secretaries and Civil Servants gasping.

Chamberlain's Secretary for War, Oliver Stanley, received a cryptic telephone message from Buckingham Palace; would Sunday be a convenient day to deliver up his seals of office? In this way Stanley learned that he formed no part of Churchill's Cabinet. The Minister of Information, Sir John Reith, more accustomed to dispense news than to receive it, heard by chance from the Assistant Editor of the London *Times* that his shoes were filled by Alfred Duff Cooper. 'Filthy treatment,' Reith raged in his diary, 'and what a *rotten* government.'

From Admiralty House, where he continued to work for the time being, Churchill daily poured forth up to fifty pink-tagged 'Action This Day' memos, probing into every aspect of the war effort. Bells rang continuously and staid civil servants were seen to run; his Chiefs of Staff, summoned to Churchill's presence at 9.30 p.m., often staggered wearily forth at 2 a.m., protracted sessions which staffers soon dubbed 'The Midnight Follies'. Intolerant of opposition, Churchill told one official who found his methods cavalier: 'I am indeed honoured to sit at the same table with a man who so closely resembles Jesus Christ, but I want to win the war.'

His 15-hour working day, which he began in bed, dictating from 8 a.m. onwards in a resplendent dragon-patterned dressing-gown, was as much a part of his life as his Cuban cigars, his 4 p.m. catnap, his nightly black-tie dinner parties. Outwardly an Edwardian figure, from his gold-knobbed cane to his 1900 taste in hats, his speed was still mid-twentieth century. He was almost never punctual and his chauffeur Joseph Bullock soon learned to clip the time schedule on journeys by shooting red lights and steering the wrong side of traffic islands. Often, at journey's end, swooning secretaries who had been taking dictation had to be revived with brandy.

'The war,' wrote his Director of Military Operations, Brigadier John Kennedy, 'would certainly have been much duller without him.'

It would have been duller, too, without the hard-bitten single-minded toe-tramplers whom Churchill brought in to aid him, men who cared for little but Britain's survival – what the Father of the House of Commons, Earl Winterton, termed 'a Government of all the toughs and all the talents'. 'Labour,' exulted Harold Laski, with some truth, 'dominates the economic organization of the war.' Not only was Attlee serving as Deputy Premier and Greenwood as Minister without Portfolio; Herbert Morrison had already left the London County Council to become Minister of Supply and Ernest Bevin, former boss of the mammoth Transport and General Workers' Union, became the new Minister of Labour, coining at the same time a new slogan: 'GIVE 'ITLER 'ELL'. But to unsnarl what Churchill called 'the muddle and scandal of the aircraft production branch' the Premier had appointed an unrepentant capitalist: bustling ruthless little William Maxwell Aitken, 1st Baron Beaverbrook.

From the first 'The Beaver', nicknamed 'Tornado' by the former King Edward VIII, seemed to vie with Churchill as to how many toes he could trample on. If Beaverbrook sought storage space he snatched it from the Air Ministry without any prior consultation, then padlocked it. To make aircraft factory workers feel 'important' he flashed messages on to cinema screens, recalling them to duty. Working from Stornoway House, St James's Park, his London home, Beaverbrook soon refused to conform to any appointment schedule. All took pot-luck, first come, first served.

Often, in an office plastered with slogans – 'Organization is the Enemy of Improvisation' – 'It is a long way from Knowing to Doing' – six officials were lined up before his desk at one time with memos to present.

When he decided to merge the industrial complex of Lord Nuffield, the 'British Ford', with the old-guard firm of Vickers-Armstrong, Beaverbrook dispatched a secretary to haul Nuffield out of bed at midnight to break the news. Nuffield's subsequent impassioned plea to Churchill fell on deaf ears. 'I cannot interfere with the manufacture of aircraft,' was Churchill's firm rejoinder.

Beaverbrook's credo was aptly expressed in a letter to Sir Samuel Hoare, soon en route as Ambassador Extraordinary to Franco's Spain: 'I don't care if the middle classes lie sleepless in their beds, so long as the workers stay active at their benches.' For what Beaverbrook was out to do, fearing the massed might of Luftwaffe bombers, was deliberately to disrupt bomber production at the expense of fighters. Out of 4,576 planes produced between May and August, 875 were new fighters and 1,872 fighter repairs.

It was not a programme achieved without the 'blood, toil, tears and sweat' which were all that Churchill had offered the British. One man, who looked in on a midnight meeting of Beaverbrook and his department chiefs at Stornoway House, never forgot it. The exchanges were as staccato as Browning machine-gun fire.

'How many planes are you producing this week? Double it!'

'I'm short of mechanics.'

'How many do you need?'

'Thirty or forty.'

'Which figure do you mean?'

'Thirty.'

'You'll have them Monday. Double your figures.'

The urgency was in keeping. At 5 p.m. on 10 May, the air-raid sirens screamed from Lyons to Newcastle-on-Tyne. Hitler had struck in the west.

The telephone wires were whispering in the night – 'René, René, René' – as the code word passed from Army post to

Army post along the Belgian frontier. Yet a curious air of unreality prevailed. In these first hours, there was nothing to indicate that this was the onset of a human event darker than any night: a day that, as Hitler had said, would 'decide the fate of the German nation for the next 1,000 years'.

At his Supreme Headquarters in the sombre casemates of the Château of Vincennes, which one officer likened to 'a submarine without a periscope', General Maurice Gamelin, the Allied C.-in-C., was conferring on the telephone with General Claudel Georges, Commander-in-Chief, North East. All reports confirmed that Hitler had just launched a concerted 136-division assault from the North Sea, to the Moselle, striking simultaneously against Holland, North-East Belgium and Luxembourg. Promptly at 6.30 a.m., Georges called General Gaston Billotte, commanding the Allied First Army Group. He ordered: 'Holland – Belgium, manoeuvre Dyle.' The Allies would move up to occupy a line based on Belgium's easterly Dyle River.

The fateful decision – to place their two strongest armies, the Seventh and the First, north of Namur, and their weakest the Ninth, to the south, in the wooded hilly region of the Ardennes – had now been taken.

Already, in olive and black 3-ton trucks, labelled 'Snow White', 'Doc' and 'Sneezy', Gort's British Expeditionary Force was on the move. Among them was the 1st Battalion, The East Surreys, whose ranks included the newly-wed Private Bill Hersey. For Hersey, who had married Augusta Six only twenty-four days back, the sudden parting had come as a wrench; the marriage seemed right from the very first. In the long twilight of the phoney war, he and Augusta had shared many warm moments; quiet games of pontoon, sing-songs, spirited evenings at the Café L'Épi d'Or's rifle range with Augusta, whose father had taught her to shoot, handling her .22 as well as any. Now, with a sprig of lilac in his steel helmet, Bill was off to fight the Germans – but he went as a conqueror, Augusta noted, perfectly confident.

At G.H.Q. Vincennes, the same air of confidence prevailed. At 6.30 a.m. Captain André Beaufre, of the General Staff, found Gamelin striding up and down the fort, humming with 'a pleased and martial air'. Gamelin had valid reasons; from this

80

day on, by courtesy of the British 'Enigma' machine,* his High Command was to be provided with the Germans' entire order of battle, situation reports and operational orders, intelligence as perfect as any commander could desire. Even so, Gamelin's total misconception of the nature of modern warfare would result in the heaviest defeat ever inflicted on a French Army in the field.

Even at Gamelin's level, the full implications had scarcely been grasped: following the incident of Major Reinberger's briefcase, Germany's strategy had changed. The original plan of attack had never found real favour with Hitler. 'This is just the old Schlieffen plan,' he objected to *Generaloberst* Wilhelm Keitel, his Chief of the Armed Forces, meaning the First World War plan of attack through Northern France and Belgium to the Channel ports, named after Alfred (Graf) Von Schlieffen, a former Chief of the General Staff. But as late as 17 February, no one had produced a viable alternative until *Generalleutnant* Fritz Erich von Manstein, Chief of Staff of *Generaloberst* Gerd von Runstedt's Army Group 'A', had come up with a plan of his own. Manstein's plan envisaged first a daring thrust to the south through the 'impenetrable' Ardennes with a sudden armoured breakthrough at Sedan and sweep to the Channel. Then, reversing the Schlieffen Plan, the main force would swing north, boring into the rear of the Anglo–French Army.

Thus Hitler's much cherished surprise element would be fully gratified, for Manstein's plan called not for eliminating France at a stroke, but for a swift advance to the Channel coast that would cut the Allies in half.

The imminence of Armageddon was hard for most men to grasp. At Metz, on the Moselle River, General Georges Boris, Inspector General of Artillery, hearing the ominous rumble of guns, inquired of an aide: 'Where are they holding the

---

* The much-discussed 'Enigma' dated from August 1939, when a model of the German cipher-machine (code-named 'Enigma'), reconstructed by the Intelligence Department of the Polish General Staff, reached London via a courier from the British Embassy in Paris, who brought it in the diplomatic bag. This model, code-named 'Ultra', was sited at Bletchley Park, a Victorian mansion forty miles north of London. Its first real contribution was to warn the Allies of Hitler's attack in the west.

manoeuvres?' 'That, *mon Général,*' the officer replied, 'is the start of the German offensive.' The Belgians were equally at a loss. In the small holiday town of Bouillon, across the frontier, the French Second Army's General Charles Huntziger, seeking to requisition a hotel, met with a blank refusal. 'Bouillon is a summer resort,' the Mayor protested. 'Our hotels are reserved for tourists!'

The sluggish incomprehension of those in command infuriated the men on the spot. On the night of 11 May, Captain René Gavoille, a reconnaissance pilot of Group II/33, took off in his twin-engined Potez 63 from Laon, some seventy miles west of Sedan, to survey the Ardennes sector. He returned agog with excitement: the forest was alive with motorized convoys. He had seen dim blue ribbons of light winding for miles through the woods. The French High Command shrugged this off as 'nocturnal illusions', so next day the incensed Gavoille took off in broad daylight. This time his Potez limped home riddled with flak holes but now Gavoille had not only seen for himself endless trucks and vehicles and a formidable array of tanks: he had photographed them. Yet even the sharp prints that emerged were rejected out of hand by the Ninth Army, whose sector this was: the Ardennes were impassable to armour. On 13 May, Gavoille, airborne to gather yet more evidence, was shot down in flames; he escaped with his life but the film was lost.

In Holland, the men at the top had also had prior warning, though scarcely putting it to great advantage. Soon after 9.30 p.m. on 9 May, Colonel Hans Oster, Chief of Staff of the *Abwehr* (German Military Intelligence) and a bitter opponent of Hitler, was dining in Berlin with his friend, Major J. G. Sas, the Dutch Military Attaché. 'The swine has gone off to the Western Front,' Oster warned Sas. 'Now it is definitely all over.' Sas promptly phoned a cryptic message to the Dutch Intelligence Service in The Hague: 'Tomorrow at dawn; hold tight.' But dawn found the Foreign Minister, Eelco van Kleffens, and his colleagues still debating what was to be done, with few conclusions reached. His wife had thoughtfully closed the window shutters tight; late passers-by must not be alarmed by the Minister's lights burning late.

Among those debating was van Kleffens' Permanent Secretary-General, Snouck Hurgronje, who a few nights back had bragged at a dinner party that he had known of the Norwegian invasion five days in advance but had warned neither the British nor the French. 'They're not *our* Allies,' was his complacent rationalization. Now, rather too late, Hurgronje realized that the bells tolled for Holland, too.

Even as they talked a new kind of fighting man was descending on the darkened tulip fields: the parachutist, neither flier nor foot-soldier but an amalgam of both, a Russian concept of five years earlier to which the Germans now gave new scope and validity. It was a phenomenon so novel that many Dutch citizens failed to react at all; as the parachutists hit the deck, milk and bread were still being delivered from door to door and many housewives were on their way to market. In the fields near Haarlem, farm workers were making an early start sowing the beet. In the Amsterdam office of the newspaper *De Groene Amsterdammer*, Editor Louis de Jong was chuckling over a rough proof of that day's cartoon; it pictured Chamberlain dressed as the dude in the Johnny Walker whisky advertisement with the caption, 'England Still Going Wrong'. Suddenly, to his alarm, de Jong realized that planes were swooping as low as 150 feet over the steep pitched roofs of the city.

It was a war so sporadic that many families hardly realized it was taking place. At her home in the fashionable Benoordenhout quarter of Holland's capital, The Hague, 13-year-old Ida van de Criendt was conscious of little more than an undefinable tension; people were crowding into the streets, craning upwards, while others peered from attic windows, shading their eyes against the brilliant sunshine. To Ida, her mother's injunction that she and her three brothers, Girrit, Jan and Hans, must pass the rest of the day beneath the stairs, seemed a cruel waste of a sunlit day, but all too soon Eitje van de Criendt had blotted the sunlight out. Sheets of black paper were spread across every window; the corridors glowed with an eerie blue light from shaded bulbs her mother had hoarded for just this purpose.

Above all, Ida envied the soldiers. Were they involved in some kind of manoeuvre, she wondered. Until today soldiers had never been seen in Benoordenhout, but by early morning they were everywhere in the street. In their green uniforms they seemed to be playing a macabre game of hide-and-seek, crouching behind bus shelters, wriggling noiselessly through bushes. Were they hiding – or were they seeking? Ida didn't know.

Everyone was agreed on one thing: the speed and ferocity of the German advance was devastating. Soon after dawn on 10 May, Belgium's much vaunted Fort Eben Emael, guarding the important city of Liège, and the Albert Canal, was captured by another weapon new to war: nine gliders weighing no more than 34 hundredweight apiece, towed from Cologne by JU 52 transports, to crashland twenty yards away. Due to a foul-up in timing, thirty-two out of the forty-one gliders that set out never made the target, yet once eighty-five trained engineers had placed hollow charges on the fort's cupolas, blasting holes in them to immobilize the guns, the garrison gave up with scarcely a fight.

By 11 May, the war was on with a vengeance in the Sedan sector. For the first time, Panzers were seen for what they were, armoured cavalry forging ahead; out of the window went decades of military theory as the motor columns cut through the Allied lines. By the late afternoon of this day, General Heinz Guderian of the XIXth Armoured Corps, whom his men called 'Hurrying Heinz', had crossed the French frontier north of Sedan, and became the first 'tourist' to reach Bouillon – where the Second Army's Huntziger had demanded 10,000 land-mines and received 200. Less than two days later, at 3 a.m. on 13 May, Hitler's directive No. 11 – an all-out assault across the Meuse – was in full swing. In boats, rubber canoes, straw rafts and even by swimming across, the Germans were gaining the west bank of the river. Joyfully *Oberstleutnant* Hermann Balck of the 1st Rifle Regiment, greeted Guderian: 'Joy riding in canoes on the Meuse is forbidden!' – the echo of a rebuke Guderian had let fall during training exercises in the Moselle.

Men who recalled an older war realized that unlike Verdun the terrors of combat were now vertical as much as horizontal. At Sedan, fifty miles up-river from Verdun, on the banks of the Meuse, the *drôle de guerre* for the French defenders ended promptly at 7 a.m. on Monday, 13 May. Endless waves of Dornier 17 and Heinkel 111 bombers pounded the crouching troops until the telegraph wires hung in useless loops and the roads were cratered and useless. Then the bombing began in earnest. While groups of Stuka dive bombers screamed like banshees towards the bunkers and the gun emplacements, their 500-pounders ripped through solid concrete, upending French artillery pieces, spreading a curtain of acrid choking fumes. Until three that afternoon, the dive bombing of the French positions on the south bank continued without cessation. 'Five hours of this nightmare was enough to shatter their nerves,' wrote their commander, General Edouard Ruby. 'They became incapable of reacting.'

At midnight on this day, one staff officer at G.H.Q. Vincennes recalled many of his colleagues were 'quite openly sobbing at having to admit the shame they felt': demoralized beyond recall, the stunned smoke-blinded defenders of Sedan had walked out of their positions and given up.

No man was more shattered by the turn of events than René de Chambrun, the former Maginot Line officer, now seconded for liaison with the British. Promoted captain one week earlier, de Chambrun was at Dibeck, a village near Brussels, when news of the débâcle reached him. His first intimation of trouble came when he glanced from the window of a small café: a captain wearing the Maginot Line badge was dismounting from an army truck, along with a group of weary helmet-less men. De Chambrun was puzzled: surely the Maginot Line was being held? He hastened out to greet the man.

At the sight of an officer wearing the same badge, the captain poured out his heart. 'The day before yesterday we received the signal to send many of our men on leave,' he expostulated. 'I had to abandon my fort without firing a shot, without seeing a German.' 'But why?' de Chambrun wanted to know. Growing more excited by the minute, the captain told of the sorry muddle: 'Orders had come to abandon the Line even before dawn on 10 May. The bridges over the Albert Canal had not been blown up. The Panzers, rumbling over them, had outflanked the Maginot Line. There had been nothing for it but to abandon their posts and retreat.'

'*C'est formidable, c'est formidable*,' the captain repeated despairingly. 'That line cost millions to build. It could have saved Belgium. I wanted to live and die in my fort. Now what can we do here without a gun?'

On 14 May, the day following Sedan's collapse, de Chambrun, at near-by Ogy, heard worse news yet from a Belgian major of the *Chasseurs Ardennais*, the unit told off to defend the Belgian sector of the Ardennes Forest. A ludicrous attempt to stall the German armoured advance by stacking mines in small dumps had literally backfired: the Germans had merely fired on them from a distance and forged ahead. 'It's too late now,' the major lamented. 'An enormous number of tanks and armoured cars are breaking through the front of your Ninth Army.'

Not surprisingly, the Ninth Army War Diary for 15 May made bleak reading: 'No information – communications cut – liaison unworkable – back areas blocked with convoys and wrecked columns – petrol trains in flames – wholesale chaos.' Already individual groups of men were cracking under the strain. 'Look, men,' one artillery colonel rallied a group of gunners. 'Here are some guns! There's plenty of ammunition. Carry on fighting!' But his answer was a disillusioned chorus: 'Colonel, we want to get home and carry on with our jobs. There's nothing to be done. We're finished, betrayed!'

On this same day, General Henri Honoré Giraud, with whom Gamelin had replaced General André-Georges Corap as head of the Ninth Army, sent to his Assistant Chief-of-Staff one of the most incredible requests ever made by a commander in the field: 'Send me some chaps who won't bolt – I mean, who'll get killed where they stand.'

In Holland, Ida van de Criendt, the 13-year-old schoolgirl who had watched the soldiers playing what looked like hide-and-seek in the green gardens of The Hague, realized that after four days' fighting her countrymen had given up.

Her mother, Eitje, had not been the only Dutch housewife to be profoundly shocked on learning that Queen Wilhelmina and the Royal family, including Princess Juliana and Prince Bernhard, had fled to London on a British destroyer. The Government had departed, too – some of them so precipitately that

Foreign Minister Eelco van Kleffens, speeding for England in a private seaplane, had made a belly-landing in the sea off Brighton, Sussex, when his fuel-tanks ran dry. To Ida, a teenage realist, the Queen's eleventh-hour departure made sense. 'Surely it's the best solution when she's a symbol,' she argued. 'How can our Queen be taken prisoner?'

In fact, Queen Wilhelmina had done her unavailing best. At 5 a.m. on 14 May, she had put through a phone call to a notably unresponsive King George VI at Buckingham Palace, to plead for planes. The King had duly informed his Chiefs of Staff, then gone back to sleep. 'It is not often one is rung up at that hour, and especially by a Queen,' he noted in his diary, 'but in these days anything may happen.' The King's reaction was predictable; at 6.30 a.m. on 10 May, the day of the invasion, a distraught Dutch Ambassador had arrived at the Air Ministry, off Whitehall, to plead for squadrons of fighters. When the Deputy Chief of the Air Staff, Air Vice Marshal Sholto Douglas, assured him that this was impossible, the diplomat dissolved in tears on Douglas's desk.

Yet, weeks earlier, when the British had proposed setting up a skeleton organization for fighter operations in Holland, the Dutch Government had refused to discuss it. Now Holland's eight million citizens were to pay the price of this neutrality.

Ida van de Criendt saw the end of everything while scarcely realizing what she saw. At 3 p.m. on 14 May, Eitje, greatly daring, had ventured to the roof, and lingered there aghast: fifteen miles away tall inky pillars of smoke were rising above the city-port of Rotterdam. 'Mother, come down, you'll be shot,' Ida was dissuading her, but despite herself she stayed on to watch. Never in her life had she seen a fire so all-consuming.

All later post-mortems suggested that the bombing was a tragedy of errors. An attack on Rotterdam had indeed been scheduled for 3 p.m., embracing a strictly military target: the powerful Dutch defence force to the north of the city's two main bridges. But by 2 p.m. a parley was already under way between *Oberstleutnant* Dietrich von Choltitz, commanding III Battalion/IR 16, and Colonel Scharroo, troop commander for Rotterdam. Shortly before take-off from Delmenhorst, Germany, *Oberst* Lackner, O.C. of Bomber Group 54, had been warned that Rotterdam was verging on surrender. Thus he was alerted that if a shower of red Very lights clustered above the target, the city had given in, and the raid was off.

At 2.15 p.m. the Airborne Corps' Signals Section at Rotterdam's Waalhaven Airport passed on a vital message: 'Attack postponed owing to parley.' But at this same hour, the 100 Heinkel 111s of Bomber Group 54 were already over the German–Dutch frontier. To reach their target by 3 p.m., an early take-off had been essential.

Now Air Fleet Two's H.Q., at Münster, stepped into the picture. They, too, were bent on recalling the raid, but Bomber Group 54's own operations room, at Delmenhorst, was the only headquarters on the same radio frequency as the speeding Heinkels. In a vain attempt to head them off, the Air Fleet's Operations Officer, *Oberstleutnant* Hans-Jürgen Rieckhoff, leapt into an ME 109 and took off from Münster.

Even this endeavour came too late. As Bomber Group 54 approached Rotterdam, the planes slid apart, as planned, into two columns: the 1st Wing's Commander, *Oberstleutnant* Otto Höhne, turned to approach from the south-west while Lackner's planes bored on. From an island in the Maas, Choltitz' men were now sending an imploring display of red Very lights soaring skywards, but in the mist and swirling smoke that blanketed the city, they were invisible. Only one man among 100 pilots – Höhne himself – spotted 'two paltry little Very lights' and shouted the order to turn back, although even he was too late to check his own automatic bomb-release.

Forty-three bombers in Höhne's wing now swung away to the south-west, but Lackner's fifty-seven Heinkels, seeing nothing, moved on to straddle the old city with ninety-seven tons of high explosive. Fanned by a gentle wind, the old timbered houses took fire like a forest, a conflagration which the obsolete two-wheeled pumps of Rotterdam's citizen's fire brigade were powerless to handle. In some sections of the city, the fires were to smoulder sullenly on until the third week of August, and many legends arose from their ashes. Thus, although 814 citizens died in the ruins, legend claimed that 25,000 had been incinerated. Even by the yardstick of 1940, the raid had been pitifully bungled – yet the legend now was that no city could resist the Luftwaffe after Rotterdam.

At 11 p.m. on this same day, all fighting in Holland ceased. To spare the people further suffering, the C.-in-C., General Henri Winkelmann, had accepted the German surrender terms. Ida van de Criendt saw it happen as she and countless million Dutch had seen it from the first: from the vantage point of her own street in Benoordenhout.

On 15 May, an olive-green *Wehrmacht* truck drove in from the southern end. A *Gefreiter* shouted a command, and from the bushes and the little walled shelters emerged the same Dutch troops that Ida had first seen five days earlier – 'just sweet farm boys putting on a big stage act as soldiers'. Orders rapped out, and one by one the soldiers came forward, throwing their rifles over the truck's tailgate. Most of them, weeping, stood ludicrously proud at attention.

To Ida van de Criendt, on 14 May, this cameo summed up Holland's surrender: the thud-thud of the rifles hitting the truck floor, the tears running down the young unlined faces.

It was a week for wake-up calls. One day after Queen Wilhelmina's call to King George VI, Churchill, in Admiralty House, was roused from sleep at 7.30 a.m. by a near-hysterical Paul Reynaud. 'We are beaten,' Reynaud hailed him dramatically. 'We have lost the battle.' Churchill was both somnolent and sceptical, but Reynaud persisted: 'A torrent of tanks is bursting through.'

Reynaud was right; the Allied cause in France was already lost beyond redemption. On this day, 15 May, with a 40-mile gap south and west of Sedan, the Meuse front was crumbling. The last chance to plug the German penetration of the Sedan bridgehead was vanishing even as the Premiers conferred.

Yet the myth of German invincibility was as much a triumph of propaganda as of military hardware. Against 156 Allied divisions, Hitler had committed no more than 136; his 2,800 strong Panzer force faced up to 4,000 Allied tanks. The Führer's secret was one as yet unplumbed by the Allies – extreme mobility backed by close air-support – and those in the Allied camp who had long advocated such tactics had spent lonely years in the wilderness. Only now was Colonel Charles de Gaulle, a 50-year-old veteran who had campaigned tirelessly for a French armoured force, given charge of a newly cobbled-up 4th Armoured Division. 'There, de Gaulle,' observed General Georges, Commander-in-Chief, North East, ironically. 'For you who have so long held the ideas which the enemy is putting into practice, here is the chance to act.'

An ardent Francophile, Churchill was loath to believe the worst, but at 4 p.m. on 16 May, intent on obtaining a clearer picture, he landed at Le Bourget airfield, Paris. But in Reynaud's office on the Quai d'Orsay, the air of gloom was palpable; from the long office windows, the bonfires of Foreign Office files, burning in the courtyard below, were clearly visible. As Gamelin, the Supreme Commander, demonstrated the Allied plight on a large-scale map, it dawned on Churchill that the French High Command were already contemplating defeat. '*Où est la masse de manoeuvre?* (Where is the strategic reserve?),' he asked, but Gamelin's reply was a terse shake of the head: '*Aucune.* (There is none.)'

Back at the British Embassy, Churchill was now more than aware that a crisis loomed. At 9 p.m. General Sir Hastings Ismay, Assistant Secretary to the War Cabinet, had dispatched a telegram – worded, for topmost security, in Hindustani – asking the War Cabinet to authorize the transfer of six more R.A.F. squadrons to back up the French. But the appeal fell on hostile ears. Though the Cabinet was at first inclined to agree, Air Chief Marshal Sir Cyril Newall, Chief of the Air Staff, took an obdurate stand. France, Newall pointed out, had neither the airfields nor the facilities to accommodate six extra squadrons; support for the French, if it was forthcoming, could be given by fighters operating from British south coast bases.

Just as in Norway, the shape of things to come was emerging. The British, with one eye cast across the Channel, were already looking to their own moat.

Franklin Roosevelt was always a man alert to danger signs. As far back as October 1937, he had deliberately chosen the isolationist city of Chicago to deliver a considered warning: 'Let no one imagine that America will escape, that America may expect mercy, that this Western Hemisphere will not be attacked.' Now, as the Panzers lanced through France, Roosevelt wondered increasingly: could America ever hope to stand aside from this conflict? To his entourage, his own sentiments were plain. Each night, as he relaxed over his stamp collection, the President would confide to his personal physician, Admiral Ross T. McIntire, 'England *has* to be saved.'

The problem was: what should the United States do? Holland had gone, and France was fast going; if Britain, too, succumbed, what would become of their empires? Should America seize such colonial outposts as Greenland, Barbados, Curaçao and French Guiana while there was still time? Should she try to establish a new relationship with an independent Canada? If Britain surrendered her Fleet to Germany, how would the United States face the resultant threat in the Atlantic coupled with the Japanese Fleet in the Pacific? Already, with each German conquest, America's export trade was shrinking – so what of her own economic future?

As things stood, America was in no immediate position to venture any gesture beyond moral wrist-slapping. Ironically, the most mechanically-minded people on earth, the builders of 65 per cent of the world's automobiles, had neither the aeroplanes to fight a Hitler-style war nor the trained men to build plants to create them. In the knowledge that America had only 178 Flying Fortress bombers to defend her own hemisphere, Secretary of State Cordell Hull had stressed to Roosevelt, on 13 May, that the United States should aim for a production of 50,000 planes a year. The President was speechless, and with reason: the figure was ten times that of current annual production.

On 16 May, Roosevelt met this challenge squarely. For defence purposes he demanded – and got – from the U.S. Senate $3,297,000,000 for the Army and Navy alone. In addition, the planes that he sought would cost $3,500,000,000 to buy, plus an additional $70,000 dollars per plane for annual maintenance. Even the Republicans, noted Secretary of the Interior Harold Ickes, 'will have to go along with this programme, because the country is for it and they dare not do otherwise'.

91

Slowly America was stirring, like a man trying not to wake from a pleasant dream. The old ideal of 'three thousand miles of good green water' on each coast no longer seemed a total guarantee of security. For the first time, American citizens were divining what Europeans had known since Munich: that life in a fear-dominated world could become less tolerable than war itself.

The realization was bringing Roosevelt unlikely allies. Colonel Charles A. Lindbergh might dismiss the risks of war as 'hysterical chatter', while author Clarence Budington Kelland charged that Roosevelt headed America's Fifth Column, but many isolationists were themselves beginning to feel isolated, consorting with such ultra-rightist bedfellows as William Dudley Pelley's Silver Shirts of America, Fritz Kuhn's German–American Bund, and the rabidly anti-Semitic radio priest, Father Charles E. Coughlin, weekly spewing forth his venom against 'Franklin Double-Crossing Roosevelt'.

Meanwhile, other voices, many of them Republican, were speaking loud and clear in Roosevelt's support. 'Neutrality has no meaning when such a merciless military machine is in full operation,' averred the *Washington Post*, 'nor can it be said realistically the U.S. is any longer neutral.' Rebutting Minnesota's isolationist Governor, Harold Stassen, the year's Republican candidate for the Presidency, Wendell L. Willkie, snapped back, 'If he ... attempts to put the Republican Party on record as saying what is going on in Europe is none of our business, we might as well fold up.' The *New York Herald Tribune* was blunter still: 'The least costly solution in both life and welfare would be to declare war on Germany at once.'

In the mid-western town of Emporia, Kansas, the renowned editor of the *Emporia Gazette*, 72-year-old William Allen White, made a move which would have been impossible before Rotterdam: the drumhead organization of a Committee to Defend America by Aiding the Allies. No utopian sentimentalist, White saw the British clear-sightedly: 'The old ... lion looks mangy, sore-eyed. He needs worming and should have a lot of dental work. He can't even roar.' Nonetheless, he felt that the risk of giving her all legal aid short of armed force must be taken.

Churchill, however, was seeking a more positive commitment, and Roosevelt was worried. As long ago as September 1939, the President, as a former Assistant Secretary of the Navy, had congratulated Churchill on his appointment as First Lord – an occasion which Churchill had exploited as a chance of plugging in a highly unorthodox private line to the White House. Now, following Reynaud's call, he had put in his first plea for the loan of forty or fifty old U.S. destroyers, following up his appeal, on 20 May, with a polite hint of blackmail. 'Putting this nightmare bluntly,' Churchill hinted that if his government fell, his successors might regard the British Fleet as 'the sole remaining bargaining counter with Germany'.

It was not a request which met with sympathy from American Ambassador Joseph P. Kennedy. 'It seems to me that if we had to fight to protect our lives we would do better fighting in our own backyard,' was his assessment to Hull. The opinion, however, was unlikely to sway Roosevelt, who thought of Kennedy as 'an appeaser ... a pain in the neck' – a verdict expressed more tartly still in Foreign Office circles: 'I thought my daffodils were yellow until I met Joe Kennedy.'

Even so, Roosevelt felt the need to bide his time. On 16 May, he replied to Churchill that only Congress could authorize a transfer of destroyers, and he was uncertain as to whether this was the time to put such a request. As Roosevelt explained to Harold Ickes, 'We cannot tell the turn the war will take, and there is no use endangering ourselves unless we can achieve some results for the Allies.'

Was Roosevelt playing his hand too cautiously? William Allen White thought so, for one; on 15 May, he warned the President, 'You will not be able to lead the American people unless you catch up with them.' But Roosevelt was less certain: as the head of the last great democracy still at peace, with only twenty-four weeks remaining of his second term, there were so many factors to be weighed. Still unresolved was the question of whether he should run for a third term at all, for what happened in Europe would be vital to that decision.

'The question of whether Mr Roosevelt will run for a third term,' noted the Assistant Secretary of State, Adolf A. Berle, on 15 May, 'is being settled somewhere on the banks of the Meuse River.'

*

At Madrid's Prado Palace, a Frenchman, who in sixty-four years of military service had known three world wars on French soil, counted the Second World War as already lost for France. It was not an opinion he sought to hide. As early as 19 March, he had stated openly that 'France's greatest mistake has been to enter this war' – a remark which the German Embassy had noted and taken pains to pass on to von Ribbentrop in the Reich Chancellery. Now, on 17 May, Marshal Henri Philippe Pétain, 84, was paying his last call as French Ambassador on General Francisco Franco, *Caudillo* of Spain.

Days earlier a desperate Reynaud had summoned him to return to France and serve as Minister of State and Vice-President of the Council. As the hero of Verdun, Reynaud felt that Pétain would be a father-figure who would inspire confidence and bolster flagging French morale. But this was not the role Pétain saw for himself. The war, he believed, was already lost. He was returning to conclude an honourable peace.

To the last Franco did his utmost to dissuade him. 'Don't go, Marshal,' he begged. 'Shelter behind your age ... You are the victorious soldier of Verdun. Don't allow your name to be linked with what other people have lost.'

'My country is calling me,' the old man replied, 'and it is my duty to go. It will perhaps be the last service I can render.'

'He embraced me, very moved,' Franco remembered later, 'and left for the sacrifice.'

The tempo of the German advance was alarming even Adolf Hitler. 'A most unfortunate day,' General Franz Halder, Chief of Staff of the German High Command, noted in his diary on 17 May, 'the Führer is terribly nervous. He is frightened by his own success, is unwilling to take any risks, and is trying to hold us back.'

Certainly the German success was unprecedented. Within seven days, they had annihilated two French armies, gained a massive foothold in France, and nullified the Allied strategic plan. Already the French First Army and the British Expeditionary Force were making a fighting retreat to the line of the Escaut River; Brussels, Louvain and Malines were to fall before the day was out. 'We were through the Maginot Line!'

exulted *Generalmajor* Erwin Rommel, commanding the 7th Panzer Division. 'It was not just a beautiful dream. It was reality.'

At the Quai d'Orsay, Paris, Reynaud was making desperate attempts to stop the rot. On assuming the Premiership, he had appointed Edouard Daladier, his predecessor, as War Minister; now, in the space of a day, he took over this role himself, replacing Gamelin as Commander-in-Chief with General Maxime Weygand, a bow-legged 73-year-old Cavalryman. On the surface, Weygand seemed spry enough; at G.H.Q., now transferred to Montry, he amazed Captain André Beaufre and other General Staff officers by sprinting 100 yards across the grass by way of relaxation, then taking the stairs to his first conference four at a time.

But by 6.30 p.m. on Sunday, 19 May, his mood was graver. At a War Ministry meeting with Reynaud and the newly-arrived Marshal Pétain, he warned them: 'You will not be surprised if I cannot answer for victory.' A chance remark to General Wladyslaw Sikorski disturbed the Polish Commander-in-Chief profoundly. France, Weygand thought, was doomed to endure a period of suffering as punishment for twenty years of laxity. 'As a Catholic you may talk like that,' replied Sikorski, shocked, 'but not as a Commander-in-Chief.'

For time was running out. On 20 May, General Heinz Guderian first took Amiens and then reached Abbeville at the mouth of the Somme, moving with such speed that his XIXth Armoured Corps caught French troops still drilling on the parade ground and captured a British battery with all its guns intact in the market place at Albert. Now, by gaining the Channel coast, the *Wehrmacht* had severed all connection between the French, British and Belgians in the north – one million strong – from the French in the south.

On 21 May, euphoric once more, Hitler bounced out of his headquarters, the *Felsennest* in the Eifel Rhineland country, twenty miles west of Remagen Bridge, and hailed Raeder's aide, *Korvettenkapitän* Kurt Freiwald: 'Isn't everything just great? This morning for the first time in ages I heard nightingales singing.'

In keeping with the Führer's mood, the German radio this

day proclaimed: 'People of France, cease thinking the world is with you. It is overwhelmingly ours.'

Despite all evidence to the contrary, Churchill still believed that French muscle would prevail. By noon on 22 May, he was once more back in France, this time at the former G.H.Q., Vincennes, to meet Reynaud and Weygand, whom he found 'brisk, buoyant and incisive'. To the scepticism of Captain André Beaufre, standing by, the three men, along with Dill and Ismay, began to improvise plans. How could they extricate the French First Army group from the disaster of encirclement? On paper, the plan they formulated seemed promising: the Belgian Army must withdraw to the line of the Yser River and stand fast. The French First Army and the B.E.F. must by tomorrow attack south-west towards Bapaume and Cambrai. Meanwhile, a new French Army Group, the Seventh, should strike northwards to link up with the British. To cohere Franco–British liaison, faulty until now, Churchill was appointing Major-General Edward Spears, who had headed Britain's Military Mission to France in the First World War, as his personal liaison officer to Reynaud.

Captain Beaufre listened in cynical silence. Men are made of flesh and blood, he thought; the troops in whom Weygand and Churchill pinned such faith had been harassed and dive-bombed for twelve days now. In his heart, Beaufre knew it was all too late. The French were finished – and most likely, he thought, the British, too.

Soon after noon on Saturday, 25 May, Major-General Spears, after presenting his credentials to Reynaud, sat in on his first meeting with the French War Committee in the Premier's Quai d'Orsay office. Along with him at the polished Louis XV table sat Reynaud, Weygand, Pétain, Paul Baudouin, the War Committee's tall handsome secretary, and Admiral Jean François Darlan, the Naval C.-in-C.

The atmosphere of defeat and distrust appalled Spears. Unknown to him, Churchill had telephoned Reynaud to question whether 'it would not be better if the British Army fought in retreat towards the coast'. At once Weygand had called General Ironside in London to insist that any suggestion of a British evacuation would be disastrous. By 24 May, however, Weygand had grown suspicious. All evidence suggested that the British were still falling back towards the Channel ports.

To Spears, an unexpected visitor was a staff officer from General Blanchard's First Army Group, who, 'in the voice of a seasick passenger asking a passing steward for a basin', told the meeting: 'I believe in a very early capitulation.'

Suddenly, turning towards Reynaud, Weygand burst out uncontrollably: 'This war is sheer madness. We have gone to war with a 1918 army against a German Army of 1939. It is sheer madness.'

Spears was badly shaken, and a meeting later that day with his old friend the Minister of the Interior, Georges Mandel, gave him no crumb of comfort. 'The men want to get out of it at any cost,' Mandel told him. 'That's what's the matter with the Army.' Almost as an afterthought, he added: 'I suppose you realize that Weygand is already thinking in terms of a surrender?'

By painful degrees, Spears was coming to accept this fact. Weygand was calculating that by mid-June the French would be fighting against odds of three to one. Pétain in turn was thinking bitterly in terms of unequal sacrifice: against France's eighty divisions, Britain had fielded no more than ten. All through that meeting, the issue of a separate peace, as yet unvoiced, had still been in the air.

It was Pétain who had worried Spears most. His defeatism seemed to communicate itself to the others. When the meeting ended, he had not risen along with the rest but sat there, head bent, staring intently at the carpet. Had he heard half of what had been said? Had he even been listening?

Or was he, Spears wondered, 'following some memory or notion of his own'?

When the deal was first broached, only five men were present. The time was 2 p.m. on Sunday, 26 May, the meeting place the Cabinet Office at 10 Downing Street, and the air of conspiracy among those seated round the green baize table palpable.

Farther along Whitehall, in an ante-room at Admiralty House, Paul Reynaud, who had flown from Paris to pose one of the year's more momentous questions, awaited on their deliberations. The point at issue was crucial: what could be offered to Benito Mussolini to keep Italy out of the war?

If Mussolini held back from declaring war on France in her hour of crisis, Reynaud had professed himself ready to offer *Il Duce* territorial gains from France's North African Empire – Djibouti, in French Somaliland, facilities in Tunisia – at the same time hinting that Germany's juggernaut progress threatened Italy's independence.

All this had originated in the fertile brain of André François-Poncet, the French Ambassador to Italy, who had initially suggested Pope Pius XII as an intermediary. The British Foreign Office, however, preferred Roosevelt in this role, and had authorized Lord Lothian to approach him. Now, on Sunday, 26 May, Churchill, after lunching Reynaud at Admiralty House, was putting the French Premier's proposals to four senior Ministers: Attlee, Chamberlain, Greenwood and Halifax.

If such an approach was made, Churchill invited his colleagues to consider what terms Italy would demand of Britain. Probably, he thought, the neutralization of Gibraltar and the Suez Canal, the demilitarization of Malta, and the limitation of British naval forces in the Mediterranean.

At first, it was plain that some were tempted. The last thing Mussolini wanted, Halifax suggested, was a Hitler-dominated Europe. *Il Duce* would be the first man to persuade Hitler to take a more reasonable attitude. If Britain could obtain terms which would not postulate the destruction of her independence, 'we should be foolish if we did not accept them'. Labour's Arthur Greenwood saw 'no objection to this kind of approach being tried'. Chamberlain, a fervent appeaser to the last, noted in his diary: 'If we could get out of this jam by giving up Malta and Gibraltar and some African territories, we would jump at it.'

Churchill himself was sceptical. He thought that little would come of an approach, but this was a matter for the War Cabinet.

At Admiralty House, where the Ministers now adjourned to meet him, Reynaud did little more than reiterate the proposals Churchill had outlined. But once he had departed to take the plane back to Paris, Churchill spoke more frankly. He thought it best to decide nothing until it was seen how many of Gort's B.E.F., now fighting towards the coast, could be re-embarked from France. But, in the long run, 'if France could not defend herself, it is better that she should get out of the war rather than she should drag us into a settlement which involved intolerable terms'.

From the first, the Foreign Office had wanted any proposals to Mussolini couched in the vaguest possible phrasing. Roosevelt, it was suggested, might offer *Il Duce* a settlement of 'reasonable Italian claims' at the war's end, and 'participation at the peace conference with a status equal to that of the belligerents', provided always that she stayed on the sidelines. But at 4.30 p.m. on Monday, 27 May, as the debate continued, Halifax reported a stumbling-block. The French Ambassador, René Corbin, had visited him that morning to press Reynaud's point still further. Any approach to Mussolini, he stressed, must be one that gave specific 'geographical precision'.

With this, the War Cabinet, now in full session, shied as guiltily as men caught with their fingers in the till. The shameful aura of Munich hung over the conference table. 'The suggestion that we were prepared to barter away pieces of British territory would have a deplorable effect,' was Sir Archibald Sinclair's outraged reaction. Labour's Greenwood, more forthright still, spoke as a true politician: the worst crime, he implied, was to be found out. If Mussolini held out for Malta, Gibraltar and Suez, Hitler would certainly get to know. And 'if it got out that we had sued for terms at the cost of ceding British territory, the consequences would be terrible'.

It was at this point that Mussolini, who had already told the American Ambassador in Rome, William Phillips, that all such overtures were 'too late', lost all hope of pickings in the Mediterranean and France was abandoned to her fate.

The only way that Britain could recover her prestige in Europe, Churchill maintained, was 'by showing the world that Germany had not beaten us'. 'Let us therefore avoid,' he urged his Ministers, 'being dragged down the slippery slope with France.'

That Sunday evening was a gloomy one at the White House.

Roosevelt sat with a small group of intimates in his study, mixing old-fashioneds, talking abstractedly. It was no time for laughter or cocktail party chatter. The dispatches came in – from Ambassador Bullitt in Paris, from John Cudahy in Brussels – and Roosevelt studied them minutely. 'All bad, all bad,' he muttered, handing them to Eleanor.

Late that evening, facing the microphones for one of his renowned 'Fireside Chats', he delivered a clarion call. In a sense it was a message all too stirring, for it held out hope that Roosevelt was at that moment powerless to give. It was no time, he said, for fear or panic, even though the last two weeks had shattered many illusions of American isolation.

'On this Sabbath evening, in our homes in the midst of our American families, let us calmly consider what we have done and what we must do ... We defend and we build a way of life, not for America alone, but for all mankind. Ours is a high duty, a noble task.'

4

'Are We Building Golden Bridges for the British?'

25 May–2 June 1940

On this same Sunday night, as Roosevelt spoke of the task that faced America, all Major-General Spears's earlier forebodings were justified. A vast military disaster was in the making. Along the canals of Northern France, from Nieuport to Seclin, from Carvin to Gravelines, the 390,000 men of Lord Gort's British Expeditionary Force, the Belgians and the French First Army gripped tight on their rifles and waited.

Retreat was now inevitable. That very morning, Secretary for War Anthony Eden had authorized a complete British withdrawal to the coast. But was a successful retreat now even possible? At G.H.Q., Premesques, a small stone château southeast of the Ypres–Comines Canal, General Lord Gort now had his doubts. 'I must not conceal from you that a great part of the B.E.F. and its equipment will inevitably be lost in the best of circumstances,' he had cabled Eden. Then, because his whole life was the army, he turned to his aide, Captain the Earl of Munster, and in a rare moment of self-revelation confided: 'You know, the day I joined up I never thought I'd lead the British army to its biggest defeat in history!'

For Gort, the prospect of defeat had come with terrifying suddenness. On 10 May, when his troops had moved up like conquering heroes to cross the Belgian frontier, the C.-in-C. had expected great things of his men. Yet within twelve days the British had abandoned riverline after riverline – the Dyle, the Dendre, the Escaut – without a fight.

The tragedy was that Gort's Army, like the French, was magnificently equipped – to refight the First World War. Against the Germans' 2,800 Mark IIs and Mark IVs, Gort could

101

marshal only such lumbering, heavily-armoured tanks as the 'Matilda', with its frail two-pounder gun. Even the French tanks, 2,400 strong, moved cumbrously, geared to infantry support, often running short of fuel during a battle.

The result had been disaster from the first. The only real armament against the tanks of von Runstedt's Army Group 'A' were 25-pounder guns detached in an anti-tank role to fire solid shot against the Panzers. Infantry used the ·55 rifle, the Boys, whose bullets bounced back from the tanks' hide like peas from a window-pane. The artillery was as bad. Not one gun which Gort possessed had much more than half the range of the latest German models – and many, due to an absence of firing locks, had never been fired before 10 May.

Thus by 26 May, Gort faced a bitter decision. King Leopold's Belgian Army, 700,000 strong but equipped only with rusty rifles and horse-drawn cannon, had begun to crack. Boulogne had fallen; Calais was under siege. Gort's sole remaining hope was to deny the French High Command who were his masters and to fight back down a corridor fifty miles long and fifteen miles wide to the thousand-year-old port of Dunkirk. But he could not overlook the grim likelihood: that 300,000 men would be prisoners by the week's end.

Few suspected this yet, and British units posting their sentries in a hundred vehicle parks and market towns and châteaux could only hope the top brass knew what they were about. 'This is Mons all over again,' a veteran assured Lance-Corporal Thomas Nicholls, a young anti-tank gunner defending Wormhoudt. 'We're forming a thin red line to throw them out.' But increasingly a note of cynicism crept in. At Ypres, when Major Cyril Huddlestone of the 4th East Yorks opened a War Office telegram routed to all units and read, 'We are holding a National Day of Prayer for you,' he snorted and crumpled it into his pocket. 'Why the hell don't they send us some 25-pounders?' he asked angrily.

Late this Sunday night Captain Harry Smith, stationed on the outskirts of Roncq, abruptly roused his East Surreys from sleep; word of the disaster was spreading now. 'We are making a general retreat to the coast,' he announced when they had shuffled into an uneasy company parade. 'The idea is to get back to England so we can return to France later.'

To Private Bill Hersey, the news was frightening. The instant the company was dismissed he approached Captain Smith and snapped to attention. 'Sir,' he asked, 'is there anything you can do for my wife?' The answer was succinct. 'Go and get her.'

Grabbing a bicycle, Hersey pedalled furiously for the Café l'Épi d'Or at Tourcoing. For the past two weeks he and Augusta had been separated by the sudden stunning war, and in the last ten days he had fought through an exhausting retreat from Brussels. Tonight his one thought was to get Augusta safely away to England. At 11.30 p.m. he reached the café and knocked thunderously.

When Augusta opened the door and saw her husband's face, she knew immediately why he had come. 'Get your things,' he greeted her. 'You're leaving.'

Augusta swiftly dressed and packed a suitcase. Her father had already gone south to find safer quarters for his family, and her mother was too distressed to speak when Augusta awakened her to say good-bye. But when Bill Hersey urged, 'Augusta is British now; only this way can she be safe,' she seemed to understand.

'Dépêchez, dépêchez (Hurry, hurry),' Bill kept imploring as Augusta wheeled out her bicycle. It seemed a night for speed. Machine guns hammered faintly in the east, and sappers were laying mines by the roadside as they pedalled to Roncq. Transport was already moving off there, and Captain Smith made a quick decision. 'Your wife can go with the driver in my truck,' he told Hersey. 'But first you had better get her kitted out.'

Bill, a company storeman, soon outfitted Augusta as a British Tommy – rifle, steel helmet, khaki greatcoat. Then she climbed into the truck, and the captain impatiently signalled 'Off'. For Hersey, who would be marching, the strangeness of it all almost numbed the pang of parting.

Across the Channel, in an office carved into the chalk cliffs 500 feet above the sea, Admiral Sir Bertram Home Ramsay, Flag Officer Commanding Dover, studied a nightmare assignment. Operation Dynamo, the evacuation of British troops from France, seemed to the aloof silver-haired admiral to offer little chance of success. Dunkirk, the one remaining bolthole in British hands, had already been bombed for a week by the Luftwaffe, and the fine harbour that had made it France's third port was now out. The twenty-five miles of tortuous, shoal-ridden coast, known as 'the graveyard of ships', was unapproachable with heavy craft; the evacuation would have to be a small-ship affair.

Quietly, clinically, Ramsay chewed it over with Captain William Tennant, newly appointed Senior Naval Officer, Dunkirk, who had been sent post-haste to help him. Only forty destroyers were immediately available from the 202 with which the Navy had begun the war; moreover, these slim, whippet-like vessels, crammed with guns and depth-charge racks, were not built to carry men. Thus the bulk of the lifting would have to fall on lightly armed merchant ships – coasters, cross-Channel ferries, flat-bottom Dutch barges. But only 129 such vessels were available on this warm May morning, though more were on the way from a score of ports.

To conduct the evacuation – which would continue as long as Gort's men could hold off the Germans – Tennant would be assisted by twelve naval officers and 150 ratings. Few on the ships knew about the project, but all through the Navy there was a pleasant tingle of expectancy. If something strange was afoot, the Navy was ready.

Some learned the news in devious ways. Chief Petty Officer Wilfred Walters, summoned from a pub in North Shields on the Tyne and now en route for Harwich in the old coalburning minesweeper *Ross*, had the romantic notion they were speeding to the rescue of the Dutch royal family, who had reached England fourteen days back. Lieutenant Victor de Mauny, skipper of the contraband-control vessel *Ocean Breeze*, thought his mission was concerned with Belgian refugees – until, at breakfast in the shore Naval base at Ramsgate, a Scots Guards officer put him right with a withering: 'Refugees? Good God, it isn't refugees – it's the B.E.F.!'

Few had it as straight from the shoulder as the officers of the minesweeper *Leda*. Finger stabbing at a map of the coast, Commander Harold Unwin told them: 'The situation is bad, almost as bad as it could be . . . we are going over tonight to bring off the B.E.F. . . . and now we are for it, boys, good and hearty.'

The way things looked, 'night' was the operative word. As Tennant left Ramsay's office, the admiral almost casually added one last word: at the most, Tennant and his staff could expect to bring off 45,000 men.

The steady retreat of the British towards the north had not gone unremarked by Weygand. As early as 25 May, following the meeting with Spears, he signalled to the B.E.F.'s commander: 'In view of the gravity of the circumstances, General Weygand appeals personally to Lord Gort. The British Army should participate vigorously in the necessary general counterattacks. The situation demands hard hitting.'

Now, at Reynaud's midday conference on 27 May, Weygand confessed to the Premier that he had just dispatched a message as strongly worded to King Leopold. 'There will probably be reactions to these rigorous telegrams on the part of the two Governments,' he warned Reynaud. 'Tell them that you can do nothing and that I am a swine. Not only do the English not attack, but they retreat, and the Belgians are giving way.'

Reynaud appeared the soul of conciliation. 'But I think your telegrams are very moderate,' he replied gently.

That the B.E.F. had any chance of reaching the coast was itself amazing, for the British held Dunkirk only because of an almost inexplicable switch in German strategy. At 6.10 p.m. on 23 May, Rundstedt had confirmed a request that was later to set the entire German High Command by the ears. In response to a phone call from *Generaloberst* Günther Hans von Kluge, commanding the German Fourth Army, who reported that 'the troops would welcome an opportunity to close up tomorrow', Rundstedt assented freely. Promptly, Kluge telephoned the chiefs of staff of Panzer Groups Kleist and Hoth to notify that neither their tanks nor the men of Fourth Army should advance on the morrow. All should hold their positions until rearward troops had closed up.

Although Rundstedt had not initiated the halt, it was in keeping with his psychology. Unlike such dashing Panzer leaders as Guderian, Army Group 'A' 's commander, a cautious 65-year-old patrician, distrusted this new concept of independent tank warfare. More than once, as the Panzers speared through the Ardennes, he had clamped down brief halt orders: the tanks were advancing too far and too fast for the infantry to catch up, leaving a long exposed flank.

Now the Army's Supreme Commander, *Generaloberst* Walter von Brauchitsch, stepped in. The tanks, he felt, were wasted in the west, since the British were no longer a force to be reckoned with. The entire Panzer contingent, von Brauchitsch ordered, along with the German Fourth Army, were to transfer from Rundstedt to *Generaloberst* Fedor von Bock, whose Army Group 'B', attacking from the east, lacked any armour at all.

Then, at 11 a.m. on 24 May, Hitler, trim in snuff-brown jacket and breeches, paid a surprise visit to Rundstedt's headquarters at Charleville, in the Ardennes – so unexpectedly that an orderly barely had time to humour the ascetic Führer and fling wide Rundstedt's window, wafting out the heavy tobacco fumes of a chain-smoker. But that day, *Oberst* Günther Blumentritt, Rundstedt's Operations Officer always recalled, Hitler was quiet, almost docile. Flicking a pointer at the big operations map, he asked finally what Rundstedt intended to do with the armour now that it was halted.

Rundstedt was puzzled. The armour, he explained, was no longer his to command. Von Brauchitsch had transferred it to Army Group 'B' twenty-four hours back.

Now every man sensed that something was wrong. Though Hitler's only comment was a quiet 'That order will be cancelled', plainly he had known nothing of the switch.

Hitler pursued his theme. The tanks, now halted, should stay halted. The marshy Flanders plain was not tank country. There was also 'Plan Red' to consider, Hitler's already blue-printed armoured thrust across the Somme River, against the heart of France. Supposing the French attacked from the south in force while the Panzers were bogged down in the marshes encircling Dunkirk?

'I hope and I believe we will come to an agreement with

Britain,' he had told Rundstedt a week earlier in this very room. '*She* should rule the globe and the seas. I should rule Europe.' The meeting over, Rundstedt had commented dryly to Blumentritt: 'Well, if he doesn't want anything else from England, we'll have peace in about six weeks.'

This story, quickly circulated among the generals, led General Hans Jeschonnek, Chief of Staff to the Luftwaffe, to remark: 'Hitler has withdrawn the tanks from Dunkirk to save the British from a shameful defeat.' Then, as the top brass grasped the full implications of this decision, there came a mighty yell of protest.

At Hitler's headquarters, near Munstereifel, General Hans von Greiffenberg, of the Operation Staff, burst out: 'What is the meaning of this insane order? Are we building golden bridges for the British?' From Brussels, General von Bock protested angrily to von Brauchitsch: 'It's essential the tanks attack at once! If Dunkirk isn't taken, the British can move their army wherever they want.'

As *Kapitän* Jesko von Puttkamer, the Führer's naval adjutant, was later to reveal, this was a truth that Hitler had signally failed to grasp. In common with General Weygand, he had always believed that the British in Flanders would stand to the last man; the concept of a pull-back by sea had barely crossed his mind. If he could contain the B.E.F. without pushing it to annihilation, he would at one and the same time render it harmless and gain a powerful political club.

Others were early in the fray, and none more eagerly than *Feldmarschall* Hermann Göring. On 23 May, hearing that the Panzers had almost reached Dunkirk, Göring had pounded the table and cried: 'I must call the Führer. This is a special job for the Luftwaffe.' 'Within minutes,' *Generalleutnant* Josef Schmid, Chief of Staff to the Air High Command, recalled, Hitler had agreed without demur – a day before he had even consulted with Rundstedt. Dunkirk should be left to the Luftwaffe.

In fact, only Göring had such faith, and General Albert Kesselring, Chief of Air Fleet Two, telephoned him from Brussels to protest. Surely Göring realized that three weeks' air war had reduced some Luftwaffe units by 50 per cent? That most available bombers were still based at airfields 300 miles from Dunkirk? At last, convinced that Göring's desire for vainglory overrode all other factors, Kesselring, with a curt 'Nicht lösbar' (It won't work), slammed down the phone.

Thus, for three days while the argument raged, the British and the French had breathing space to reorganize, to re-group their forces to defend the shattered port. And though by Monday, 27 May, Hitler had agreed to a limited use of tanks within thirteen miles of Dunkirk, they were still to bypass the port. On this point, the Führer remained adamant: Dunkirk remained the Luftwaffe's job.

Late on the Monday afternoon, Captain William Tennant and his party set out from Dunkirk aboard the old destroyer Wolfhound. Soon enough their task became a chill reality; scarcely had the ship cleared Dover than German dive-bombers came snarling from the hazy sky. For the next two hours, with the ship swerving from port to starboard to dodge the rain of bombs, Tennant's men crouched on deck beneath the 'X' gun, straining their ears to catch their captain's briefing.

But the salient points were clear: Commander Jack Clouston was to meet incoming ships, Commander Renfrew Gotto would handle troops from the harbour end, Commander Harold Conway would reconnoitre the beaches, each officer to be assisted by a dozen ratings.

Yet, as Dunkirk came in view, Tennant's heart sank. Never in his wildest dreams had he imagined such havoc. Black smoke from the burning oil refineries at St Pol enveloped the harbour. The miles of warehouses and quays seemed on fire from end to end. In the sky above, dive-bombers wheeled and turned and bombs screamed down incessantly. Even as they watched, a stick of bombs fell beside the nearest quay with hammer-blow precision, to send concrete and white water founting. 'A nice welcome to Dunkirk,' Commander Gotto murmured.

It was just 6 p.m. when Tennant landed and took swift stock of the appalling situation. For four days there had been no water supply in Dunkirk. Only one telephone line remained open to London. Through an error in interpreting orders, 100-odd heavy anti-aircraft guns had been destroyed, leaving almost no defence against planes. And on that Monday alone 30,000 incendiaries and 15,000 high-explosive bombs had been dropped. The 115 acres of docks and five miles of quays were reduced to rubble, and in the ruins of the town 1,000 men, women and children lay dead.

Defeat and shame had bred a savage anarchy, and whole groups of men, deserted by panic-stricken officers, prowled through Dunkirk in an ugly mood of violence. As Tennant's party marched through the blazing town they saw sights to turn them cold: soldiers smeared with lipstick, howling and screeching, a sergeant, blind drunk, sporting a woman's feather boa, a litter of pigskin brandy flasks and toilet cases dropped by hastily departing officers.

Suddenly there was a crack, and a bullet whined past Tennant's head. A snarling, trigger-tense mob of British soldiers, rifles at the ready, was advancing towards them through the dusk. To Commander Harold Henderson, it seemed high time to turn back. But Tennant, confidently approaching the ringleader, quietly but firmly disarmed him.

'Here, old chap,' he invited, producing a hip flask. 'Have a drink. You'll feel better.'

For one electric moment, Henderson thought the troops might open fire. But the ice was broken. Convinced the Navy was there to help them, the men became pathetically docile, forming readily into queues.

Now Tennant gave crisp orders to his staff. The troops were to line up on the dunes and advance to the water's edge in groups of fifty. No man was to embark without arms. The Admiralty's last order had been: 'Mind you bring back the guns.' If Britain itself was to be the last line of defence, even rifles might soon be at a premium.

Aside from the beaches, which lay open to the roaring northern winds, the sole remaining embarkation facilities were the east and west moles – long wooden gangways, merging into concrete substructure that thrust 1,400 yards into the roadstead. These had been erected to protect the harbour, and were not designed for berthing ships. At this season, a surging three-knot tide raced between the concrete piles and made it extremely difficult to bring craft alongside.

Later that evening Tennant saw that at low tide Channel waters had receded a full half mile. Medical corps men, stretchers lifted head high, were struggling towards two solitary lifeboats that had been rowed within 100 yards of the shore. The parent ships were merely dark specks a mile offshore, and every lifeboat that rowed in would face a back-breaking 20-minute pull, and could load, at most, twenty-five men.

With two of his staff, Tennant thoughtfully tramped to the east mole. 'This would certainly be quicker,' he said, 'if only we could get a ship alongside.'

For a grim moment he considered the alternatives. 'We'll try it,' he announced. 'Signal the nearest ship to come in.'

As the *Queen of the Channel* responded, cutting a path towards them, the minutes seemed to crawl. First the bow had to be nosed in gingerly. Next a head rope was made fast. Then, as Tennant watched tensely, the ship's stern swung around and against the pier. Minutes later she was secure fore and aft, and men were filing aboard.

Tennant breathed a sigh of relief. At least it *could* be done – with luck.

During the first experimental day, 7,669 men were safely transported to England.

At 11 p.m. on that Monday night, Gort arrived for a conference at Bastion 32, the vast underground headquarters of Admiral Jean Abrial, French commander at Dunkirk. Their main task now was to finalize the Dunkirk bridgehead – though for political reasons no mention was made to Abrial of a total British withdrawal. (Even the French Naval Liaison Officer in London, Admiral Odend'hal, only learned through a chance visit to Dover; the Admiralty had not seen fit to tell him.) But suddenly General Koeltz, Weygand's personal emissary, asked nonchalantly: 'Is Lord Gort perhaps aware that the King of the Belgians has asked for an armistice from midnight?'

For a moment Gort sat quite still, palms outspread on the table, staring into space. Now for twenty miles the whole left flank of the British Army lay open to the sea.

But Gort's poker face was born of foreknowledge. Three days earlier Leopold had warned him that such a surrender was forthcoming, an intimation that Gort had shrunk from sharing with Churchill or Eden. 'My God, Geordie, they're shits!' he had burst out to Captain George Gordon-Lennox, one of his staff officers, but in more sober moments he knew this was unfair. Twenty-four hours before the Belgian surrender, Gort had begun the slow withdrawal of *his* Army, without informing Leopold – and the King, like Finland's Field-Marshal Mannerheim, had a duty to his troops. 'Do the Belgians think us awful dirty dogs?' Gort had asked Admiral Sir Roger Keyes, Britain's representative in Belgium, shamefacedly.

No news of the Belgian surrender reached Augusta Hersey that night, yet somehow she had known. A French liaison officer had sought shelter for her in a farmhouse east of Dixmude, but all his pleadings had not softened the Belgian farmer's heart; he had no beds for the British and their kind. Augusta had settled for a heap of dry straw in the farmyard. Next morning when she and Captain Smith's driver sought to quench their thirst, they found that the farmer had locked the well.

Augusta understood this hostility. As a Frenchwoman, she knew better than most the anguish that had befallen the land. Two weeks earlier the Belgians had pressed wine and flowers on the British, and priests had blessed the army as it streamed past. But now the liberators were pulling out. Belgium had surrendered, and for the second time in their lives these people were to be overrun by the Germans.

Sudden despairing signs of defeat were everywhere: white flags flapping from soldiers' bayonets; white sheets hanging from the windows of houses until it resembled washday; a Belgian general in a car, hastily changing into civilian clothes. And every village gave the British the same bitter, hostile glances.

'Why have they turned against us?' one puzzled sergeant asked, unaware that the British troops were going back to England. 'Search me,' a sergeant-major replied. 'But you never know who's going to win this flaming war!'

René de Chambrun, now far from the Maginot Line, was fast reaching one conclusion. Whoever won the war, it could scarcely be the French. Weygand's army was cracking, and de Chambrun knew it.

On Tuesday, 28 May, de Chambrun reached Dunkirk for a near-implausible reason: vital papers from the First Army's General Blanchard must be delivered to Weygand in Paris. But with the Allies surrounded, there was now only one way to reach the French capital: by hitching a speedboat ride from Dunkirk to Dover, then crossing the Channel once more in a plane from London to Le Bourget airfield.

'You'll have to take a chance if you really want to go this morning,' a naval officer told de Chambrun when he reported at Bastion 32. 'Our defences at sea will only be well organized tomorrow.'

As de Chambrun's car raced for the harbour, he saw what the officer had meant. Already eight bombers were over the port, and gutted ships leaned on their keels in the oily muddy water. Taking cover in a bomb crater, with a group of British officers, de Chambrun listened intently to a naval petty officer's instructions: when his whistle blew they were to form two groups and dash for the incoming speedboats.

Piling aboard the second boat, de Chambrun could see the bombers still circling the harbour. 'What are they doing?' he asked the pilot, as the craft slipped away from the ruined pier. 'Dropping mines for us. They've been doing that for days,' was the laconic answer.

But the crossing was uneventful, and four hours later, de Chambrun was thankful to reach London's Victoria Station. Almost at once he sensed that something was wrong. Small groups of people were clustered silently round the news-stands. The first poster he saw contained just two words:

CALAIS
FALLS

In London there was now no escaping the facts. At 2.45 p.m., packed tensely on the green leather-padded benches of the House of Commons, the Members heard out Churchill in shocked silence: following a brave unequal struggle, the Belgians had thrown in their hand. 'Meanwhile,' Churchill warned, 'the House should prepare itself for hard and heavy tidings . . .' In just four minutes he had given them the worst.

Later, in the Cabinet Room at 10 Downing Street, he called in a score of Ministers outside the War Cabinet and told them plainly how bitter the future might be. Almost casually, he concluded: 'Of course, whatever happens at Dunkirk, we shall fight on.'

There was a split second's silence. Then, to Churchill's astonishment, there were cheers. Twenty-three sober politicians were cheering as one ... the First Lord, A. V. Alexander ... the Minister of Food, Lord Woolton ... some pounding the table with their fists, others leaping up to slap Churchill on the back. The room rang with their loyalty.

Although dozens of ships had now brought more than 25,000 survivors from Dunkirk, the process was still too slow. The east mole could berth only sixteen vessels at top high water, and Tennant sent word to Ramsay that the crying need was for small ships – motor boats, whalers, lifeboats, any craft capable of inshore ferrying.

Ramsay called Rear Admiral Tom Phillips, Vice-Chief of Naval Staff, then handed the phone to Tennant's emissary, Captain Eric Bush. 'Here,' he said, 'you tell him.'

Phillips listened to Bush for a time, and then asked, 'Well, how many small boats *do* you want? A hundred?'

To Bush it didn't seem that anyone as yet appreciated the full gravity of the situation. His voice tight with emotion, he answered, 'Look, sir, not a *hundred* boats – every boat that can be found in the country should be sent if we're even to stand a chance!'

All that day, thirty miles to the south, the perimeter of the escape route was held open only by the grim determination of some 3,500 men, the crack battalions of the B.E.F. Along the line of the Ypres–Comines Canal, units like the 3rd Grenadier Guards, Lord Gort's old battalion, the North Staffordshires, and the famous Highland regiment, the Black Watch, stemmed the German advance. Farther south, on La Bassée Canal, the line held, too, though with appalling losses: the whole of General Noel Irwin's 2nd Division, 13,000 strong, was reduced to brigade strength, 2,500 men.

Towards noon, the 3rd Grenadiers faced a situation as desperate as any. Armed with 100 rounds per man at the outset of the battle they were now, after sixteen hours, running short. When Captain Stanton Starkey, commanding one of the forward companies, opened the last ammo boxes available, an eerie chill settled over his men. A hard pressed ordnance officer had slipped up; the boxes contained Very signal lights.

But Starkey had noted one salient fact: the Germans were attacking by a rigid pattern. To keep the Grenadiers pinned down they first called for a withering mortar barrage, signalled by a red-white-red Very light. Then another Very cartridge – white-red-white – signalled the barrage to stop so the infantry could advance.

As the day wore on, Starkey resolved on a last fling of the dice. As the German infantry again surged forward, he raised his pistol and sent a red-white-red pattern into the evening sky. On all sides the Germans doubled in confusion as molten mortar fragments showered among them like an upended brazier.

From the German forward positions an urgent 'stop' signal went soaring: within seconds the barrage died. Recovering, the infantry once more moved forward. Again Starkey fired, signalling a mortar barrage.

Now, as the Germans strove to countermand the order, red and white signals spangled the sky like a millionaire's firework display. But as Starkey kept firing, the Germans gave up. Abruptly the mortaring ceased.

At a cost of more than 1,000 lives along the eight-mile front, the Ypres–Comines Canal had been held. On that Tuesday, the second day of the evacuation, 17,804 troops were lifted from Dunkirk.

In the pre-dawn darkness of Wednesday morning, Captain Eric Bush, having made his plea for small ships, returned to the evacuation area on the minesweeper *Hebe*. One fact now consoled him: the Admiralty, which had begun a register of privately owned craft two weeks earlier, had agreed to call on every available small boat in England.

But in the waters off La Panne – where Gort had established his headquarters, nine miles up the coast from Dunkirk – Bush sensed something strange about the beaches. 'What do you make of those dark shadows over there?' he asked Lieutenant Commander John Temple, for the dawn mists made it hard to see.

'I can't think, sir,' Temple replied, 'unless it's shadows thrown by the clouds.'

But the sky was perfectly clear. Then as the mists parted, the appalling truth dawned and the two men caught their breaths in awe. 'Soldiers,' Captain Bush exclaimed. 'Yes, by God it is . . . ten thousand of them!'

In huge dense squads they blocked the beaches, long queues of them winding like black serpents from the sandhills. Every few yards of the nine-mile stretch from La Panne to Dunkirk, the piers seemed to jut a long way into the sea – human piers, the front ranks up to their necks in chill grey water, patiently waiting for boats.

And more were coming, as Bush soon discovered – thousands more, streaming across the countryside towards Dunkirk, in the strangest retreat a modern army ever made. Some came on scooters and children's bicycles, some pushed their wounded in wheelbarrows. Sergeant Bob Copeman rode on a white hunter twenty hands high. A bombardier drove a tractor, towing a gun. Trooper Paddy Kennedy and his mates journeyed in a Brussels garbage truck; others came astride dairy cattle. Some Lancashire Fusiliers rode in a truck; when the radiator ran dry, they solemnly passed a watering can to relieve the needs of nature, filled the radiator, then drove on. 'Make for the black smoke,' they were told for the fiery destruction that was Dunkirk was visible almost thirty miles away.

It was a tragic cavalcade. Not since Corunna, more than 100 years back, had a British Army fallen back like this – leaving ruin behind it, shocked and in defeat. At dusk, fevered with mosquito bites and nettle rash, they slumped thankfully on to the dry straw of barns or into ditches lined with boughs. They were always hungry – so hungry that Driver Percy Case, of the Service Corps, remembers 29 May, his nineteenth wedding anniversary, as the day he washed down mouthfuls of cattle cake with gulps of stagnant ditch water. They were harassed by leaflets, which read, 'Your generals have gone home', and often

115

they were in pain; their feet misshapen with huge blisters, they marched with their insteps bound in sacking or with the blood seeping through the soles of their boots.

Despite themselves, they absorbed shameful skills that the years cannot blot out, for a man had to eat. Gunner Hugh Fisher still recalls: 'God help me, I learned to pick dead men's pockets – but someone had always been there first.'

Only one thought sustained them all: if they made Dunkirk the Navy would see them through.

But Tennant and his staff had no such confidence: the pace of the evacuation was still maddeningly slow. At the east mole a 15-foot tide made it difficult to board ships at top speed, and a heavy surf thwarted loading on the beach. By Wednesday afternoon eleven ships lay at the east mole's seaward end, and the inshore waters swarmed with destroyers, ferryboats and other craft. Worse, after days of overcast, the skies had cleared – an open invitation to General the Baron von Richthofen, who commanded a force of 180 Stukas from the farmhouse headquarters of VIII Flying Corps near St Pol, fifty miles away.

Close to 4 p.m. the skies to the west of Dunkirk seemed to darken. Within minutes the first wave of Stukas swelled into an inky cloud sliding beneath the sea and the sun. Richthofen had rigged both planes and bombs with toy whistles, and as the bombers came lower and lower their unearthly screaming chilled the blood. Now, in a long plummeting dive they fanned out over the harbour, over the nine miles of water between Dunkirk and La Panne.

It was worst for the ships at the east mole; tight packed like pleasure-steamers at a jetty, they did not stand a chance. But as long as a boat remained afloat, the troops continued to file defiantly aboard. From the personnel ship *Canterbury*, Captain Bernard Lockey watched them neatly closing their three-abreast ranks, while man after man was blown to smithereens.

Close by, the Stukas screeched for the destroyer *Grenade*, three bombs plunging home, one going plumb down her funnel, to leave the sailors floundering in a slippery film of blood and oil. Then, blazing like a pine brand from stem to stern, the *Grenade* swung slowly into the fairway out of control. For seconds it seemed certain the destroyer would sink, blocking the entrance to the harbour, to bring the entire evacuation to a standstill. Captain Tennant's party saved the day. Commander Jack Clouston shouted for a trawler to take the destroyer in tow, and slowly the stricken ship was pulled clear of the fairway. The next instant her magazine ignited, and with a violence few men have witnessed, 1,000 rounds of ammunition went sky-high.

As the sand quaked with the force of the bombing, smothering those whose foxholes were too deep, some men went as completely to pieces as Major-General Auchinleck had foreseen at Narvik. Stripped to a loin cloth, one man raved in circles, proclaiming himself Mahatma Gandhi; others roamed distractedly, clutching children's teddy bears and weeping hysterically. Now as an inferno of flame engulfed the harbour, molten metal dripped from the buckled cranes; waving an axe atop a truck's bonnet, a sergeant yelled, 'Come down and fight fair, you bloody bastards.' Through the dunes a man ran wildly, crying like a lost soul, 'Lord have mercy on us, Christ have mercy on us.'

Vast columns of water geysered 100 feet high, and in the sunlight men were screaming.

Yet, faced with unimagined horror, others summoned up matchless courage. On the coaster *Bullfinch*, a high-hearted Tommy whipped a bugle from his lips, knocked a hysterical mate cold and resumed playing 'Land of Hope and Glory' without missing a note. On shore *Chef de Peloton* Jean Demoy, finding the blind fury of the raid unbearable, suggested to a British major that they take shelter. But the major, blandly manicuring his nails, refused; he must guard some mortars. Later, Demoy returned to find his friend mutilated beyond recognition. Turning to his men, he burst out: 'The British are brave. This officer died with his hands well-groomed but now, look – even his finger nails are blown to pieces.'

Unknown to the men who survived this hell on earth, an incredible armada of small craft had for two days been assembling along Britain's south coast. They came from Margate and Dover, Portsmouth and Sheerness, and from down the tidal rivers, a fleet almost a thousand strong – salt-stained trawlers, motor launches, sleek cabin cruisers, barges, tugs and

117

lifeboats. On Thursday, 30 May, knowing nothing of the devastating raid that had put twelve ships out of action, their skippers were given their final briefing at the small fishing port of Ramsgate, near Dover.

'Off you go and good luck to you,' Commander Eric Wharton of the Small Boats Pool told them, 'and steer for the sound of the guns!' Then to the distant thunder of the Dunkirk guns, reverberating over the water, the little boats moved out.

There had never been an armada like it. Manned by the rich and famous, the poor and unknown, the old and young, it was an international mercy fleet: a true United Nations of boats and men. A Dominican monk in a reefer jersey skippered the yacht *Gulzar*. Bank of England clerk Wilfred Pym Trotter reported for duty on a lifeboat with an umbrella, bowler hat and pinstripe pants. Chinese steward Ah Fong brewed tea aboard the *Bideford*, the Earl of Craven served as third engineer on the rescue tug *St Olave*. California-born John Fernald commanded one of the twelve lifeboats towed by the tug *Racia*; an Irish crew worked with its own Gaelic interpreter on the minesweeper *Fitzroy*.

Some had talked their way into it despite official qualms. Stewardess Amy Goodrich, the only woman to rate a Dunkirk decoration, had sworn that as long as nurses were sailing on the hospital ship *Dinard*, she would sail, too. When the Navy tried to commandeer the 70-ton motor vessel *Bee* without also taking her crew, Engineer Fred Reynard objected so violently that he was hustled before Admiral Sir William James, Commander-in-Chief, Portsmouth.

'Beg pardon, sir, what do your young Navy gentlemen know about Swedish engines?' Fred asked obstinately. 'I've been looking after them since 1912.'

'We've no guarantee you'll get back,' the admiral said dubiously. 'Ever been under shellfire?'

A First World War soldier, Fred had the answer to that one: 'Ever heard of Gallipoli?'

The Admiral knew when to surrender, and Fred Reynard and his crew set off for Dunkirk – though they had never before sailed wider waters than the 4-mile channel of the Solent between Portsmouth and the Isle of Wight.

Hundreds of boats, built for short-run river work, had never before put out to sea. Few had protection against mines and almost all lacked adequate weapons or provisions. One crew set out with no more food than a bottle of malted-milk tablets. Aboard the tug *Sun IV*, Charles Jackson's ambulance team discovered a shortage of surgical dressings; without further ado they stripped off their underclothes and began slicing them into bandages. Not to be outdone, the skipper soon had men shearing through towels, pillowcases, even his shirts.

And still they streamed across the water: the *Count Dracula*, former launch of a German admiral, scuttled at Scapa Flow in 1919 but salvaged years later; the fishing trawler *Jacinta*, reeking of cod; Tom Sopwith's famous racing yacht, *Endeavour*; the Yangtze gunboat *Mosquito*, bristling with armament to ward off Chinese river pirates; the beach boat *Dumpling*, built in Napoleon's time, carrying a 70-year-old skipper.

As the cockleshell armada fanned out towards Dunkirk even seasoned naval officers felt a lump rise in their throats; absurd yet magnificent, it was without all precedent in the world's naval history. On the bridge of the destroyer *Malcolm*, Lieutenant Ian Cox was moved almost to tears to see the boats led by the *Wootton*, the old Isle of Wight car ferry, wallowing like a sawn-off landing-stage through the water. His voice shaking with emotion, Cox burst out with the classic lines from Shakespeare's *Henry V*, which spoke of another battle in France:

> And gentlemen in England, now abed,
> Shall think themselves accurs'd they were not here:
> And hold their manhoods cheap, whiles any speaks
> That fought with us upon St Crispin's Day.

They sailed into an inferno which was now almost beyond description. Two million tons of oil from the port's bomb-shattered tanks roared in a vast conflagration, 11,000 feet high and a mile wide. The air reeked with an unholy compound of smoke, putrid horseflesh, rank tobacco, cordite, garlic and rancid oil. Unearthly sounds smote the ears; the frenzied braying of a jammed klaxon in an abandoned ambulance; the screams of French cavalry horses, wheeling and plunging in panic; and incongruously, the far keening of bagpipes from the dunes.

Along twenty miles of beaches, which for two days were now mercifully shrouded by fog, endless lines of men still stretched across the sands. Sometimes the seeming nearness of the waiting ships caused scores to throw aside all caution and rush into the waters, often to their deaths. From the deck of the destroyer *Impulsive*, Stoker Walter Perrior watched a slow-motion horror: men in full kit, rifles raised above their heads, were wading out towards his ship. On and on they struggled, apparently completely bemused, until the sea engulfed them for ever.

By now, thousands of troops were near starvation. With its railhead bombed out, Dunkirk had been cut off from almost all supplies for days, and desperate men scavenged anything their jaws could chew. Lance-Corporal Syd Garner and his mates fell on a 14-lb chunk of corned beef soaked in diesel oil and carved it up with their bayonets. Private James Wilson, serving up sausage and tomato from a field cooker, piled it on the hands of senior officers who gobbled like hungry dogs.

It was now that Major-General Harold Alexander, the imperturbable commander of the 1st Division, hit on an inspiration. Gort had ordered all but essential transport destroyed so that nothing left behind would be useful to the Germans – 'Burn, smash everything that belongs to Britain!' And on all sides men had been wielding sledge-hammers and blowtorches with the fierce energy of vandals. Truck after truck was shunted into appointed fields and burned in great funeral pyres.

Now Alexander reasoned: why not wreck the vehicles and make good use of them at one and the same time? If the Navy had a dire need for piers, why not drive a pier of trucks as far as possible into the sea?

Within hours the plan was under way. At Braye Dunes, Sapper Bill Searle was one of scores sitting grimly at the wheel of a 30-cwt truck, careering down the beach and far into the sea until the water had almost reached the windshield level, while a jolting groaning line of trucks followed behind. Other sappers took up the task, sawing planks and lashing them to the truck roofs until jetties twenty trucks in length had taken shape. By Friday, 31 May, troops were marching three abreast along these gangways out to lifeboats and whalers they might otherwise never have reached.

It was none too soon. Every hour now, the traffic snarl along the retreat lines was getting worse; the rattletrap laundry vans and milk carts which had served the men as emergency transport were breaking down. Everywhere vital roads were blocked.

One private was so baffled by the chaos that he stormed up to General Alexander and snapped, 'You look like a big brass hat – perhaps *you* can tell me where we get a boat for England?' Though his staff officers bristled with anger, Alexander was unperturbed: 'Follow that lot there, son.' In tribute, the private flashed back: 'Thanks a lot – you're the best pal I've had in 100 kilometres.'

The disrespect was typical. For many officers – and troops too – a bitter truth was dawning: the true qualities of leadership, rather than the rank and birth that had dominated the Army hierarchy hitherto, would see this war through. For thousands of Britons, Dunkirk would mark a sombre milestone in military history; as the rank-and-file realized that officers could equally show the yellow streak the old idols were tumbling, and forever.

In a foxhole close to Private Sidney Grainger, a senior officer, paralysed with dread, was explaining to all who would listen that he couldn't venture out to comfort his men: he must guard a basket of eggs. Approaching, Grainger saw no eggs – only the man's hands hovering protectively over nothingness. Not far from Private James Wilson, a major cracked up, too – thrashing wildly through the water, bypassing the queue, and almost capsizing a ship's whaler. Without hesitation, the naval officer in charge drilled him between the eyes.

At La Panne, Private Bill Hersey, at last reunited with Augusta, felt a flash of the same rebellious spirit. In the clammy heat, Augusta had discarded her army greatcoat and her blue topcoat was plainly visible. Now an army beachmaster stepped forward: 'No women allowed on the beach.'

'She's my wife,' Hersey explained. But the officer's voice was curt, final: 'I said no women on the beach.'

As the officer rapped out his veto, Hersey, eyes blazing, jerked his rifle to the ready, snicking back the bolt: 'I said she's my wife!' After an ugly pause, the officer turned and walked away.

The Herseys were just in time. At midnight on 31 May, time

was running out for Gort's Army. Of the last 5,000 souls to be lifted from La Panne beach, Bill and Augusta numbered two. Yet against almost impossible odds, 68,014 troops were ferried to England that Friday, against 53,823 men on the Thursday: the evacuation's highest 24-hour total.

But the cost was horrifying. By Friday, the Dover waterfront had become a vast shipyard in which carpenters, engineers and divers worked frantically to repair crippled vessels; and every approach to Dunkirk was a navigator's nightmare, a forest of sunken masts and superstructures. A high wind blew up that morning, and as the surf rose in the shallow waters, dozens of small craft beached and grounded. Moreover, the defence lines had contracted to the point where German guns were finding the range of the harbour. All morning the docking berths rocked under artillery fire; at La Panne shells were falling along the water's edge for three-quarters of a mile.

Rarely had ships or troops taken such a beating. To Ramsay and Tennant it seemed that only a miracle could save these men – more than 100,000 of them – still waiting for boats.

But Britain was in the mood for miracles. The crews of the little ships worked dazedly on; and more and more small craft joined them until *Capitaine de Corvette* Toulouse-Lautrec, on the French ship *Sirocco*, was reminded of the Champs Élysées in the rush hour. All through the day they kept coming – river barges with massive oars and russet-coloured sails, an R.A.F. seaplane tender, the naval pinnace *Minotaur*, manned by teenage Sea Scouts, even the fire float *Massey Shaw* from the London Fire Brigade.

Few of the crews had steel helmets to protect them against the hail of shell; the men on the oyster-dredger *Vanguard* shielded their heads with enamel bowls and zinc buckets as they ferried troops to a yacht. But even under shellfire many boats returned to the shore time and again.

At 5 a.m., Saturday, 1 June, Lord Gort, expressly 'ordered home' by Churchill to avoid capture, reluctantly stepped ashore at Dover from a motor anti-submarine boat. A Whitehall official met him with a government limousine and bustled forward to express relief that the commander-in-chief was safely back.

'That I've come back safe?' Gort flashed angrily. 'That isn't what matters – it's that my army gets back!'

Much of it *was* back. Most of the B.E.F. (as well as thousands of French troops who Churchill had wholeheartedly agreed were to be evacuated, too) were now in England. But more than 65,000 British soldiers, including the best rear-guard defence troops, were still at Dunkirk, as were 50,000 French soldiers. Gort feared that the Germans would reach the beaches, and thus end the evacuation.

An impressive number – 64,429 – were lifted to England that day, despite another all-out attack by the Luftwaffe. But by 6 p.m. it seemed to Captain Tennant that now the fog had lifted the Navy was paying too dear a price for daylight evacuation. Only nine destroyers were left now, and shipping losses were mounting out of all proportion to the number of men still to be saved.

Even as he watched, six Stukas attacked the old destroyer *Worcester*, pounding her every five minutes without mercy, sending her staggering from the harbour with a casualty list of 350 dead, 400 wounded. Leaping to his feet, Tennant told Gort's successor, General Alexander, flatly: 'I'm sorry, but that finishes it. I'm signalling Ramsay to stop any more stuff coming in by day.'

Ironically, the Luftwaffe men ended the day with a sense of bitter disappointment and frustration. For when the last of the Stukas limped home in the dusk, Baron von Richthofen knew that the bombing of Dunkirk was all but over. Hitler had ordered a change of target: from Monday on, all planes must be in readiness to bomb the airfields around Paris. If the Führer had indeed laid plans to spare Gort's Army, his wish had been fulfilled to the letter. In his diary, Richthofen penned his bitter epitaph on the whole campaign: 'The Luftwaffe can't halt the Dunkirk embarkation at this last moment ... a victory over England has been thrown away.'

As the minesweeper *Speedwell* inched into Dover late Saturday afternoon, an embarkation officer hailed her captain from the quayside: 'How many aboard?' By megaphone the reply boomed back: 'Five hundred and ninety-nine men – and one woman!' As a shock-wave of laughter travelled through the ship, Augusta and Bill Hersey knew they were safely home at last.

They had come back to an England bursting with welcome. As tens of thousands of troops continued to stream ashore, it was obvious that most of the British Army had been saved, and a joyous, carnival atmosphere filled the port.

All day Sunday, huge crowds lined every street and embankment along the forty miles from Dover to London, cheering the troop trains. Everywhere there were signs of tribute; the gay bunting and flags saved from King George VI's 1937 Coronation, the slogan 'Well Done B.E.F.' daubed on garden walls, bands playing 'See the Conquering Heroes Come'. The *Daily Mirror* summed up popular feeling with one jubilant headline: 'BLOODY MARVELLOUS!'

Aboard a tug fussing into Ramsgate Harbour, one French liaison officer voiced an outsider's query: 'If this is how the British celebrate a defeat, how do they celebrate a victory?'

The query was apposite. True, the vainglorious British Expeditionary Force was home – but with its tail between its legs. Only a handful of men – above all, Major-General Bernard Montgomery's 3rd Division – remained mobile to repel Hitler's next onslaught.

Already, for 68,000 fighting men, the war had ended. Of those, 40,000 faced only the cruel monotony of five years behind bars. Incredibly, the evacuation, now conducted by night, continued until the early hours of Tuesday, 4 June – to bring the final total to an amazing 338,226 men. But to rescue them, Britain had paid a staggering price.

To many Germans, not least the Führer, the combat was now numbered in weeks. When General Ewald von Kleist demurred at the halting of the Panzers, Hitler gave him an airy assurance: 'We will not hear much more of the British in this war.' But a few far-sighted men had doubts. On Saturday, 2 June, *Generalleutnant* Hans von Salmuth, Chief of Staff to Army Group 'B', in Brussels, took time out to make up his diary. 'In the discussions between the Führer and von Rundstedt on the 24th,' he noted carefully, 'were born those decisions which cost us an assured victory in Flanders.' The corollary seemed evident, even then: '. . . and which perhaps have lost us the whole war.'

In London, Winston Churchill had business to do. Two days from now he must render his report to the nation. In the long room at Admiralty House pacing slowly, he marshalled thought. On the far side of the room, poised at the noiseless Remington typewriter, only Mary Shearburn, his secretary, stood vigil. To sit closer – within earshot – would never do. The Old Man liked freedom to pace.

Almost thoughtfully, Churchill began: 'We must be very careful not to assign to this deliverance the attributes of a victory. Wars are not won by evacuation.' Swiftly Mary Shearburn's fingers flew over the keyboard, each paragraph in the triple spacing that was the Premier's whim.

By the unlit fireplace, Churchill marched: from fireplace to velvet draped french windows and back. Often he rumbled, 'How many?' and the answer must come pat: the total of words dictated already. Sometimes he growled, 'Gimme!' ratcheting paper from machine to scan a phrase.

Still he marched. Once he took thought on history: 'When Napoleon lay at Boulogne for a year with his flat-bottomed boats . . . he was told by someone "there are bitter weeds in England"!' He mused on a parallel: there were certainly a great many more since the B.E.F. returned.

Past midnight now. The room was colder. As yet Miss Shearburn had no sense of a disciple's role. She was tired and now, as often, Churchill was gripped by the pain of gestation. His voice had grown faint. She could barely hear.

Moving myopically, head bowed, he struggled with tears.

Loving him because his feelings were naked to the bone, Mary Shearburn yet invoked a silent curse on his mumbling. Now sobs shook the firm foundation of his voice.

'. . . we shall not flag or fail. We shall go on to the end. We shall fight in France, we shall fight in the seas and oceans . . . we shall defend our island whatever the cost may be. We shall fight on the beaches, we shall fight on the landing-grounds, we shall fight in the fields and in the streets, we shall fight in the hills . . .'

It came home to Mary Shearburn then as the most painful of

all dictations. Racked by grief for his stricken land, he could not go on.

A full minute passed. Almost trumpeted, the next sentence hit her like a fist: 'We shall NEVER surrender.'

It was the turning-point. 'All the tears,' Mary Shearburn recalls in wonder, 'had gone from his voice.' Her fingers had flown to the keyboard. Churchill was marching again.

'. . . and even if, which I do not for a moment believe, this island or a large part of it were subjugated or starving, then our Empire beyond the seas . . . would carry on the struggle . . .'

On and on Churchill marched, faster and faster, his voice a drumbeat, charged with faith, thundering to a finale.

'. . . until, in God's good time, the New World, with all its power and might . . .'

'Thank God We're Now Alone'

2 June–27 June 1940

'. . . step forth to the liberation and rescue of the Old . . .'

In a dimly lit studio at London's Broadcasting House, Churchill was concluding a broadcast of his fighting speech to the United States, via the Columbia Broadcasting System. Then the speech delivered, he grinned mischievously, clapped his hands over the live microphone and told the commentator, Ed Murrow: 'And if they do come we shall hit them on the head with beer bottles, for that is all we shall have to fight them with . . .'

Despite his brave words to rally the nation, Churchill's sally was not far from the truth. Against Germany's 200 divisions, Britain could now muster but a score – without equipment for a tenth of that number. To repel a German assault on England, Britain had just 500 18-pounder guns and howitzers, many of them stripped from museums. The equipment of ten divisions was gutted or strewn across the fields of Flanders.

Worse, of 200 destroyers, only 74 were out of dockyard hands – and the R.A.F. had fared no better. Of their first line bomber strength, 40 per cent had been lost in the battle of France.

At Seaford, Sussex, Second Lieutenant John Watney, of 19th Holding Battalion, was one of many officers seeking arms, ammunition and billeting accommodation for men returning with little more than the uniforms on their backs. When Area H.Q. hopefully requested rifles for 10,000 men, Watney was incredulous: 'All we've got here is thousands and thousands of men with hardly a rifle between them.'

The position was as grave across the almost thirteen million square miles that made up the British Empire. From Scapa Flow to Singapore, from Alexandria to New Delhi, men, ships and aircraft were scattered in small vulnerable units across one-fifth of the globe's surface. East of Malaya, only one British infantry brigade, plus an Indian battalion, defended the Crown Colony of Hong Kong. No R.A.F. fighter squadrons were based in India, or in the entire Far East. Only twenty-three naval destroyers were available to patrol the Western Approaches; the security of Scapa Flow depended on the presence of nine destroyers and three cruisers. 'We must have eight battalions from Palestine home at the earliest possible moment,' Churchill had minuted Ismay on 29 May, but such far-flung elements could scarcely buy time for the British if the crunch came.

True, the Dominions were rallying to the flag, but time was of the essence. Australia had undertaken to raise 20,000 men for active service, and New Zealand had promised one infantry division. South Africa had agreed to expand her special service battalions to two brigades, but it became plainer daily how hopelessly over-extended Britain's overseas commitments had become. On 10 May, the Government in Ottawa had agreed to hasten the 2nd Canadian Division to Britain to join the 1st, already encamped, but here, too, shortage of supplies was a crucial factor. As late as January, Canada had been unable to mobilize 100,000 men; shoes, uniforms and guns to equip them simply did not exist.

For once, the gloomy prognostication of the American Ambassador, Joseph P. Kennedy, that 'to suppose the Allies have much to fight with except courage is fallacious' accurately summed up the situation.

At War Cabinet level, even the courage was in doubt. Stressing the need 'to take a leaf out of the Germans' book and to organize special squadrons of Storm Troopers', Secretary of War Eden had to admit that 'many of the Territorial officers who joined in peacetime were not really suitable men'. From now on leaders lacking in drive 'had to be ruthlessly eliminated'. Over lunch with the Vice-Chief of the Imperial General Staff, General Sir John Dill, Chamberlain heard his estimation that the troops were 'demoralized ... and may not be steady when the time comes'. At a top-secret conference of senior officers at the Royal Station Hotel, York, Eden heard much the same verdict. Regular officers and non-coms might dutifully soldier on, even continuing the fight from Canada, if need be, but wartime inductees would take their chance with their families or not at all. The conscript army would desert en masse rather than fight on from Canada.

In truth, they were unlikely to have the chance. This far-fetched suggestion was originally mooted by the isolationist Key Pittman, Chairman of the United States Senate's Foreign Relations Committee, in the hope of appeasing Hitler, but on 25 May, Roosevelt and Cordell Hull, discussing the proposal with the Canadian Premier, Mackenzie King, had advised against it. If King George VI arrived in Canada, with Roosevelt's backing, the President might be accused of 'establishing monarchy on the North American continent'. Nor did the Canadian opposition party want any truck with Churchill, whom they deemed a Victorian imperialist. The one non-controversial refuge for King George and his subjects was thought to be the Bahamas – where the King's brother, the former King Edward VIII, now Duke of Windsor, was soon to take over as Governor and Commander-in-Chief.

But more than the British Army's morale was faltering after Dunkirk. The 300 scrutators of the Mass Observation Organization, who reported on current topics to the Ministry of Information, adjudged morale in many areas as zero. Only 50 per cent of the population expected Britain to fight on alone – 'everyone is going around looking as if they want to put their heads in a gas oven', ran one report. Ten million citizens were so apathetic they had not yet applied for their ration books.

In an era when it took a munitions worker eleven hours to earn £1 sterling as against a Cabinet Minister's twenty-four minutes, the feelings of thousands were summed up by one determinedly articulate man-in-the-street: 'This is not our war – this is a war of the high-up people who use long words and have different feelings.'

Most felt, perhaps with reason, that some of their leaders were as out of touch as the denizens of another planet. The radio sneer of the Minister of Information, Alfred Duff Cooper, that Hitler was not a gentleman because he did not drink wine and ate grapefruit jarred oddly with workers hard put to it to find the coppers for carrots at 6d. a lb. Instead, perversely, the admiration was all for Hitler, like an astrologer whose predictions persistently came true. 'He's done everything he said he would – he really is a wonderful bad man.'

'Hitler,' urged one Ministry of Information memorandum, with what sounded like desperation, 'must be reduced in status to the level of a man who eats and drinks and cleans his teeth.'

A handful of British scientists had farther-reaching ambitions. Their aim was to reduce Hitler to a loser's level in the technological war that already loomed on the horizon.

On Thursday, 12 June, Dr R. V. Jones, a 28-year-old adviser to A.I. l(c), the Air Component of M.I.6, the British Secret Intelligence, called by invitation on Group Captain L. F. Blandy, chief of the R.A.F.'s 'Y' Service, which intercepted German radio signals, in his Whitehall office. Even as Jones was seating himself, Blandy, pulling a scrap of paper from his desk drawer, asked, 'Does this mean anything to you? It doesn't seem to mean much to anybody here.'

The message read: KNICKEBEIN, KLEVE, 1ST AUF PUNKT 53 GRAD 24 MINUTEN NORD UND EIN GRAD WEST EIN-GERICHTET. (Cleves Knickebein is confirmed (or established) at position 52°24' north and 1° west.)

Jones was elated. 'Yes, it means a lot!' he told Blandy, simply.

For Jones, the details of three months' patient scientific investigation were now slotting into place. Back in February, studying a transcript of a bugged conversation between two German prisoners of war, Jones had chanced on a casual mention of something called the 'X-Gerät' or X-Apparatus. Over tea at the Bath Club with Squadron Leader Denys Felkin, head of the R.A.F.'s P.O.W. Interrogation Centre, Jones had learned more. The conversation had suggested that the X-Gerät was an apparatus used in a bomber and involving radio pulses

March had seen further progress. A page Felkin had salvaged from a shot-down Heinkel 111 of Bomber Group 26 translated as follows:

NAVIGATIONAL AID: RADIO BEACONS WORKING ON BEACON PLAN A. ADDITIONALLY FROM 0600 HOURS BEACON DÜHNEN. LIGHT BEACON AFTER DARK. RADIO BEACON KNICKEBEIN FROM 0600 HOURS ON 315.

This had been the first hint of Knickebein. From the context Jones adjudged it to be a beamed beacon, set to transmit in a north-westerly direction, from which a bomber's navigator might take rough bearings. Now, on 12 June, Knickebein had surfaced once more

Jones's interpretation was shrewd. The geographical position pinpointed was in the rough vicinity of the Great North Road, a mile or two south of Retford, Nottinghamshire. Thus Jones deduced that a radio beam transmitter code-named Knickebein (Crooked Leg), set up at Cleves, in North Rhine-Westphalia, provided for a crudely-effective system of intersecting beams for bombing England – 'a blunt instrument', as Jones was later to put it, 'rather than a finely-honed tool'.

Were Knickebein and the X-Gerät one and the same – or variations on a theme? As yet, Jones did not know, but the circle was narrowing daily. At his headquarters at Cockfosters, Middlesex, Felkin questioned sundry German bomber pilots but drew a blank. Then a further fragment of bugged conversation put Jones on the right scent; no matter how hard the British tried, one P.O.W. told another, they would never find the equipment. The challenge seemed implicit. The evidence was there for the British to see, but they would never have the mother-wit to find it.

In his office at 54 Broadway, by St James's Park Underground Station, Jones fell to studying the technical report on a Heinkel 111 shot down in an early raid on the Firth of Forth. It struck him that the one possible item was the receiver installed for a normal blind landing on the Lorenz beacon system, by then standard on many aerodromes. On the off-chance, Jones phoned the technician who had evaluated the radio equipment at the Royal Aircraft Establishment, Farnborough, Hampshire.

'Is there anything unusual about the blind landing receiver?' Jones asked.

'Now you mention it,' the technician replied thoughtfully, 'it is much more sensitive than they would need for blind landing.'

Jones was within sight of success. Knowing the receiver, and the frequencies to which it could be tuned, he thus knew those on which the Knickebein beam must operate.

On the afternoon of Sunday, 16 June, Jones reported to Air Marshal Sir Philip Joubert, who had just now taken charge of Air Ministry work on the beams. Also present was Air Chief Marshal Sir Hugh Dowding, the remote taciturn Commander-in-Chief of Fighter Command. Both men listened in silence as Jones presented his evidence.

'Well, C.-in-C.,' Joubert asked finally, 'what should we do?' Dowding answered with just one word: 'Jam!'

Jones was in complete agreement, but one formidable problem still remained. First he must find the beams.

By now, the French had ceased to hope for much from the British. On 1 June, Roland de Margerie of the French Foreign Office approached General Spears with a bizarre request: could not all the British troops saved from Dunkirk be sent back to France, armed only with rifles, to dig strong positions behind the Somme front? Three days later, on 4 June, Weygand asked for the dispatch of no less than twenty British fighter squadrons. Neither request was to be granted, and as a result Captain René de Chambrun became involved in one of this year's most fraught missions.

It was the American Ambassador, William C. Bullitt, who first set events in motion. A long-time friend and an ardent Francophile, Bullitt no sooner heard that de Chambrun had successfully returned from London and completed his mission as a courier than he summoned him to the Embassy beyond the Place de la Concorde. To Bullitt's astonishment, de Chambrun gave him a novel assessment: 'We have lost – but England will never be attacked.'

Bullitt was incredulous. What prompted such a certain judgement, he wanted to know.

De Chambrun elaborated. He had seen British fighters in action over the Channel, and he believed they were second to none. Moreover, the British had committed little more than twenty squadrons to the Battle of France; they were husbanding them for their own defence. And despite Germany's sweeping victories, de Chambrun seriously doubted whether she had enough reserves to assault and conquer England.

Bullitt was impressed. 'Would you be prepared to see Franklin Roosevelt and tell him that?' he asked. De Chambrun, assuming this to be a joke, burst out laughing. 'Bill,' he protested, 'I'm just a captain in the French Army.' But Bullitt was in deadly earnest. 'I'm going to see Reynaud and General Weygand tomorrow,' he promised.

Thus, at 7 p.m. on 1 June, de Chambrun found himself in the bare dungeon-like office at Weygand's Vincennes headquarters. Weygand, 'as alert as a company commander', at first questioned him intently as to all he had seen and heard in the field, then ordered him to write a report. Next day, he instructed, de Chambrun must also wait on Marshal Pétain. Then he added: 'I've decided to appoint you Assistant Military Attaché to our Embassy in the United States. I wish you to leave by the first Clipper from Lisbon.'

He wound up sombrely: 'Please explain in the United States to what extent the odds are against us. We have neither the men nor the needed equipment.'

At the Quai d'Orsay, Reynaud, a darting five feet three inches, harrying secretaries with his *Vite! Vite! Vite!*, was now trying every expedient. On 5 June, impatient for action, he called Roosevelt long-distance and was immediately buoyant again: the President saw a possibility of sending 150 planes. At once as sanguine as Weygand and Pétain were dejected, Reynaud was now pinning all his hopes on another long-shot: a Breton Redoubt, entailing the withdrawal of all French forces to Brittany, with the Government transferring to Quimper, south of Brest.

But by 6 June, the French had abandoned five river-lines: the Bresle, the Aire, the Oise, the Seine, the Ourcq. The concept of stand-and-take-it warfare was dying beneath the treads of German tanks, blasted into extinction by Stukas.

Before catching the Clipper that left Lisbon on 9 June, René de Chambrun submitted his report. All told, it was a lamentable tale: he skimped nothing of what he had seen. The sheer negligence of the *Chasseurs Ardennais*, who had neglected both to fell trees and place mines, had enabled the Germans to cross the forest in less than forty-eight hours. Anti-aircraft and service corps units had fallen back without orders: the appearance and conduct of many troops had been 'deplorable,' their morale bad. Nor were the civilians by any means blameless. Almost all the Mayors of Northern France had fled their towns, adding to the panic.

This much de Chambrun conveyed to Marshal Pétain, an old friend of his father, in his office at the Hôtel des Invalides. As always, the Marshal seemed calm and serene, but now somehow remote from the anguish that was besetting France – as if he had 'just left a world of agitation and chaos to penetrate into a refuge of quiet and peace'.

As de Chambrun left, Pétain's faithful aide in the outer office asked him reverently: 'What would we do if we did not have him?' De Chambrun didn't know – but before long he was to divine the answer to that question.

Given the tools of war, the French could still fight to the death, as *Hauptmann* Werner Mölders, of the Luftwaffe, acknowledged in grudging admiration on 6 June.

It was no idle tribute, for at twenty-seven Mölders, the leader of Fighter Group 53's 1st Wing, was known as the Luftwaffe's deadliest ace. Two years earlier, in the Spanish Civil War, Mölders, as commander of the German-staffed Condor Legion, had notched up fourteen confirmed 'kills', at the same time evolving fighter techniques which were as yet a closed book to the British and the French: the 'Finger Four' formation, which saw pilots flying in pairs, one man swooping for the primary attack while a wingman protected his tail, the staggering of altitudes to eliminate the distraction of flying in precise formation.

A lean dark youngster with piercing eyes, his solicitude for the squadron's new boys had already earned him the nickname 'Daddy Mölders'. Few divined that his calm confident manner was a façade concealing many doubts. In the Spanish Civil War, Mölders, giving air support to Franco's Nationalists, had seen it as a straight anti-Communist combat, but the Second World War found him less certain. A devout Catholic, the Nazi

Party's attacks on his religion disturbed him profoundly, and he was worried, too, by Hitler's inexorable advance. 'If only he won't talk himself into the role of Ghengis Khan,' Mölders confided in his intimates.

There was no time for such introspection at 5.15 a.m. on 6 June. Only this morning, Mölders had shot down his twenty-fifth fighter plane, but suddenly, over Amiens, he was involved in a whirlwind combat with six French Moranes who fought back as tenaciously as furies. As fast as he lined up one Morane in his sights, it jinked mischievously to port, then re-appeared to starboard; soon his Messerschmitt 109 was a hawk-shadow swooping only 2,400 feet above the Somme valley. Suddenly his cockpit seethed with sparks; the throttle lever shattered into jagged fragments and the control column tilted uselessly. As the ME went into an uncontrollable power dive Mölders baled out.

Grimly he realized that he was over enemy territory, at least forty-five miles behind the French lines, to the west of Compiègne. As he hit the brown baked earth, releasing the parachute harness, shots from French sporting rifles were detonating close to his ear-drums.

Throwing off his fur-lined flying jacket, Mölders doubled forward, diving head-first into a field of lupins. Inch by inch, using his knees and elbows, he began to crawl forward, but the shots and the shouting had redoubled. The bright flower spikes quivered in the evening light; the farmers were systematically working over the field like beaters at a shoot. Rising reluctantly to his feet, Mölders found himself hemmed in by a tight ring of fifty men. As a French officer led him to a car, the German ran a painful gauntlet of kicks, punches and accurately-swung rifle butts.

Towards 10 p.m., Mölders was undergoing the makeshift lot of all P.O.W.s as the French front crumbled; bedded down on straw in a goat shed and guarded by two sentries, he had at least enjoyed a scratch meal of tinned sardines, bread and wine. Next day he and nine German infantry officers were shunted by truck to Chantilly, and from there, on 9 June, through Paris, Versailles and Chartres to a prison barracks at Alençon.

Mölders took all of it phlegmatically; in the days to come,

he thought, he would need calm nerves. Rooting round the barracks he found spare wood, and at once began methodically to carve himself a chess set. Like all the Germans, he knew that now it was only a question of time.

Time was at a premium in Norway, too. The tragi-comedy of Narvik was reaching its last act.

Now the indecent haste of the Flanders campaign decreed that the whole venture was to be abandoned as capriciously as it had been launched. Yet, although the War Cabinet had finalized this decision on 24 May, prestige demanded that Narvik must still be taken, on 28 May, and destroyed before the final evacuation. 'Norwegian Government have not repeat NOT yet been informed,' ran the Cabinet's orders to the Earl of Cork and Orrery; they, like the French, were to be kept in the dark until the last.

Even a man unaccustomed to question orders, like Lieut.-Colonel Magrin-Vernerey, commanding the French Foreign Legion's 13th Demi-Brigade, was moved to bitter comment. On 28 May, his troops had stormed ashore to win the Legion's first victory in the Second World War; now on 6 June, they were pulling out. 'Well,' he asked his officers, 'what do you think of the Norwegian campaign? Not even a little bit of glory. We take Narvik, and then we clear out like a lot of blasted idiots.'

More senior commanders, privy to the deception, felt an acute sense of shame. 'Why?' the Norwegian C.-in-C., General Otto Ruge, had earlier asked Major-General Bernard Paget, commanding 15 Brigade, 'when your troops are undefeated?', and Paget could find no words to answer him. 'One feels a most despicable creature in pretending that we are going on fighting,' Major-General Claude Auchinleck wrote to Dill, newly-appointed C.I.G.S., 'when we are going to quit at once.'

No bystander who watched the Allies depart was more shocked than Polly Peabody, the New York socialite who had brought her American Scandinavian Field Hospital ashore at Bergen on 6 April, unaware that the German ore freighters in the harbour had been crammed with hidden troops. No sooner had Polly's team reached Stockholm than news of the Norwegian invasion reached them; at once they had decided they must return to give succour. Within days, their 18-truck convoy adorned with the Red Cross emblem and the Stars and Stripes, led by Polly's white Ford, 'Leaping Lina', had set off on its long journey north.

They had equipment enough to support a 200-bed Field Hospital for six months, including three mobile surgeries, but at Namsos, the first port they struck, the war had passed them by. For the first time, Polly saw a devastation that would soon become commonplace: bombs and shells had reduced a trim white-painted Norwegian town to a waste of black and dripping ruins. To her horror – for, like all her team, she had believed that Namsos and the North could be held – she heard that the port was to be abandoned.

By the light of a blazing ammunition dump, Polly Peabody witnessed 'one of the most poignant scenes of my life'; Tommies and *poilus* embarking by night, shuffling silently through the gutted wreckage of the port, the warships' heliographs blinking and flashing offshore. At this moment she reached a snap decision: if the State Department forbade her unit to operate in hostile territory, she would make for France on a one-woman mission, signing up with the International Red Cross at Geneva on her way in.

More troops were pouring along the dockside as she watched, cursing monotonously as stretcher bearers shouldered them aside, their words lost in the strident blast of ships' whistles, the long black files standing out in silhouette against a red, unearthly glow. Behind them they were leaving three million Norwegians to their fate – among them, Theodor Broch, the Mayor of Narvik, now, for the second time, awaiting sentence of death.

His friends the British *had* come, Theodor Broch thought wryly, confounding the prophecy a German lieutenant had made him as far back as 17 April, but only to depart as swiftly.

Once more under armed guard, this time in the dining room of the Nobel Hotel, Harstad, forty miles from Narvik, Broch thought the events of the past two months had taken on a near-surreal aspect. On 26 May, when a combined task force of British, French and Poles streamed ashore at Narvik the

National flag was the first to fly above any Norwegian City Hall since the Germans came. Alongside it streamed the Union Jack, which city wives under Ellen Broch had stitched with their own hands while sheltering from air raids. Food had been scarce and beer non-existent, but at least the liberators had been made welcome with an impromptu feast of anchovies, bread and bilberry jam.

But the elation was short-lived. On 2 June, acting on a hunch, Broch sent Ellen and Siri north to Tromso, a wise precaution, for the Luftwaffe were returning in strength. As the bombs hailed down, Broch sensed with pain that his life in Narvik now lay in the past. Danielsen's Building, where he had first set up as a young lawyer, had vanished in a corona of flame. The harbour which had formed the hard core of Narvik's prosperity was now the graveyard of more than thirty ships.

Most townsfolk heard the news that the Allies were leaving with anger as much as incredulity. Broch tried to damp down passions which were close to flashpoint. 'They have to go back to their own country and fight there,' he excused the British. Already it had crossed his mind to wonder: could the Germans be aware that in the days before the Allies came ashore the unerring accuracy of the naval broadsides had been aided by harbour plans which Broch had smuggled out to them by rowboat?

The Germans were well aware. On 6 June, as the British left Narvik, Broch, hitching a ride in a friend's car, went north to Tromso to find Ellen and Siri. King Haakon and his government were just then leaving for England in a British cruiser, but now the quixotic streak which had been the mainspring of his municipal life betrayed Broch. Word reached Tromso that refugees in sorry shape were arriving on Harstad Island. Broch, determined to help, took his family back south by ferry.

On 15 June, he was crossing Harstad's main square when a squad of German soldiers halted him. By chance, General Dietl's adjutant, *Korvettenkapitän* Reichmann, had spotted him from the hotel window. 'We have some very interesting information about you, Mr Mayor,' he greeted Broch ominously. 'You are under arrest.'

In the Nobel Hotel's dining room, guarded by two sentries,

Broch thought fast. Once Narvik's City Council had interceded to spare him from death under Section 36 of German Military Law, but the Council no longer existed, and even disarming a German non-com paled beside the crime of overt espionage, passing maps to the British. Acknowledging that he was on his own, he strolled casually across the dining room, reconnoitring prospects. The room lay on the first floor, its windows over-looking the street, although one, already open, gave on to a back yard piled with barrels. Behind the bar, in one corner, a staircase led directly to the cellar. Still strolling, Broch glanced through the back window into the yard. A young boy prising open a cask looked up and caught his eye. Nodding confidentially, Broch whispered: 'For God's sake, get me a taxi. Tell it to wait in the second cross street to the north.'

Turning back, he saw the sentries eye him thoughtfully. Broch lit a cigarette, perching nonchalantly on a high stool, as if awaiting a bartender. Presently the sentries turned away. Out-side, trucks were groaning up the street from the dockside and they grew curious. Flinging wide the windows, they craned out. Now or never, Broch thought.

Dropping lightly from the stool he ducked behind the bar, taking the cellar stairs three at a time. Now he was in the yard, doubling between the barrels, sprinting into the street at the rear. Mercifully, his sense of direction held good, taking him due north. Just as he had prayed, a taxi was parked, ticking over. Broch flung himself flat on its floor, blurting out garbled directions. From the lodgings where Ellen and Siri were bil-leted, the taxi sped them on across the island, one already-packed knapsack crammed with everything they possessed.

Luck was with them; in the island's tiny port of Hindö, white wraiths of mist were drifting in from the sea. On the dockside, Broch did a quick deal with a fisherman to row them to any offshore island with a sizeable fishing harbour. From there, he knew, another bargain could be cemented: a passage for all three on any fishing vessel voyaging further north.

Soon the rowboat was drifting out across the grey waste of the Atlantic. The fog was still thickening; from a few hundred yards out, Hindö was no longer visible. But where they were going, and when they would at last find refuge, Broch did not know.

At dusk on Monday, 10 June, Paris was a melancholy sight to all who loved her. Out through the Porte de Châtillon, in the fading light, groaned an endless line of trucks and private cars – Citroëns, Mercedes – heading south-west by day and by night for Tours, 145 miles distant. After much heart-searching, Paul Reynaud's administrative machine was abandoning the capital as an open city – leaving only the Préfet, Roger Langeron, and 25,000 gendarmes to represent the French Government in Paris.

To the very end, there had been bitter argument for and against. Weygand himself was anxious to stay, convinced that if he fell into German hands, he would be cleared of all blame. On 8 June, de Gaulle, the new Under-Secretary for War, saw signs that Weygand was throwing in the towel. 'When I'm beaten here,' he prophesied, 'England won't wait a week before negotiating with the Reich.' One of the few opposing voices had been Reynaud's, convinced that any armistice could bring only dishonourable terms. Pétain all along veered between pessimism – 'It is our duty to get out of it' – and sentiments devoid of reality. 'We don't seem to be making much use of carrier pigeons,' he interrupted one Cabinet meeting. 'There should be a dove cote in the rear which is permanently linked up with Supreme Headquarters.'

Now, as the Government quit Paris, hope in France vanished, as a dam gives way before an inexorable flood. On this hectic Monday night, all the city – and soon all France – became obsessed by one single thought: to get away.

By dawn on Tuesday, an endless cavalcade jammed the highways leading south. Like animals fleeing before a forest fire, a bizarre array of vehicles was streaming from the city: fire engines bearing firemen and their families, tricycles, furniture vans, coal and ice-cream carts, street sweepers with rotating brushes, even eight funeral hearses crammed with living freight. Whole stud farms had taken to the roads, headed by grooms riding stallions, along with manure carts and little trailers for the stud books.

In their desperate effort to get away, people surprised even themselves. A lecturer, Peter Fontaine, realized that he had not mounted a bicycle for twenty-five years, but he clocked up 400 miles on one now, daily drying his underwear on the handlebars as he headed south for Bordeaux.

Black smoke from burning fuel dumps cast a sooty pall over the city – at times so dense that no man could see across the Place de la Concorde, where lowing cattle now wandered untended. Soon every railway terminus was closed save the Gare de Lyon, where a frantic trampling horde of would-be refugees clawed at the iron railings. By now more than a million had gone, and Paris was dying by inches. Newspapers closed down, Maxims put up its shutters and rare taxis were stormed on sight. The sight of expensive Vuitton luggage piled outside the Ritz showed that the rich had been among the first to go.

On the roads leading south it was worse. No man or woman who made the journey would ever forget the stripped and silent villages, where not a crumb of bread or a thimbleful of milk remained as sustenance. The main café at Le Mans more resembled a stage set for a poorhouse, littered with orange peel, and refugees bedding down on the banquettes. In this chaos, where petrol was priced at fifty francs a litre, and ten sous charged for a glass of water, profiteers were having a field day. One woman was even mulcted £50 for a racing bicycle.

The panic was spreading from town to town, to the very foothills of the Pyrenees. Whole communities, like Evreux in Normandy, evaporated as swiftly as morning mist, reduced from 20,000 to 172 overnight. At Alois, a fear-stricken woman in a heavy fur coat, afraid that engineers would blow the bridges, swam the breadth of the river, looking like a 'drowning bear'.

In this week, the French writer, Paul Valéry, wrote what might have been the epigraph for 1940: 'Nothing that we could fear is impossible; we can fear and imagine absolutely everything.'

By now, almost ten million were on the roads, mindless of a destination, coursing blindly on, like lemmings, although to travel 200 yards an hour was now a rare achievement. In one column, the inane cries of a wheel-of-fortune man, shouting to keep himself awake, jarred the nerves: 'No blanks, ladies and gentlemen, no blanks! Every number wins.' In other columns, some men, numb with fatigue, just gave up. Bone-weary *poilus*, clinging to the tailgates of trucks, fell insensible, and the rearmost trucks rolled on over them.

'The Middle Ages,' wrote the deeply-shocked General Guderian to his wife, Gretel, 'were humane compared to the present.'

The deep disgust of defeat gripped civilian and military alike. On the Boulevard Sebastopol, Paris, the writer Arthur Koestler greeted a waiter from his favourite bistro, mobilized in March but no longer in uniform: 'I thought you were at the front?' The man merely grimaced: 'The front is where the Lieutenant is, and the Lieutenant has beaten it in his car.' As disillusioned with their officers as many of the English, some *poilus* made their feelings even plainer. On the outskirts of Nantes, one young soldier flung a fistful of mud through a limousine's window, splattering an officer's cheek. The officer's lips tightened, but he drove on without comment.

The tired old slogan *Il faut en finir* had abruptly become *Il fallait en finir* (It should have been stopped). In this mood Breton housewives mobbed retreating troops to tear the rifles from their hands, putting an end to all resistance. At Vierzon, near Bourges, a tank commander preparing to defend the town was seized by citizens anxious to avoid German reprisals and battered to death.

To one 6-year-old boy, Pascal Jardin, at Trouville, that week, in retrospect, would always be associated with 'a revolting noise in my memory – forty million Frenchmen were shitting their pants at the same time'.

In his office on Rome's sixteenth-century Piazza Venezia, a room so lofty (seventy feet long by thirty-nine feet wide) that he had to communicate with his orderlies by hand-signals, Benito Mussolini had reached a decision destined to change the face of the war in Europe – and ultimately to topple his own Fascist régime. On 26 May, standing hands on hips behind his writing desk, he broke the news defiantly to two key officials: Marshal Pietro Badoglio, the cunning 68-year-old Chief of the Supreme Staff, and Marshal Italo Balbo, Governor of Libya.

'I wish to tell you,' Mussolini announced abruptly, 'that yesterday I sent a messenger to Hitler with my written declaration that I don't intend to stand idly by with my hands in my pockets. After 5 June, I am ready to declare war on England and France.'

To both men, the decision came like a thunderclap. As Badoglio, the first to speak, was quick to point out: 'Your Excellency, you know perfectly well that we are absolutely unprepared – you have received complete reports every week.' The gist of those reports, Badoglio hammered home, had made one thing plain: Italy's military involvement throughout the thirties – in Ethiopia, the Spanish Civil War, and Albania – had left her a spent force. With twenty Army divisions possessing only 70 per cent of their equipment, another twenty only 50 per cent, she could wage no war worth the name.

'We haven't even sufficient shirts for the Army,' Badoglio expostulated. 'How is it possible to declare war? It is suicide.'

The crippling shortages were everywhere apparent. Italy's annual imports totalled twenty-five million tons of food – none of which might be available in the event of conflict. The Air Force had fuel for just forty sorties. Italian colonies such as Tripolitania reported weapons better suited to a war surplus dump: rusting water-cooled machine-guns, tanks so frail that trucks were needed to transport them into battle. In Libya, Balbo had only cannon dating from Garibaldi's wars of the 1870s, precariously mounted on garbage trucks. Only the Fleet, numerically powerful and including six battleships, nineteen modern cruisers and 120 destroyers, offered a challenge which Churchill was to sum up as 'formidable'.

The Minister for War Production, General Carlo Favagrossa, had most aptly summed it up: if industrial plants worked non-stop shifts, Italy might conceivably enter the war in 1949. Failing this, he would set the date at 1959.

But ever since 1922, when his Fascists seized power with their much-publicized March on Rome, *Il Duce* had been obsessed with dreams of Italy's military destiny. Thus, the concept of non-involvement was ultimately unthinkable, for Mussolini, all his life veering between abject self-abasement and overweening confidence, could only equate his country's inadequacy with his own. 'We should be like Switzerland multiplied by ten,' was his shamefaced definition of total neutrality.

Yet for days before the meeting with Badoglio and Balbo, Mussolini had been tugged by the winds. His Minister of Justice, Count Dino Grandi, a man so bitterly opposed to the Axis alliance that three years later he would mastermind a conspiracy deposing Mussolini, never forgot his 17 May visit to Palazzo Venezia, only nine days earlier. Standing before a beflagged wall-map of France, studying troop dispositions, Mussolini had declared that, despite the Germans' belief in victory, they would never reach Paris.

'There will be a new Battle of the Marne,' he told Grandi with characteristic lack of prescience. 'The hated Boches will break their heads for a second time and all Europe will be liberated from them.'

This curiously wishful thinking had been known to the British War Cabinet as long ago as 7 April, through a cable summarizing a private conversation between Amadeo, Duke of Aosta, nephew of King Vittorio Emmanuele III, and the British Ambassador's wife, Lady Loraine. Mussolini, the Duke had stressed, felt threatened on all sides – by the prospect of an Allied flank attack on Germany through Italy, by a sudden German invasion of Italy from the north. Although Mussolini 'was aware of, and shared, the hatred of the whole country for Germany, he feared Germany's military strength'.

The lessons of Hitler's sneak attacks on Norway, Denmark and Belgium, which the Führer had never deigned to reveal to his junior partner, had been far from lost on Mussolini. 'Even if Italy were to change her attitude and go over bag and baggage to the Anglo–French side, she would not avoid an immediate war with Germany,' he had argued in a top-secret memorandum of 31 March, 'a war which Italy would have to carry alone.' Following reports that the war scare had brought booming business to furriers and jewellers in the north, a hedge against the collapse of the lira, Mussolini rapped out, 'The Milanese should know that it's better to negotiate than have the Germans in Milan.'

Racked as always by his own inferiority complex, he would admit no fears of Hitler to Badoglio or Balbo. 'You are not calm enough to judge the situation, Marshal,' he told Badoglio condescendingly. 'I can tell you everything will be over by September, and that I need only a few thousand dead to sit at the conference table as a belligerent.'

But at the Palazzo Chigi, Italy's Foreign Ministry, the diplomats knew that any warning word from Germany swiftly brought Mussolini into line. On 27 May, the day following Mussolini's meeting with Badoglio, one official, Count Luca Pietromarchi, received a swingeing rebuke from the Palazzo Venezia. After months of negotiations, Pietromarchi had worked out a *modus vivendi* which had that day been announced in London; although the British fought shy of the territorial concessions that Reynaud had urged, they had still agreed to relax their contraband controls in the Mediterranean. But the news, simultaneously relayed to Berlin, had brought a sharp reprimand from Hermann Göring.

'You're to cancel every agreement you've made with the British and the French,' Pietromarchi was instructed. 'The Duce says that he's not a brigand, doing business with a gun in one hand and a Bible in the other.'

From this moment on, Mussolini was to see life as in a splintered mirror – the reality that he was shrewd enough to perceive, the distorted image that he urged himself was the truth.

For Italy the ultimate tragedy was that no lack of sycophants existed to assure him that all was well. Despite his token protest, Badoglio stayed on in his post – loath to resign and forego emoluments of two million lire a year. The Under-Secretary for War, General Ubaldo Soddu, obligingly put on a show of martial might – upping the Army's on-paper strength from forty to seventy-three divisions, stripping every division of one regiment to swell the totals. At military reviews, Mussolini never spotted that fourteenth-century brass cannons stood in for more lethal hardware – or that the armoured cars were loaned by the police, painted khaki for that day's parade.

At 6 p.m. on Monday, 10 June, for the first time following his nine months of indecision, the glass doors swung open on to the Palazzo Venezia's balcony, and Mussolini – who twelve days earlier had appointed himself Supreme Commander of the Armed Forces – stepped forward. His voice strangely high-pitched, he told the well-drilled crowd mustered by the Party Secretary the fate that awaited Italy – at the moment that the code-word announcing his decision, 'Duplicity', flashed to all British Ministries.

Among those listening in the tight-packed square was Erik Seidenfaden, the Danish reporter whose thirst for news had thus far netted him notable scoops in both Stockholm and Oslo. But as *Politiken*'s newly-appointed Rome correspondent, Seidenfaden felt no professional pride in the story he was about to file – merely 'a terrible feeling that I'd seen all this before'. There had been just such a scene, he recalled, in Hamburg, in 1932, the year before Hitler attained power, yet still, eight years later, Seidenfaden could ask himself, how is it possible that all these teenagers are wild for war?

In truth, the bulk were party hacks, a handful of them fanatics but more of whom had sworn allegiance to a meal ticket. Most Italians felt only a true sense of horror as Mussolini's voice crackled out through amplifiers all over Italy; in Genoa and Turin, the crowds massed in ominous silence, without a cheer, without a handclap. And in Milan's cathedral square, men were seen crying that day, under the clear and windy sky.

'A declaration of war has been handed to the ambassadors of Great Britain and France,' Mussolini trumpeted vaingloriously. 'Italian people, rush to arms and show your tenacity, your courage, your valour!'

Yet, at 5 p.m. in the Villa Camilluccia, on Rome's Monte Mario, Myriam, the 20-year-old sister of Mussolini's mistress, Claretta Petacci, had answered the phone to hear the Duce sounding palpably shaken. 'In one hour's time,' he told her, 'I shall declare war. I'm forced to declare it.'

Like most Italians, Myriam was thinking only of a token *coup-de-grâce* against France. 'But it will be short, Duce,' she reassured him.

'No,' Mussolini disillusioned her, 'it will be long – not less than five years.' His final prophecy made Myriam shiver: 'Hitler's tree reaches as high as the sky – but it grows only towards ruin.'

The Presidential train was racing through the red and green Virginia foothills. Aboard it, Franklin Roosevelt was making the final changes in the speech of a day that would become history. One hour before leaving Washington, the President had heard of Mussolini's decision. Now he was angry.

A light rain was falling as the train reached Charlottesville, but Roosevelt, pale and strained when he embarked on the journey, now seemed relaxed. Whatever decision he had reached had seemed to strengthen him. His mind was made up as he drove to the Memorial Gymnasium of the University of Virginia, there to don his cap and gown, and address the graduating class.

It was a fighting speech that the world heard, powerful and more determined than any since the war began – specific in its promise of aid, bitter in its condemnation of the dictators. When Roosevelt spoke of Italy's preserving its 'freedom of action', it was plain he meant freedom to murder.

Now came the crunch; the phrase that the cautious Sumner Welles had already excised from the speech but which had lodged all day like an obstinate burr in Roosevelt's brain. 'The old red blood said "Use it",' he was to recall later, and now he did: 'On this tenth day of June, 1940, the hand that held the dagger has stuck it in the back of its neighbour.'

With that one sentence, America had taken sides, and many myths were ended. The myth of U.S. neutrality, for one – 'Let us not hesitate – all of us – to proclaim that victory for the gods of force and hate will endanger the institutions of democracy in the Western World . . .' The utopian hope that America could remain an island of democracy in a totalitarian world was ended, too – 'Such an island represents to me . . . a helpless nightmare of a people without freedom, a people lodged in prison . . .' The vacillating talk of the value of aiding the Allies was dead. One thing now remained: to get on with the job.

To be sure, there were still cautious voices, sensing in Roosevelt's non-belligerent intervention a pull towards war. 'Whoa, Mr President,' cried the *Detroit News*, in alarm. Hundreds of citizens approved, by eight to one, the *St Louis Post-Dispatch*'s round declaration that the President, unless checked, would take the U.S. to the brink of war. But there were contrary manifestations, closer to the core of current fears and feelings. On this same day, in New York's Century Club, thirty private citizens combined to voice the unspeakable in a nation-wide news-

147

paper advertisement that both the *Los Angeles Times* and the *Boston Globe* refused to run: 'Let us declare war on Germany.' Among the signatories: Henry W. Hobson, Episcopal Bishop of Cincinnati, Admiral William H. Standley, retired Chief of Naval Operations, the urban planner Lewis Mumford, and Harvard's President, James Bryant Conant.

'Only a tightrope walker could keep his balance here,' lamented the German Chargé d'Affaires in Washington, Hans Thomsen. 'They want Britain to win.' Belatedly, America was taking to heart the warning that Ambassador Lothian had delivered to the alumni of Columbia University. 'Let our Navy disappear and Hitler will be thundering on your doorstep.'

In the *New York Times*, the plea of the poetess Edna St Vincent Millay seemed to say it all:

> Oh build, assemble, transport, give,
> That England, France and we may live . . .
> Lest . . . we be left to fight alone . . .

In France, the fruitless Anglo–French sessions, where no meeting of minds seemed possible, dragged on for three more days. On 11 June, the day after Roosevelt's speech, Churchill returned yet again, supported by Eden, Dill and Ismay, for a meeting at Weygand's new headquarters, the Château du Muguet, near Briare. But the talk, in Spears's view, was little more than a recital of familiar recriminations. When would more British squadrons be forthcoming? Where were Britain's divisions? De Gaulle, watching Pétain closely all through, sourly diagnosed him as 'suffering from senility, pessimism and ambition, a fatal combination'.

Next morning, Churchill, who had remained as an overnight guest, raised a gnawing preoccupation with Admiral Jean François Darlan. Whatever the outcome of the battle, he urged, Germany must never lay hands on the French Fleet. Darlan emphatically shared his concern. Rather than that, he would give the Fleet sailing orders for Canada.

A constant spectre at this feast was Reynaud's mistress, Madame Hélène des Portes, whose harsh importunate voice was heard offstage all through the conference. As defeatist as Reynaud was staunch, surrender was the one thought on her mind. Once, as Reynaud and de Gaulle conferred privately, debating the last-ditch Breton Redoubt, Madame des Portes burst in unannounced to berate her lover: 'What is this ridiculous talk about going to Quimper? I certainly don't propose to go and sleep in Breton four-poster beds.'

On 13 June, when Churchill, along with Beaverbrook and Halifax, arrived for a last melancholy meeting with Reynaud at the Préfecture in Tours, Madame des Portes was again in evidence. Twice, using Baudouin as her emissary, she sent strident messages to Reynaud: 'Tell Paul we must give up, we must make an end of it. There must be an armistice.' From an anteroom came the angry voice of Weygand, shouting like a barrack-room lawyer, 'They sit there with their arses on their chairs and don't give a damn that all this time the French Army is being massacred.'

As Churchill left the building, Madame des Portes attempted to accost him, crying imperiously, 'Monsieur Churchill! Monsieur Churchill! My country is bleeding to death.' Pink with annoyance, pretending that he had not heard, Churchill bored on, butting head first into his Citroën.

It was 5.50 p.m. on Thursday, 13 June, just thirty-seven days after Hitler had launched his blitzkrieg, and only one thing had been settled. 'America is our only hope,' Reynaud had put it to them, 'without her we are powerless.'

Beaverbrook, a man to whom time had always been money, agreed wholeheartedly. 'Telegraph to Roosevelt,' he advised Churchill, 'and await the answer.' Suddenly irritated, he rattled his loose change. 'We're doing no good here,' he said tersely. 'Let's get along home.'

At first, there was only one man to be seen: a solitary German motor cyclist in field grey with a coal-scuttle helmet tut-tutting across the lonely expanse of the Place Voltaire, in Paris. It was 3.40 a.m. Friday, 14 June.

But by 8 a.m. they were coming in their hundreds, a solid goose-stepping phalanx moving across the heart of Paris, past the posters that since February had proudly proclaimed, '*Nous vainquerons parce que nous sommes les plus forts.*' (We shall win because we are the strongest.) Simultaneously, braking their landing speed to 25 m.p.h., two Fieseler 'Storch' spotter planes set down on the Place de la Concorde, to disgorge, among other officers, *Oberst* Walter Warlimont of Hitler's Operations Department. Within the hour, the swastika was floating from the Arc de Triomphe and from the 985-feet Eiffel Tower, where, since the elevators were not working, the flag-bearers had to climb 1,671 steps.

To bewildered Parisians, now undergoing what Finns, Danes, Norwegians, Dutch and Belgians had already undergone – the humiliation of surrender – the first Germans they encountered seemed ebullient to a degree but reassuringly human. Outside the Hôtel de Ville, a beaming officer hailed a woman in the crowd: 'Madame, without doubt you eagerly await your husband's return?'

'Yes!'

'Well, so's my wife looking forward to seeing me again. Once we've signed the peace with you we'll settle the whole thing with the British in fifteen days.'

They came, it seemed, less as conquerors than as hungry tourists. In the bistros that night, men who had lived on Army tack for two years were demanding one kilo steaks and 12 egg omelettes, even buying chocolate bars and smearing them thickly with butter. Every man seemed to have a camera and was busy focusing on the Arc de Triomphe, Notre Dame and Les Invalides. With a nice sense of what was due to them, senior officers took over the Crillon, the Meurice and the Plaza Athénée Hotels. At Rundstedt's H.Q. at St Germain, orderly officers set up a new type of ops map that promised pleasures to come; blue dots for the best gourmet eating, red dots for the apartments of compliant Parisiennes.

In those regions of France still nominally free, there was no such rejoicing. At Brest, in Brittany, on the evening of 14 June, Second Lieutenant Zygmunt Litynski, of the Polish Highland Brigade, who had shared in the fiasco of Narvik, never forgot the pitiful appearance of the French soldiers on the quayside – 'useless pathetic wrecks', innocent of weapons, cap peaks pulled down, tunics unbuttoned.

Suddenly, from the open doorway of a garage, a woman's

voice was heard over the radio – a soft melodious voice, but unmistakably an English accent.

'I, who have always loved France deeply,' the woman was saying, 'I now share with you your sufferings. France is now defending with heroism and courage not only her own land but the lands and liberty of the whole world . . .'

Queen Elizabeth of England was speaking to the people of France. As Litynski watched, first one soldier, then a second and third, got slowly and heavily to his feet, drifting towards the door of the garage. Soon there was a crowd, listening intently, 'the strange weaponless remnants of an army'.

The Queen's tribute continued. '. . . A nation defended by such men, loved by such women, sooner or later is bound to conquer. Such a nation is the mainstay and hope of the whole world . . .'

Suddenly the irony became unbearable. A murmur rippled through the men, and one, raising his empty hands towards his face, cried out: 'Oh God, oh God!' Still the Queen went quietly on, recalling her visit to a hospital of wounded French soldiers. When she had asked them how they were, 'all of them, even the most gravely wounded, replied with one voice "*Ça va*".'

'I do believe with all my heart that when these dark days are gone the time will come when our two nations will be able to say with one voice once more: "*Ça va*".'

All through the afternoon of Friday, 14 June, aboard the Presidential yacht, *Potomac*, René de Chambrun was conscious, as men rarely are, of living through history. In the three days since he had arrived in the United States to carry out Weygand's mission, he had realized the magnitude of his task. Both in New York and Washington, D.C., the polite consensus was that France and Britain were finished.

The young Captain sensed no personal hostility. At the White House, Roosevelt had welcomed him warmly as one of the family, which de Chambrun indeed was; as the nephew of the redoubtable Alice Longworth, Theodore Roosevelt's daughter, he and the President had blood ties. It had been 'Dear René' from the first, and de Chambrun was relieved to learn that the only week-end guests aboard the yacht would be 'family' too: Harry L. Hopkins, Roosevelt's Secretary of Commerce and most intimate adviser, Marguerite 'Missy' Le Hand, the President's secretary, Averell Harriman and his wife.

At 4 p.m., as the *Potomac* slipped away downstream from the Navy Yard, the heat was torrid. Sipping tea on the quarter-deck, de Chambrun watched Roosevelt and Hopkins intently. These men were symbols of the free world – but how would they react to a chain of events in which total war looked more and more like world revolution?

The answer, it seemed, was with despair. Towards 5 p.m. a bluejacket handed the President a radiogram and Roosevelt silently passed it over: the Germans had entered Paris, and were marching towards the Loire. In that moment, de Chambrun saw only defeat in Roosevelt's face; his arms had dropped helplessly to his wheel chair. 'René,' he said, 'the show is over. I don't think that Great Britain can hold out.'

De Chambrun's answer was identical to his response to Ambassador Bullitt back in Paris. 'Mr President, unfortunately you're right so far as France is concerned. But I think you're completely wrong as far as Great Britain is concerned.'

For almost an hour thereafter, de Chambrun held the stage. Conscious that both Roosevelt and Hopkins were weighing every pro and con, he advanced the same argument he had given Bullitt: if France kept her Fleet and America supplied Britain with food and bombers, the day would come when air attacks could hit Germany's most vulnerable region, the Ruhr.

Unexpectedly, Roosevelt cut in: 'René, you have convinced me.' Then, after a moment, 'I am going to ask you to fulfil an important mission – convince this country.'

De Chambrun smiled uncertainly. 'Mr President, there are 130 million Americans and they all seem to believe in Germany's victory.' But Roosevelt, smiling in return, merely countered, 'What I have just asked you to do is less difficult than that which you have already done. Isn't that right, Harry?'

Taking de Chambrun's silence for assent, Roosevelt got down to cases. Even before dinner was announced, he had scribbled out, on one of the *Potomac*'s telegraph forms, a list of twenty-two influential people whom he wanted de Chambrun to see.

Some, Cabinet Ministers or intimate friends, were already more than half-way convinced – Hull, Ickes, Eleanor Roosevelt, the financier Bernard Baruch – but others, like Senator Key Pittman and Republican Minority Leader Joe Martin, were hardcore isolationists. De Chambrun would begin on Monday by addressing the Senate's Foreign Relations Committee.

Still de Chambrun wondered: what hope lay ahead for France? In an appeal which likened his country to 'a drowning man', Reynaud had besought Roosevelt to send 'clouds of planes', but America, as Roosevelt gently explained, had no clouds of planes to give. The provisions of the Neutrality Laws decreed that even those he might dredge up – ninety Navy bombers, 173 Army attack planes – must first be flown to tiny Houlton, Maine, towed across the border into Canada, then sold to private manufacturers who in turn would sell them to the Allies.

On Saturday, 15 June, as the yacht once again neared the Navy Yard, de Chambrun drafted a hasty cable for Paul Reynaud. In part it read: [THE PRESIDENT] IS CONVINCED THAT HIS COUNTRY, THE BRITISH EMPIRE AND ALL THAT REMAINS OF THE FRENCH FLEET AND COLONIES CONSTITUTE THE ONLY RAMPART AGAINST WORLD DOMINATION BY GERMANY STOP AS THE CHAMPION OF A CAUSE HE HAS AN ALMOST MYSTICAL BELIEF THAT THE EVENTS OF TODAY MAKE HIM THE ONLY MAN WHO CAN STOP HITLER STOP THE PEOPLE WILL FOLLOW HIM EVEN TO WAR ON TWO CONDITIONS . . . THAT ENGLAND . . . AFFIRM THAT SHE WILL WIN IN SPITE OF THE SETBACKS . . . THAT FRANCE KEEP HER FLEET AND HER EMPIRE.

Thinking back on all he had seen over nine months, de Chambrun had only one reservation. To him it was less than puzzling that France was losing the war. The puzzle was: How could anyone have ever expected her to win it?

In Bordeaux, 360 miles south of Paris, where his government had now transferred yet again, Reynaud, on Sunday, 16 June, was anticipating far more than the cautious measure of comfort offered by de Chambrun's cable. Buoyant to the last, he still nourished hopes that Roosevelt, with the classic timing of a

153

Seventh Cavalry squadron, would come to France's aid by declaring war on Germany.

On this day, too, Reynaud was pinning his faith in another last-ditch project: a mooted Franco–British Union, reviving an earlier abortive union effected by Henry V through the Treaty of Troyes in 1420. The brainchild of René Pleven, of the French Economic Mission in London, who had discussed it with both Chamberlain and Churchill, it looked to a joint Franco–British War Cabinet to carry on the struggle, the subjects of both nations to enjoy a common citizenship and a common flag. Even more to Churchill's taste, it called for a mass evacuation of French troops across the Channel, 'to make the island stiff with soldiers'.

Over lunch at the Carlton Club, de Gaulle, on a brief visit to London, had discussed it further with Churchill, who was cautious but impressed. A two-hour Cabinet session at Downing Street had followed, but at last Churchill emerged to tell de Gaulle that the plan was agreed. Promptly de Gaulle had telephoned the details to Reynaud in Bordeaux. At 5 p.m. Reynaud met with his Council of Ministers, determined 'to die defending these proposals'.

But to a French Cabinet half of whose members were bent on capitulation, the Franco–British Union was stillborn. 'France would be nothing more than a dominion,' one Minister protested. 'It would be fusion with a corpse,' Pétain shrugged. Reynaud had at length reached stalemate, for although no votes were taken, his supporters numbered thirteen, while those in favour of an armistice totalled eleven.

The day held another painful shock for Reynaud. A message whose contents de Chambrun had already discerned arrived from Roosevelt. Its gist was plain; although war matériel would be forthcoming, 'you will understand that these declarations imply no military commitments. Congress alone can undertake such engagements.'

As he read it, Spears noted that Reynaud's face grew paler and contracted, 'his eyes became just slits'. 'Our appeal has failed,' he said, in a small toneless voice, 'the Americans will not declare war.'

*

154

Late that night, a small false hope flared through Bordeaux like a fading comet. For four unavailing hours Reynaud had pleaded with his Cabinet to go with him to North Africa and carry on the fight from there. In a forlorn hope that he would prevail, he had asked U.S. Envoy-Extraordinary Anthony Drexel Biddle to return at midnight, at which time he could give him news.

Somehow word had spread through the port that America *had* declared war – and as Biddle's car nosed through the darkened street it was greeted by a storm of cheering: '*Vive Les États-Unis*' – '*Vive Les États-Unis!*'

'I sat there in that car,' Biddle recalled later, 'and I had a lump in my throat, because I knew we weren't going to do a damn thing.'

By 10 p.m. in a 'sarcastic disparaging voice', Reynaud had resigned, and Pétain was confirmed as France's new Premier. It was to this end that the old Marshal had worked all along, for promptly he pulled from his briefcase the list of Cabinet members he had selected. Foreseeing this, Churchill had released France from her obligations as an ally and given her freedom to negotiate an armistice – but only provided that the French Fleet now sailed for British harbours.

At noon on Monday, 17 June, Pétain, through the Spanish Ambassador, set his armistice negotiations in train. Half an hour later, the nation first heard of his intention through a studio broadcast from Bordeaux, where Pétain, in a fine fury, deliberately kicked an errant radio technician on the shin. But the calculated pathos was there as the quavering voice, broken by a dry cough, began hesitantly: 'With a broken heart I tell you that fighting must cease.' One man remembered with shame: 'An old man with the voice of an old woman told us he had asked for peace.'

All over France, on Town Hall steps, in bistros and tenements, people listened as if turned to stone, uncomprehending. Exactly ninety-six days after the Finns had acknowledged defeat, France, the last of the prosperous complacent democracies, had succumbed.

At Ligny-en-Barrois, in the department of the Meuse, the

heart of the champagne country, the face of France in defeat showed plain that sunlit Monday afternoon. Marooned in the station was an entire train, twenty waggons long, loaded with champagne and liqueurs. Soon after noon, whole columns of infantrymen, debouching on the station, chanced upon it.

By mid-afternoon, a man approaching the platform had to wade through a sea of broken glass. Hundreds of bottles had been emptied and smashed on the spot; a sticky light brown syrup of cognac and champagne oozed from the looted cars. An old drunken woman who had fallen from a champagne crate lay bleeding face downwards in a glittering mosaic of glass.

The whole station reeked of drink. Soldiers lay recumbent between the rails, snoring or humming in their sleep. Along the tracks, a horde of soldiers, joined by an officer and two non-coms, had set up champagne bottles like ten-pins, bowling at them with other bottles. Each time glass splintered against glass, the players joined hands, yelling and capering and kissing one another. A Bedouin in a bright-coloured turban leaned out of the station-master's office and vomited on the platform.

Only one man seemed to care, a middle-aged captain slumped on a crate, his head buried in his hands. '*La ligne Daladier*,' he moaned repeatedly. '*La ligne Daladier!*' But nobody heeded him, or even understood what he meant. The Maginot Line had already passed into history.

It might have been one of Churchill's most historic wartime broadcasts – yet for reasons of state he was never to deliver it.

Its aim was to demonstrate yet again to the Americans that Britain, if down, was not out, whatever poison Ambassador Joseph P. Kennedy might drop in the collective ear of the State Department – and its delivery was timed for the evening of 18 June. Among its enthusiastic proponents was A. V. Alexander, the new First Lord of the Admiralty, who encouraged Churchill: 'The U.S.A. must be on tiptoe for an authoritative voice from this country.'

It was as American-oriented as Churchill, the son of an American mother, could make it. Hitler, he declared, was 'using men's souls and bodies as poker chips'. True, on the basis of territory gained, 'the German supreme gambler has met with success; and success flushes a gambler like bad liquor'. But the end was not yet. 'An army much greater than the entire standing army of the United States today' had been ferried across the Channel to fight again. 'I say to you,' ended the Premier's peroration, 'what your John Paul Jones said: "*Surrender?* We're only just *beginnin'* to fight." '

But at the last moment Churchill decided against it, unwilling to give ammunition to the American isolationists with whom Roosevelt must contend. Instead he wisely preferred to rely on his private link with 'Potus', as Churchill called the President of the United States, and he didn't hesitate to pressure Roosevelt unmercifully with every passing day. On 11 June, his cry was 'The only counter is destroyers ... Not a day should be lost.' On 14 June, he urged the President to publish his message to Reynaud – a plea which Roosevelt and Hull flatly refused to countenance. On 15 June: 'Events are moving at a pace where they will pass beyond the control of American public opinion.' Later on the same day: 'If your reply does not contain the assurance asked for (the entry of the U.S. into war) the French will very quickly ask for an armistice.'

Presumably, Roosevelt's silence on this last one gave Churchill cause to feel he was pressing too hard. As he was later to tell Herbert Morrison, who was unaware of this intimate White House link: 'Only events will serve to turn public opinion in America.'

This was sound thinking. Roosevelt was moving gingerly, a step at a time, like a man testing thin ice, though on 19 June he took a giant one. Out of his Cabinet went the isolationist Secretary of War Harry Woodring, in came the stalwart Republicans, Frank L. Knox and Henry G. Stimson, as Secretaries for Navy and War. It was Roosevelt's first step towards a coalition government, prompting outraged cries of 'Dirty politics!' from those Republicans still wedded to isolationism.

But France's fall had clinched one resolution in Roosevelt's mind. With the spectre of Britain alone standing between America and the Axis conquerors, to run for a third term had become imperative. Until now he had kept the options open – 'his decision had been to reserve a decision' as one biographer put it – but by early July his mind was made up. He told the

Democrats' Party Chief, James A. Farley: 'Jim, if I'm nominated and elected I could not in these times refuse to take the inaugural oath.'

In Knox, for one, the President had picked a doughty ally. 'Frank,' wrote Harold Ickes, '...knows that we must prepare and lose no time about it. He believes that as soon as Germany has consolidated its gains in Europe ... it will proceed to penetrate South America – and then we will have our work cut out for us in this country.'

Secretary Knox's prediction was premature. In this week, Adolf Hitler's thoughts were occupied solely with France's fall and the avenging of the Treaty of Versailles. From the first, the armistice proceedings were to be as carefully stage-managed as a Nazi Party rally. To be sure, the peace terms would not be so harsh as to drive France closer to Britain; the Führer looked as unfavourably on the prospect of a potential French Government in North Africa as on the Free Frenchmen now rallying to General de Gaulle in London. Thus, while Germany would occupy three-fifths of France, including the rich industrial areas north of the Loire, the remaining two-fifths would come under Pétain's aegis. From the first, Hitler was as intent on recognizing the Marshal's Cabinet as the official French Government as he was to disavow interest in her Fleet. 'If need be,' Hitler snapped, 'let them sink it.'

But for the rest, the subtle undercurrents of humiliation would be there. The French delegates under General Huntziger, arriving on 21 June, were to meet in the Forest of Compiègne, where Marshal Foch had confronted the Germans who came to sue for peace at the end of the First World War. Moreover, the French would hear Hitler's terms in the very same coach, Dining Car 2419 D, which for twenty-two years had been preserved in a near-by museum, complete with printed cards indicating the former seating arrangements.

The frenzied preparations gave rise to some bizarre sights. Under Dr Paul Schmidt, the official interpreter, teams of translators worked all night in a candle-lit church to ensure the terms of surrender were made plain. In a forest glade near by, so quiet that a woodpecker could be heard tapping against a beech tree, one German diplomat, Erich Tuch, chanced on Hitler quite alone – pirouetting, rehearsing salutes and gracious smiles, the entire act performed in dumb show like a pantomimist at rehearsal.

This was truly the Führer's hour, and once the French delegates had arrived at 3.15 p.m. on 21 June, he lingered no more than fifteen minutes for the ceremony round the green baize table. The mundane details of surrender were left to *Generaloberst* Wilhelm Keitel, nominal Chief of the German Armed Forces, for Hitler, like his soldiers before him, was in a mood to play tourist in Paris. The Battle of France had cost him barely 150,000 casualties, 111,000 of them wounded men, who would most likely fight again, while his troops now patrolled the Atlantic coast from the North Cape to the Pyrenees. It was the hour wherein a conqueror might relax.

For the most part, Hitler was in rare high spirits. He revelled, like any globe-trotter, in the glory of the Paris Opéra and the Panthéon. At the Dôme des Invalides, he launched into a soliloquy beside Napoleon's sunken tomb: 'They have made a big mistake ... you should look up at Napoleon, feeling small by the very size of the monument.' Three days later, touring Alsace, he rallied one mass parade: 'Do you like this beautiful country?' When the troops chorused, 'Yes, *mein Führer*,' Hitler promised, 'Well, we shall hold on to it forever then.'

It was at this stage that Hitler's architect, Albert Speer, was given the charge of reconstructing Berlin, Nuremberg, Munich, Linz and twenty-seven other cities by way of celebration – most of them to be recast in Swedish granite which had been ordered as long ago as February.

In Berlin, Göbbels, too, was formulating grandiose victory plans: whole oxen were to be roasted at street corners, with free cuts and cold beer for all comers, plus a brand new production of Hitler's favourite operetta, Lehár's *The Merry Widow*. But even Göbbels was careful to keep from the press the alcoholic victory fantasy of Minister of Labour Robert Ley: the construction of five million new apartments and ten 20,000-bed hotels.

In the lower echelons, too, there was an implicit belief in a total and speedy victory. Werner Mölders, transferred from

Alençon to a prison camp near Toulouse, recalled a long-standing vow with his fellow fliers: the first drinks on reaching London would be in the R.A.F. Club, Piccadilly. A non-com billeted on the Van Duren household in Breda, Holland, told them nonchalantly: 'Any day now I'm off to Downing Street.' In an Antwerp jeweller's, a *Hauptmann* haggling for a bargain in diamond rings, finally pushed the tray aside – 'Probably I'll do better in London.'

At the Staff H.Q. of Schützenregiment 11, 9th Armoured Division, *Gefreiter* Wilhelm Prüller was as fiercely confident as any. 'Give us the right to live of our own free will, Mr Churchill,' he wrote in his diary, 'and . . . you will spare the English nation useless mountains of corpses.' He ended on a note of challenge: 'Choose, Mr Churchill!'

In London, Winston Churchill had chosen – to fight tyranny with tyranny.

On 22 May, the mild-mannered Clement Attlee had risen in the House of Commons to ask Parliament to approve the Emergency Powers Defence Bill – technically an extension of one passed in 1939, giving the King wide powers to govern by decree in wartime, following his Privy Council's advice. In effect it gave Churchill and his Ministers wider powers than had been vested in any caucus since the death of absolute monarchy.

It had been sparked off only twenty-four hours back by a memorandum from General Sir Hastings Ismay, Assistant Secretary to the War Cabinet – a thesis which credited Hitler with plans he had never remotely formulated. 'It can be taken for granted,' Ismay posited, 'that the Germans have the plan for an invasion of this country worked out to the last details . . . We can be sure that Hitler would be prepared to sacrifice 90 per cent of the whole expedition if he could gain a firm bridgehead on British soil with the remaining 10 per cent . . .'

'The counter to such forces,' Ismay maintained, 'is a scheme of well-planned demolitions covered by resolute troops.' But he warned, 'no real progress can be made unless the powers over persons and property, which it is intended the Government should assume in a grave emergency, are taken at once.'

Next day, within two hours forty-three minutes, and opposed

by only two dissenting voices, the Bill became law – as momentous a step as any in British history. To resist Hitler, Britons had surrendered the rights over persons and property which they had wrested from King John at Runnymede 725 years earlier. From this day on, for example, an Englishman's home was no longer his castle: any man with a uniform or badge could enter his house, search it, turn out his lights, send him to bed or take him to gaol.

Not only his house, but his factory, his car, and his bank account were now the intimate concerns of the State. Supply Minister Herbert Morrison not only assumed powers to control factories needed to produce munitions and equipment but to prescribe the hours of work, the labour employed, the price of the goods. By a strange irony, Minister of Labour Ernie Bevin, who had battled all his life for a 40-hour week, now commanded workers to ban strikes, work a 7-day week, and toil uncomplainingly alongside unskilled non-union labour.

Although Bevin at first used his powers sparingly, the Act empowered him to march into any Pall Mall club, demand details of a member's war effort, and if need be, direct him forthwith to the nearest Labour Exchange.

Overnight, after nine months' stagnation, Britain was on a total war footing. As early as 14 May, Eden, as Secretary of State for War, had made a radio appeal for what he privately called 'a broomstick Army', known to the public as the Local Defence Volunteers. Soon to be re-christened the 'Home Guard' by Churchill – and dubbed by a later generation 'Dad's Army' – the force consisted of any man not in uniform, aged between sixteen and sixty-five, who was committed to a minimum ten hours' duty a week scouting for paratroops.

The response was overwhelming. The first volunteers were besieging police stations within four minutes of Eden's appeal – although only one in three of the 500,000 strong force could be equipped with rifles.

Even in this hour of crisis, *The Times* felt moved to make a nice distinction: 'It would not be correct for country gentlemen to carry their guns with them on their walks and take flying or running shots as opportunity is offered ... Such action would put them into the position of *franc-tireurs* ...'

From 28 May on, as the Dunkirk evacuation gathered momentum, Britain was honeycombed with ghost towns. To the bafflement of 117,000 London schoolchildren evacuated to remote villages by the Great Western Railway, all signposts, milestones, village signs and street names now came down – an idea to fox potential invaders thought up by the thriller writer Dennis Wheatley in a strategic plan submitted to the War Cabinet. Already pillboxes, three and a half feet of solid concrete, bulked as tank traps in thousands of village streets. In South Wales, the miners made plans to blow up the pits and take to the hills armed with picks and shovels.

But what gravely preoccupied Churchill and his Ministers was not only the vulnerability of the south and east coasts, but the potential threat to their own back door through the green republic of Eire. On 4 June, the First Sea Lord, Admiral Sir Dudley Pound, had urged his chief, A. V. Alexander: 'Would it not be worth while trying to get de Valera to agree to British forces being sent to Eire, on the understanding that at the end of the war our troops would be immediately removed?'

The bones of contention were the Irish treaty ports of Queenstown (now Cobh), Berehaven and Lough Swilly, Royal Naval bases in the First World War, which Chamberlain, to Churchill's fury, had handed back to Eire in 1938. 'A more feckless act can hardly be imagined,' Churchill had fulminated then, and now, fearing their seizure by Germany, he debated the idea of seizing them first, as bases against U-boat operations in the North Atlantic.

But even as France fell, Eire's leader, 58-year-old Eamon de Valera, was still bent on a neutrality as unswerving as Sweden or Switzerland. On 18 June, he made his position abundantly clear to the German Ambassador, Dr Eduard Hempel: if England invaded Eire, the Irish would fight them shoulder to shoulder with the Germans. But if Germany invaded, the Irish would make common cause with the English.

One day earlier, a 'tired and frightened de Valera', afflicted by near-blindness, had put this same viewpoint to the British Minister of Health, Malcolm MacDonald, an old friend and son of a former Labour Prime Minister, who had journeyed to Dublin as Churchill's secret emissary. His every action was being studied and analysed, de Valera complained bitterly, lest he strayed from the path of strict neutrality.

What maddened the ailing *Taoiseach* past all patience was that the British refused to take no for an answer. Almost as if the first interview, lasting three-and-a-half hours, had never taken place, MacDonald was sent back on 25 June to propose the unthinkable: a joint union of Eire and Northern Ireland, with Eire not only affording sanctuary to British troops and offering the use of her ports but entering the war as Britain's ally.

'An invasion of your country would embarrass us but it would be disastrous for you,' MacDonald had hinted. But de Valera was unyielding. The presence of any foreign troops on Irish soil would destroy Eire's national unity, he maintained. Thus he would resist either belligerent to the utmost limit of his power. The situation was so frustrating that even the law-abiding Chamberlain was tempted to consider entering the ports by force – though he counselled caution 'in view . . . of the possible unfavourable reaction which would be caused in the United States'.

In the last resort, the War Cabinet placed infinite faith in MacDonald's powers of persuasion. On 27 June, the weary Minister returned to Dublin, to continue, in Halifax's words, 'the process of educating Mr de Valera as to the dangers of invasion'.

At Miss Coffey's boarding-house in the genteel Dublin suburb of Dun Laoghaire, a morose stranger whom the other guests knew as a commercial traveller named Mr Robinson was debating his dubious future.

Since early May, when a Heinkel 111 airborne from Kassel, Germany, had dropped him near Ballivor, County Meath, seventy miles wide of his target, *Hauptmann* Dr Hermann Goertz, a 50-year-old agent of the *Abwehr* (German Military Intelligence) had seen everything go as wrong as it feasibly could.

Briefed by the *Abwehr* to explore chances of stirring up 'a partisan war in Ulster', Goertz had had all the strikes against him from the first. At the moment that he baled out and hit

Irish soil, his second parachute containing not only his radio set but the spade to bury the chute by which he descended, had drifted far from sight. When he was forced to swim the Boyne River, because the footbridge was guarded by police, the invisible ink pad concealed in his shoulder padding had been ruined, staining his underwear a sickly yellow.

Goertz' intention of travelling in full uniform to establish his 'international status' had thus been doomed to failure. Discarding his sodden flying suit and service dress jacket, he soldiered on in a pullover, breeches and riding boots, a black beret perched on his head. Four days later, keeping scrupulously to by-roads, he reached Laragh, in County Wicklow, the home of his one and only Irish contact, Professor Francis Stuart. Stuart, a lecturer in Anglo–Irish literature at Berlin University, was a patriot of the de Valera stripe, but he had no links with the *Abwehr* and few with the Irish Republican Army, the paramilitary force whose goal was a united Ireland.

Stuart's wife, Iseult, given no warning of Goertz' arrival, was at first highly suspicious. Finally she agreed to travel to Dublin and buy him a civilian suit, at the same time tipping off Jim O'Donovan, a one-time I.R.A. agent, who obligingly took Goertz off her hands. Hidden up in O'Donovan's garage in the Dublin suburb of Shankill, Goertz next became the concern of I.R.A. activists. Willy-nilly, he found himself shunted to another 'safe' house – the home of Stephen Carroll Held, who had once visited Berlin to urge the Germans to invade Ulster.

Only when a police raid turned over Held's house, narrowly missing Goertz, as he took off over the garden wall, did the German realize that de Valera's Eire and the I.R.A. were not as one, as the *Abwehr* had always believed. Then as now, the I.R.A. were proscribed terrorists and as such, hunted men. But the raid was to cost Goertz more than a loss of faith. In Held's safe, the police had found $20,000 in American currency, the bulk of Goertz' travelling expenses, which he had entrusted to the Irishman.

Thus by the first week in June Goertz was a fugitive who had lost his money, his transmitter, his secret ink, his uniform and all faith in the I.R.A.; he alone could have told both Churchill and de Valera that the Germans had absolutely no plans for

Ireland at all. In fact, on 25 May, having had no radio contact, the *Abwehr* had written him off – at roughly the same time as Goertz wrote off the I.R.A.

'The organization,' he went on record bitterly, 'was rotten at its roots.'

On the night of 21 June, Dr R. V. Jones, the ebullient young scientist who sought the elusive German detector beams called Knickebein, was a preoccupied man. In the flat which he and his wife Vera rented at Richmond Hill Court, South London, Jones twisted uneasily in bed, counting the hours. In spirit, he was far from Richmond; he was a passenger in a twin-seater *engine* Anson trainer plane, airborne from Wynton airfield, Huntingdonshire, flying steadily north.

The Anson's pilot, Flight Lieutenant Hal Bufton, had reason to view the flight more phlegmatically. Knowing nothing of the Knickebein story, he had been told only to scout for Lorenz-type transmissions – but this was the third night that he and his wireless operator, Corporal Mackie, had searched without success.

Earlier that day, Jones had been startled to find himself in the Cabinet Room at 10 Downing Street, expounding the story of his Knickebein investigations to Winston Churchill. Conscious that most men present – Professor Lindemann, Sir Archibald Sinclair, Dowding, Sir Cyril Newall – were some thirty years his senior, Jones had left the meeting elated by the reception of his far-flung theory.

For Churchill had shown a lively interest. If the beams did exist, he had asked, what could be done? Jones had ready answers. Once found, they could be jammed, as Dowding had earlier suggested. Or false cross-beams could be introduced, to fool the Germans into dropping their bombs too early. The question arose: where should an aircraft search for the beams? Jones, remembering the Germans had pinpointed a location near Retford, Nottinghamshire, played a hunch. Supposing the director beam was laid on Derby, where the Rolls-Royce works were turning out Merlin engines for Beaverbrook's Hurricanes and Spitfires?

The hunch paid off. Around 10 p.m., as Jones was retiring

uneasily to bed, Bufton and Mackie struck lucky. A series of dots, sixty to the minute, were suddenly mosquito-shrill in Mackie's headphones. As the Anson flew on, the dots merged into a steady monotone, then abruptly broke up. At the same steady rate of sixty to the minute, the dots had been supplanted by dashes.

What the two-man crew had chanced upon was a narrow beam, not more than 500 yards wide, passing just south of Spalding, Lincolnshire, with dots to the south and dashes to the north. A second beam, intersecting with the first, was passing over Beeston, Nottinghamshire – but this time with dots to the north and dashes to the south.

Although Knickebein could be roughly traversed over any sector of eastern England on a line between London and Edinburgh, Bufton and Mackie had struck it where Jones had predicted – trained on Rolls-Royce, Derby.

Next day, 22 June, saw such exultation at the Air Ministry that one elderly Air Commodore actually skipped like a faun across his office. Now counter-measures could be brought into play against Knickebein. A special anti-beam organization, No. 80 Wing, R.A.F. was set up at Radlett, north of London, under Wing-Commander Edward Addison. At Swanage, Dorset, the Telecommunications Research Establishment, under Dr Robert Cockburn, got even higher priority. Their first jammers were electro-diathermy sets hastily snatched from hospital wards, to set up a 'mush' of noise on the Knickebein frequencies, but soon high-powered custom-built jammers, nicknamed 'Aspirins', were superimposing powerful morse dashes on the German beam wavelengths. Thus the steady monotone the bomber pilot needed to guide him to the target was now lacking; he heard only a nonstop sequence of dashes. If he swung to the dot zone by way of correction, he met up with a mind-boggling confusion of both dashes and dots.

The beams were never 'bent', as legend claimed, merely confused enough to ensure that many bombs aimed at provincial industrial targets went wide of their mark. Such technical details were too trifling for Churchill; for him, thereafter, Jones was always 'the man who broke the Bloody Beam'.

*

In the air, the British were thus far holding their own. On the ground their chances looked slimmer.

In the quiet south-coast resort of Bognor Regis, Sussex, 11-year-old Sonia Bech watched the landscape transformed with each passing day. The daughter of a Danish porcelain dealer, who had stayed on in London, Sonia, her mother, 14-year-old Barbara and 9-year-old Derek had remained at the family's summer home, for fear the capital was bombed. But now even Bognor, beloved of King George V, where the Royal Norfolk Hotel had always insisted on black ties at dinner, had become a cat's cradle of mines and barbed wire. Sentries were posted everywhere, manning pillboxes and even bathing machines filled with pebbles. Bognor had become the front line.

Sonia wondered how long the Bechs would stay put; her mother, Marguerite, was becoming uneasy over Britain's future. Her memories of bombing in the First World War were all too vivid, and the sight of the beaten men from Dunkirk beaches, unshaven, swathed in bloody bandages, reeking like polecats and prone to sudden bursts of hysteria, did nothing to reassure her. The idea of the whole family seeking refuge with a relative in Montreal, was already in her mind.

The sights that Sonia saw on her way to school were being re-enacted in scores of coastal towns. By early July, the voluntary evacuation of the 185-mile coastal area between Sheringham, Norfolk, and Folkestone, Kent, had been extended 180 miles further, as far south-west as Portland, Dorset. The hardships were manifold – one town, Lowestoft, Suffolk, was already in the hands of a bank – and many houses blocking a field of fire were flattened out of hand. On hand to supervise their demolition was one of the new fire-eating commanders whom Eden had sought, Major-General Bernard Montgomery, zestfully gesticulating with his swagger stick: 'Have them out. Blow up the house. Defence must come first.'

The ground defences were pitiful. If only one Home Guardsman in three had a rifle, the Army was in poor shape too. To defend 2,000 miles of coastline, of which 800 were assailable, the new C.-in-C., Home Forces, General Ironside, had in theory twenty-six divisions – fourteen badly mauled from France and Norway, twelve totally unequipped raw training divisions.

From Dover to Southampton, there was one machine gun to defend each 1,500 yards of beach. At Deal, Kent, the men of the 5th Battalion, Shropshire Light Infantry, had one Bren gun between 750 men.

All along the coast, the weird barricades showed the shape of the war to come, a guerrilla war with the people caught up in its midst. At Chilham, Kent, Home Guardsmen manhandled tree trunks from the sawmills; at Tonbridge, near by, it was tar barrels from the distillery. At Goring-by-Sea, in Sussex, the locals made do with a flimsy latticework of old iron bedsteads. Inland, at Sidcup crossroads, the police had dumped 100 tons of broken glass, as if for a medieval siege.

Spy scares abounded. At Winchester, a clergyman's daughter even denounced as a spy a British officer billeted at her father's rectory; he had shown 'un-English' behaviour by visiting the lavatory and failing to pull the chain afterwards. But other authorities, who should have known better, over-reacted too, none more so than the Home Secretary, Sir John Anderson, 'Pompous John', a one-time Governor of Bengal. From June onwards, 'alarm and despondency' fines ranging from £50 to £100, and wholesale incarcerations in goal, were visited on all who spoke their minds too freely. 'It'll be a good thing when the British Empire is finished,' was one man's opinion: it netted him a year in gaol. 'You're bloody fools to wear those uniforms,' a woman told a group of soldiers: her reward was three months' gaol and a £20 fine.

'Begging your pardon, Sir John,' scolded the *News Chronicle*, 'we would remind you that you are no longer in Bengal . . .' After seventy such prosecutions, Churchill, who had never relished the idea, vetoed all further proceedings.

More at risk in this climate of fear and suspicion were Britain's 100,000 aliens, of whom the heavy-handed Sir John gaoled fully 30,000 in sub-human conditions – so many that Churchill chided the Cabinet that it was 'unjust to treat our friends as foes'. Why not, he asked, consider forming a Foreign Legion?

But for many months yet, thousands were to suffer like the 4,000 interned at Huyton, Lancashire, housed under appalling conditions, without hot water; two-thirds of them were sleeping in tents on raid-sodden ground, in a camp where rations were so scarce that the rueful commandant could do no more than console them: 'I can only prevent you from starving.' Hemmed in by the very sentries and barbed wire that many of them had fled Hitler's Europe to escape and faced with the prospect of deportation to Canada, at least one each day committed suicide.

'I can't believe,' wrote one shocked observer to the Deputy Director General of the Ministry of Information, Sir Walter Monckton, 'that English people would allow it to go on.'

Unhappily, the English would. The humiliations of France, Belgium and Norway had nourished a fierce irrational xenophobia, a hard and unforgiving core, which the Ministry's Mass Observers were swift to perceive. 'There ought to be an earthquake in France and swallow the whole bloody lot up' ... 'They might be spies – they're a dirty lot' were two typical comments. Noted one observer in despair: 'It is becoming the socially done thing to be anti-refugee.'

In the week that France fell, Air Chief Marshal Sir Hugh Dowding, C.-in-C. of Fighter Command, summed up the way most Englishmen felt as Britain awaited the worst. Staring across the rose garden from his office window at Stanmore, Middlesex, Dowding turned back abruptly to his guest, Lord Halifax.

'Thank God we're now alone,' he said.

'I am . . . the Victor Speaking in the Name of Reason'

27 June–7 August 1940

The fate of the French Fleet, a major prize for any warring nation, was causing Britain grave concern. Until now, the British and the French had between them dominated the Mediterranean, but without France the British faced an Italian challenge. Although marginally superior in battleships – seven against Italy's six – plus the added might of two aircraft carriers, the British Mediterranean Fleet was still outnumbered in cruisers and destroyers. Italy, by contrast, boasted the world's largest submarine fleet, and ten land-based aircraft for every plane that the R.A.F. could spare. If France joined the war on the Axis side, the British could be swept from the Mediterranean.

Ironically, the seeds of distrust were first sown in the British by a Frenchman, René Cambon, of the London Embassy. On 17 June, Orme Sargent, the Foreign Office's Deputy Under-Secretary of State, minuted Sir Alexander Cadogan: 'Cambon remarked to me this morning that the new French Govt would behave worse than King Leopold, and that we should not put too much trust in Ad. Darlan.'

This led the First Sea Lord, Sir Dudley Pound, to speculate that the French would sink their Fleet rather than undergo the humiliation of surrender – adding 'if the French would not sink their Fleet we could perhaps do it for them'.

The idea did Darlan, Pétain's new Minister of Marine, less than justice, both as a patriot and as a politician. France's intention was to keep firm hold on her Fleet as a prime bargaining card – a card she was in no way disposed to yield to Britain despite Churchill's insistence. Already, on 18 June, Darlan had ordered the unfinished battleship *Richelieu* to leave Brest for Dakar, Senegal, at full speed. One day later, although also incomplete, the battleship *Jean Bart* left St Nazaire for Casablanca.

The stumbling-block Darlan sought to overcome was Article 8 of the Franco–German Armistice treaty, which laid down that warships were to be returned to their peacetime stations and disarmed under Axis supervision. Under these conditions, two-thirds of the Fleet would lie at anchor in German-occupied ports.

Thus, Darlan took no chances. By 29 June, the bulk of his Fleet was assembled at Oran and Mers-el-Kebir, harbours in the Bay of Oran, Algeria, 200 miles east of Gibraltar. From his flagship, the *Dunkerque*, Admiral Marcel Henri Gensoul, C.-in-C. of the Atlantic Fleet, held a watching brief over the great battle-cruiser *Strasbourg*, as well as two battleships, seven light cruisers, four submarines and a torpedo boat.

Three days later, unknown to the French, the British War Cabinet had evolved four courses of action for their Fleet to follow: to sail with the British Fleet to fight the Axis, to sail under supervision to British ports, to sail with reduced crews to the West Indies, or to scuttle their ships within six hours. Failing this, the British would use 'whatever force may be necessary'.

This last alternative appalled Churchill. On the night of 2 July, Beaverbrook was summoned to the Cabinet Room to find a highly agitated Premier closeted with Pound and Alexander. If the French did not comply with one of the first three alternatives, Pound favoured an all-out bombardment, and Churchill could not stomach it. He saw an alliance between France and Britain, born thirty-six years ago and twice sealed with blood in Flanders, rushing towards a nightmare end.

Beaverbrook did not hesitate: there was no choice but to attack. He foresaw that the Germans would force the French Fleet to join the Italians, thus taking command of the Mediterranean. 'The Germans will force this,' Beaverbrook prophesied, 'by threatening to burn Bordeaux the first day the French refuse, the next day Marseilles, and the third day Paris.'

Suddenly, overcome, Churchill seized Beaverbrook's arm and

ran almost headlong into the garden of No. 10. 'I had trouble keeping up with him,' Beaverbrook was to recall, 'and I began to have an attack of asthma.' He remembered, too, Churchill's words: 'There is no other decision possible.' A high wind had blown up through the garden, and Churchill was crying.

Soon after 4 p.m. on Wednesday, 3 July, five men met in the stifling cabin of Admiral Marcel Henri Gensoul aboard the flagship *Dunkerque*. It was a meeting which Gensoul and his aides had been seeking to avoid since 9.30 that morning, so that until now all the efforts of Captain Cedric Holland, R.N., the former Naval Attaché in Paris, to come aboard, had been unavailing. Since Gensoul had refused point-blank to receive him, Holland had been forced to negotiate aboard a barge in the broiling heat of mid-harbour with the Admiral's Flag Lieutenant, *Lieutenant de Vaisseau* Bernard Dufay.

At their first, 10 a.m. meeting, Dufay had warned that Gensoul was mortally offended by Britain's threats of force – and by the ships of Force 'H', under Vice-Admiral Sir James Somerville, making steady legs to seaward in the Bay of Oran. It was to Dufay that Holland had been forced to entrust Somerville's ultimatum to Gensoul.

Gensoul, when he scanned it, was in no way mollified. Not only was he angered that Britain suspected Darlan of operating under Axis duress; he felt slighted that the British, by implication, doubted his capability to scuttle his own ships if the need arose.

As early as 9.45 a.m. Gensoul had signalled a précis of the situation to Darlan's temporary headquarters near Bordeaux, though strangely he made no mention of the West Indies option. But Darlan, at this hour, was absent from the office, and his Chief of Staff, Rear Admiral Le Luc, was momentarily at a loss. At 1.30 p.m., however, unable to reach Darlan, Le Luc, on his own initiative, sent fifty French warships full steam ahead for Oran to back Gensoul's resistance.

Meanwhile, in London, the last chance to avert imminent tragedy had been thrown away on this same morning. Although Pound had drafted a signal authorizing Somerville to accept the

172

de-militarization of the French ships where they lay, the War Cabinet rejected it, 'since this would look like weakening'.

'The deadly stroke', as Churchill was to call it, was coming nearer by the hour.

By 1.30 p.m., the mining of the outer harbour entrances had been carried out by planes from the aircraft carrier *Ark Royal*. Gensoul was all but trapped and he knew it. However, stalling for time and planning to make a break after nightfall, he finally agreed to see Captain Holland and his party. By this hour, 4 p.m., the mining of the inner harbours had effectively sealed off his Fleet inside Oran and Mers-el-Kebir.

The atmosphere was hostile from the start. 'The first shot fired . . . will be tantamount to a declaration of war between France and Great Britain,' Gensoul told Holland, stiffly. 'Is this what you want?'

'Of course not.'

'Do you not trust my word of honour?' asked Gensoul coldly.

'I am quite sure you will do everything possible to prevent your ships falling into enemy hands,' Holland conceded. 'However, we do not trust the Germans or Italians.'

Holland, like Somerville, who called the whole venture 'a filthy job', was sickened by the role he had to play. By accepting any one of the alternatives, he urged Gensoul, he would be yielding to *force majeure* and the blame would fall on the British. Gensoul, stubborn and correct, rejected this: 'I have my code of honour.'

Then, to Holland's total dismay, Gensoul unbent sufficiently to hand him a copy of Darlan's top-secret instructions, dated 24 June. Rather than have them fall into Axis hands, Gensoul was authorized either to scuttle his ships or to head for the United States. 'It's so nearly what we are asking you to do now – to sail for America,' Holland pleaded. But Gensoul's pride was also involved. 'Yes, but not under the threat of your guns,' he answered.

But already two signals had decided the fate of the French Fleet. At the same time as Gensoul learned from Admiral Le Luc's Message 3309 that 'all French forces in the Mediterranean will rally to you immediately', the Admiralty, on receipt of an 'Enigma' intercept, cautioned Somerville with their own Message 1614/3: 'Settle matters quickly or you will have reinforcements to deal with.'

From his own flagship, H.M.S. *Hood*, Somerville at once issued his final ultimatum: if the French had not complied with one or other alternative by 5.30 p.m., he would open fire. Sick at heart, Holland left *Dunkerque* for the last time.

In fact, not until 5.54 p.m., to enable Holland to get clear, did Somerville's battle squadron open fire, but the timing was immaterial. In this first Franco–British sea battle for over a century, fought between the sworn allies of two weeks back, the French never stood a chance. As the 15-inch shells came screaming through a drifting smokescreen over a 7-mile range, only *Dunkerque* and the battleship *Provence* were even close enough to hit back.

As columns of water and oil spouted 300 feet high, there was little for the other ships to do but die bravely. Aboard the blazing battleship *Bretagne*, orders were given to abandon the crow's nest, but the ladder descending to the deck was red-hot; as the burning ropes frayed and parted, the look-outs plummeted to their death. The duty officer, *Lieutenant de Vaisseau* Etienne Sicard, grasping a handrail, found himself hurtling into space along with the bridge; as he sank forty feet below the water he thought quizzically of a ski-jump. Fighting slowly back to the surface, he witnessed astonishing sights.

With a tortured howl of escaping steam, *Dunkerque*, caught by a shell in a starboard boiler room, was drifting slowly aground like a killer whale beached in the shallows. *Provence*, hit in the stern by a salvo, split apart and capsized with a loss of 900 lives. In the thick 2-inch film of fuel which covered the harbour, dotted with bobbing red matelots' pom-poms, exhausted men choked on the oil, then died.

At the moment the destroyer *Mogador* was hit, blown up by her own depth charges, Sicard and his fellow survivors took comfort from a sight which moved them to tears: the battlecruiser *Strasbourg*, escaping for Toulon amid the confusion, speeding full ahead past the pier, all guns firing, her guard presenting arms, a band playing full blast on her stern.

After ten minutes all firing ceased. The massacre was over. Within hours on this day, which had also witnessed bloodless

French surrenders at Alexandria and Plymouth, the world's fourth fleet had been knocked out of action to an astonishing extent: 84 per cent of its battleship strength, 48 per cent of its cruiser strength, all its aircraft carriers, 16 per cent of its destroyers, 14 per cent of its submarines, 50 per cent of its sub-chasers.

Yet this was a battle, unusually for 1940, where the aggressors felt only guilt. 'It was an absolutely bloody business to shoot up those Frenchmen who showed the greatest gallantry,' Somerville wrote to his wife. 'We all feel thoroughly dirty and ashamed.' Most British naval officers echoed whole-heartedly the bleak words of Admiral Gensoul at the mass funeral of 1,297 Frenchmen in the cemetery at Oran: 'If there is a stain on the flag it is certainly not on ours.'

Only one man, it seemed, approved unreservedly, for to him it demonstrated a truth which Ambassador Joseph P. Kennedy had long been at pains to deny: that the British were mean fighters when roused. On the bottom of the daily military report submitted to Franklin Roosevelt, Lord Lothian noted in longhand: 'You will see that Winston Churchill has taken the action in regard to the French Fleet which we discussed and you approved.'

On the day that news of Mers-el-Kebir hit the world's headlines, René de Chambrun had almost talked himself hoarse. For eighteen days, with missionary fervour, de Chambrun had travelled non-stop across the United States, as Roosevelt had urged him, clarifying, persuading, arguing. The President's first list of twenty-two contacts had long since been ticked off. From there de Chambrun had gone on to talk with Lord Lothian at the British Embassy, with influential publishers like Henry Luce and Roy Howard, and with pollster George Gallup. In the midwest he had conferred with farmers, bankers and civic leaders. He had dined with men as loyal to Roosevelt as William Allen White and with Roosevelt-haters like Governor Harold Stassen of Minnesota. Wherever he had journeyed, his theme had been the same: Great Britain needed arms and planes to survive; southern France, where Pétain held sway, needed food and medicine.

To de Chambrun's surprise, his own father-in-law, Pierre

Laval, had been called upon to serve as Pétain's Vice-President. A canny businessman from Auvergne, whose drooping moustaches and white piqué ties were the delight of cartoonists, Laval was no stranger to politics: twice Premier of France and Foreign Minister from 1934–6, he had openly opposed all involvement in a war he knew that France would lose. Now, by letters and cables, de Chambrun learned from his wife, Josée, that her father had taken office with rueful resignation, comparing himself to the receiver of a firm in bankruptcy. On one count, de Chambrun had no doubts: France's role as combatant had now ceased. When Pétain, bristling with rage, proposed bombing Gibraltar to square accounts for Mers-el-Kebir, Laval replied wearily: 'We have just lost one war. Are we about to start and lose another?'

Some American politicians foresaw another stumbling block: the inevitable clash of interests between Laval, who must seek accommodation with the Germans, and the first cadre of 2,000 Free Frenchmen who had rallied to de Gaulle in London. In reply, de Chambrun quoted Laval's words to Josée: 'There are two policies, that of resistance abroad and that of mine in France. Both must be carried out.'

In all these weeks, de Chambrun had been sure of one thing: he had put the case for Great Britain as forcefully as any native son. Even as early as 17 June, Secretary of the Treasury Henry Morgenthau had assured him: 'You have galvanized the President.' One day later, Senator Robert Taft, until now an isolationist to his fingertips, had conceded: 'I am ready to envisage going to war if I were absolutely certain that by doing so it would save England.' On 27 June, Cordell Hull told de Chambrun: 'You have given our President courage. He and we need it.'

The most heartfelt tribute came later, in a personal letter dated 9 August, from a man who was more involved than most, Lord Lothian: 'Practically single-handed you were able to sway official opinion over here in favour of my country ... Great Britain will never forget what you did for her in her days of plight and distress.'

The climate of opinion, de Chambrun saw, had swung over-

1a Count René de Chambrun

1b General de Gaulle in London with Major-General Edward Spears

2a Erik Seidenfaden
– skilled observer
of Europe's turmoil

2b Sumner Welles, U.S. Under Secretary of State (*left*) in London with
Winston Churchill and the American Ambassador, Joseph P. Kennedy

3a Polly Peabody

3b Theodor Broch, Mayor of Narvik

3c Vidkun Quisling

4 Oil tanks ablaze at Vaagso

5a Werner Mölders on the eastern front

5b Oran

6 London burning

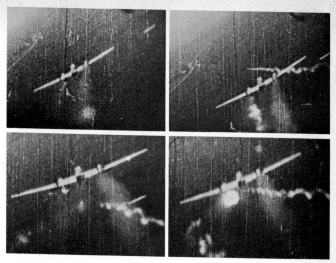

7a The killing of a German Messerschmitt 110

7b The morning after, near Marble Arch

8 Coventry Cathedral

whelmingly towards Britain. But how would his own country fare?

It was Roosevelt himself who raised this issue, in a White House meeting on 1 August. The young Captain had done everything that had been asked of him. 'Now,' the President queried, 'what can *I* do for France?'

'There is only one policy to embrace,' de Chambrun answered incisively, 'feed her.'

Roosevelt seemed reluctant. 'I would like to – but if I send supplies there the Nazis will grab them.'

De Chambrun was sceptical. 'Mr President, do you think the Nazis would dare cross the demarcation line to take from French mouths condensed milk that Americans may have sent over? It is true that they have made many mistakes, but I doubt that they would make this one.'

Already, he explained, he had worked out a formula with Lothian and Harry Hopkins. There would be successive deliveries, three or four weeks apart, to limit the risk of cargo confiscation. From these cargoes, America would derive major political and moral benefits, which would help arouse French public opinion against Germany.

Roosevelt thought hard, then finally came up with a plan. De Chambrun must return to see France and see Pétain. The Marshal must call a press conference and make a pro-American statement in favour of the democratic ideal. At the same time Pétain must silence the floodtide of press vituperation that had followed Mers-el-Kebir. If those conditions were met, 'I shall see to it that the free zone receives regular food shipments ... for the duration of hostilities.'

'Bring me back a good letter from the old Marshal,' Roosevelt rallied him. 'I shall release it during one of my press conferences.'

Only one query was still unanswered: the reaction of Churchill and the War Cabinet. But at 6 p.m. on this same day, de Chambrun called at the British Embassy to receive Lothian's assurance. 'My government agrees,' Lothian told him, 'on the condition that the quantities shipped are reasonable and that the ships have a rather low tonnage.'

De Chambrun was ecstatic. For almost two months he had worked with everything he knew to ensure two prime essentials: arms for free Britain, food for impoverished France. His last call before returning home was at the White House to tender his thanks.

Roosevelt, he always remembered, winked at him hugely as they said good-bye. 'René,' were his parting words, 'it's a deal.'

True to her vow, Polly Peabody arrived in Unoccupied France, still convinced that she could in some way help the French. It seemed logical to head for the spa town of Vichy, once just a name on a bottle of mineral water, where the Pétain Government was now established, and where Polly was to witness 'some of the saddest and most amazing pages of French history'.

What struck her most forcibly, six days after Mers-el-Kebir, was the pervasive hatred of England. Pétain had at once broken off diplomatic relations with Great Britain, but the timely warning Roosevelt had voiced to de Chambrun was still some weeks away; the columnists of the Vichy press had traded in ink for vitriol. 'To those who recall the clarion calls of ... a fortnight ago for sacrifice,' cabled Ambassador Bullitt to the State Department, 'it is revolting to watch the complete about-face of the French Press.'

In part due to Bullitt and the U.S. Chargé d'Affaires, Robert Murphy, Americans were still accepted in Unoccupied France. But Polly sensed that feelings ran high. 'Hell, we'll be just as well off under German rule,' a French soldier sneered aboard the crowded train bound for Vichy, but when Polly rebuked him, the entire compartment flew at her as one. 'An American! If you're as patriotic about France as all that, why didn't you send us some guns instead of cotton wool and pills?'

In defeat, Polly felt, the people of Vichy France were determined that all should share in the blame. In a mass-wave of self-recrimination, they saw their débâcle as Weygand had done, the price of laxity: paid holidays for workers and the 40-hour week, changes which the leftist Léon Blum's Popular Front government had wrought in the thirties, were now blamed along with such strange concomitants as adultery and

178

aniseed aperitifs. 'Better Hitler than Blum,' many had said then, and now they reaffirmed this view.

The messiah of this new asceticism was Pétain himself, who was soon to ban both Pernod as decadent and nail varnish for women as 'a demoralizing Jewish–Oriental habit'. On 10 July, winding up the Third French Republic with a new and inward-looking slogan, '*Travail, Famille, Patrie.*' Pétain told Bullitt morosely, 'It's all been the fault of Socialist schoolteachers.'

Polly Peabody was appalled by the 'snake's nest' that was Vichy, though she was willing to stay on if her help was needed. Through the intercession of Gaston Henri-Haye, an old family friend and Vichy's Ambassador-designate in Washington, she counted herself lucky to get a fourth share in a hotel room for five francs a week. Already the little spa was bursting at the seams with refugees from the German-occupied zone; hundreds were sleeping in armchairs, bath tubs and even parked cars.

All over France, as the world crumbled, refugees were on the run. The Baron and Baroness Robert de Rothschild had fled to England on a tramp steamer, along with former French Air Minister Pierre Cot, Eve Curie and the political commentator Geneviève Tabouis. The Grand Duchess Charlotte of Lux-embourg and the jeweller Pierre Cartier were among thousands seeking refuge in Spain; former Premier Édouard Daladier was en route to Lisbon, soon to be followed by ex-King Edward VIII. Homeward bound from Genoa on the U.S.S. *Manhattan* went 2,000 American expatriates, along with artificial tree trunks for forty dogs.

In this strange new world of topsy-turvy values, the most anachronistic refugee was perhaps Archduke Otto – 'Otto the Last' – returning to Lisbon with his mother, the Empress Zita, to plot the restoration of the Habsburg Empire.

As a socialite, Polly Peabody had known many of them, but now she was impatient of that old life. She wanted to help, but the problem was how. Her American Scandinavian Field Hospital was still stranded in Sweden, forbidden transit through Germany to France, yet nursing skills were needed here as everywhere. Through an introduction from Ambassador Henri-Haye, Polly often met Marshal Pétain in the lounge of the Hotel Parc et Majestic, and Pétain, rising gallantly to the occasion, offered her coffee and *petit-fours*, listened drowsily to her adventures and praised American women as *débrouillardes* (resourceful). But even he had no helpful suggestions; his main concern was to quit Vichy for Paris, to assert an authority he did not possess. 'I am going to Versailles in two weeks,' he told Polly sharply, 'I have quite made up my mind. I have sent word to the Germans to evacuate the premises.'

Polly had no more luck with Vice-President Pierre Laval, de Chambrun's father-in-law – a convenient post-war scapegoat but one whose moves accurately reflected contemporary opinion. Bidden to lunch, Polly found Laval good company and a witty raconteur, but the excesses of the sycophantic women who dogged his table at mealtimes nauseated her. No sooner had one pressed a little gold saint's medal on him than another snatched away his glass of Vichy water, replacing it with her own – '*Monsieur le Président*, do me the honour of dipping your lips in my glass.'

One belief that Laval shared, in common with many Vichyites, was that a Franco–German entente now formed the only possible basis for world equilibrium, and that all things could be subtly arranged to France's advantage. *C'est enfantin* (child's play) was a phrase much in vogue.

Polly Peabody wondered. Although no student of politics, the lessons of Poland, Austria and Czechoslovakia suggested otherwise. In the meantime, while awaiting transit to Paris to work for the American Red Cross, she toyed with the concept of a one-woman Relief Plan for refugees from the north, spending her afternoons as a hospital visitor.

Every afternoon, for two hours, she sat at the bedside of the red-haired Private Auguste Gringer, a 26-year-old hairdresser from Paris. On many days, crossing the hospital's threshold, she could hear his screams from as far away as the second floor. For two months he had been in constant unendurable pain from a bullet in his bladder, which had nicked the base of his spine. Clutching her wrist until she thought it would snap he would time and again ask Polly the question all France seemed to be asking: '*Mademoiselle*, why must I suffer so? Surely it can't be right?'

*

As July dawned, the fear that René Chambrun would express to Roosevelt was already being realized. Vichy France, the two-fifths of the country that Hitler had assigned to the Pétain government, was suffering. To support Germany's army in the Occupied Zone she was mulcted of 400 million francs a day, while her own armed forces, on Hitler's *diktat*, were reduced to 100,000. To his French counterpart, Huntziger, General von Stülpnagel of the German Armistice Commission expressed himself in terms reminiscent of a riding school: 'If France rears, we will tighten the curb. We will loosen it to the extent that France is amenable.'

It was worse in the Occupied Zone. No French citizen there had a right to a radio, a telephone, to send cables or to leave town without permission. At 7 p.m. a curfew was clamped down. In the long silent evenings, the citizens were forbidden to read authors as diverse as Thomas Mann, Vicki Baum, Sigmund Freud, Erich Maria Remarque and André Maurois. In Alsace, a German domain from 1871 to 1919, the rules were harshest. Gallic symbols such as berets were forbidden, French Christian names were Germanized (Yvonne became Irmgard), and even thermometers, with their blue casing, white background and red alcohol were banned as reminiscent of the Tricolor.

The clampdown affected all occupied Europe. In The Hague, Holland, 13-year-old Ida van de Criendt noted that prayers for the Queen in church were now forbidden, and no cleric could preach a sermon based on Psalm 130: 'Out of the depths have I cried unto Thee, O Lord.' The word 'Royal' was erased from streets and parks. Here, as elsewhere, Jews were early forced to register, then excluded from public office.

Under newly-appointed *Gauleiters*, *Reichsleiters* and *Reichskommissars*, arbitrary decrees multiplied. In Norway, where the inhabitants faced a bill of 360 million kroner for the costs of occupation, Quisling's successor, *Reichskommissar* Josef Terboven, lost no time in tampering with the economy. Wages were reduced by 7 per cent and peasants were summarily set to work ploughing 80,000 hectares of land to create new farms. Though dairy cattle and pigs were cut down to conserve fodder, sheep were upped to a four million high. No forester, fisherman, farm worker, seaman or any member of his family could change jobs or place of residence.

To the badgered inhabitants, some decrees had a ring of Alice-in-Wonderland. Hitler's man in Belgium, General von Falkenhausen, abruptly forbade the supply of soap to any save manual workers, women pregnant at home, the habitually incontinent or colostomy patients.

By contrast, the Third Reich was thriving. Into a Germany depleted by years of sacrifice flowed a tide of Danish butter, Dutch vegetables, Polish coal and Norwegian timber: at least 200 tons of prime-quality Norwegian fish were shipped to the German Army daily. In Belgium, whose levy was 8,000 tons of industrial coal a day and 100 dairy cattle a week, one Brussels doctor, Paul Duner, beheld an astonishing sight: a convoy of trucks, forty strong, heading for the German border loaded solely with pots of jam.

In Paris alone, machinery from the Simca, Blériot and Hispano-Suiza factories were stripped and transported to Germany, but what the U.S. Chargé d'Affaires in Vichy, Robert Murphy, described as 'scientific looting' was going on all through the Occupied Zone.

In Germany it was confidently expected now that peace was just round the corner. Brand-new 'Visit Heidelberg and the Rhineland' posters blossomed in the tourist agencies in Berlin's Kurfürstendamm. Mileage tickets were in the course of preparation by German Railways, enabling citizens to gratify their long-harboured desires to visit Paris and the Riviera. Most inquiries, though, centred round a monument in Occupied France, which was soon to become the world's most expensive and elaborate tourist attraction: the Maginot Line.

Suddenly the world was talking peace. There were rumours of it everywhere, although with what degree of reliability nobody knew. In Washington, D.C., there was talk of a peace personally negotiated by Roosevelt. In New York, it was reported that Germany was offering Britain peace with 95 per cent of her Empire intact.

Any unguarded utterance nourished fresh rumours. In Madrid, the Duke of Windsor, the former Edward VIII, remarked incautiously to an American diplomat: 'The most important thing now is to end the war before thousands more are killed or maimed to save the faces of a few politicians.' By noon next day, Ambassador Alexander Weddell had put it on the wire to Cordell Hull. The Swedish Minister in London, Bjorn Prytz, heard from the Under-Secretary of Foreign Affairs, R. A. Butler, that Halifax thought 'common-sense and not bravado' would prevail. From this remark, Prytz drew his own pacifist conclusions.

In Berne, Switzerland, the British Minister, David (later Sir David) Kelly talked several times that summer with Prince Max of Hohenlohe-Langenburg, who repeatedly passed on an offer said to come from the German Foreign Ministry: guarantees for the British Empire in return for giving Germany a free hand in Europe. Each time, affecting keen interest, Kelly passed on the information without comment to the Foreign Office. If it served no other purpose, Kelly thought, he was buying time.

There was no lack of self-appointed and self-important doves. The founder of the Royal Dutch airline, K.L.M., Dr Alfred Plesman, flew into Berlin from The Hague to propose a three-fold carve-up to Hermann Göring, just then appointed *Reichsmarschall*: Britain should have her Empire, Germany the Continent, the United States, Latin America. But after ten days the talks fell down – at the same time as Malcolm R. Lovell, an American Quaker, made an abortive attempt to bring the British Ambassador, Lord Lothian, and the German Chargé, Hans Thomsen, together for peace talks in Washington.

On 19 July, Hitler himself, although he cavilled at the idea of 'crawling up English backsides' decided, in a rabble-rousing Reichstag speech, to 'appeal once more to reason and common-sense in Britain . . . I consider myself in a position to make this appeal since I am not a vanquished foe begging favours, but the victor, speaking in the name of reason . . .'

But the British, it seemed, were too short-sighted to realize they were beaten. 'The Germans,' Halifax noted in his diary, 'have got to be more knocked about.'

As Hitler's victories were recognized as inescapable, restive voices were heard once more far to the east of the Suez Canal.

In India, following the fall of France, Subhas Chandra Bose had once more urged Mahatma Gandhi to launch a passive resistance campaign: it was clear now that the British Empire would be overthrown. But the canny little Mahatma was still sitting on the fence. 'We do not seek our independence out of Britain's ruin,' he reiterated in his reedy high-pitched voice. 'That is not the way of non-violence.' He ended ambiguously: if Bose's efforts to win India's freedom succeeded, Gandhi's telegram of congratulations would be the first through Bose's letter-box.

Bose bearded other Indian leaders with equal lack of success. Mohammed Ali Jinnah, the elegant monocled leader of the Muslim League, was cool; the British, he thought, might one day help realize his dream of Pakistan and a divided India. Vinayak Damodar Savarkar, the President of the *Mahasabha*, a right-wing nation-wide Hindu political party, saw other uses for the British. By entering Britain's army in India, members of his Fascist para-military army might receive valuable training in weaponry.

On 2 July, khaki-clad police officers calling at 38/2, Elgin Road, Bose's Calcutta villa, temporarily put an end to his career as a freedom-fighter. For the eleventh time in his forty-three years, Bose was clapped into gaol.*

In Burma, other voices had taken up the cry. The former Premier Ba Maw had united three parties into a Freedom Bloc akin to Bose's, but the one concession they wrested from the British was a promise of full self-government after Britain's victory. 'Not even a world in flames could teach these people anything new,' Ba Maw flared to his confederate Aung San, a student who had attended Gandhi's Ramgarh congress as an observer and been sorely disappointed by the Mahatma's pacific stand. Both men resented bitterly the assumption that Burma must fight alongside Britain to free enslaved nations of

* Bose's rejoinder, in November 1940, was to notify the Governor of Bengal that he intended to fast himself to death. Six days later the authorities released him. At the end of January 1941, Bose slipped away from Calcutta, finally reaching Berlin, via Afghanistan and Moscow, at the end of March. In 1943, he took over the Indian National Army, a force of 10,000 dissident officers and men made up from former Japanese P.O.W.s. to fight against the British in Burma. He was killed in an air crash in 1945.

whom they had never heard. 'What must be, must be,' Ba Maw decided, 'and this revolution of ours must be.'

As August dawned, Ba Maw's plans met the same setback as Bose's. For contravention of the Defence of Burma rules he was gaoled for one year in Mandalay.

But in more than one region of the Far East, the British writ did not run, and the voices that hailed Hitler's triumphs sounded loud and clear throughout the Empire of Japan. 'Japan,' warned the U.S. Ambassador, Joseph C. Grew, in a dispatch to the State Department, 'is in a state of political turmoil of unusual intensity.' 'The German victories,' Grew noted, 'have gone to their heads like strong wine.'

Already Grew anticipated that the 'present (Yonai) Cabinet may fall, with the result that a pro-German Cabinet will take over – with disastrous results for Japan'. Such a Cabinet, he thought, would likely be headed up by 49-year-old Fumimaro Konoye, an insomniac who doped himself with ten different kinds of sleeping pills, a certified hypochondriac who sterilized his food with boiling water and alcohol and used an antiseptic mask as a germ-trap in crowded meetings.

Konoye himself saw nothing but catastrophe looming ahead – but by now it was too late for Japan to turn back.

The reasons were inescapable: the Japanese were prisoners of history. Unable to support a population increasing by millions annually, Japan had been expanding compulsively for years – into Korea in 1910, into Manchuria in 1931, into China in 1937. By 1939, when Admiral Isoroku Yamamoto became Commander-in-Chief of the Japanese Combined Fleet, this obsession with a southern Eldorado had become a grandiose project.

The fall of France and the Low Countries now made the expansion feasible. But to counter this came hints from Washington's Japanese Embassy of a massive U.S. naval building programme. Action, if it came, must come before the U.S. tipped the naval balance against Japan in the Pacific.

Japan's needs were now paramount: to obtain metals and raw materials solely within their own sphere of control – for a victorious Germany might equally hamper Japan's expansionist programme. Thus, April 1940 had already seen the move of the

Japanese Fourth Fleet to the Palau Islands, in the Western Pacific, to move against the Dutch East Indies if any other power tried to seize them. By 20 June, operational research on the Southern advance – against British Malaya, the Dutch East Indies, even the Philippines – had begun, even though it was plain that this would mean war with the United States, Britain and Holland. By mid-July, Japan had accepted this: if need be they would meet any American challenge with war.

At the prospect of this head-on encounter, the Yonai Cabinet vacillated, so that, as Grew had predicted, a Konoye-headed Cabinet replaced them by mid-July. Ironically, Konoye had been pressured into acceptance of the programme by the military before even being considered for office, though the last thing he sought was an Axis alliance.

Yamamoto, equally, was categorically opposed to war with the United States. As Naval Attaché in Washington, D.C., between 1925 and 1927, he had seen their industrial might at first hand. In the event of Japanese attack, Yamamoto saw the U.S. fleet in Hawaii no longer as a potential threat to Japan proper but as an actual danger to the flank of the Japanese southern expansion force.

To his trusted friend, Admiral Ryunosuke Kusoka, Yamamoto mused: 'If we are ordered to fight the United States we might be able to score a runaway victory and hold our own for six months or a year.' But in the second year, he thought, America would increase its strength.

The logic seemed inescapable: the only way to secure Japan's threatened flank was to destroy the United States Fleet before it ever left its Hawaiian base of Pearl Harbor.

Meanwhile, with Britain and France in no position to resist, the Japanese were stepping up the squeeze play. On 17 June, France was instructed to close the road from Hanoi, French Indo-China (later Vietnam) to China. The British were ordered to close both the Hong Kong border and the Burma Road.

This was a body-blow for the Chinese, for the Burma Road, literally clawed by coolies' hands out of the 715 miles of mountain and ravine between Lashio, Burma and Chungking, China, was China's lifeline in her three-year-old war with Japan, carrying 3,000 tons of supplies a month.

Promptly, through a lower-level Lothian–Hull meeting, Churchill appealed to Roosevelt: would the United States back up Britain in resisting this? But Hull saw no way to oblige. America could not leave the Pacific wide open to aggressors to send warships to Singapore; moreover they were so weak in military hardware that at that summer's manoeuvres trucks marked 'This Is A Tank' had stood in for the real thing. Nor could Roosevelt risk involving America in a war to rescue British Imperial possessions.

All Halifax's instincts, as he told Hoare on 8 July, had been 'to tell the Japanese to go to the devil', but Churchill was more cautious. At this stage in history, Britain could not risk war on another front, nor did Churchill believe the Japanese were bluffing. The Japanese Director of Military Intelligence in Tokyo had been quite blunt with the British Military Attaché: 'If you do not close the Burma Road, we shall seize Hong Kong.'

Rationalizing it, the British took the easy way out. For the next three months the rainy season would make the Burma Road near-impassable in any case. From 12 July, the Burma Road would be closed to 'military supplies, arms, munitions, trucks and gasoline'.

In Chungking, the foggy walled city above the Yangtse River that was China's wartime capital, one man heard of the Burma Road's closure with a burst of uncharacteristic rage.

'*Nimen ta suan pan!* (You people are counting beads on the counting board!),' he railed at the British Ambassador, Sir Archibald Clark-Kerr, for to 53-year-old Generalissimo Chiang K'ai-shek, President of China, the British preoccupation with trivial detail – rounds of ammunition and gallons of gasoline – was a truly galling factor. A man of far-reaching historical perspective, Chiang looked back not on the three years of the China Incident, as the war with Japan was known – years in which the Japanese had captured 465,000 square miles of Chinese territory, including Shanghai and Canton – but on the larger

187

picture, the seventeen years in which he had marched north, beaten the war lords, province by province, and united China.

'Let the Japanese come,' Chiang threatened. 'If they drive me back to Tibet, in five years I will be back and will conquer all China again.'

It was appropriately fighting talk. Five months back, on Chinese New Year's Eve, the Year of the Rabbit had been succeeded in the Chinese zodiac cycle by the Year of the Dragon, the nation's patron beast – sharp of claw, smoky of breath. On the stroke of midnight, an auspiciously fierce dragon, fashioned from tinsel and crêpe, borne aloft by six men, had led a stamping snaking conga-style dragon dance of cabinet ministers, generals and lovely ladies across the ballroom of Chungking's Visitors' Hostel.

Now, for three long months, Chiang's troops would be denied the crucial supplies which would have enabled them to wage a dragon-war against the Japanese invader. In those three months, Chiang would face another problem: a group of Chinese, ostensibly loyal, but waging war against the Japanese in their own territory, on their own terms, with their 400,000 strong Eighth Route Army under General Chu Teh. Chiang tolerated these Chinese Communists solely because he had to; without them, there would have been no trickle of Russian supplies to sustain him. It was Chiang's uneasy espousal of Mao Tse-tung and Chou En-lai that had transformed him, in *Pravda*'s eyes, from a 'Fascist reactionary' to a 'national leader and hero'.

'The Japanese are a disease of the skin,' Chiang would observe shrewdly. 'The Communists are a disease of the heart. They say they wish to support me but secretly all they want is to overthrow me.'

But the 'Gissimo', as his followers called him, was giving hostages to fortune. In his fine walled villa at Hoangshan, across the Yangtse, his strategy, like the British and French during the phoney war, was one of masterly inactivity. He had no plan for victory: only for survival. Like the British and French before him, he believed that sooner or later America would enter the war – and when that time came he would be rewarded for tying up a million-odd Japanese soldiers. So why fritter away strength – when the real confrontation, with the Communists, was still to come?

Meanwhile, the Communists sedulously fostered two myths which the world came to believe in earnest: that Mao's men alone bore the brunt of the Japanese war and that none among them were true Communists, merely mild agrarian reformers. Passive in his Chungking eyrie, Chiang was little by little relinquishing the prize for which he had striven all his life: China.

The Communists were getting their message across. Some months would elapse before one of Roosevelt's administrative assistants, Lauchlin Currie, reached Chungking for meetings with Chiang, bearing an oral message from the President. The 'Gissimo' found its tenor profoundly disturbing. For the first time but not the last, Roosevelt, so canny in keeping his finger on the pulse of the United States' feeling, was to minimize the Communist danger. 'Your Communists,' his message ran, 'seem more like Socialists to us. Surely you should be able to work together?'

Now was the time when all nations who could took up a minatory stance. Even tiny Switzerland made brave noises. On 25 July, 65-year-old General Henri Guisan, Swiss Commander-in-Chief, though handicapped by a pro-Nazi President and 1,200 miles of frontier to defend, took a decisive step. Along with his staff, his senior and junior commanders, Guisan repaired to the Rütli, a meadow on the shore of Lake Lucerne, symbolic in Swiss history as the meeting place which in 1291 saw the birth of the Swiss Confederation. 'We are at the turning point of our history,' Guisan told his officers. 'The existence of Switzerland is at stake.'

Who threatened Switzerland's independence? This was a question to which Guisan prudently gave no answer, but the will to resist was made plain. From this time on, the Swiss Army was to press forward with the concept of a National Redoubt, an Alpine stronghold covered by Switzerland's three principal forts, Sagans in the east, St Maurice in the west, the Gotthard in the south. In this mountain fortress, 400,000 militiamen would have adequate supplies to hold out against attacks from all sides, ready in the last resort to blow up the Gotthard and Simplon Tunnels and all roads over the Alps.

As always, Josef Stalin had moved faster than any. Now apprehensive that Britain and France might sue for peace, leaving Hitler free to turn eastward, Stalin consolidated an earlier gain. In September 1939, the Baltic states of Lithuania, Latvia and Estonia had capitulated where Finland held out – agreeing to provide Russia with bases, and if need be to support 20,000 Russian troops apiece. On 15 June, Red Army troops moved in. Russia was now virtually on a war footing – and as separate entities Lithuania, Latvia and Estonia ceased to exist.

One hapless group of nations could take no stance at all: the Balkans. Despite ethnic differences, Yugoslavia, Hungary and Romania had three things in common: they depended on Germany, feared Russia, and looked vainly to Italy for police protection. Hungary's Premier, Count Paul Teleki, like Yugoslavia's Regent Prince Paul, balanced all the time on a tightrope of evasion. 'Why should Hungarians be slaughtered if Britain and France are ill-prepared?' Teleki would demand rhetorically, for he knew that his country's officer-caste dreaded Communism more than Nazism. Many saw Hungary's true future as a German model dictatorship supplying raw materials to the Third Reich, with Parliament, trade unions and political parties abolished.

In Bucharest, the tawdry capital of Romania, a city where, legend had it, 'the flowers had no scent, the men no honour and the women no shame', King Carol II, a flabby green-eyed descendant of Queen Victoria, also emulated Bunyan's Mr Facing-Both-Ways. Britain and France, the King prophesied to his Secretary-General for Foreign Affairs, Alexandre Cretzianu, would ultimately triumph – 'but we must avoid the destruction of our country in the meantime'. For this reason, seeking to be all things to all men, Carol had been privy, on 6 April, to an amateurish British attempt to block the Danube at Giurgiu with ninety-four barges crammed with cement and dynamite, towed by six British tugs and crewed by 100 British agents. This clandestine manoeuvre, to which the Romanian authorities were prepared to turn a blind eye, was designed to check the flow of oil from Romania, the world's fifth oil-producing country, into Germany.

But the agents dallied too long at Giurgiu, drinking and flirting with the local girls, and the port authorities, tipped off by *Abwehr* agents, searched the barges to uncover both cement and dynamite. The mission ended in a fiasco, as the British agents were hastily spirited back to London.

Hitler, incensed, stepped up the pressure on Carol. Even though the bitter winter of 1939 had played havoc with the crops, he demanded $10 million worth of wheat, more even than Romania had exported to the Reich in 1939. When Carol expostulated, Germany's Trade Negotiator, Dr Karl Clodius, proposed a simple solution. If Romania delivered the wheat, Germany would relax her demands for oil which had now risen to 1,820,000 tons a year – up to 300 tank cars a day. To sow the wheat, Clodius suggested, Carol could demobilize 500,000 peasants from his army – and Germany would send 6,000 agricultural experts to show them how to do it.

The last thing Carol wanted on Romanian soil was 6,000 German experts of any kind. To stay their coming, the four million boys and girls of Romania's National Youth movement were given staggered two-week leave periods from school, bundled into overalls and put behind ploughs.

As France crumbled, the Balkan nations reacted like dogs, fawning round Hitler's table for scraps, and it was now that Carol began to hand Romania to Hitler lock, stock and barrel. He actively sought a German military mission in Bucharest. He restored freedom to the pro-Nazi Jew-baiting Iron Guard, replacing his pro-Ally Foreign Minister Grigore Gafencu with the pro-Axis Ion Gigurtu. Finally on 21 June, with one decree, Carol made Romania totalitarian with a single new Party of the Nation.

As sophisticates of *Realpolitik* had guessed, it was now Stalin's turn to apply the screws. On 26 June, Premier Molotov brusquely demanded from Carol the 17,000 square miles of Bessarabia, eastern Romania, formerly a Russian domain. The Red Army, Molotov announced, would be marching in at 2 p.m. that day. The Romanian Army had four days to vacate the territory.

King Carol flew into a most unregal panic. All that night, his cheeks smudged with tears, he paced his study, chain-smoking until every ashtray was overflowing with butts, downing tumblers of neat Scotch. At first, in desperation, he sought help from Hitler, but the Führer was unresponsive: above all he wanted peace in the Balkans, to ensure his oil supplies. He advised Carol to yield to the Russians.

Carol might have called Hitler's bluff by threatening to destroy the oil-wells, but fearing for his personal fortune he did not dare. Even before his Cabinet met to debate the matter he had surrendered.

Personal fortune was an intimate concern of both Carol and his red-haired mistress Magda Lupescu. To finance a palace larger than Buckingham Palace with a 100-seater theatre and portraits of Carol looming twenty feet high, they had for nine years treated the country as a cash register to be milked at will – with regal rake-offs from both the State railways and the State textile mills. Not surprisingly, Carol listed 'designing uniforms' as his principal hobby. In nine years he had even changed the uniforms of the Boy Scouts three times to keep the State looms humming.

But Carol's climb-down, after boasting early in January that no foot of Romanian territory would ever be yielded, lost him face with his people. On 1 July, he let drop the mask, denouncing all the British guarantees offered him in 1939. In future his orientation was with the Axis.

Germany, however, would offer no military alliance, or any other crumb of comfort. If clarification had been needed, the position of small nations in the world had been clarified afresh.

Theodor Broch, no longer Mayor of Narvik, saw that truth as plainly as any man. As long as Hitler's armies held sway, a small nation such as Norway was no more than a geographical location on the map of Europe – and there was no longer any place in Norway for Theodor Broch.

On 15 June, following his breakneck flight from the Germans on Harstad Island, Broch had had no clear idea where he and his family would find sanctuary as the hired rowboat pulled out across the foggy Atlantic. From a near-by harbour, together with Ellen and Siri, he had journeyed north on a two-man fishing vessel, still uncertain as to their destination. But by degrees it dawned on Broch that over the years he had forged an endless chain of goodwill throughout the Lofoten Islands. On a score of farmsteads he had drawn up wills and wrestled with tax complaints for crofters and farmers often enough, when times were hard for them, deliberately waiving his fee.

At Tysfjord, near the island of Torghatten, Broch located just such good friends, a retired doctor and his wife. But the couple warned Broch that he was already a hunted man: the radio had broadcast his name. For the time being, it was safer for Ellen and Siri to hide up here. Later Broch could send for them; now he must journey on alone.

Broch decided to head for Sweden. With Leif, an 18-year-old Laplander, as his guide he set out on the long mountain trek towards the border. Bowed beneath his knapsack, pausing only for catnaps beside birchwood fires, he toiled on for ten hours until the cairn that marked the border of neutral Sweden came in sight.

In Stockholm, a tranquil brightly-lit enclave in a blacked-out Europe, Broch sought out an old friend from Oslo days, Erling Falk, a Socialist professor whose teachings had inspired a generation of students. Now Falk was in the Royal General Hospital, dying of a brain tumour, but as Broch sat miserably at his bedside, his mind seemed diamond-clear. For twenty years, Broch knew, he had lived and taught in America, and now his thoughts reverted to those times. 'This is a revolutionary era,' Falk told him, 'and the United States will become the deciding power. Go there.'

Broch was in luck. Hearing that Mrs Florence Harriman, American Minister in Norway, had just arrived in Sweden, after accompanying King Haakon on much of his journey north, Broch, who had met her in the past, sought her out at Stockholm's Grand Hotel. Over dinner, Mrs Harriman proved solicitous: what were his future plans? 'I'd like to go to America,' Broch confessed, 'to make propaganda for Norway. But perhaps a visa would be difficult?'

Florence Harriman saw no difficulty. Once Broch had secured a loan from the Norwegian Embassy to cover his passage money, a debt he contracted to pay off by instalments, his visa was granted. Like all who travelled in 1940, he embarked on a cramped and snail-paced journey: by air from Stockholm to Moscow, thence by slow train to Vladivostok, Siberia, finally on a battered Norwegian freighter via Tokyo and Yokohama. On 18 August, still bearing only the knapsack he had toted across the Swedish border, he reach his final port of destination, a world away from Narvik and the cold high mountains: the noisy sprawling sun-drenched city of Los Angeles.

The auditorium of the Renacimento Theatre in downtown Buenos Aires was jammed, and the mood was ugly. Across the screen flickered a German propaganda film of Hitler's triumphs in the west, *The Siegfried Line*, a heady brew for the 200 young Nazi Party supporters, who had come to pay homage to their Führer. As the Panzers rolled victoriously forward, staccato cries of '*Heil Hitler*' resounded through the stalls.

It was too much for 100 young Argentine hot-bloods, mostly athletes and amateur boxers, who had also chosen that night to see *The Siegfried Line*. As counterpoint they set up an angry barrage of '*Abajo* (Down with) Hitler'. Suddenly a fusillade of jumbo fireworks was lobbed through the darkness towards the hostile Nazis. As the lights came up, the air was blue with spent gunpowder and women were screaming. With a massed yell, the Argentines went to work on the Hitlerites, pounding, kneeing, gouging. Police flooding in to break up the mêlée had the clubs torn from their hands and used mercilessly on the Germans. Two score Argentines were arrested, only to be released next day. Further showings of *The Siegfried Line* were banned by President Roberto M. Ortiz.

All over Latin America, the twenty-one republics which, like the United States, had won their freedom from Europe by revolution, were reacting in the same way. Unlike the United States, they were already wide-awake to the dangers posed by the Axis presence. In La Paz, Bolivia and Montevideo, Uruguay, students stoned Italian commercial establishments, and staged monster rallies outside the German and Italian Legations. Other countries acted more coolly but no less decisively. Colombia's Government-owned airline, Avianca, fired all its

German employees. Ecuador gave marching orders to its Italian Military Mission. Hitler's man in Mexico City, Arthur Dietrich, heard sourly that he was no longer *persona grata.*

Late in June, as the U.S.S. *Quincy* steamed slowly up to the quay in Montevideo Harbour, the only show-the-flag gesture that America, vigilant in the Pacific, could afford to make, her reception was rapturous – '*Viva Roosevelt! Viva Los Estados Unidos!*' The reason was plain: the *Quincy* was berthing in the wake of a Trojan-horse scare prompted by the arrest of Hitler's man, Julius Dalldorf, and twelve other agents operating under German Minister Otto Langmann.

Shocked Uruguayans now learned that they had unwittingly been the headquarters of a movement to fuse all Latin America into a German-dominated economy. Nor was there any doubt that Germany had a powerful lever, for fully 55 per cent of South American exports went to Europe – Brazilian coffee, Peruvian tin, Argentine beef. Those exports must be sold, even to a Europe dominated by Hitler, or Latin America faced an imminent crisis.

Cordell Hull, the courtly Tennesseean, had as much to fear, for if Latin America became an Axis bloc this threatened the security of the entire United States. Every country, Hull warned in his habitual log-cabin language, 'could be swallowed as a boa constrictor swallows a squirrel'.

All this was grist to the mill of Getulio Vargas, the affable smiling dictator of Brazil's Estado Nôvo who four years earlier had consolidated his ten-year reign with Nazi support, then proceeded to declare the party illegal. Now the canny Vargas – the man they said could be silent in ten languages and remove his socks without taking off his shoes – saw a way of extracting some long-sought concessions from the United States.

On 7 June, Brazil's Foreign Minister, Oswaldo Aranha, dubbed by the Nazis 'a hireling of North America', gave a gentle nudge to the U.S. Ambassador, Jefferson Caffery: 'You hold conversations with us, and the Germans give us arms.' On 14 June, he was blunter: 'If [the United States] are interested in stopping this country from going Nazi ... good will and speeches will no longer satisfy our people. We need a few results.' On 16 July, he was quite specific as to the results he had in mind: United States credit to finance a monster Brazilian steel plant, thereby saving foreign exchange.

On 21 July, delegates from twenty-one republics, in neat white suits that would soon wilt in the sticky heat, met at the Capitolio, Havana, Cuba, for a Pan-American Conference hastily convened by Cordell Hull. Prominent on the agenda were four crucial items: to secure some form of mandate over European colonies in the Western Hemisphere, to control Fifth Column activities, the defence of the hemisphere, and the disposal of surplus exports.

It was a conference that some attended with misgivings. Costa Rica, Guatemala, Honduras, El Salvador and Bolivia had had veiled threats to stay away – but all realized that, ultimately, delay could be fatal. Proof was daily forthcoming that General Wilhelm Faupel, President of Berlin's Ibero-American Institute, had planted Axis eyes and ears all over Latin America: Alfred Muller, an able henchman, in Buenos Aires, H. H. von Cossel, Press Attaché at the Rio de Janeiro Embassy, even a von Ribbentrop – Erich, the Foreign Minister's nephew – in Bogotá, Colombia.

Five days later, on 26 June, when Cordell Hull was the first to scrawl his name on the Act of Havana, he was tired but satisfied. If a piece of paper would keep the Americas free from the Axis, he had that paper. Above all, he had wanted Pan-American support for the Monroe Doctrine – and this he had got in the Convention of Havana, which set up the machinery to seize and administer any European possession in the Western Hemisphere threatened with transfer of sovereignty. But he also needed Pan-American sanction, in case the United States found it necessary to seize a colony before the Convention went into effect. An emergency resolution had granted him this, too.

But in exchange for the execution of the Monroe Doctrine, Hull had pledged the United States to mammoth responsibilities – virtually to guarantee a military protection to the entire Western Hemisphere. And many of the signatures that crowded after Hull's on the Act were prompted by the hope, soon realized, that Congress would authorize half a billion dollars in aid to Western Hemisphere countries. 'It was,' exulted *El Mercurio* of Santiago, Chile, 'the most important and significant agreement ever reached in the American hemisphere, and perhaps in the world.'

The happiest delegate after Hull was perhaps Getulio Vargas's Secretary-General to the Ministry of Foreign Affairs, Mauricio de Nabuco. Like Hull, he, too, was bound for Washington, to collect a few favours for Brazil in return for his staunch pro-American stand in Havana. Brazil, deprived of her European coffee and cotton markets, was soon to be amply compensated in her struggle for economic recovery. A hefty $20 million loan from the United States Export-Import Bank would help establish Brazil's first steel plant at Volta Redonda, ninety miles from Rio, with the help of United States equipment and United States technicians.

'When I go back to my country,' mused Foreign Minister Aranha in Washington, D.C., 'I shall propose that we erect a statue to Herr Hitler. It is [he] who at last succeeded in drawing the attention of the United States to Brazil.'

Afterwards, Werner Mölders looked back to those July days on the French Channel coast as no more than an illusory calm. He sensed that a bitter battle lay ahead, for if Churchill had promised the British only 'blood, toil, tears and sweat' the same would be true for Germany. The Luftwaffe had an awesome task ahead of them: first to destroy the R.A.F. and with them the Royal Navy before the *Wehrmacht* could cross the English Channel.

Mölders knew that Göring was supremely confident – perhaps too confident. Following his release from the prison camp near Toulouse, Mölders had been flown as guest of honour to Karinhall, Göring's mighty mansion outside Berlin, and *Der Dicke* (The Fat One), as the pilots called him, had scarcely mentioned the combat to come. Instead he had delighted, like any new-rich host, in showing off Karinhall's glories: the private cinema, his elaborate model railway, silver tapestries and gold-plated baths, even canary cages shaped like dive-bombers. Once, in an ebullient moment, he had commented, 'We'll beat up the Tommies,' but that had been all.

Mölders's only hint of misgiving had been when Göring, half-way through dinner, had clapped an empty water glass over the gleaming white cloth and hailed his wife, 'Look, Emmy! Look what I've got! A flea! A present from Mölders from captivity!' As he shook with crazy laughter, the first faint doubt crossed the embarrassed Mölders's mind.

Other Luftwaffe officers shared Mölders's conviction that the fight would be long and hard. On 19 July, now promoted Major, Mölders took command of Fighter Group 51, at Wissant, near Calais, where the regional fighter commander for Air Fleet Two, *Oberst* 'Uncle Theo' Osterkamp, took pains to dispel any complacency. An Anglophile, to whom the British were always 'The Lords', 'Uncle Theo' warned: 'Now we're going to fight "the Lords", and that's something else again. They're hard fighters and they're good fighters – even though our machines are better.'

On this score, Mölders fully agreed. As Group Commander, he had been privileged to carry out test flights on two captured British fighters: the Vickers-Supermarine Spitfire and the Hawker Hurricane. Neither plane, in his view, measured up to the Luftwaffe's ace machine the Messerschmitt 109. Easy to handle and faultless in a curve, the Spitfire was as fast as the ME 109, but its Merlin engines sometimes cut out for a split second, reducing its manoeuvrability. The Hurricane, though a tougher plane, was a slower performer, sluggish in the ailerons.

Nine days later, on 29 July, Mölders knew what 'Uncle Theo' had meant about the British pilots. North of Dover, he and Fighter Group 51 chanced on a swarm of Spitfires above the Straits. True, he scored a hit on one Spitfire, but instantly the others were on him like a swarm of hornets, so eager to close that they blocked each other's field of fire. Their flight discipline, Mölders thought, was lamentable, but their courage and determination were awe-inspiring. His radiator and starboard tank shot up, Mölders broke hard for France, bellylanding at Wissant, his landing-gear jammed like a concertina.

In the flaring excitement of battle, he had felt nothing; only now did he notice that his flying overalls were thickly daubed with blood. The Tommies had peppered him with everything they had; shell splinters had punctured his knee-joint, his thigh, the calf of his left leg. Mölders felt no pain, only intense chagrin. Until further notice he was transferred as a patient to the Luftwaffe Hospital, Berlin, and the battle hadn't even started.

For one élite arm of the German war machine, the battle was already on – and the fortunes of war were with them all the way.

In less than a year, *Kapitänleutnant* Otto Kretschmer, 28-year-old commander of U-Boat 99, and the fifty-six other skippers operating under the submarine chief, *Konteradmiral* Karl Dönitz, had seen their war transformed from a kid-glove affair to a no-holds-barred combat. At first, still hopeful of Anglo–French acquiescence, Hitler had insisted that all U-Boats must surface when sighting merchant vessels, ensuring the safety of both passengers and crew before sinking the ship. Those days were long past. Now the U-Boat war had become a threat that was, in Churchill's words, 'the only thing that ever frightened me'.

The logistics were simple. The very survival of Great Britain depended on 3,000 ocean-going merchantmen importing fifty-five million tons of supplies annually: every gallon of oil, half of the food consumed, most raw materials. Yet such was Britain's plight that only fifty-six special escort vessels were available to protect them.

Otto Kretschmer knew early on that the Royal Navy were as yet no match for the U-Boats. The reason was strategic ignorance. The Admiralty's policy favoured the random tracking of individual submarines instead of the staid but effective policy of escorting convoys en bloc. Moreover, their faith in the Asdic submarine detector device was misplaced; Asdic could operate only at a fixed angle, for a range of rather less than a mile, and was of little use when U-boats were travelling faster than eight knots. No more than 180 warships had been equipped with Asdic in 1939, and of these 150 were destroyers, which were needed to protect the fleet. And since Admiralty Plans refused even to accept that submarines could operate by night, Britain as early as January 1940, had lost 150 merchant ships, half a million tons of shipping. As the year dawned, even bread rationing had been a possibility.

At the same time, the war had taken a ruthless turn which Kretschmer, like his fellow commanders, accepted but did not relish. Hitler had now forbidden the rescue of survivors and the care of ships' boats, although Kretschmer, like most others, blandly ignored these orders.

June alone had seen 300,000 tons of shipping lost to Dönitz's torpedoes – a fact reflected on every British breakfast table, where sugar was now limited to half a pound per week, butter was reduced, the bacon ration in jeopardy, and tea limited to two ounces a week for every citizen. Now was the beginning of what the U-Boat skippers would always remember as *Die Glückliche Zeit*, The Happy Time, for with the Admiralty concentrating their destroyer flotillas on anti-invasion patrols, the U-Boats, heading for the Western Approaches, were to enjoy a field-day.

On 5 July, Kretschmer set out from Wilhelmshaven on Heligoland Bay, for the first of his Atlantic adventures. Until now, like the other commanders, he had operated in the Fair Isle Passage, between the Orkneys and the Shetlands. As always, when the 500-ton U-99 put out to sea, her conning tower marked with the insignia of two golden horseshoes, her 44-strong crew knew that things would be done the Kretschmer way. Despite leavening qualities of humour and compassion, Kretschmer ran a tight ship, intolerant of weakness or slovenly demeanour. A schoolteacher's son from Lower Silesia, 'Silent Otto's' only betrayal of inner tension was the non-stop chain of black cheroots he smoked when U-99 was surfaced.

At 4.15 that day, Kretschmer spotted his first Atlantic prey: the 2,000-ton Canadian steamer *Magog*, approaching on a zig-zag course. Almost by rote, Kretschmer gave the order: 'Engineer, prepare to fire one torpedo. Keep the bows steady at trim.' All this was routine, and so, too, was the sight of the steamer breaking in two like a riven plank, her crew scrambling to launch the lifeboats clear of her rear section. But far from routine, to newcomers aboard U-99, was Kretschmer's flaring anger as a young petty officer rushed to the conning tower, sub-machine gun at the ready, anticipating trouble. Furiously ordering the man below, Kretschmer, part-educated in Devonshire, hailed the bobbing lifeboats in fluent English: 'Sorry about that gun. We don't intend to harm you.'

By way of farewell, Kretschmer first gave the Canadians bearings to reach the Irish coast, then passed down a full bottle of brandy. Baffled by a U-Boat commander who had first sunk him and then stood him drinks on the Third Reich, the skipper could only mumble a bewildered thanks.

At midnight that day, U-99's look-out reported a convoy heading out from the Western Approaches. Tossing his cheroot from the conning tower, Kretschmer ordered action stations. His manoeuvre was already decided: to steam at full speed on the surface and attack the convoy's port bow before dawn. Only one thing perturbed him: against all the law of averages, the convoy seemed to be screened by a strong destroyer escort. Soon after dawn on 6 July, caution prompted him to submerge ahead of the convoy, dropping back at periscope depth.

One freighter, the *Humber Arm*, broke up in a yellow-white flash as the first torpedo struck, but it was enough to alert the escorts to Kretschmer's presence. Soon after 8 a.m., he noted in his War Diary: 'Propeller noises heard approaching to starboard. I believe my crew are going to get their baptism of depth charging.' Four minutes later: 'Escort picking up speed. This is the attack.'

Within seconds, it came. In fact, Kretschmer's pursuer was not a destroyer but a corvette, one of the first to join the Atlantic escort groups, but to the crew of U-99, fast submerging to 350 feet, the distinction was academic. With the first pattern of ten depth-charges, the submarine rocked like a truck hitting a brick wall; there was a noise 'like the grating of a thousand chisels on steel'. At once Kretschmer ordered emergency precautions: all electrical equipment, save hydrophones and gyro compass, to be shut down, speed was reduced to the point where only the propellers were turning over, enabling U-99 to maintain depth. But after two hours of these concussion-like blows, the oxygen supply cut out. The crew donned breathing masks, connected by tubes to cases of alkali.

Stealthily, maintaining listening speed, U-99 was creeping away from the path of the convoy. But the corvette, implacably, was keeping pace, and now Kretschmer's crew strove to remember the training school's text-book rules for survival:

to conserve precious air for breathing, each man lay prone at his action station. Unable to use the lavatory, in case the telltale discharge rose to the surface, all of them in turn shamefacedly fouled their overalls. Often, for twenty minutes at a time, they drifted into a deep trance-like sleep. The shuddering impact of the depth charges continued and, as the carbon dioxide content mounted, the men began to pant like dogs behind their masks. Their heads ached abominably; a cold dew of sweat bathed their bodies. Soon the batteries would run dry; without power, U-99 would sink like waterlogged jetsam to the sea-bed.

Twelve hours passed ... fourteen ... then nineteen. In the War Diary, Navigator Petersen now marked up the 127th depth charge. Yet to the puzzlement of Radio Operator Jupp Kassel, Kretschmer, sitting placidly on the control deck, seemed absorbed by a paperback whodunnit. Only later, peering over his commander's shoulder, did Kassel realize that Kretschmer was calling on all his iron reserves of will to stiffen his crew's morale. Not only had he neglected to turn the pages; the book was held upside down.

But the depth charge that Petersen had noted was the last. Around 12 July, U-99 limped into harbour at Lorient, France, the new headquarters of Dönitz's submarine arm. All her movable parts had been put out of action; everything breakable had been smashed to smithereens. On the quayside, Dönitz, no man to betray his emotions, felt a twinge of anxiety as the crew came ashore: their sea-overalls caked with excrement, leather jackets stained with salt and oil, their faces strained and emaciated, bristling with untended beards.

The hell of their first depth-charging would stay with them a long time yet, but Kretschmer was undeterred. 'Now we have received all the presents the enemy can give us,' was his last entry on that voyage. 'We all have a fresh confidence in our ship.'

Kretschmer's confidence was not misplaced. On 24 July, U-99 was ordered to sea once more. Caught up in a convoy of twenty merchant ships, Kretschmer sent three freighters to the bottom, then, down to his last four torpedoes, sank three tankers and a freighter. On 8 August, U-99 steamed triumphantly back into Lorient. Seven victory pennants, each bearing the golden horseshoe insignia, flew from her raised periscope. For Otto Kretschmer, it was still The Happy Time.

If the successes of Otto Kretschmer and his fellow aces were costing Winston Churchill sleep, his Cabinet were unaware of it. Immersed in minutiae, he often failed to see the wood for the trees, driving his Ministers to distraction in the process. Many would have endorsed the verdict of Lord Halifax: 'I have seldom met anybody with stranger gaps of knowledge or whose mind worked in greater jerks.'

A titanic leader, though by no means a great strategist, Churchill was by turns ardent, inspiring, impetuous, voluble, stubborn and determined to poke his finger into every pie, often spurred on by the sometimes erratic advice of his scientific adviser, Professor Sir Frederick Lindemann (later Lord Cherwell). The newly-appointed Commander-in-Chief, Southern Command, Lieutenant-General Alan Brooke, summed it up: 'The more you tell that man about the war, the more you hinder the winning of it.'

Ideas – not always welcomed by his colleagues – poured from Churchill in a spate. Long before the war he had been urging on the then Minister of Air, Kingsley Wood, an idea of Lindemann's to beat the night bomber which he thought surpassed the tank: a million air mines a week to 'create a lethal drizzle very unpleasant for aeroplanes to fly through'. Since the idea involved suspending the mines on parachutes at the end of 2,000 feet of piano wire, defending R.A.F. fighters were equally prone to tangle with them, but it took one R.A.F. squadron a year of experiment to convince Churchill they were useless.

The R.A.F.'s shortage of pilots puzzled Churchill, too – even when Air Minister Sir Archibald Sinclair pointed out that R.A.F. squadron strength had been upped from thirty-nine to sixty, preparing for the air battle to come. The Premier was unconvinced: why then were only three pilots out of every ten with wings operational?

The horrified Sinclair had to explain that a pilot was awarded his wings after eighty to ninety hours' flying training – 'but he was in no circumstances operationally qualified at this stage'. To attain this pitch, at least 200 hours were needed.

This led Professor Lindemann, on the strength of his stint as a First World War test pilot, to interpose: 'Are not our training standards too high? The final polish should be given in the squadrons.'

As a result, the training period was reduced from three months to one. At a fearful cost to the R.A.F. that 'final polish' would be given them by aces like Werner Mölders and others.

The Minister of Food, Lord Woolton, felt the same sense of frustration when dealing with Churchill. Despite mounting shipping losses, Churchill took him severely to task for rationing diners-out to one main course. A resolute trencherman, Churchill grumbled: 'Is it worse for the country for a man to eat a little of three or four courses of food, daintily cooked out of scraps, or a good solid plate of roast beef?' . . . 'Is it wrong to eat up the luxury foods already in the country, or ought they to be wasted?'

Woolton was unrepentant. A spot check had revealed no less than eighty items on the menu at London's smart Grosvenor House Hotel – too large a choice by far in a Britain at war. Moreover, he reminded Churchill shrewdly, 'it is important from a political point of view. My mail shows that the working class is concerned that rich and poor should be treated alike, and the reason why I introduced the phrase "luxury feeding" [in a broadcast] was in order to balance the rationing of tea and margarine, which undoubtedly affects the poorer classes the most.'

His whole world centring round No. 10, Chequers, the Prime Minister's country residence, or 'The Hole', a six-acre honeycomb of offices beneath Whitehall, where one in ten of War Cabinet meetings were held, Churchill did not realize that the England he had known was changing irretrievably. To the naked eye the changes were there for all to see. In Piccadilly Circus, Eros was a shrouded obelisk of sandbags; the railings had gone for scrap metal from the London parks; restaurant entrances had long been heavily sandbagged against possible bomb blast. As host to five governments-in-exile, London was now more cosmopolitan and colourful than at any time in history: the black *képis* of Free Frenchmen who had rallied to Charles de Gaulle, vying with the vivid electric blue of Dominions pilots' uniforms and the black silver-braided uniforms of the Dutch police.

This was a world where shortage was the established norm: a world of newspapers whittled to six pages, where waiters had been replaced by waitresses in clubs, where teashop customers had grown used to one lump of sugar and a thin shaving of butter with their bread.

But these were only surface changes. All over Britain one woman in three now went hatless and wore slacks – 'Horrible!' lamented the couturier Victor Stiebel. 'Women seemed to think that now at last they could forget about fashion and go about as they liked.' On 26 July, one theatregoer noticed lounge suits in the stalls replacing black ties for the first time. Even at the Ritz Hotel, august dowagers dined with portable radios on their table, keeping up with the war news.

The mood of Britain was changing fast. Clothes, style, wealth, the King's English, suddenly mattered less. 'In the England of the future,' conceded the novelist Somerset Maugham, 'evening dress will be less important than it has been in the past.' Already a Socialist tomorrow was looming. 'Either we turn this war into a war of revolution,' warned the left-wing *New Statesman* in mid-July, 'or we shall be defeated.' Ernest Bevin, on taking office as Minister of Labour, had made his concept of the future abundantly plain: 'When this war is over, the task of rebuilding the world has to be done by the working class. We are taking none of the promises . . . the plausible stuff of the last war. This time it must be the economic reconstruction of the whole foundation of society.'

In this climate, a friend's assurance to Lady Cunard at a party – 'Don't worry, Emerald, within three weeks of the declaration of peace, all the classes will be back in their proper places' – was less than prophetic.

This vision of an egalitarian future, which by degrees was stiffening the British will to resist, was ironic, for much of the world, the Axis apart, had already written them off. 'The German victories are putting great heart into my Opposition,' noted the South African Premier, Jan Smuts, on 10 July. 'The Allies are finished, they say' – and he predicted that the opposing Nationalists, if returned to power, would plump for secession from the Commonwealth and an alliance with Germany. In Washington, D.C., the isolationist Senator Arthur Vandenberg infuriated the Australian Minister, Richard Casey, by suggesting that a German victory would be 'unpleasant, but not catastrophic'. The British, Vandenberg thought, could be re-housed in Canada and the U.S.A. and a self-contained democracy built up again in North America.

Few men were more aware of Britain's unpopularity than Ambassador Sir Samuel Hoare in Madrid. 'Whenever I go out, I have to have an army of gunmen, as if I was going to have to fight a battle in the streets,' he complained in a letter to Beaverbrook. On 22 June, having granted Hoare an audience after keeping him waiting for three weeks, General Francisco Franco was bold enough to put into words what the rest of the world was thinking. 'Why do you not end the war now?' he asked Hoare contemptuously. 'You can never win it. All that will happen if the war is allowed to continue will be the destruction of European civilization.'

Five weeks after Franco's prediction, Hitler unwittingly ensured that European civilization would, however precariously, survive.

The first hint of a change in priorities came on 29 July to *Oberst* Walter Warlimont of Hitler's Operations Department (Section L) and his three senior officers. The four men were assembled in the restaurant car of their special train, code-named Atlas, in a siding at Bad Reichenhall station, Bavaria, hard by Hitler's Berchtesgaden retreat. Briefed to wait on a visit from the newly-promoted General Alfred Jodl, all of them had one thought in mind: promotion for their good work in the West was on the cards. But to their astonishment, Jodl, like a spy in a melodrama, prowled through the car checking every door and window tight-shut.

Then, in a quiet dry voice, Jodl let fall his bombshell. The Führer had decided to rid the world 'once for all' of the danger of Bolshevism. A surprise attack on Soviet Russia was scheduled for May 1941.

At first, gripping on to his chair arms for support, Warlimont couldn't speak. Then, just as when Hitler had halted the tanks before Dunkirk, a torrent of objections arose. The struggle against England, the projected invasion, code-named 'Sea-Lion' only seventeen days earlier, was not yet accomplished fact. What about the two-front war they had always been careful to avoid? Jodl was emphatic: the victory over Russia, 'the last force on the continent', would be the best possible method of forcing England, shorn of a potential ally, to make peace.

'That's impossible,' objected *Oberst* Bernhard von Lossberg, one of Warlimont's officers. Surely, he protested, England was first priority? Jodl's answer was revealing: 'The Führer is afraid that the mood of the people after a victory over England would hardly permit him to embark on a new war against Russia.'

Warlimont's own objections were clamant. What about the 'pact of friendship and non-aggression' concluded with Moscow only eleven months back? Had not Russia delivered all war material promptly and in full, as promised? Again Jodl had pat answers: the collision with Bolshevism was bound to come, so it was better to fight it out now while Germany was at the height of her military powers. And by the autumn of 1941, the Luftwaffe, tempered by victories in the east, could bring its full brunt to bear against England.

Finally, Jodl, who had himself presented similar arguments to Hitler, clamped down on further dissent. 'Gentlemen, it is not a question for discussion but a decision of the Führer.' From this time on, Warlimont and his staff were to concentrate on planning papers under the code-name Build-Up East.

None of the officers privy to this astonishing about-face were even aware that Hitler had been debating this decision as far back as 3 June. On that date he had told *Generalleutnant* Georg von Sodenstern, Chief of Staff of Army Group A: 'Now that things have got to this point, I can begin settling my accounts with Bolshevism.'

There were many factors to account for this resolve. All his life Hitler had dreamed of winning a great Eastern empire. Now he saw urgent reasons to achieve this aim before an unbeatable coalition of enemies united to oppose him. The Soviet forces were bound to modernize; by 1942, the United States might have entered the war. Moreover he was convinced that the Slavs, whom he despised, were 'ripe for dissolution', and since they 'bred like vermin' they would be a fertile source for slave labour.

In the weeks that followed, Hitler's conviction slowly assumed the proportions of an obsession. At first he was bent on an attack in the autumn of this year, until the impassioned arguments of Jodl and Keitel persuaded him to postpone it.

Throughout July, Halder's diary recorded the determined progress of Hitler's thoughts. 3 July posed the problem: 'The main question is how to deal Russia a military blow which will force her to recognize Germany's preponderant role in Europe.' On 13 July: 'England still has some hope of action on the part of Russia.' On 22 July: 'The problem of Russia must be dealt with.'

What hardened Hitler above all was the memory of the Red Army's lamentable showing in the Finnish campaign. Architect Albert Speer, summoned to Hitler's presence, always remembered how the Führer was pacing the gravel drive at Berchtesgaden along with Jodl and Keitel as he approached.

'Now we have shown what we are capable of,' Hitler was saying. 'Believe me, Keitel, a campaign against Russia will be like a child's game in a sand-box by comparison.' He was, Speer noted, in radiant good humour.

'The Battle of France is over,' Churchill had warned the nation as long ago as 18 June. 'I expect the Battle of Britain is about to begin.' Now the world held its breath. 'The future of our Western civilization,' Ismay told General Raymond E. Lee, U.S. Military Attaché in London, 'rests on the shoulders of the Royal Navy and about 5,000 pink-cheeked young pilots.'

7

'The Whole Bloody World's on Fire'

8 August–7 September 1940

Across the English Channel from France, the pilots of whom Ismay had spoken – the crew of twenty-three fighter squadrons, preparing to defend a 250-mile front from thirteen south coast airfields – waited for the worst that would happen.

Although every man was aware that the first Luftwaffe sweeps marking the prelude to the Battle of Britain had been evident from 8 August, none as yet suspected that Göring's plan was to knock out the R.A.F. in four days flat, an air battle that would be the harbinger of a full-scale 13-division invasion of England from Ramsgate, Kent, to the Isle of Wight.

'The British Air Force,' stressed Hitler's Directive No. 16, 'must be eliminated to such an extent that it will be incapable of putting up any substantial opposition to the invading troops.'

Few men gave much for their own chances – an estimate which Fighter Command's C.-in-C., Sir Hugh 'Stuffy' Dowding, accepted as the painful truth. Although a few pilots were natural-born aces – among them 242's Squadron-Leader Douglas Bader, whose tin legs, the result of a pre-war crash, were already legend, and 257's Robert Stanford Tuck, who sported monogrammed silk handkerchiefs and long cigarette holders – they were the exception. As the battle gained momentum, scores of R.A.F. pilots were to be swept brutally from the sky; hundreds more would survive by luck rather than judgement.

Their morale was never in question. On the south coast airfields that were now Britain's front line – Hawkinge, Manston, Tangmere – the legends on their planes testified to their don't-give-a-damn spirit: Leslie Charteris' The Saint, Walt Disney's Figaro, the little cat swatting a swastika as blithely as a mouse, even a sharp-edged scythe, dripping blood, to symbolize death, the grim reaper. But on all these airfields the pilots were as hard-pressed as any men alive. At least 100 would be at readiness – at their dispersal points, life-jackets already adjusted – since dawn. Others, more sorely tried, would be on stand-by – strapped in their cockpits, facing the wind, engines ready to turn over. Only the fortunate few would draw 'available' – in the mess and ready to take off within twenty minutes. Garbed in flying overalls or polo-neck sweaters, with silk scarves for comfort, they lolled on the grass or on canvas cots, the thump-thump of the petrol bowsers' delivery pumps dinning in their ears, lucky enough to breakfast off lukewarm baked beans and tepid tea.

For many food, even a bed, was a luxury. At Rochford, Essex, 151 Squadron's pilots bedded down in their cockpits; the airfield's dew-soaked grass was the one alternative. At North Weald, Essex, one squadron, starting lunch soon after noon, were airborne so often they didn't reach dessert until 3.30 p.m.

It was a battle the English shared as they would share no other throughout the Second World War. For five long weeks, the sights they saw did not vary: the cold white contrails scoring the enormous bowl of the sky, the dragonfly glint of silver wings spinning and snarling over Kentish apple orchards and Sussex valleys. On many days the sky became a place of terror, raining blazing planes, shell splinters, parachutes, even flying boots. On the chalk hills, farm workers would find rabbits, bolt upright on their hind legs, paralysed with sheer terror.

These were heart-stopping sights, but everywhere along the southern coast hundreds who had never been under fire now walked taller, as if conscious it was now fashionable to be a front-liner. At Dover's Grand Hotel, one luncheon guest complained of shrapnel in his soup, but head waiter George Garland coaxed him to rise above it, and greeted newcomers to the dining-room: 'Good morning, sir! A nice table here, sir, away from the broken glass . . .'

Whatever the inconvenience, people were careful to shrug it off. At Homefield, Kent, ancestral home of the wealthy Smithers family, William, the butler, did the rounds of the velvety lawn after each dog fight, sweeping up spent machine-gun bullets as deftly as ever he had brushed crumbs from a damask tablecloth. Fifty miles south-west, at Worthing, Sussex, Miss Vera Arlett's maid was equally matter-of-fact: 'Shall we have plums and custard for dessert – oh, and they're machine-gunning the back garden.'

But still the R.A.F.'s losses mounted, for on most days the pilots fought against odds of three to one. By 23 August, Beaverbrook's Ministry of Aircraft Production was to achieve the battle's highest ever total – 440 fighters delivered from the assembly lines – but what Dowding lacked was the trained pilots to man those planes. It was a need so dire that on 16 August – the day the Luftwaffe struck the airfields at Manston, Tangmere and West Malling – Dowding was 209 pilots below strength.

Haggard, scarcely able to snatch more than three hours' sleep a night, it was the pilot shortage that plagued the weary Dowding above all.

It was no idle concern. The casualty rates now made plain that a pilot's expectation of life was no more than eighty-seven flying hours, and many were so near collapse their reactions were a long way off the medical board's touchstone: one-fifth of a second quicker than average. At Hawkinge, pilots taxied in, then slumped in their cockpits dead to the world like men under morphia. After eight daily sorties, Peter Hairs, another Hawkinge Hurricane pilot, would stare at his log-book, unable to remember how to write.

Many cushioned their fears with drink; as 32 Squadron's C.O. John Worrall recalled it: 'If you weren't in the air, you were plastered.' But some couldn't drink at all. At Northolt, near London, Canadian Roland Dibnah, though no teetotaller, found that one jigger of liquor drove him vomiting to the lavatory.

Despite Churchill's immortal tribute in the House of Commons on 20 August – 'Never in the field of human conflict was so much owed by so many to so few' – no pilot saw himself as a hero. At North Weald airfield, Pilot Officer Michael Constable-Maxwell, on hearing the Premier's words, grinned, 'He must be thinking of our Mess bills.' Flying Officer Michael Appleby, at Warmwell, Dorset, thought of the fourteen shillings and sixpence a day at which the country valued his services. Irreverently he capped Churchill's speech: '. . . and for so little.'

But the public had taken Churchill's words to heart. The R.A.F.'s crucial losses, the acute shortage of pilots, was still a closely guarded secret; on all sides there seemed cause for jubilation, even complacency. In south coast towns, newspaper sellers chalked up each day's result in terms of a cricket match: 'R.A.F. v. Germans, 61 for 26 – Close of Play Today. 12 for 0.' For now, after many false starts, the English knew why they were fighting. The battle had moved away from distant fjords with unpronounceable names and cobbled streets that smelt of *caporal* tobacco in the Pas de Calais. Now they were fighting for things that were dear; for His Majesty King George VI, King and Emperor by the Grace of God, for hedgerows and village greens, thatched roofs and sooty chimney-pots, for bewigged judges and horses with heart, for Yorkshire pudding and overcooked cabbage and verbal sniping in the House of Commons. Chamberlainism was dead, the Old School Tie was going fast; a strange radiant calm had invested their world.

Hard as each pilot strove, it was bitter uphill work; many had never flown a fighter sortie before 8 August. One Spitfire pilot, Dudley Williams, of 152 Squadron, airborne over Portland, never forgot opening fire on an ME 110 and seeing the chips of metal showering. A glow of joy was followed by a sober realization; though he had been once allowed to fire his Browning machine guns into the sea for practice, this was the first time he had ever fired them in anger.

He was no lone example; barely 10 per cent of Dowding's pilots had undergone more stringent gunnery practice. Their training had stressed only disciplined pre-war air display flying in rigid V-shaped formations – a copybook procedure which baffled Luftwaffe aces like Mölders. Most, unaccustomed to sighting their guns, opened fire at 600 yards – then, at the surer range of 200 yards, broke from combat. Still doing things by the book, they flew the four standard Fighter Command attacks on bombers – based on the theory that German bombers would fly in straight unwavering lines, without rear gun turrets, and would be unescorted by fighters.

Thus even the newest trainees perfected the No. 1 Fighter

Command attack where every man in the squadron swung into line behind their leader, queueing to deliver a 3-second burst before breaking away, their underbellies a sure target for the German tail gunners.

By 18 August – the day that the Luftwaffe pounded the airfields at Kenley, Biggin Hill, Croydon and West Malling – Dowding was at his wits' end. One day earlier, the Air Ministry had at last acceded to his pleas so that Fighter Command's thinning ranks would now be stiffened by pilots trained on Fairey-Battle day bombers, by Army Co-Operation Command pilots, by allied pilots like No. 1 Royal Canadian Air Force Squadron. But again the training period had been slashed – from one month to two weeks. Many of the pilots who bore the brunt of the battle that lay ahead had never fired their guns, could not use a reflector sight, and had done no more than twenty hours on Spitfires and Hurricanes.

Now the steady induction of novices into the front line only accelerated the rate of attrition. At Croydon, down to nine pilots, 111 Squadron's Squadron Leader John Thompson greeted two unfledged sergeants: 'I'm sorry, but I'm afraid you'll have to go in today – you see, we're so terribly short.' Outside the mess, he saw their old rattletrap car, jam-packed with luggage. By 5 p.m. the same day, one of them was dead, the other in hospital – their gear still unpacked.

The man in hospital was Sergeant Raymond Sellers, who had earlier noted twenty minutes' dog-fight practice in his log-book. Now he was so deep in shock that despite the medical orderlies' probing he couldn't even remember his name.

By the third week in August it was not surprising that many R.A.F. pilots were growing angry. To them these thin-red-line tactics, geared to foolhardy sorties from coastal strips like Manston and Hawkinge, made increasingly less sense. If the squadrons withdrew to the airfields north of London – North Weald, Duxford, Debden – they would be beyond the range of the ME 109s – and could steadily gain operational height as they came south. True, the northern airfields would still be within German bomber range – but without the protection of their fighters, who could not range so far north, the bombers would be easy meat. At Manston and Hawkinge, the R.A.F. had always to climb under the surveillance of hovering German fighters, knowing they would be jumped at 18,000 feet.

It was hard for the pilots to grasp, but Dowding and senior commanders like Air Vice-Marshal Keith Park, of 11 Group, saw the show of front-line strength as paramount. Large-scale air-raids on British cities were still an unknown bogey; gloomy estimates still predicted 200,000 casualties within ten days, and four million mental cases after six months of bombing. Even Churchill believed that up to four million would flee from London once the first bombs fell.

Thus even retaining advanced bases, like Manston, though tactically wrong, was politically expedient. To keep British morale at peak, every one of Dowding's planes must be up there in the sky – fighting against any odds that Göring chose to decree.

Across the English Channel, the growing concern of Dowding and his pilots would have puzzled Werner Mölders and his comrades. As each day passed, the clear-sighted among them realized that their onslaught was being slowly but irrevocably repulsed.

The inescapable truth was that the Luftwaffe was as unequal to its task of neutralizing the R.A.F. as Gort's British Expeditionary Force had been to stem the onrush of the Panzers in the West.

Designed primarily to support the Army in the field, its main strength lay in short-range fighters, dive-bombers like the Stukas that had pounded Sedan, and twin-engined level-flight medium-weight bombers. Though on paper it was the world's largest air force, fielding 4,093 first-line aircraft (of which 3,646 were operational) it totally lacked night bombers, bombs larger than 1,000 lb, air torpedoes, modern mines, modern armaments and bomb sights.

Incredibly, Göring all along was to pin his faith in two planes supremely unfitted for the combat. His special pride was the twin-seater, twin-engined ME 110, christened the Zerstörer (destroyer), a long-range escort fighter, designed to clear the way for mass bomber attacks, with a maximum cruising range of 680 miles. Yet when loaded the 110 outweighed the streamlined ME 109 by almost 10,000 lb. Despite the easy laurels the 110s had won in the French campaign, their lack of manoeuvrability and speed were a byword with every pilot.

In combat their stock tactic was what the R.A.F. called 'the circle of death' – a defensive gambit which had the machines circling, warily, each guarding the other's tailplane, perilous to friend and foe alike. In the first days of the combat, Major Hennig Strümpell of Fighter Group Two had found himself in one such circle dog-fighting with a Spitfire – while 110s blasted tracer at both of them impartially.

Yet to all arguments Göring was obdurate: 'If the fighters are the sword of the Luftwaffe, the ME 110 Zerstörer is the point of that sword.'

Göring's unwavering belief in the Stuka troubled his commanders, too. Unrivalled in precision bombing and close infantry support when the Luftwaffe held the sky, they now made up one-third of the Luftwaffe's bomber force. Yet one disastrous Channel attack on a convoy of merchantmen on 8 August had written off 13 Stukas; the ME 109s, lacking diving brakes, found themselves screaming for the sea at 375 miles per hour, while the Stukas' air brakes throttled them back to half this speed. Time and again, as they flattened out unprotected at the end of their dive, the R.A.F. had picked the Stukas off with deadly accuracy.

On 18 August, when 28 Stukas attacked targets around Portsmouth Harbour in an effort to draw up British fighters the losses were appalling: 18 Stukas lost or severely damaged. Beside himself with fury, Göring had still been forced to withdraw the remaining 280 Stukas from the battle.

Another bitter bone of contention with Mölders and his fellows was the use of the 109. It was a fine plane, to be sure, but playing nursemaid to the lumbering Heinkel and other bombers – 'furniture vans', the fighter-men called them – was not the task for which they had been designed. Often 120 fighters were slated to protect a bomber formation forty miles long, so that the ME 109s, with an operational radius of 125 miles and a tactical flying time of ten minutes, were severely hampered. If the R.A.F. were in the mood for combat, the 109s were left with just eight minutes to fight before breaking away.

Soon, as with the R.A.F., every pilot was feeling the stress. Many a man found himself watching his fuel gauge as anxiously as he scanned the sky; the red warning bulb on the instrument panel that showed fuel running out now prompted a code-cry: 'Trübsal' (Distress). One pilot, *Oberleutnant* Hans von Hahn of the 3rd Fighter Group, reported the plight of all of them in a letter home: 'There aren't many of us who haven't made a forced landing in the Channel in a badly shot-up plane or without a propeller.'

Above all, Göring's tactics puzzled the pilots, for day by day the attacks jumped spottily from target to target, seeming to lose all technical advantage. On 12 August, the crack Luftwaffe unit Test Group 210 had struck at the R.A.F.'s key southern radar stations: Dunkirk, near Canterbury, Pevensey, Rye, Ventnor and Dover. As the R.A.F.'s sole early warning system, these were vital targets, the eyes and ears that alerted Fighter Command's Sector Controllers how many raiders were in cross-Channel flight, and thus how to deploy their defences. By mid-afternoon on 12 August, all these stations, save Ventnor, a write-off for three weeks, were functioning again on stand-by generators – yet never again were they to figure as targets for Luftwaffe bombers.

Were the stations vital or not? Which factories should be attacked to neutralize Beaverbrook's Spitfire and Hurricane production? Which airfields most merited attack, and when attacking them which targets mattered most – the hangars and buildings or the planes on the ground? None of these questions had been adequately studied or thought through by Luftwaffe planners.

At Karinhall, on 16 August, Göring still steadfastly ignored the implications of the battle to date. The losses of the ME 110 Zerstörer were mounting steeply, for inevitably the span of the plane – fifty-three feet as against the 109's thirty-two feet – led the R.A.F. to single it out. Stubbornly insistent that the planes could do the job, Göring could no longer ignore the losses – and now he reached a well-nigh unbelievable decision.

In future, he decreed, every ME 110 unit must be shepherded into battle by an escort of ME 109s – a fighter in the ludicrous position of itself needing fighter protection.

It was then that *Oberst* Werner Junck, regional fighter commander for Air Fleet Three, made a telling point. If extra burdens were to be thrown on the 109, surely serious thought must be given to stepping up fighter production? Aircraft production had been virtually static since war began; in the last four months of 1939, only 1,869 aircraft had been delivered.

Even in July, Junck pointed out, German aircraft factories had produced only 220 ME 109s – less than half Beaverbrook's total output. By the end of August the figures would have slumped again to 173.

Mock-solicitous, Göring stretched out his hand. 'I must take your pulse to see if you are all right physically – it seems you have taken leave of your senses.'

This was not the first time that Göring had heard such an argument from his production experts, and as summarily rejected it. Others had stressed that at the present rate of attrition, the Luftwaffe would need to shoot down four British fighters for every one they lost – yet even so, the ME 109 factories at Regensburg and Augsburg often worked a minimum six-hour day against the ten or twelve needed.

Only recently, when General Thomas, Göring's production coordination chief, raised the question of non-stop shifts, Göring had crimsoned with rage. Any such move would be fatal to home-front morale.

Thus all German strategy was becoming increasingly subordinate to Göring's inflated estimates of his Luftwaffe's potential, a private war waged with no attempt to coordinate with the needs of the Army or the Navy. Dazzled by the public's concept that he himself was leading the battle from the front line, Göring had even been surprised in a Paris hotel suite by his signals officer, clad only in a sky-blue silk dressing-gown and describing by telephone to Emmy, his wife, how he was at that moment on the cliffs at Calais, with squadrons of aircraft thundering overhead to England.

And little by little, on every Luftwaffe airfield, from Vannes, in Brittany, to Amsterdam-Schiphol, disillusion was setting in. Though the pilots lacked inside knowledge, many still had the uncanny hunch that Hitler saw the much vaunted 'Operation Sea-Lion' as no more than a study plan. 'If he didn't invade after Dunkirk,' opined *Oberleutnant* Victor Bauer, of the 3rd Fighter Group, 'he can't really mean business.'

Bauer and his fellow pilots were more sceptical still when the only visible signs of invasion planning materialized off the coast at Le Touquet: a fleet of weatherworn apple barges. The men of Major Max Ibel's 27th Fighter Group, near Calais, felt the same: in the one combined operation that they carried out with the Army, thirty pontoons had broken loose from their moorings and been carried away by the tide. Before the exercise could proceed, the Luftwaffe had to lay on rescue launches to tow the drifting engineers back to safety.

It was near Calais, too, that *Hauptmann* Hans-Heinrich Brustellin, one of Mölders's flight commanders, felt a mingled sense of mirth and disgust at the unit's only glimpse of the great invasion armada. Overnight, a fussy flotilla of old Rhine steamers had assembled near the harbour mouth. Somehow it seemed to debase all they had striven for over the Channel: had the blood and the fear and the young lives lost been just for this? '*That* is Sea-Lion?' Brustellin asked Mölders incredulously. 'But it's like a travelling circus.'

Six hundred miles from the Channel coast, in the pine-scented air of the Baltic at Peenemunde, a frustrated coterie of German scientists knew that they could succeed where the Luftwaffe was failing. But the one obstacle standing in their way was then insuperable: Adolf Hitler's profound distrust of technological innovation.

Their project had been launched ten years back, when the Germany Army Weapons Office appointed *Hauptmann* Walter Dornberger, a 35-year-old chemist's son, to explore the chances of developing military rockets on a massive scale. Two years later, Dornberger recruited a scientist to his team who was to achieve world renown: Dr Wernher von Braun, then aged twenty.

From 1937 on, von Braun's team had conducted secret full-scale trials along Peenemunde's 300-mile water-range, fringing the Baltic's southern shores. Test stands, laboratories, workshops, even the world's most powerful supersonic wind-tunnel, capable of developing velocities in excess of Mach 4, mushroomed among the pine forests, all of them geared towards the perfection of one rocket-prototype, the A3. This was a remote-controlled missile powered by the combustion of 75 per cent ethyl alcohol in liquid oxygen, lending its motor a $1\frac{1}{2}$-ton thrust. Still in the drawing-board stage was the A4, a rocket forty-two feet long designed to carry a ton of high-explosive warhead over a 160-mile range.

But Hitler, who had briefly viewed an abortive test of the A1 prototype in 1933, had shown little interest. In November 1939, convinced by his Polish victory that rockets would never be needed, he halved Peenemunde's steel allocation. That the project was still in being as late as August 1940 was due to two secret benefactors: Hitler's architect, Albert Speer, who connived with the Army Ordnance Officer to continue building, and Walter von Brauchitsch, now promoted *Feldmarschall*. Both men were excited by the potential of a missile which von Braun believed might be brought to such a pitch of accuracy it could level Whitehall.

Four years later, the first A4s (now rechristened the V-2s) were to shower on southern England. Von Braun, a belatedly-enthused Hitler now declared, was a young man 'who would change the face of the future'. But in August 1940, he and his team were merely the Cinderellas of the Third Reich, powerless to play any determinant role in Operation Sea-Lion.

In the Hotel Terminus, at Lorient, France, six U-Boat commanders were grouped anxiously round the bedside of Admiral Karl Dönitz, who had taken to his bed with a heavy cold and a stomach ache. Despite the pain, Dönitz could not refrain from chuckling wryly at the concern on their faces. 'Don't worry,' he reassured them, clutching a pillow to his midriff, 'I'm only having a child.' Then, conscious of the sensation he was about to cause, he explained the reason for their summons: 'Gentlemen, you are here to receive your orders for Operation Sea-Lion.'

Kapitänleutnant Otto Kretschmer felt an almost palpable tingle of excitement pass through the room. Now every man was craned forward, listening intently.

'The day for invasion has been set,' Dönitz told them,

'September 15. Those of you on patrol in the Atlantic will receive orders directing you to proceed to Cherbourg to refuel and reload with torpedoes. Your task will be to bar entry to the Channel through the western approach. No warship of the British Navy is to get through to interfere with our cross-Channel supply lines.' He paused meaningfully: 'I must stress this point. No British ship must enter the Channel.'

Along with the others, Kretschmer now waited expectantly. Surely further details of the overall operation would now, on 26 August, be forthcoming? But if Dönitz knew more he did not choose to reveal it – and Flag Lieutenant Hans Meckel now signalled dismissal. Kretschmer and his fellow commanders left the room none the wiser – though with no reason to doubt that Sea-Lion was going according to plan.

If the rank and file of the Navy still had faith, *Kriegsmariners* in the higher echelon were less sanguine. Some, like *Grossadmiral* Raeder, felt that Hitler was not wholeheartedly committed. Sea-Lion was always to be a last resort, he had stressed, against an enemy already broken by blockade and air attacks – but since Sea-Lion was less of a seaborne assault than the transportation of an army to occupy a defeated nation, the British collapse would have to be considerable. Yet Hitler had never once convened any conference with Göring to discuss aerial strategy.

Moreover, even on 31 July, before the Battle of Britain began, the Führer had ordered significant increases in the Army's strength – to 180 divisions – but only sixty were slated to garrison the west. The remaining 120 were earmarked to attack Russia.

In the days that France toppled, Hitler, perhaps playing devil's advocate, had gone out of his way to decry the whole concept of an invasion. 'How can we do an operation of this sort?' he had demanded of his naval aide, Puttkamer, rhetorically. 'It looks completely impossible to me. Losses would be heavy and no guarantee of success. How can we take on such casualties after conquering France with none to speak of?'

Nonetheless, from 16 July, physical preparations of a kind had been ordered – to the great perturbation of the Navy, for the dateline was initially set for 15 August, and the prerequisites seemed daunting. A defeated R.A.F. was the first essential, but the use of mine-free routes, the laying of flak mine-barriers, the readiness of the coastal artillery and a completely neutralized Royal Navy were of equal importance.

Yet, incredibly, Hitler had given no man overall authority for coordinating the operation, and Raeder and von Brauchitsch never met until mid-July. Only one man, forgotten by history, General Georg-Hans Reinhardt, director of technical experiments at Putlos, on Kiel Bay, had grasped the need for landing craft, since this was primarily an assault from the sea on a beach position.

By dint of much wire-pulling, Reinhardt rounded up 2,000 river and canal barges, called *prahms*, each capable of carrying 2–4 vehicles and 150 troops, though all needed much modification. But all these craft between them could ferry no more than six divisions, four infantry and two armoured, and Reinhardt thus advised the Army to scale down their requirements.

From 22 July a great air of bustle was apparent. The Todt Labour Organization was engaged on harbour clearance, and 24,000 troops had been inducted to man the invasion craft, for paradoxically, after Hitler's 29 July Barbarossa bombshell, the estimates for Sea-Lion requirements were stepped up. Now the planning called for at least 1,800 barges but also for 274 tugs, 156 steamboats, 1,586 motor boats, 137 trawlers and 127 motor coasters. Many of the smaller craft, though, could do only 4–5 knots and bow waves were likely to sink them en masse.

But their naval losses off Norway had left the *Kriegsmarine* stripped of formidable ships, and Raeder ultimately refused to guarantee the Army's safety on their ambitious 150-mile Ramsgate–Isle of Wight front. Thus the front was scaled down to encompass the coastline from the Thames Estuary to Brighton, to be assaulted by three waves, in all 700,000 men.

By 12 August, Hitler's thinking more closely resembled the waverings of a psychograph than the reasoned deliberations of a war lord. 'Independent of the eventual decision,' the War Diary of the German Navy noted, 'the Führer wishes the *threat* of invasion to be maintained against England in every way. The preparations must therefore proceed, however the decision may fall.'

'The fiction of an invasion', as the War Diary put it, now became the order of the day. Landing barges were still assembling at the seven main invasion ports: Rotterdam, Antwerp, Calais, Boulogne, Le Havre, Ostend, Dunkirk. The swank Paris Plage at Le Touquet, fifteen miles south of Boulogne, was set up as a propaganda exercise beach for manoeuvres watched by Halder, Admiral Friedrich Ruge and von Brauchitsch, but not by the sceptical old Gerd von Rundstedt, whose opinion was summed up by one explosive, 'Sea-Lion, rubbish!'

In truth, Hitler was in a quandary. By refusing to sue for peace, the British had thrown all his plans awry, but he knew full well that all his senior men – Kesselring, Guderian, Göring, Milch – were lukewarm on Sea-Lion. Only Halder was full of a drive which nobody else shared, and on 6 August he noted their half-heartedness in his diary: 'The Navy is full of misgivings, the Luftwaffe is very reluctant to tackle a mission which at the outset is exclusively its own, and O.K.W., which for once has a real combined-forces operation to direct, just plays dead.'

Two days later, Halder scented further naval obstructionism, when the Navy opined that a broad-front invasion could drag on for forty-two days. 'I might as well put the assault troops straight through a sausage machine,' Halder declared furiously.

Other officials meanwhile were going through the motions. Plans formulated by the Reich Central Security Office for the total occupation of Britain went steadily ahead. All able-bodied men between seventeen and forty-five – approximately eleven million in all – were to be shipped to the continent as slave labour. The rate of exchange was pegged at 9.60 Reichsmarks to the pound sterling. S.S. *Standartenführer* Dr Franz Six prepared to take up headquarters in London, to implement the rounding up of all persons ranging from Churchill to Noël Coward on a 2,700-name black list. 'My dear,' Rebecca West, also prominent on the list, commented drily to Coward, 'the people we would have been seen dead with.'

One British family, however, was singled out for élitist treatment from the first, the special responsibility of S.S. *Haupsturmführer* Otto Begus, who was based near Boulogne. On

D-Day Begus, along with twenty-three young officers and a task force of 100 men, was to parachute directly into the grounds of Buckingham Palace to seize King George VI, his Queen and their two daughters, Elizabeth and Margaret, for with them held hostage Hitler foresaw a speedy end to the war.

The only Wehrmacht unit to have pin-ups of the British Royal Family in their billets, for recognition purposes, Begus and his men had firm instructions to give the Army, not the Nazi, salute when face to face with Royalty. By now they had rehearsed their greeting so often they knew it by heart: 'Good morning, your Majesties. The German High Command presents its respectful compliments. My duty, on the instructions of the Führer, is to inform you that you are under the protection of the German Armed Forces . . .'

As the British steeled themselves for what Churchill called 'their finest hour', Roosevelt took time out to examine the budding evidence of budding U.S. defence.

At Ogdenburg, New York, on 17 August, along with Secretary of War Stimson and Governor Lehman, the President rode in brilliant sunshine through the rolling green of St Lawrence County to witness a formidable display of manpower. Eight times in six hours his motorcade pulled up before stiffly-assembled divisions of the 94,000 men of the First Army of the United States. Eight times he heard the 21-gun salutes, followed by ruffles and flourishes; eight times he sat at attention for the national anthem, while Old Glory stirred in the breeze above the regimental colours dipped in salute.

When it came to war machines, the picture was bleaker. The President saw just five anti-aircraft guns, forty First World War 155-mm howitzers, a large number of 75-mm guns and approaching 100 aircraft. There were no automatic rifles in sight, and no anti-tank guns, with good reason: there were no tanks. How was the equipment of the 44th Division, Roosevelt asked Major General Clifford Powell. 'It's pretty good, what there is of it,' Powell conceded. 'But we are using broomsticks for machine guns and rain pipes for mortars.'

The President laughed ruefully. Everybody, he admitted, seemed to be in the same boat.

In a sense, the nation's growing awareness of its fragile frontiers was working to Roosevelt's advantage. Much had changed since the June day when he had confided his misgivings to Secretary Ickes as to the wisdom of supplying destroyers to Britain. Despite heated isolationist speeches against conscription in Congress, Gallup polls showed that 71 per cent of American citizens now favoured it. The fall of France had influenced more than the President's decision to run for a third term. On 28 June, Congress had passed the Naval Defense Act, which now permitted the sale of naval equipment provided the Chief of Naval Operations, Admiral Harold Raynford Stark, certified it as surplus. Now Roosevelt saw a way of belatedly acceding to Churchill's long-standing plea for destroyers, for the United States had 200 old four-stackers in cold storage.

On 13 August, four days before setting out on his defence survey, he had hit on a way to break the log jam. It would be a straight Yankee horse-trade, for if, in return for fifty over-age flush-decker destroyers, Britain gave the United States the right to fortify and defend eight crucial British-held bases in the Atlantic – Newfoundland, Bermuda's reefbound Great Sound, the Bahamas, Jamaica, Antigua, St Lucia, Trinidad and British Guiana – Roosevelt, invoking the Naval Defense Act plus his executive privilege, could successfully bypass Congress, provided that Stark agreed.

Thus Stark could, on 21 August, endorse the transfer with a clear conscience, pencilling at the end of his memo, 'This is the time when a "feller" needs a friend.'

It was, Roosevelt would claim to Congress on 3 September, 'the most important action since the Louisiana Purchase', for the bases offered much-needed protection to the Panama Canal, Canada and Mexico. The gesture won him unexpected allies. As a Republican, Stimson was in frequent touch with William Allen White and his Committee to Aid the Allies, and White could give him assurance that the Republican candidate for the forthcoming election, Wendell Willkie, would in general support the plan, although Willkie later castigated the bypassing of Congress as 'the most dictatorial and arbitrary act of any President in the history of the United States'.

Support came, too, from the doughty old General John J.

Pershing, Commander of the First World War American Expeditionary Force, who advocated backing the 'destroyer deal' in a broadcast on a nation-wide radio hook-up. 'If the destroyers help save the British Navy,' Pershing reasoned sagely, 'they may save us from the dangers and hardships of another war.'

Even so, it was a colossal political risk for Roosevelt to run, one which he admitted might have cost him the election. 'Congress is going to raise hell over this,' he prophesied to his secretary, Grace Tully, anticipating the storm of protest that was to arise from Capitol Hill, though the Republican press gave him an even rougher ride. 'If we want to get into war,' the *Chicago Tribune* opined, 'the destroyers offer as good a way as any of accomplishing the purpose.' 'The United States,' claimed the *New York Daily News*, 'has one foot in the war and one foot on a banana peel.' 'Of all the sucker real-estate deals in history, this is the worst,' sneered the *St Louis Post Dispatch*, 'and the President of the United States is the sucker.'

The Third Reich thought otherwise. On 6 September, the first eight of the old destroyers, looking like absurd little floating factories with their flat decks and four tall funnels, steamed into the hill-fringed harbour of Halifax, Nova Scotia, where 2,000 Canadian and British tars were waiting – 'by the long arm of coincidence', as Churchill explained guilelessly – to receive them. 'The deal,' exploded the German Chargé in Washington, Hans Thomsen, 'is evidence of Roosevelt's ruthless determination, devious modes ... and total disregard of congressional and military advice.'

Roosevelt had acted none too soon. Like a running torch applied to tinder, Hitler's New Order was engulfing much that remained of free Europe.

Ever since the Führer began his redemption of minorities in Czechoslovakia and Poland, Romania, too, had been ripe for partitioning. The first step had come in June, when Russia, to the anguish of the venal King Carol, had moved into Bessarabia and northern Bucovina. Now Hitler, intent on maintaining absolute peace within the Balkans, became painfully conscious that Romania was still pockmarked with islands of foreigners

225

whose parent states coveted their return. Two such large and solid islands were the Bulgarian minority in Dobruja and the Hungarian minority in south-east Transylvania, almost at the country's dead centre.

King Carol, who had wooed the Axis too late in life, now realized that Hitler was exacting his price. As the summer of 1940 neared its end, Hungary was preparing to go to war for Transylvania, which Romania had taken from her following the First World War. To Hitler such a war was unthinkable. Not only would it cut off the Reich from its main source of crude oil; it could conceivably prompt the Russians to step in and occupy all Romania.

Hitler acted fast. On 2 August, he ordered Carol to settle the claims of both Hungary and Bulgaria before 1 September. When the King stalled and vacillated, Foreign Minister von Ribbentrop and Italy's Count Ciano lost patience. Romania was ordered to submit the dispute to arbitration at an Axis-convened conference held in Vienna's Belvedere Palace on 30 August. When the Romanian Foreign Minister, Mihail Manolescu, saw the map that the Axis powers had drawn up, ceding not only Dobruja to Bulgaria, but 16,000 square miles of Transylvania to Hungary he fainted dead away across the conference table. Physicians had to revive him with spirits of camphor.

Though the 'Vienna Award' was received sourly by Stalin, who had not been consulted, Hitler, for the time being, had achieved all that he wanted. Both Romania and Hungary would continue vying for his favours, the one in the hope that she might regain what she had lost, the other in the hope of further bounty.

In Bucharest, Romania's capital, the smouldering resentment of the people at Carol's sell-outs now exploded into rage. Shocked and sullen crowds milled before the King's Palace and the German and Italian Legations, shouting, 'Fight the Hungarians.' Across the muddy Pruth River, dividing Romania from Bessarabia, the Red Army lay in waiting. Promptly Hitler sent word to the capital that unless the disorders stopped Germany would occupy all Romania with troops, ringing down the curtain on the land of Carol.

The King saw the red light. On 5 September, he entrusted the reins of power to General Ion Antonescu, Chief of the Fascist Iron Guard and a friend of Hitler's. Antonescu responded by giving his sovereign marching orders. Romania wanted no more of its king; if he valued his life he should leave while the going was good.

One day later Carol agreed to abdicate in favour of his son, 18-year-old Prince Michael.

His farewell to the land he had mulcted for so long was suitably Ruritanian. He and his red-haired mistress Magda Lupescu, under the travelling aliases 'Mr and Mrs Carol Caraiman', fled the country by night in a 9-coach train with three bullet-proof automobiles, the Royal stamp collection, four Rembrandts, sixteen poodles, six pet white turkeys, $2,500,000 worth of jewels, a flock of peacocks and a million dollar haul of gold coins.

As the Royal special careened towards the Yugoslavian frontier, armed members of the Iron Guard were lying in wait at the railway station of Timisoara. Forewarned, Carol had told the engineers to stop for nothing and nobody. Amid a hail of bullets the train pounded through Timisoara, as Carol dived into a bath-tub and his foppish former Lord Chamberlain, Ernest Udarianu, took refuge in a lavatory. Only Madame Lupescu remained superbly unruffled.

The King's fellow dictator, Benito Mussolini, at once sent a pilot train full of Italian police to lead Carol's special from Yugoslavia across Italy to Switzerland. At journey's end, Lugano, the King became belatedly aware that one of the locomotive's firemen, in running the gauntlet of bullets, had been wounded in the arm. To mark his gratitude, Carol handed him a two-dollar tip.

The engineer surveyed the coin judicially. Then he flung it in the former monarch's face.

The British were soon aware that Hermann Göring had switched his aerial priorities yet again. For threefold reasons – reprisals for an R.A.F. raid on Berlin, the hope of flushing up the R.A.F. fighters into free combat, to wield a lethal blow against dockland traffic – the Luftwaffe's target was now London.

Now it would become a war against people, a war that Londoners had not known and would not relish.

One man with cause for concern was Assistant Divisional Officer Geoffrey Vaughan Blackstone of the London Fire Brigade. Aged thirty, a six-foot-plus ex-public schoolboy, Blackstone had been three years with the Brigade and was already noted for his trenchant views. On the afternoon of Saturday, 7 September, Blackstone had no apparent motive for worry; stretched out on the grass at a friend's tennis party in Dulwich, South London, he was enjoying a rare spell off duty from Fire Brigade Headquarters, Lambeth.

But Blackstone was looking to the future. Of the 30,000-strong Brigade, 28,000 were wartime auxiliaries, some conscripts, more of them volunteers, but all with one thing in common: at least 90 per cent of them had never tackled a fire of any kind.

In Blackstone's view, the auxiliaries had had a raw deal from the first. Unlike peacetime firemen, who were fully kitted-out, the newcomers lacked not only topcoats but a change of uniform; any man getting wet in line of duty had to shiver in his underwear until his tunic and trousers had dried out. In the long lull of the phoney war, the public had singled them out as scroungers and parasites, deriding them as 'the darts brigade', a lot so unenviable that many men had quit in protest. By June 1940, alarmed by the exodus, the Home Office had been forced to 'freeze' them in the service, and thus Blackstone wondered how such unwilling volunteers would face up to danger if danger came.

Few others on this warm sunny afternoon gave danger a thought. Couples lay flirting on the grass in St James's Park; others were queueing for theatre matinées – Celia Johnson in *Rebecca* or Robert Donat in *The Devil's Disciple*. Even over many coastal districts, random raiders were now commonplace; as the first London-bound raiders of *Oberst* Johannes Fink's Bomber Group 2 swept over the cattle-market at Canterbury, Kent, a newsboy by the traffic signals hailed them cheerily: 'Hey, wait for the lights to turn green!' At Shepperton, on the Thames, spectators at a Saturday afternoon cricket match broke into brisk applause from the pavilion as a batsman's stumps flew: 'Oh, well bowled, sir – a beauty!'

Looking upwards, they saw Heinkels at 15,000 feet sliding towards the blue haze that marked the city's boundary and thought complacently: they'll never get to London.

One man was determined that they should: *Reichsmarschall* Hermann Göring, who had already arrived at Cap Blanc Nez, on the Channel, in his private train, code-named Asia, with its ornate mahogany-panelled saloons. For Göring, at this eleventh hour, all the magic and soon-discarded formulas of the past weeks – Stukas, Zerstörers, radar attacks, close fighter escorts – had boiled down to one solution: *he* must infuse the fighter pilots with the bellyfire they so obviously lacked.

To a reporter with a recording van, Göring announced that he personally had taken command of the battle. Watching him, Werner Mölders wondered why he was wearing pink patent-leather boots.

But as the teleprinter chattered out its first reports Göring grew more angry still: of the 247 bombers dispatched to the target, forty would not return. The reason, although the *Reichsmarschall* refused to admit it, was plain enough to commanders like Mölders. By insisting that a fighter escort 600-strong accompany the bombers, Göring had created such a mêlée in the sky over London that fighters had been too busy dodging each other to stop the R.A.F. taking toll of their bombers.

On 7 September, Göring was blind and deaf to any such logic. Without further ado, each fighter group and wing-commander was ordered to report to his private train for a bitter diatribe. 'Your job is to protect the bombers,' he assailed them, 'and each time you fall down on it.' When one man next to Mölders raised the question of British fighters, Göring swung on him: 'Don't tell *me* the sky is full of enemies – I know they haven't more than seventy fighters left.'

It was in vain that Mölders and the others sought to defend their men. Impatiently, Göring brushed their arguments aside: the pilots were cowards.

In London, where the air-raid sirens wailed around 5 p.m., the realization that the city was under attack was slow to dawn at first. Armed with little more than a whistle, a white tin hat marked 'W', the knowledge that Lewisite gas smelt of geraniums, and that bomb blast travelled in all directions, 9,000 London air-raid wardens and their part-time unpaid volunteers set out to face their first blitz. For others the first intimation of disaster came in observing an apparent freak of nature. Tonight, it seemed, the sun was not setting in the west, over Putney and Wimbledon, but in the east. Above the docks at Poplar and Whitechapel, the whole skyline was a shifting orange glow.

From his office roof by St James's Park, the scientist, Dr R. V. Jones, watched the blaze with a sense that he was beaten before he started. Three months after identifying the Knickebein beams, Jones was on the eve of coming to grips with the mysterious X-Gerät system – a device he believed to be a vastly more sophisticated refinement of Knickebein. Now the gloomy thought struck him; even if the beams were traced and jammed, a fire like this would be a marker beacon in itself.

In Chiswick, West London, a social worker, Nesca Robb, recited to herself, scarcely crediting that it could be true, an old childish jingle: '*London's burning, London's burning, Fire, fire! Fire, fire! Pour on water! Pour on water!*'

It was an apt jingle, but in some areas the fires were already so intense that water was useless. At Surrey Commercial Docks, on the Thames at Rotherhithe, Geoffrey Blackstone, who had hastened from his tennis party to take command, found 250 acres of resinous timber stacked twenty feet high burning with a dry and terrible crackling; from his control car he watched water pumped by fireboats from a river already choked with blazing barges evaporate in hissing clouds as it struck the warehouses. Closer to, even the wooden blocks that formed the dockland roadway burned with a merry glare. From Paget's Wharf Fire Station, in the heart of the conflagration, the hardpressed Station Officer Plimlett, using the professionals' word for fire-engines, phoned Fire Brigade Headquarters: 'Send every pump you've got. The whole bloody world's on fire.'

It was a night when every man and woman had cause to hold their breath, for as dusk fell it was plain that London's ordeal was far from over. Under cover of darkness, the bombers were still coming, unimpeded now by British fighters, to stoke up the fires that the pathfinders had lit until 4 a.m. on the Sunday. From the Colonnade of St Paul's Cathedral, the Dean, the Very

Reverend William Matthews, dressed, like the other volunteers on his watch, in battle-dress and steel helmet, gazed with silent awe on a city whose Fire Brigade had now logged 1,000 separate calls.

Close at hand, someone muttered, 'It's like the end of the world,' and another voice replied quietly, 'It's the end of *a* world.'

By 8 p.m., on this apocalyptic night, the British saw this as the truth. Nobody viewed it as a raid to preface peace terms, to avenge Berlin, or to draw the R.A.F. into combat. This non-stop air armada could mean one thing only.

The invasion fleet was coming. It was H-Hour.

'The Way Across the Channel
Will Soon be Clear'

7 September–27 September 1940

From the War Cabinet downwards, this belief was common: Hitler was making good his boast. At 8.07 p.m. Lieutenant-General Alan Brooke, from his headquarters at St Paul's School, West London, issued the codeword 'Cromwell', signifying Alert No. 1, to the Army's Eastern and Southern commands – 'Invasion imminent and probable within twelve hours.'

At Gosport Army Co-operation Command Station, on Portsmouth Harbour, Pilot Officer 'Nobby' Clarke, R.A.F., in a Skua target-towing plane, had word: 'Get cracking – light all the points, working from east to west.' From Weymouth, 150 miles east along the coast to Beachy Head, Clarke knew that on every available landing beach petrol pipelines jutted almost level with the water's surface. Now his task was to dive-bomb each with incendiaries, to transform the inshore waters into a raging cauldron of fire.

Since early July, the newly-formed Petroleum Warfare Department had been working all out to install some 200 'Defile Flame traps', ranging from Dover, Kent, to Fowey, Cornwall. Now their testing time had come. On the main roads leading inland to Canterbury and Maidstone, in Kent, and Horsham, in Sussex, troops stood by beside 600-gallon tanks, sited ten feet above road level, ready to spray a petrol and gas-oil mixture on to the advancing Germans – pumping at a rate of thirty gallons a minute, to burn at a heat of 500 degrees Fahrenheit. Professor Lindemann had grimly assured Churchill: 'Nothing could live in it for two minutes.'

But why had the Germans delayed? Flying east towards Littlehampton, Pilot Officer Clarke could see no invasion barges: only the grey wash of the sea at sundown, white surf creaming on the sand. Then abruptly his radio-telephone crackled. Without explanation he was recalled to Gosport.

Along the south coast confusion multiplied. At Folkstone's Hotel Mecca, panicky officials whipped out Mrs Lillian Ivory's telephone, then remembered that her boarding house was Intelligence Corps Headquarters and hastily brought it back again. Inland, on the Berkshire downs, Land Girl Barbara Hornsey, mounted on her black horse, Nero, was one of a select vigilante patrol, anxiously scanning the sky for descending paratroops. If she spotted them, her instructions were clear: to gallop helter-skelter for the nearest telephone box and use the twopence provided from Government funds, and returnable after each mission, to call the nearest Home Guard unit.

It was a night of strange alarms. On the drive from Brighton to Worthing, motorists kept their passes at the ready: bayonets glinted eerily at every checkpoint. At Dover, bugles sounded along the white cliffs; in a score of villages from Portsmouth to Swansea, Home Guardsmen, unbidden, rang the church bells, to warn against invasion, a lonely tolling over dark fields. In Reg Cooke's little coastguard cottage at Pett, Sussex, the telephone shrilled and the Home Guard was on the line: 'They've landed at Lydd.'

Peering east through the darkness, Cooke could see nothing – and in any case he had only a duck gun. He and his wife Lydia went to bed.

All that night, the Home Guard stood by, half a million men alerted for the first invasion in more than a century, gripping a weird armoury of weapons – from assegais, the relics of a spectacle supplied from London's Drury Lane Theatre, to boarding pikes from Nelson's *Victory*. At Stubbington, Hampshire, Colonel Barrow told his Home Guard company: 'They may be landing paratroops behind you, but there will be no turning back.' Doggedly his farmworkers and shepherds agreed – though only one among them had a ·22 rifle, and the rest had stout sticks.

All next day, Sunday, 8 September, strange rumours multiplied in the Channel ports. In Folkestone, the people numbered Dover's fate in hours: the Germans had completed a cross-

Channel tunnel and were preparing to launch bombs against Dover torpedo-fashion. Dover knew the worst about Folkestone: their ground defences had caved in, and German planes were already operational from near-by Hawkinge Airfield. Station Officer Thomas Goodman, a London fireman on relief at Dover, heard of an attempted landing at Sandwich Bay, fourteen miles north: the inshore waters, it was said, were black with German dead. Taking a staff car, Goodman set off – to find only baking sands and blue sea, not a soul in sight.

In Whitehall, hastily recalled civil servants made contingency plans to transfer the Government en bloc to Malvern College, Worcestershire, although one key figure had made it plain that he was staying put to the last. 'I do not think much will be left of Downing Street after a few weeks,' Churchill wrote to Chamberlain's wife, Anne. 'I propose to lead a troglodyte existence with several "trogs".'

Unknown to all save the Cabinet and the General Staff an invisible army, now almost 5,000 strong, was preparing for a similar existence. Operating under Major (later Major-General) Colin McVean Gubbins, a veteran of Narvik, the bulk of these Auxiliary Units Groups were concentrated on a southern coastal strip no more than thirty miles deep – men dressed, for security reasons, in the khaki battle-dress of ordinary Home Guardsmen. But no Home Guardsman, in 1940, ever saw weapons such as theirs.

The inside pockets of their battle-dress blouses bulged with charges of 'plastic' – a form of cyclonite three times as powerful as TNT. Their underground caches in outbuildings and chicken runs were stacked with weapons unknown to the men of Dunkirk: the first Thompson sub-machine guns imported from the United States, Piat anti-tank weapons, phosphorus handgrenades, tyre-bursting mines disguised as lumps of coal or horse manure. Selected snipers among them carried ·22 B.S.A. rifles, fitted with powerful telescopic sights and silencers, capable of picking off German officers and their tracker dogs from a mile away.

Their hide-outs were a triumph of ingenuity. By December, there were more than 300 of them, sited six feet below ground, twenty feet by ten feet wide, designed to house up to seven men for days at a time if need be. At Charing, Kent, Captain Norman Field's 'operational base' was a converted rabbit warren sited beneath a sheep trough – but other men were holing up in one-time badger setts, camouflaged by rotting farm carts, in abandoned Cornish tin-mines, even beneath cucumber frames. On the Bowes-Lyon estate in Berwickshire, Scotland, owned by King George's brother-in-law, resistants had first to scale a cliff overhanging a salmon river, then leap for their cave through a waterfall.

Most of this Army were men attuned to move by night – poachers, gamekeepers, fishermen, ghillies – but others were natural-born soldiers of fortune, unable to resist a challenge. At Bilting, Kent, Captain Peter Fleming, Old Etonian, author and jungle explorer, had already mined every house in the district likely to attract the Germans, using milk-churns packed with high explosive. North of the Thames at Kelvedon, Essex, Captain Andrew Croft, one-time A.D.C. to the Maharajah of Cooch Behar, and former secretary of Cambridge's Fitzwilliam Museum, ran his private army from the sanctuary of his father's vicarage. Captain Anthony Quayle, a Shakespearean actor more used to grease-paint than burnt cork, now spent his nights on the moors of Northumberland, dogging imaginary tanks.

All these men had their secret letter-boxes – in garbage heaps or abandoned birds' nests – where messages could be left for collection by 'cut-outs', along with out-station transmitters, sometimes sited in pub cellars or in disused farm privies. For camouflage, their radio aerials were buried half an inch deep in the trunks of trees, the channels filled in with plaster of Paris and painted to match the bark. All of them were geared to one purpose, and would remain so for the foreseeable future: to go under cover if the Germans invaded, to remain there, living rough, by day, to launch hit-and-run raids by night, to fight on as they had been taught to fight – killing until they triumphed or until they themselves were killed.

Meanwhile on Saturday, 14 September, one week after the dockland blitz, a heated argument was taking place in Berlin between Hitler and his service advisers. The Chief of the

Luftwaffe General Staff, General Hans Jeschonnek, was maintaining stubbornly that there had been 'no mass panic [in London] up to now because residential districts have not been attacked or destroyed'. Jeschonnek now sought permission to extend his target area, a plea backed by Admiral Raeder, who felt that without that 'mass panic', Sea-Lion stood little chance of success.

Hitler did not agree. 'Attacks on military objectives,' he ruled, 'are always the most important because they destroy irreplaceable war material.' This was sound reasoning. After three nights of blitz, the Port of London had been closed to ocean-going shipping and vessels were being re-routed to ports all over Britain.

Jeschonnek, Hitler conceded, could extend his area to railway stations and power supplies but 'bombing with the object of causing a mass panic must be left to the last'.

To some it seemed that the spectre of Franklin Roosevelt hovered over the conference table, for Hitler went further still. 'Terror bombing might invite reprisals against German towns,' he pointed out, 'to say nothing of having an adverse effect on neutral opinion in the United States.' In Rome, the U.S. Ambassador William Phillips had already warned Count Ciano that a bombardment of London with many civilian deaths might yet induce America to intervene.

The alternative – one last massed London raid to induce the R.A.F. to come up and be destroyed – was timed for Sunday, 15 September.

At 11 a.m. on this historic morning, the German formations were soon apparent as V-shaped blips of light on the convex glass screens of the coastal radar stations: wide deep steadily-beating echoes swimming into focus, arising from the mists of the morning.

By 11.03 a.m., Wing Commander Eric Douglas-Jones, Duty Controller in the Operations Room at H.Q. 11 Group, Fighter Command, could wait no longer. Already every bulb on the panels lining the opposite wall was glowing red – a signal that every squadron throughout Fighter Command's six sectors was standing by. He reached for the first of six telephones, and automatically, thirty-five miles away, a bulb lit up on the Sector

Controller's desk at Biggin Hill, in Kent. The day's first squadrons were to patrol Canterbury at 20,000 feet.

At 11.25 a.m., with every 11 Group squadron now committed, a 60-strong wing from 12 Group were speeding from Duxford, Essex, to lend support over London.

To the first pilots airborne, it seemed that this morning the Luftwaffe, as never before, held the sky – as if a dense black swarm of insects was advancing, trailing ever-lengthening miles of black ribbon. As they drew nearer, a high and watery sun picked out their strange and colourful insignia: the green heart of Major Hannes Trautloft's 54th Fighter Group, the poised black sledgehammer of *Oberst* Johannes Fink's Dorniers, the frowning eagle's head of Werner Mölders.

Of the twenty-one R.A.F. squadrons airborne, twenty-one intercepted the raiders, though not all with equal success. Over Biggin Hill at 18,000 feet Squadron Leader Ernest McNab's No. 1 Canadian Squadron never saw the group of 109s that bounced them from the sun; only two of their Hurricanes even closed with the raiders. Above Gravesend, 41 Squadron, equally baulked, watched yet more bombers sliding towards London.

As Big Ben boomed noon, 148 bombers broke through to the centre of the capital, raining bombs to the south-west and south-east, one Dornier landing an unexploded bomb in King George VI's back garden at Buckingham Palace. For this *lèse-majesté* the pilot paid dearly; Sergeant Ray Holmes, of 504 Squadron, hot on its trail, delivered a burst so lethal that his victim crashed with pile-driving force in the forecourt of Victoria Station. At the same time, Holmes, his Hurricane hit, baled out, landing feet first in a dustbin in near-by Ebury Bridge Road.

By now, Mölders and every German fighter pilot was anxiously watching his fuel gauge, knowing that the moment to break for the Channel must come within seconds. At this psychological moment, the 60-strong 12 Group wing led by the legless Squadron Leader Douglas Bader fell like falcons from above.

The sky over London was suddenly a whirling wheeling arabesque of fighters – in Bader's words 'the finest shambles I'd ever been in'. But for the German bombers, suddenly shorn of protection, these were moments of naked terror. High above the city, crewmen were baling out from a Dornier which broke ludicrously in half, level with the black crosses. Another Dornier fell from the sky before a shot had been fired; to those watching it seemed the pilot must have reached the peak where the strain could be borne no longer.

As Major Hannes Trautloft of Fighter Group 54 noted in his diary: 'Who'd know that it was Sunday if it hadn't been announced on the radio?'

By 2 p.m., in this last effort to force the R.A.F. into a fight to extinction, the Luftwaffe had committed every plane they could muster – and every R.A.F. plane still serviceable was airborne to meet the challenge. At H.Q. 11 Group, Winston Churchill, who had arrived to join the Controller on the dais, asked the Air Officer Commanding, Air Vice-Marshal Keith Park, 'What other reserves have we?'

Noting that every bulb was glowing red once more, Park admitted soberly: 'There are none.'

At this moment, Sector Controllers all over southern England were marshalling their squadrons as Wing Commander Douglas-Jones instructed them and the radio telephones were crackling with the weird call-signs in use between sectors and squadrons. 'Hello, Garter, this is Caribou, your message received and understood' ... 'Turkey leader, this is Runic, patrol Maidstone, angels twenty' ... 'Laycock Red Leader to Calla Leader ... watch it, Calla Leader, here the bastards come!'

They were coming in force; Pilot Officer Patrick Barthropp, who after his very first sortie that morning had noted in his log-book, 'Thousands of them,' now added a mental rider, '*Still* thousands of them.' But the Luftwaffe were destined to pay a bitter price; a two-hour respite had given the R.A.F. the chance to refuel and rearm, and even though Dowding was 170 pilots below strength, many pilots were gripped, as rarely in the past, by the fierce elation of combat.

The sky was suddenly a clawing, stalling mass of fighters, bent on destruction, fighting within a cube eighty miles long by thirty miles broad, more than five miles high: a battle that within thirty minutes would number above 200 individual dog-fights.

Once more deprived of fighter cover, the bombers were to suffer most. Above Maidstone, Pilot Officer Mike Cooper-Slipper, 605 Squadron, knew that his Hurricane had taken fire, then saw three Dorniers dead ahead of him, closing in. With a sudden snap decision to ram them, Cooper-Slipper bored in on the middle plane, conscious only of 'a swishing and a swooshing' as the shattered Dornier fell steeply to port. At 20,000 feet, ripping three fingernails from his right hand, Cooper-Slipper baled out.

Over Appledore, Kent, seeing two unescorted Dorniers approaching, Pilot Officer Paddy Stephenson, 607 Squadron, came to the same decision. With no time to take aim, Stephenson charged both with a left and right blow from both wings, then baled out above the blazing bombers – probably the only Battle of Britain pilot to bring down two German aircraft without firing a shot.

To more than one bomber pilot, glimpsing no fighter escort above and astern, it seemed fruitless even to attempt the journey. Airborne from Juvaincourt, in a Junkers 88 of the 77th Bomber Group, *Oberleutnant* Dietrich Peltz found the whole sky empty of 109s; without hesitation he sent his entire 4,000 lb bomb load tumbling towards the Channel, then turned for home. Even the fighter pilots, who for six weeks had heard Göring's hollow promises that the R.A.F. were a write-off, found their cynicism hard to contain. As yet more glinting cohorts of Spitfires hove into view, *Oberleutnant* Ludwig Franzisket of Fighter Group 27 broke radio silence with a sardonic comment: 'Here comes those last fifty Spitfires!'

At 3.50 p.m., as the last raiders receded across the Channel, it seemed a day for tributes. At Marden, Kent, a gang of field-labourers lifting potatoes rose as one man when a squadron of Spitfires roared overhead, lifting their caps in salute. At Maidstone, near by, a shot-down German pilot acknowledged his opponent's merit to his captors: 'Well done, Spitfire.' To the surprise of Wing Commander Douglas-Jones, the 11 Group Controller, Churchill suddenly clapped him on the shoulder with a heartfelt, 'Good show, old boy.'

It was hours before Fighter Command knew the extent of their losses – twenty-six planes, thirteen pilots – though the legend of their counter-claim was to persist for many years: a total bag of 183 German planes. Within days, Air Ministry crash investigators had arrived at the truth: the German losses totalled no more than fifty-six, of which thirty-four were bombers. Yet another truth was becoming equally apparent: the Luftwaffe's attempts were slackening, and the R.A.F. was still a force to be reckoned with.

One day earlier, in Berlin, Hitler had noted: 'Four to five days' good weather are required to achieve decisive results.' But, by 17 September, Raeder had dictated for the War Diary: 'The enemy air force is by no means defeated. On the contrary, it shows increasing activity. The Führer therefore decides to postpone Sea-Lion indefinitely.' From now on, the onslaught on Russia, Operation Barbarossa, would assume full priority.

In a rare moment of honesty, Göring confessed ruefully to General Student: 'We'd forgotten that the English fought best with their backs to the wall.' But within days he had retreated into fantasy, assuring himself that night bombing alone would break British morale. 'After all, man isn't a nocturnal animal,' was his solemn reasoning.

Did the decision rankle with Hitler? No man could be sure. To *Oberst* Martin Harlinghausen, Chief of Staff of 10th Flying Corps, the Führer seemed to take it philosophically: 'I want colonies I can walk to without getting my feet wet.' Werner Mölders, though, was less certain. On 23 September he flew to Berlin to meet Hitler for the first time, and receive the award of the Oak Leaves to the Knight's Cross. At first Hitler seemed 'almost fatherly', taking both his hands, steering him to a settee in the Reich Chancellery, appearing well informed about the Channel battles.

Suddenly Mölders made a random remark: 'The way across the Channel will soon be clear.' Abruptly Hitler's face clouded. Totally disregarding Mölders's remark, he turned away from him. 'It was as though, spiritually, he was enclosed within himself,' Mölders was to recall. 'Like a snail in its shell. No one may enter.'

Again Mölders felt a twinge of doubt. Wasn't Sea-Lion

going to come off after all? And, if the project had been abandoned, one factor was more perplexing yet: why were they still fighting?

Aboard the S.S. *City of Benares*, three days outward bound from Liverpool, ninety British youngsters, aged between five and fifteen, some accompanied by their parents, along with a sprinkling of adults bound on business, rejoiced that they had left bombs and battles behind.

None of the 408 souls aboard was more content than Sonia Bech, the 11-year-old schoolgirl from Bognor Regis, who in June had watched the war transform her quiet Sussex coastline into a cat's cradle of barbed wire and concrete pill-boxes. After Dunkirk, just as Sonia had anticipated, Marguerite, her mother, had finally taken the plunge and written off to an uncle by marriage in Montreal. Could he offer her and her three children a home for the duration?

Since the fall of the Low Countries, 3,000 children – some State-aided, some financed by their families – had gone to start new lives in the United States, Canada and South Africa.

There had been the pang of leaving her Scottie, Mackie, behind with relatives, but Sonia, romantic and impulsive, had revelled in the voyage from the start. The 11,081-ton *City of Benares*, flagship of the Ellerman line and formerly on the India run, was Sonia's idea of a dream ship: the Lascar stewards, with their pale blue and white uniforms and ornate blue sashes, the mountains of American ice-cream on which the youngsters gorged themselves twice daily, seemed part of a vanishing world. After rations that had now scaled down to 8 oz of sugar, 4 oz of butter and tea, 2 oz of bacon and 1s. 10d. worth of meat weekly; life aboard the *City of Benares*, for Sonia, was filled with a glamour known only at secondhand from books and movies.

For three days now the weather had been choppy, but the Bechs didn't let this deter them. Barbara, fourteen, the family bookworm, had found the ship's library. Derek, aged nine, displayed to envious friends the sackful of hardware he had gleaned during the Battle of Britain from the fringe of Tangmere airfield: blackened ME 109 pistons, part of a charred flying helmet. Sonia preened herself over her new camel-hair coat from D. H. Evans' department store and her six pairs of new silk stockings.

At eleven, Sonia was too extrovert to have premonitions, although some adults had been disturbed when the ship sailed on Friday, 13 September. Nor was Sonia aware that the U-Boat menace coupled with the shortage of flotilla craft decreed that the Royal Navy could not provide ocean convoys with anti-submarine escorts more than 300 miles west of Ireland.

If the passengers were ignorant, the crew had no illusions. Fashion designer Digby Morton, on a business promotion trip for the Board of Trade, along with his wife Phyllis, had been chatting on the first day out with the ship's Master, Captain Landles Nicholl. 'Why,' the Mortons asked, 'hadn't Nicholl, a family man, evacuated his own children along with the others?' The Captain met their gaze steadily. 'I'd rather put their hands in the fire,' was all he said.

At 1 a.m., on 17 September, the escort – a destroyer and two sloops – withdrew. Convoy OB 213, nineteen ships strong and wallowing at eight-and-a-half knots, half the *Benares*' speed, was now adjudged to be in safe waters.

As night fell, a Force 5 gale was raking the Atlantic. Towards 10 p.m., the *City of Benares* was 600 miles off the British coast, approaching latitude 56 43 North, longitude 23 15 West. At this hour, most of the children, Sonia included, were sleeping soundly. None aboard the ship was aware that half a mile to port *Kapitänleutnant* Heinrich Bleichrodt, of U-Boat 48, had the merchantman squarely in his periscope. Bleichrodt already knew the ship's name through monitoring her wireless traffic, but not her cargo or her destination. At 10.05 p.m., as 500 lb of torpedo streaked through the water, the *City of Benares* to Bleichrodt was no more than a routine naval target.

For most passengers still awake, the first impact was minimal. Fifteen-year-old Anthony Quinton, sitting with his mother in the first-class lounge, noticed a mighty cloud of dust arise from the pile carpet – but the Lascar steward, serving coffee, was still inquiring politely, 'Black or white, sir?' Phyllis Digby Morton, already in her cabin ready for bed, was conscious of a strange smell 'as if a huge wax match was dying out'.

Others came swiftly face to face with disaster. Mary Cornish, a 41-year-old music teacher and volunteer escort for the Children's Overseas Reception Board, was groping through the darkened alleyway towards the children's cabins when she stopped short. Where the cabin class bathrooms had been there was only a black abyss. A vast hole had been blown in the liner amidships.

In fact, the torpedo had exploded in No. 5 Hold on the ship's port side, blasting away the hatches. Water was rushing into the lower hold, and the vessel was settling slowly by the stern, where the State-aided evacuees were quartered.

Now alarm bells were jangling urgently through the darkness – plainly audible to Barbara Bech, still awake and browsing through a library book. Shaking the sleepy Sonia awake, she ran to the next cabin to arouse her mother and Derek.

Dazedly, groping their way through a misty blue curtain of high-explosive fumes, the Bechs followed the instructions they had been given: if the alarm bells ring, muster in the first-class lounge for further instructions. But in the brightly-lit lounge a curious calm prevailed. Some passengers were still drinking, others playing bridge, wondering what the 'bang' had portended. Suddenly a ship's officer rushed in: 'My God, what are you all doing here? Don't you realize the ship is sinking? Get to the boats fast!'

At No. 4 boat station, the Bechs found more confusion. A bitter sleet was driving from the sea; distress flares were livid against the night sky. Though the lifeboats should have been slung from the davits for the passengers to climb into, most had already been amateurishly launched and were bobbing far below. The resourceful Barbara Bech shinned down a rope and scrambled aboard one, but all the time the lifeboat was drifting clear across the choppy sea. The last thing Barbara saw was Derek, incongruously wearing his school cap, outlined against the rails, cradled in a seaman's arms.

Now the presence of a B.B.C. technician, Eric Davies, saved the remainder of the Bech family. 'Come quickly,' he called to Sonia, motioning them forward. 'We'll find rafts.' Somehow, though the rafts were 6 feet square, three feet deep, and buoyed with canisters, Davies managed to lift them clear of the deck and hurl them in. In the howling darkness of the Atlantic night, the Bechs found themselves scrambling down a rope ladder and jumping into space, Sonia dismally conscious that her new camel-hair coat was slicked with black oil. As they sought to maintain hand-hold on the raft, Davies was all the time swimming beside them, pushing them away from the terrible suction of the dying ship.

Already the sea bobbed with flotsam: potted plants, wicker chairs, life-jackets, the floating bodies of men and women desperately treading water. Not far away the *City of Benares* was listing like a black leviathan heavily to port. At 10.45 p.m., as she sank by the stern, Phyllis Morton, waist deep in a waterlogged lifeboat, looked up to see a never-to-be-forgotten sight: Captain Nicholl, still leaning over the bridge, as the *Benares* reared as if alive, then sank in a column of flame.

At the same moment, Sonia Bech felt a great buoyancy, as the wash lifted their raft high on the water. It was then that she caught Derek's eye, and the same thought occurred to both of them: 'What a rotten waste of good ice-cream!'

Then for most there was only darkness, and thin cries for help, and a deepening silence in which all of them felt small and afraid. Twice Sonia, slipping from the raft, resigned herself to die. 'A rather soothing feeling,' she recalls now, 'a humming in my ears, a whiteness before my eyes . . . all rather calm.' With implicit faith in a world beyond, she pondered: 'I wonder what God's going to be like.' Twice a ship's engineer on the same raft saved her life, hauling her back, spitting and spluttering salt water, from eternity.

Now scores of adults and children who had lived on the sidelines of war acknowledged a painful truth: they would plumb the secrets of survival or they would perish.

One secret was to maintain morale. Escort Mary Cornish was one of forty-six people, among them six boys, huddled into a lifeboat thirty feet long. For eight days thereafter, as the boat pitched and yawed, Miss Cornish kept their minds alert and occupied. At first there were sing-songs – *Roll Out the Barrel*, and *There'll Always Be An England*, but later there was storytelling on a Homeric scale. Racking her brains for a non-stop cliff-hanger, Mary Cornish singled out 'Sapper's' hero, Captain

Bulldog Drummond, somehow contriving to spin yarns which involved him in an unending battle of wits with slinky sirens and Nazi agents.

At noon each day, a steward inched with difficulty along her boat doling out rations: half a ship's biscuit with a fragment of sardine, and, once only, an eighth of a canned peach.

In other boats, the going was harder. Escort Lillian Towns recalled how, as the dawn of 18 September broke over her lifeboat, 'the children started to go into a coma one by one ... we slapped their hands and faces and then we kept their heads above water until we could tell it was no use'. As the day passed, boat after boat over the wide waste of water gently committed their dead to the sea.

Overnight, many children came suddenly of age. In the Mortons' lifeboat, 11-year-old Colin Ryder-Richardson spent hours with a dying woman's head cradled in his lap, stroking her hair, assuring her that rescue was at hand. Thirteen-year-old Bessie Walder and her friend Beth Cummings stayed for twenty hours glued precariously to the keel of a capsized boat, their only company two delirious Indian seamen calling on Allah.

Bessie Walder did not know it, but her brother, 10-year-old Louis, in another boat, had struck it luckier. At the outset his friend Jimmie, the bartender, had pressed on him half a bottle of neat Scotch to ward off the chill. Swigging it down like Coca-Cola, and topping it up with four cans of condensed milk, Louis felt no more pain for twenty-eight drowsy hours.

It was the sense of challenge that ultimately saved Sonia Bech. Her mother, far gone, was on the point of giving up. 'Darling,' she murmured, 'I think we'll take off our lifebelts and go to sleep in the water.' But all Sonia's instincts rebelled against this. 'Oh, no, Mummy, don't do that yet – I'm sure we'll be picked up.' For Sonia the worst thing was holding on to the wood of the raft. Her fingers had begun to bleed, for under the buffeting of the waves the canisters were working loose, and she sensed the raft was doomed to disintegration.

At dawn, with swooping gulls, and wreckage 'as big as houses' looming, Sonia sighted a sail. All of them whooped and hollered and soon it was bearing down on them. Their saviour was Skipper Leslie Lewis, of the S.S. *Marina*, another torpedoed merchantman, who had rigged a sail on his ship's lifeboat, sent radio messages to Land's End and was now all set to row to England. At last gasp, with barely one hour of life left to their raft, the Bechs were hauled aboard, along with an elderly Australian woman and the *City of Benares*' second engineer.

Now, as Sonia and her family gulped down rum – 'which tasted horrible' – and condensed milk, which was better, Lewis circled, picking up survivors, many of them Lascars, near-dead with cold. Around noon, H.M.S. *Hurricane*, a destroyer hastily rerouted from the Mediterranean, for rescue operations, sighted them. Cold and drenched, caked with black oil and brine, the Bechs were hauled aboard.

Not until three hours later, when Sonia and the others, dried out, fed with bacon, eggs and baked beans and reattired in tropical whites, were resting on the wardroom floor, did *Hurricane* sight Barbara Bech's lifeboat. By this time, Marguerite Bech had alerted the entire crew that she was missing. As Barbara scrambled on to the deck, a sailor greeted her for all the world as if she had been playing truant from school: 'Are you Barbara Bech? Your mother's been very worried about you.'

Then there was a brief period when the bitter battle for survival was succeeded by a strange aura of surreal glamour. At Greenock, the port of Glasgow, where *Hurricane* landed them at noon on 20 September, reporters and cameramen were already waiting. Newly attired in clothes from a top department store, Sonia now embarked on a marathon press conference, revelling in it all as she had revelled in the luxury of the *City of Benares*. She was still posing for photographs like a newborn Hollywood starlet long after 10 p.m. – clad now in pyjamas and dressing-gown outside her bedroom in Glasgow's Central Hotel.

Later that week the Bechs returned to Bognor Regis. Their house at Aldwick Bay was not yet up for sale; Sonia's grandmother, along with Mackie, the Scottie, was still in residence. For Sonia, the final accolade came as the taxi drew up outside, and Marguerite Bech asked the driver: 'What do I owe you?'

The chauffeur brushed her request magnificently aside. 'Mrs Bech, it's been an honour.'

*

Afterwards, for all the Bechs, the sheer joy of being alive faded like an anaesthetic. Instead there came the pain of knowing from the press reports that few had been so fortunate. Of the ninety children aboard the *City of Benares*, only thirteen – among them Bessie and Louis Walder, Beth Cummings, Anthony Quinton – had been saved. Of the adults, the Digby Mortons, Lillian Towns and Mary Cornish had come through, but 181 others had not. In all, 258 out of the 408 passengers and crew aboard had perished.

From this time on, no more British children were evacuated overseas. They stayed and took their chances with the adults.

Appropriately, it was for those children who would not celebrate New Year's Day, 1941, that the Children's Hour programme of the B.B.C. held its own memorial service. The speaker's closing text, from Revelation XXI, 4, seemed almost a lament for a waning civilization:

. . . And God shall wipe away all tears from their eyes; and there shall be no more death, neither sorrow, nor crying, neither shall there be any more pain: for the former things are passed away . . .

*

As September dawned, Polly Peabody had quit Vichy. After six weeks in the capital, she had almost given up hope for France. In Vichy, the French seemed prostrated, apathetic, indifferently accepting defeat. Most banks were closed or scattered to the four corners of the land and the collapse of money, with credit unobtainable and cheques refused, seemed to bring out the worst in the Vichy French. Polly was among the lucky ones; her few dollars would still fetch 100 francs each on the black market.

Typical of Vichy's topsy-turvy fortunes was the dapper Frenchman with the rosette of the Legion of Honour in his buttonhole whom Polly saw ordering lamb cutlets and champagne in a smart restaurant. A few days later she saw the same man standing in line before a soup kitchen.

Some citizens were burrowing little holes in their gardens hiding jewels, banknotes and gold, but this stifling preoccupation with greed sickened Polly. She resolved to leave for Paris and the Occupied Zone, and join a relief organization

247

there. She would give her beloved France one more chance to redeem itself.

It was still a shock to enter the Occupied Zone. All through her six-hour drive to the capital in a Red Cross car, past arrows that pointed the way *Nach Paris*, France teemed with Germans. Paris itself seemed one vast garrison. From the Bois de Boulogne to Montparnasse, millions of shining black boots thronged its pavements. A cloud of sadness hung over the city.

Friends had loaned Polly a variety of apartments on the left bank of the Seine, hoping that her presence would exempt them from German occupation. From here, since no taxis, buses or trams were running, Polly set out on foot for the American Hospital at Neuilly, to sign on as an ambulance driver, transporting food and clothing to the prison camps. It was here she heard by chance that her old outfit, the American Scandinavian Field Hospital, were just then on their way back to the States. Good luck to them, Polly thought. She meant to stay where the action was.

By degrees she took heart. Armed with a German pass issued only to relief workers and prostitutes – 'Mademoiselle Polly Peabody is allowed to walk the Paris streets at night for professional reasons indispensable' – she was able to ignore the curfew and go everywhere. What she saw of the native Parisians gave her new faith.

At first, the mood of the people was shown only through surreptitious graffiti. Overnight, as the Métro began to run again, posters on the tiled walls were adorned with slogans: *'Vivent les Anglais!' 'Vive de Gaulle!'* Propaganda posters designed by Dr Göbbels to cash in on French bitterness at the British assault on the fleet at Oran were wittily defaced. *'N'oubliez pas Oran!'* ('Don't forget Oran') ran the original slogans, above a cut of a French sailor drowning in waters reddened with blood. By night, unseen hands changed this to *'N'oubliez pas votre costume de bain'* ('Don't forget your bathing costume'). The gibe was not lost on German troops awaiting the Channel crossing to England.

To deface posters was punishable by a 10,000-franc fine, but Polly noticed that the mutilations did not cease. At first policemen were kept busy with knives and wet sponges to erase the scribbling. Later they could not keep pace; Göbbels's posters had to be sited higher and higher, beyond human reach.

Imperceptibly, the manifestations grew bolder. As German officers entrained in their first-class carriages on the Métro, the train drivers kept up a steady tuneless whistling of the British Tommies' song from the First World War, *It's a Long Long Way to Tipperary*. In those parts of France where Italian soldiers were garrisoned, French girls boldly sported short lengths of macaroni in their buttonholes.

Polly Peabody was encouraged. At the A.B.C. Music Hall, where the reigning queen was suddenly an unknown waif from the slums, Édith Piaf, the nightly running gag was the two clowns who leaped upon the stage in the middle of a Piaf number. When one of them insisted on speaking English, his colleague, in mock embarrassment, pointed out that most of the audience were German and took a poor view. 'You are in *France!*' the stooge expostulated. 'Can't you speak French like us?' To which the clown, provoking a scream of delight from the French, responded solemnly '*Jawohl!*'

One evening, on the terrace of Fouquet's Restaurant, on the Avenues des Champs-Élysées, Polly was dining surrounded by German officers. Suddenly a drunken old Parisienne, wisps of white hair straggling down her neck, hands planted belligerently on her hips, began abusing them from the street. '*Eh, bien,*' she bawled, '*moi, je vous dis* MERDE!' The waiters began to snigger. Polly and the few French present chuckled discreetly into their napkins. The Germans merely stared ahead of them, saying nothing, betraying nothing.

All is not lost, Polly thought, there is still hope. For the time being she was staying put.

Three thousand miles from Paris, in the Ritz Hotel, New York City, Count René de Chambrun felt bitterly disillusioned. He felt that Franklin Roosevelt had betrayed not only him but France besides.

No sooner had de Chambrun returned from Vichy than he had phoned 'Missy' Le Hand. When would the President find it convenient to see him? But 'Missy' had seemed patently evasive, explaining that the meeting would be with Harry Hopkins and not in Washington but New York. Indeed, learning of de Chambrun's return, Hopkins was on his way and would be with him before dinner.

'It was then that I was to know a terrible disappointment,' de Chambrun recorded later, for Hopkins, pallid and unemotional, had wasted no time on small talk arriving at the Ritz. Roosevelt, he told de Chambrun bluntly, had renounced his 'project' of supplying France with food and medicine. It was all, Hopkins explained disingenuously, really Churchill's fault. He had insisted that the President apply the blockade integrally.

De Chambrun was appalled. He harked back to his August meeting with Roosevelt, the mission on which he had returned to France, and the President's final words, 'René, it's a deal.'

Now Roosevelt was reneging on that deal and de Chambrun was outraged. The President, he pointed out to Hopkins, had made a treaty with Pétain, and he, de Chambrun, had been the instrument of that treaty. On 19 August, as Roosevelt had requested, Pétain had duly called a press conference in Vichy, laying on champagne and canapés – 'the first time I shall hold a press conference' – and the American press had run his words in full. 'France will remain firmly attached to the ideal she shares with the great American democracies, an idea founded on the respect for individual rights, the family, the country, and love of justice and humanity.'

Angrily, de Chambrun told Hopkins that he should make sending food to France a condition for continuing to supply arms to Britain.

Hopkins was unyielding. Roosevelt's mind was made up. Only years later did de Chambrun learn from General George Marshall that Churchill's about-face had been occasioned by de Gaulle, who had pressured him to tighten the screws on Vichy, strongly backed by Hugh Dalton's Ministry of Economic Warfare.

De Chambrun was in a quandary. Republicans like Herbert Hoover and Thomas Dewey were campaigning for supplying Europe – but since an election was coming up they were the President's political opponents. Even now, de Chambrun could not bring himself to stoop low and confide in them the details of this double-cross. He must work on his own to raise funds for sending American Red Cross packages.

In the last resort, there was the letter Roosevelt had requested from Pétain, which de Chambrun had helped the old Marshal to draft. One paragraph in particular had been carefully calculated to appeal to the President's sense of compassion. 'Millions of refugees from the most fertile regions of France are bringing (to Unoccupied France) nothing with them except their retinue of fatigue and misery ... sharing with Belgian, Austrian and Czechoslovakian refugees ... the pain and problems of Frenchmen in Free France ...'

That evening, following Hopkins's departure, de Chambrun took his letter to the lobby and sent it by registered mail to the White House.

Days passed, but there was no reply. He never heard from Roosevelt again.

The smouldering resentment that Polly Peabody was noting in Occupied France was no lone example. By degrees a palpable spirit of resistance was arising in all of occupied Europe.

Its slow genesis was only to be expected; history had set no precedents. In past centuries, countries like Belgium had endured occupation under Spanish, French and Dutch rulers with rueful grace. But now there was more than an alien presence in streets and squares to breed opposition. The slow encroachment of Hitler's New Order, with all its ideological implications, was an outrage to many.

That autumn, following a decision that Norwegian schools should devote time to 'introducing children to the New Order', the history teachers went on unanimous strike, and were promptly arrested. Attempts to force them to join a political union resulted in 12,000 out of 14,000 resigning. The schools closed down, but after six months *Reichskommissar* Terboven ordered the puppet government to 'relent'. Like most of Hitler's appointed overlords, Terboven wanted no trouble so early in the war.

On all sides, the occupied peoples sought solidarity. One such occasion was 26 September, the seventieth birthday of King Christian X of Denmark. The fact that for five months the old

King had ridden out on horseback each morning, acknowledging the greetings of his humblest subjects, stonily ignoring the punctilious salutes of the Germans he passed en route, was known to every Dane. Now, on his birthday, the square before Amalienborg Palace was jampacked with Danes chanting patriotic songs and hymns. Nor was this loyalty confined to Copenhagen alone. Even in smaller towns like Odense, crowds 3,500 strong packed out every public hall.

Early Danish resistants took their tone from the King, offering the coldest of shoulders to the invader. If a German civilly asked the way in the street, passers-by walked blithely on as if no one had spoken. The same technique caught on early in Oslo, Norway. When German officers sought membership of an exclusive tennis club, the committee ostensibly welcomed them – then held a drumhead meeting to convert the courts to a potato patch in the interests of the national economy.

Emblems and lapel badges conveyed sentiments that it was prudent not to utter. Danish badges stamped DKS (Den Kolde Skulder) showed where a man's sympathies lay. Norwegians sported wire paper-clips, which meant 'Stick together', or advertising slogans cut from milk cartons: '100 per cent Norwegian'. Patriotic dairy farmers even branded their milch cows with the emblem of King Haakon VII.

Gradually, resistance became more overt. Hand-made Danish printing presses began churning out leaflets called strewslips, crudely printed fragments of brown adhesive paper that could be gummed on walls or lamp-posts: 'DON'T BECOME A TRAITOR', 'HELP HITLER LOSE THE WAR'. As the Battle of Britain was joined, Danish students sported red, white and blue woollen caps, the colours of the R.A.F. rondel. As the battle swung in Britain's favour, the wearers, accused of 'provocative conduct', often faced fines or gaol.

Even the smallest gestures assumed significance, for they gave back to the occupied peoples something they had forfeited at the time of Hitler's conquests: self-respect. Alert for trouble, the authorities in Holland early forbade the wearing of flowers in the buttonhole: both the white carnation that was the trademark of Prince Bernhard of the Netherlands and the marigold that symbolized the House of Orange spelt resistance. But as early as 29 June, Bernhard's birthday, many Dutch citizens defied the ban – and the bullyboys of Anton Mussert's pro-Nazi N.S.B., swift to snatch them from lapels, recoiled with bleeding fingers. Behind each innocent flower lurked a sharp-edged razor blade.

The will to resist bred many new routines. In The Hague and other Dutch cities, 13-year-old Ida van de Criendt recalled that no one ever answered a phone call around 7 p.m. Like Ida's family, most were tuned in to hear Radio Oranje, broadcasting from London with its message from the exiled Queen Wilhelmina. Already hiding places had been devised for these radios; Ida's family kept theirs under the floorboards of the cupboard that housed the family bicycles.

Sometimes the clandestine broadcasts posed a problem. In Verviers, Belgium, one woman, believing her husband had died in the 18-day campaign, appointed a day for the funeral and sent out invitations. On the eve of the burial, she was in a quandary: Radio London had announced her husband was safe and well in England. Should she cancel the funeral and thereby reveal that she listened to the freedom radio – or go ahead?

Playing safe, she asked the priest to go ahead, but found herself the sole mourner. All her friends had listened in, and felt that condolences were unnecessary.

Underground news-sheets were another way to hit back, though their circulation was limited at first. In Copenhagen, Erik Seidenfaden's newspaper, *Politiken*, printed one solely for distribution to the reporters, to up-date them on the news the censors kept from the public. In Belgium, 1940 saw the birth of no less than ninety-five resistance journals, though the total print was no more than 20,000 copies. Some sheets were little more than chain-letters, like the one called *Geuzenactie* (The Giants), produced by Bernard Ijzerdraat, a carpet weaver in Haarlem, Holland. Lacking carbon paper, the diligent weaver had to write it out by hand, one copy at a time.

Only one country – the tiny Duchy of Luxembourg – knew the savage satisfaction of publicly registering their distaste for the invader. On 10 October, their Nazi *Gauleiter*, Gustav Simon, a man unafflicted by doubt, ordered a plebiscite in favour of Hitler's occupation. The Luxembourgers, trudging to the polls, recorded a verdict that spoke for all of occupied Europe: a 97 per cent hostile vote.

From his Thames-side eyrie atop Fire Brigade Headquarters at Lambeth, Assistant Divisional Officer Geoffrey Vaughan Blackstone watched eight million Londoners, day by day, waging their own war of resistance.

On these bitter autumn nights, Blackstone's routine, as Deputy Chief of the Southern Division, almost never varied. Jolting in his control car through the high-risk dockland area that was his bailiwick – Southwark, Bermondsey, Rotherhithe – he coordinated the battle plan against the scores of warehouse fires threatening London's food supplies. Often it was mid-morning next day before he could return to his quarters for a bath and a change of uniform. At dusk, following office routine and a brief catnap, he was once more alert for the wail of the siren.

Afterwards, looking back, no single fire stood out above the others. The nights merged into one like an enveloping flame: intense heat and nipping cold, the eyes inflamed by smoke and the feet sore from the chafing of rubber boots, hasty snacks of coffee and meat pies from the mobile canteen van.

On one score at least Blackstone had ceased to worry after 7 September: the courage of London's auxiliary firemen, despised until then, had become a byword. Often, as they returned at dawn, smoke-grimed and sodden, early-morning shift workers lined the streets to cheer them; at the sight of them on a news-reel screen the audience broke into applause. One fireman, pointedly ignored for a whole year by the barmaid in his local pub, was now always served first, frequently out of turn.

Other fire-fighting problems were far from resolved. Every firm employing more than thirty workers was obliged to furnish night-time fire-watchers, but few drew up such rosters and the new Minister of Home Security, Herbert Morrison, seemed oddly reluctant to enforce the law to the letter. A bigger head-ache still was London's water supply. In a large-scale fire-raid, a square mile of the city needed 600,000 gallons of water a minute to keep the flames in check. Yet the cast-iron public mains, sited barely three feet below street level, could be fractured by the impact of a 50-kilo bomb. At low tide, the Thames was almost unapproachable, separated from the shore by fifty feet of black mud.

The answer, Blackstone and his chief, Lieutenant-Commander John Fordham, argued, was on-the-spot emergency reservoirs – a solution condemned as too costly by the Home Office, the Treasury and the London County Council. Their own compromise was a series of 5,000-gallon steel dams scattered at remote intervals. Blackstone's reaction was scathing: a trailer pump delivered 500 gallons a minute, so a 5,000-gallon drum ensured just ten minutes' supply. 'It's like pissing against a thunderstorm,' was Blackstone's acid comment.

Although backed by Fordham and Major Frank Jackson, the Fire Brigade chief, his arguments were brushed aside by Sir Arthur Dixon, chief of the Home Office Fire Department. If an all-out fire-raid ever came, London might burn like a prairie in a drought – but Blackstone, for his pains, was dismissed as 'a cheeky young man'.

Despite these drawbacks, Blackstone had no doubts on one score; morale would hold up. Like the Finns before them, Londoners were adapting. From 11 September, when General Frederick Pile's Anti-Aircraft Command loosed off its first box-barrage over 200 square miles of Greater London – firing 13,500 rounds without damaging a single bomber – Londoners had had a buoyant sense of hitting back. Not more than 6 in 100 ever resorted to ear-plugs; the fearful martial music was like a lullaby.

Other sounds became an integral part of this life: the bombers circling, as one woman noted, 'like dogs trying to pick up a scent', the aching empty silence after a bomb fell, broken only by small sounds, the rustle of water from fractured pipes, the little cries of the trapped and wounded, the stealthy shifting of debris. Dawn brought the most welcome sound of all: the notes of the All Clear, like a liner nearing safe haven, crying over the city.

Each night thousands of Londoners burrowed underground like gophers into damp shelters and subways. Many with gardens slept in corrugated-iron outdoor so-called Anderson shelters, buried four feet deep. By September's end, 177,000 of them had taken to the Underground railway, squatting figures throwing forlorn shadows on the tiled walls, bedded down on floors gritty and buff-coloured from leaking sandbags.

Armed with suitcases, blankets, rugs and pillows many queued in the street for places as early as 10.30 a.m.; by 4 p.m., the permitted hour of descent, every yard of platform and passage space would be staked out behind the painted line that reserved the front yard of platform for passengers.

Those who could afford twopence bedded down on copies of *The Times*, by far the thickest paper. Sanitation was primitive, confined to bucket latrines behind hessian screens. Privacy was non-existent, and at least one marriage was consummated in full public view in a shelter in London's slatternly Tottenham Court Road.

In scores of shelters, from the sandy caves at Chislehurst, Kent, thirteen miles south, which the denizens had equipped with double beds, to Mickey Davis's in Stepney's dockland, kept by a hunchbacked East End optician, Londoners gathered each night from 7 p.m. to 7 a.m. At dawn they emerged to what were soon familiar scenes: vast mounds of timber and lath and plaster, torn window curtains, the fine glitter of powdered glass that covered the pavements like hoar frost.

In time, the smells became familiar, too: the harsh acrid smell of cordite from high-explosive bombs, leaking gas and blue London clay, charred wood and pulverized plaster.

It was a weird unnatural life, even for the birds, which awoke and sang when the searchlights turned night into day, and no man or woman who took part in it was ever to forget it. International order had given way to universal insanity, and even the laws of nature had become mixed up. In some communities, the blind now offered their services as guides during total blackouts.

London was now a city where strange sights had become the norm. Thus one man would always remember a girl kneeling by night in fashionable Pall Mall, smothering the sizzling thermite of a foot-long incendiary bomb with her evening cloak. Others recalled a man striding down Piccadilly in black coat and striped trousers, shielding himself from falling shrapnel with an open umbrella. On one night waiters and chefs were seen racing

256

a raw sirloin of beef from a club that had been hit into a club whose kitchen still functioned.

Between 7 September and 13 November, 13,651 tons of high explosive and 12,586 incendiary canisters were showered upon the city. Now not only tiny red-brick homes were at risk, but those parts of London charted by that indefatigable German tourist, Karl Baedeker. Names of heroes and works of great memory were trampled. Somerset House, where Shakespeare's will, among others, was filed, lost its superb staircase. John Nash's curving Regent Street was ripped by a delayed-action bomb. So, too, were the National and Tate Galleries, William Hogarth's panelled house in Chiswick, the Gothic House of Lords, Westminster Abbey and that haunt of dandies, Savile Row. St Giles, Cripplegate, where John Milton's remains lay, did not survive the bombings as it had the fire in 1666. Other churches suffered: Christopher Wren's St James's, Piccadilly, and his much-admired St Stephen's, Walbrook, St Mary-at-Hill, St Dunstan-in-the-East and the Church of Our Lady of Victory.

'We are as continuously alive to danger as animals in the jungle,' noted a Canadian diplomat, Charles Ritchie. This was true, but by degrees the pattern was changing. At first, Londoners went religiously home each evening to an established routine: blacked-out windows criss-crossed with transparent paper against blast, the shelter with a sixpenny Penguin Book for company, sometimes a bath in five inches of tepid water to conserve fuel, a breakfast egg from a bucket of isinglass. But ultimately the lures of cinemas (open until 9 p.m., although theatres were closed), friendly pubs and the opposite sex proved too potent. To socialize, defying bombs and landmines, became part of the pattern, too. 'See you tomorrow,' one warden heard a girl promise her boyfriend, 'same time, same sandbag.'

Whatever the hazards, Londoners were determined to keep their cool. Posted on the notice-board of one golf-club outside London was a new emergency rule: 'Players may pick out of any bomb crater, dropping ball not nearer hole without penalty.'

To outsiders, it seemed that the security bred by three centuries of immunity from warfare on their own soil had given the English an invincible sense of their own superiority. Few among them could now conceive of being beaten. Pierre Bourdan, chief of the London-based Agence Française Indépendante news agency, never forgot an interview he was granted around this time by Sir Archibald Sinclair, Churchill's Secretary of State for Air.

Studying a huge wall-map of the world, Sinclair told Bourdan seriously: 'We shall probably lose Egypt, Malta, Aden, the Middle East, perhaps the Indies, Singapore, and I'm very much afraid, dear old Gibraltar, too.'

As he reeled out this formidable list like a geography master, Bourdan gazed at him in awe. Then, shaking his head and frowning, Sinclair confessed: 'Yes, I very much fear it will be five or six years before we win this war.'

'Dead Lucky if We See
the Sun Again'

15 October–15 November 1940

In the vast Hall of the Ambassadors of Berlin's Reich Chancellery, at 1.15 p.m. on 27 September, a long-awaited pact was in the making. As Adolf Hitler entered with a nervous cat-like tread, three men seated at the long table, a thin document printed in triplicate lying before them, rose to greet him: Ribbentrop, Italy's Count Ciano, and a newcomer to the scene, the slim suave Saburo Kurusu, Japan's man in Germany. A moment's pause, then Ribbentrop swivelled to confront a battery of microphones. In a staccato 419-word preamble he announced to the assembled foreign correspondents that Japan had joined the Axis.

'The pact which has been signed,' Ribbentrop proclaimed, 'is a military alliance between three of the mightiest States on earth ... It is to help bring peace to the world as quickly as possible ... Any State, should it harbour the intention of mixing in the final phase of the solution of these problems in Europe or Eastern Asia, or attacking one State signatory to this three-power pact, will have to take on the entire concentrated might of three nations with more than 250 million inhabitants.'

What Ribbentrop was making clearer than crystal was a fact that was crystal-clear already: the treaty was an alliance against the United States.

If America were to join Britain in the European war, its text implied, Japan would attack in the Pacific. If America interfered in the Chinese war, Germany and Italy would attack in the Atlantic. In sum, with the United States scared into isolation, the Rome–Berlin–Tokyo Axis could dismember the British Empire piecemeal.

The treaty was, in fact, no bombshell through the roof of the State Department. Though no man could deny that it was a diplomatic defeat for the United States, which for the first time in its history was now surrounded by enemies, the treaty did no more than confirm the warnings that Ambassador Joseph C. Grew had been routing to the State Department for months past. 'The era of democracy,' predicted Japan's Foreign Minister, Yosuke Matsuoka, in a press interview on 21 July, 'is finished', amply justifying Grew's later report of 5 September, 'The new [Konoye] Cabinet has every earmark of a totalitarian régime.'

The tenor of events had so alarmed Grew that on 12 September he had dispatched an uncompromising telegram to Cordell Hull: 'Japan today is one of the predatory powers; she has submerged all moral and ethical sense, and has become frankly and unashamedly opportunist, seeking at every turn to profit by the weakness of others.'

But if the Axis hoped to frighten the United States out of its everything-short-of-war policy to help Great Britain, it had almost certainly failed. Since American security in the Atlantic – hence liberty to maintain her Fleet in the Pacific – depended on the British Fleet, the U.S. could now do no less than help Britain more.

'We should profit by Mr Chamberlain's bitter experience in Europe,' was Grew's considered counsel. 'We know by experience out here that Japan's word of honour can be trusted no further than Hitler's word of honour . . .'

Certainly there was no hint of irresolution in either Washington or London. In the face of a muttered Japanese threat that the gesture would mean war, the British, on 11 October, reopened the Burma Road. At Lashio, Burma, on this cold clear night, 5,000 coolies were busy loading some $20,000,000 worth of China's future into 2,000 U.S.-built trucks – including such vital cargoes as aeroplane wings, high-octane gasoline, rifle barrels and raw cotton.

The U.S., it seemed, was beginning to meddle in earnest. After France's fall, Roosevelt had stopped the export of aviation fuel and top-grade scrap to Japan. Then, in September, he had cut off scrap iron and steel. Within two years' time, these embargoes, designed to halt Japan's march to exploit Allied difficulties, would have sapped her economic strength. Thus, in the naval race, America would have begun to outstrip Japan.

The message was not lost on Prince Fumimaro Konoye and his Cabinet: Japan must act fast. 'Anglo-Saxonism,' declared Matsuoka's deputy in Tokyo, Chuichi Ohashi, 'is about to become bankrupt and will be effectively wiped out.'

Despite the seeming invincibility of the Axis, some commanders were beset by doubts. In mid-October, Major Fritz von Forell of the Wehrmacht visited his old friend Major Werner Mölders at the headquarters of Fighter Group 51, which lay at Pihen, near Calais.

That evening Fighter Group 51 had nothing more martial in mind than an uproarious stag party: Göring had awarded silver cups to three young officers of merit, *Oberleutnants* Joppien, Pape and Fleig, and first, in the elegantly-furnished villa that served as the officers' club, Mölders had to make the formal presentation. 'Let this be a happy day,' he rallied them by way of conclusion. 'Let us forget the struggle for tonight. I will celebrate with you!'

As the evening wore on, the champagne flowed faster. Each pilot in turn was hoisted shoulder high and borne in whooping triumph through the brightly-lit salons. But as the party reached fever-pitch, it seemed to Forell that Mölders could not forget the struggle, not even for that night. Though he smiled mechanically and matched toast for toast, his face was drawn and earnest. Forell was troubled. In the past, Mölders had always thrown himself into a party as if there was no tomorrow.

Towards midnight, Mölders abruptly strode from the villa. Forell followed. The night was dark and without stars; a cool wind blew from the sea. For a moment the two walked in aimless silence, towards the dispersal ground where silver Messerschmitts stood camouflaged beneath tall poplars. Suddenly, jerking his head towards them, Mölders broke out: 'I am terribly worried.'

Forell said nothing. 'I am *terribly* worried,' Mölders repeated. 'We're not making any progress. What's happening to Operation Sea-Lion? When are we going over to England? I've spoken to high naval officers. They don't know either. "The Tommies are still flying," they said.'

Deep in thought, Mölders had stopped walking, scuffing at the sand with his toe. 'My boys shoot down one after another,' he complained, 'but it's as though they grow new heads on the other side of the Channel, like a hydra. For every Briton shot down, two new ones seem to rise up!'

'Has the Reich Marshal been told?' Forell asked.

Mölders was sombre. 'Of course. But I have the impression he either doesn't want to believe it – or that he doesn't know what to do about it. But God in Heaven, something has to be done!'

Forell was deeply disturbed. Mölders was voicing doubts dangerous to a man when he is fighting an air war: doubts as to the whole meaning of the combat, doubts as to whether it was worth going on.

'Shall we be able to overpower England?' he asked with increasing agitation. 'And will she be the last enemy? And if the worst comes to the worst, and America comes in to help the British, what then?'

Forell was realistic. America was already helping wherever she possibly could. 'Wouldn't it be helpful,' he suggested, 'to talk things over with Göring?'

Mölders ran his fingers through his hair. ' "It will turn out all right," is what he says when told of such things, "Everything's been all right so far." ' He ended gloomily: 'So far! I wonder if Göring really is the general, politician and strategist that we need? It isn't enough to be able to lead a mass of mercenaries . . .'

Forell watched him in silence, miserably, wanting to help. He wished that there was something he could say.

In Britain, the War Cabinet's uncertainty as to Hitler's intentions decreed that 'The Happy Time' of *Kapitänleutnant* Otto Kretschmer and his fellow U-Boat aces continued undisturbed. Still intent on countering Operation Sea-Lion, if it came, the Chiefs of Staff were insistent that the bulk of the British Fleet was scattered throughout the east and south coast ports, effectively stripping the Atlantic convoys of their escorts.

From September on, what Dönitz termed *Rudeltaktik* (pack attacks) – U-Boats hunting in tactical groups – came into being. On his undersea forays, Kretschmer was now supported by other seasoned skippers: Günter Prien, whose U-47 had slipped cunningly into Scapa Flow to sink the battleship *Royal Oak*, Günter Kuhnke, of U-28, Heinrich Bleichrodt, whose U-48 had accounted for the *City of Benares*, Joachim Schepke, commanding U-100.

In October, one date alone – Thursday, 19 October – marked Kretschmer's greatest triumph in the U-Boat war.

At dusk on that day, operating with seven other U-Boats, Kretschmer, in U-99, was edging ever closer to the convoy code-named SC (for Slow Convoy) 7, outward bound from Sydney, Nova Scotia, for Liverpool. He had counted her escort as strong for these days – three destroyers and several smaller warships – but the fact did not deter him. What Kretschmer now planned was to cause maximum havoc by a new tactic of the Atlantic war – striking from within the convoy itself.

At 10 p.m. the classic attack began. As seven other U-Boats, including Schepke in U-100 and Prien in U-47, attacked from outside the convoy screen, firing salvo upon salvo, Kretschmer headed for the starboard side covered by the three destroyers – one ahead of the convoy, one on the beam, another on the bow.

Now, as he headed between the beam and the bow destroyers, neither showed any signs of spotting him, gliding one mile distant from each. Three minutes later he was through, fast approaching the convoy's outer column. Closing to 700 yards range U-99 fired at the first ship – and missed by yards. But on this calm clear night, with the targets standing out in vivid silhouette against a hunter's moon, the life of his quarry was destined to be short. Again U-99 fired, her second torpedo striking amidships. Within twenty seconds, the ship had wallowed from sight.

Suddenly, as two more explosions sounded from the other side of the convoy, the long line of ships abruptly altered course, and Kretschmer seized his chance. Sweeping down the outer column, now only 100 yards distant, he spied a gap and slipped through it. Now U-99 made part of the convoy itself.

One large cargo ship spotted her and tried to ram, firing star-shell as she came, but Kretschmer dodged prudently back towards the escort screen. By now he was near the convoy's stern, aiming at the end ship of the outer column. Missing, the torpedo went home on another ship in the next column. As she broke in two, her radio signal for help marked her sole claim to identity '*Empire Brigade*'.

At the front of U-99's conning tower, Kretschmer now told Sub-Lieutenants Elfe and Bargsten, 'We're going to tear this convoy down.'

It was an attack that was to go down in Allied naval history as the worst convoy disaster of the war. At midnight, another of U-99's torpedoes struck a large freighter forward. Seconds later, in a huge spurt of red and yellow flame, she tore apart before their eyes, a cloud of smoke mushrooming 500 feet high. In fifty seconds she had vanished from sight. At 1 a.m. another torpedo capsized a fifth merchantman, her red-hot plates hissing and boiling as she sank. Next it was the turn of S.S. *Fiscus*, broken in two near the stern.

In the unholy confusion of this night, the destroyers were dropping depth charges at will, and starshells made frenzied, spangled patterns of light across the water. Unperturbed, Kretschmer turned hard to starboard, conning U-99 to the freighter *Shekatica*. At 300 yards' range, he ordered, 'Stern tube, fire,' watching the ship rear in the air like a wounded beast. His next target, the *Sedgepool*, executed as perfect a crash-dive in her death throes as if she herself was a submarine, propellers churning the water as she drove towards the sea-bed with a roar of ruptured girders.

Enough was enough, Kretschmer decided then. It was surely only a question of time before the escort guessed where he was, and effectively barred his escape route from inside the convoy. One small straggler lying to the stern, the S.S. *Clintonia*, was U-99's last victim this night. She settled slowly in the water, seemingly unremarked, as the main convoy drove ahead at maximum speed.

On 22 October, U-99 arrived at her cleaning up anchorage in the island bay off the approach to Lorient. Kretschmer was well satisfied. In three hours of one night he had sent nine merchantmen to the bottom, while his fellow U-Boat commanders, between them, had accounted for another eight.

The loss of seventeen ships had cost the Allies 80,000 tons of shipping, 100,000 tons of supplies, and this was only the beginning. For all October, the month's total losses would escalate to one third of a million tons. Kretschmer and all of them felt that victory could not be far away.

In a suite in the Palace Hotel, Estoril, outside Lisbon, the phone was ringing stridently, and Polly Peabody hastened to answer it. Earlier that day, acting on impulse, she had cancelled a liner passage to the States, deciding that bombed and beleaguered London was where she most wanted to be. After two months, Paris under German occupation had finally palled.

To her surprise, the switchboard operator announced, 'Senhora Peabody, New York is calling you.' It was the evening of 5 November, a date which for Polly held only one significance. Even before she had exchanged greetings with an old friend she was shouting, 'What about Roosevelt?'

'To hell with Roosevelt,' the friend rejoined. 'Tell me about you.'

'I'm going to London,' Polly told him triumphantly, but her friend demurred. 'You'd better come home,' he advised. 'New York is very gay. There are lots of good plays. Your old hangouts are going strong . . .'

'I want to go to London,' Polly insisted.

'Haven't you had enough?'

Polly was adamant. 'No! Now tell me about Roosevelt!'

'Oh him,' the voice announced, with monumental indifference. 'He's been re-elected.'

That ended the conversation. As Polly saw it, if the election of the one man who could open American eyes and lead them into the fight for freedom was of no importance to her New York set, that clinched it. In future her New York set could get along very well without her – and she without them.

It was a night when all the traditions were faithfully observed. Inside the big house at Hyde Park, on the Hudson

River, a bevy of family and friends had celebrated with a scrambled egg supper, as the teletype machines in the pantry clattered out the irrefutable returns. The President had sat tensely at the dining-room table, coatless, his necktie loosened, studying the final tallies. Towards midnight, the familiar jostling crowd of neighbours thronged the entrance road to the mansion, torches flickering ruddily on the white painted balustrade and the hemlock hedge that bordered the rose garden. A drum-and-bugle corps launched into *The Old Grey Mare*, and Harry Hopkins, standing to the rear of the portico, executed a sudden spontaneous pirouette of triumph, smacking right fist into left palm. More plainly than any words, the gesture spelled out: 'We made it.'

For the first time in history, an American President had been elected to a third term of office – 'SAFE ON THIRD', proclaimed one jubilant banner – with 27,243,460 votes against the Republican Wendell Willkie's 22,304,755. He had opened a door that no other president had ever opened; now he prepared to walk through it.

Ironically, it had been a campaign in which Willkie had seemed to have more in common with his adversary than with his party's hard core. Though he embarked on 560 speeches in fifty days, until his voice died to an inaudible croak, many issues that were a sore point with Republicans were barely raised. Even the passage of the Selective Service Act, which on 16 October saw the registration of all American males between twenty-one and thirty-five for the first peacetime conscription, met with Willkie's favour – as did the earlier 'destroyers for bases' deal. Only as his opponents began to link him with Fascist sympathizers did Willkie belatedly yield to temptation, charging that Roosevelt sought a third term to assume a dictator's mantle and involve America in Europe's war.

It had not been a campaign in which the President had visibly exerted political muscle. All through the fall, jauntily confident, he studiously ignored Willkie's bandwagon. Only in the third week of October did he announce that he would make five addresses in the two weeks preceding Election Day to answer 'deliberate falsifications of fact by the Republicans'.

Roosevelt's confidence was by no means shared by other

Democrats. From all over America, a steady stream of messages from jittery politicians warned him that the cause was lost unless he guaranteed to American mothers that their boys, though inducted into the armed services, would never be called upon to fight. In vain they even sought to dissuade him from presiding over the drawing of the first draft papers from a mammoth goldfish bowl in Washington, D.C., while the cameras recorded his presence for history.

On 30 October, in Boston – the same night that Willkie charged stridently, 'You may expect war by April 1941, if he is elected' – Roosevelt finally yielded to party pressures. 'I burn inwardly whenever I think of those words,' his speechwriter, the playwright Robert E. Sherwood, confessed later. 'And, while I am talking to you mothers and fathers, I give you one more assurance,' Roosevelt told them roundly, 'I shall say it again and again and again. Your boys are not going to be sent into any foreign wars.'

Always before, he had qualified this statement 'except in case of attack', but at the last when this was raised, he flashed back irritably, 'If somebody attacks us, it isn't a foreign war, is it? Or do they want me to guarantee that our troops will only be sent into battle in the event of another Civil War?' But the statement was to haunt him 'again and again and again' in the months that followed – and so, too, did his pronouncement in Buffalo: 'Your President says this country is not going to war.'

Yet the hysterical demands for reassurance at any price had been there, as none knew better than Theodor Broch, the former Mayor of Narvik.

Ever since arriving in Los Angeles in August, Broch had embraced Roosevelt's cause – 'I felt I had him with me from the start,' he confessed later. For three months, as a lecturer on the books of the Redpath Agency, Chicago, Broch, in an old second-hand Ford, had travelled everywhere in the United States where Norwegian immigrants had settled – to Montana, North and South Dakota, Minnesota, Iowa and Wisconsin. Often speaking in children's schools, Masonic lodges, or neat white prairie churches, he gave three lectures a day, sometimes in hamlets so remote that third-generation Norwegians on the streets still spoke the dialects of Narvik and Trondheim.

Yet the dichotomy of emotions disturbed him. Tough Norwegian farmers who wept unashamedly at the strains of Norway's national anthem played on a church organ recoiled at Broch's message that Hitler posed a threat to all mankind. 'You can't expect us to declare war and send our boys abroad?' they asked incredulously.

Wherever Broch journeyed, a tidal wave of isolationist fear seemed to be sweeping the country. Insurance companies warned their policy-holders that Roosevelt's election would reduce their policies to worthless scraps of paper. Telegrams warned doctors that Roosevelt's return meant the socialization of medicine. One Chicago bank solemnly advertised: 'In a last stand for democracy, every director and officer of this Bank will vote for Wendell Willkie' – a broad hint to depositors to do likewise or lose their money.

To the people of this land of plenty, Europe seemed very far away, and many counted her cause as lost. 'Do you think you'll ever get back?' the Norwegians would ask Broch, and most were dubious when he affirmed his faith. 'But the Germans are overwhelming,' they would point out. 'They are,' Broch agreed quietly, 'and in the end they'll provoke the whole world against them.'

Scurrilous rumours, designed to damage Roosevelt's reputation, abounded. Some isolationists charged that Crown Princess Martha of Norway, who had sought sanctuary in the United States, had become the President's mistress, and that Eleanor Roosevelt, to spite her husband, had taken a Negro for a lover. Even Broch himself, as a man who sought American commitment, was not immune. Some Norwegian businessmen circulated the smear that he had never set foot in Narvik. He was a Roosevelt agent, paid to embroil America in the war.

On 5 November, Broch, in Minneapolis, heard of Roosevelt's triumph with undisguised joy. But still it seemed to him that many hurdles lay ahead. By paring his expenses to around two dollars a day, he was slowly saving the 6,500 Swedish kroner (almost $2,000) that would finance a passage from Stockholm for Ellen, his wife, and daughter Siri. But that was four months away, and America had not yet reached the hour of decision.

What turn of events, Broch wondered, could ever involve her in this war?

Six days after Roosevelt's re-election, the British, quite unwittingly, brought America's involvement in the Second World War perceptibly closer.

At 10 p.m. on the bright moonlit night of 11 November, twenty-one Fairey-Swordfish torpedo-bombers of the Fleet Air Arm, operating from the aircraft carrier, H.M.S. *Illustrious*, and escorting cruisers, swooped 170 miles from off the coast of Cephalonia to attack the Italian fleet at Taranto, the major naval base in the Ionian Sea.

'A black day,' noted Count Galeazzo Ciano, Mussolini's Foreign Minister, in his diary, for the planes of what the British styled 'Operation Judgement', venturing as low as 150 feet, had sunk the dreadnought *Cavour* and severely damaged the 35,000-ton battleships *Littorio* and *Duilio*, faster and more up-to-date than any warships the British possessed.

The moral of this operation was not lost on Roosevelt's Secretary of the Navy, Frank Knox. 'The success of the British aerial torpedo attack against ships at anchor,' he wrote to Secretary Stimson in the War Department, 'suggests that precautionary measures be taken immediately to protect Pearl Harbor against surprise attack in the event that war should break out between the United States and Japan.'

Knox could not know it, but Admiral Isoroku Yamamoto, Commander-in-Chief of the Japanese Combined Fleet, had also taken the lesson of Taranto to heart. In a locked drawer of his desk aboard the flagship *Nagato*, there already reposed a 500-page mimeographed book, titled *The Habits, Strengths and Defenses of the American Fleet in the Hawaiian Area.* Every fact of relevance to Pearl Harbor was in that book – its berthing plans, training areas, defences and zones of reconnaissance.

Already, having scouted the Japanese coastline, Yamamoto had found a place that strikingly resembled Pearl Harbor – south of Kyushu in Kagoshima Bay. This, like Pearl, was accessible only through a single entrance channel, which all ships, coming and going, had to use.

Now had come Taranto – simon-pure proof that an attack on

Pearl was as feasible in a shooting war as the aerial exercises carried out over Kagoshima. From 12 November on, 'Operation Z', as Yamamoto called it, was allotted priority above and beyond all other projects.

By 3 November, the bombs had rained on London for fifty-seven nights, and Churchill was in his element. 'Let us go on together through the storm,' he rallied his former chief Neville Chamberlain in a letter written as October dawned. 'These are great days.' The sentiment was inopportune, for Chamberlain was to die of intestinal cancer before the year was out, but Churchill was now mindful of little else but the nightly stimulus of danger.

To his anxious bodyguard, Detective-Inspector Walter Thompson, 'The Old Man' often proved a sore trial. When raids were heaviest, Churchill often chose for sheer devilment to sleep on the top floor of 10 Downing Street or duck from doorway to doorway along Whitehall dodging a hail of shell splinters. When Thompson urged him to move to safe quarters, Churchill, irked, replied: 'Thompson, the Prime Minister of this country lives and works in this house – and until Hitler puts it on the ground, *I* work here!'

The sufferings of London's East Enders, the Cockneys, who had most to lose in the raids on East London dockland boroughs like Poplar and Stepney, moved him profoundly. He took pains to visit them after each heavy raid – always stepping out briskly, Thompson noted, to boost morale – and the Cockneys warmed to his presence in these mean streets. 'We are with you, Winnie,' the cry would go up. 'Give it to them, Winnie.' Turning to Ismay, his eyes filled with tears, Churchill blurted out: 'What fellows they are. Did you hear them? They cheered me as if I had given them a victory, instead of getting their houses bombed to bits.'

King George VI and his Queen were as instrumental as Churchill in boosting Londoners' morale. 'I'm glad we've been bombed,' Queen Elizabeth confessed after 15 September. 'It makes me feel I can look the East End in the face.' After one East End visit, the Queen sent sixty suites of furniture from Windsor Castle, along with linen, carpets and rugs, and the gesture was not forgotten. Nor did the Queen lack the common touch, as Minister of Food Lord Woolton had cause to observe during one Royal tour of communal feeding centres in South London.

At one centre, a grime-smeared baby in its mother's arms grabbed for the Queen's rope of pearls. Minutes later, the Queen moved on – too late for a hapless photographer who was trying to snap a picture. 'Your Majesty,' Woolton murmured under his breath. 'You've just broken a press man's heart.' With no indication that she had heard, the Queen moved discreetly back, within the baby's reach. Next day the picture made most front pages – prompting one Cockney housewife's spontaneous tribute: 'Ain't she just *bloody* lovely!'

In all these weeks of Calvary, no Londoner was fighting to win a battle, as at Ypres or Waterloo, but merely to survive, yet this in itself was a kind of victory. And, significantly, anxiety states diminished as the blitz continued; in the first three months of bombing, less than three patients a week reported sick with nervous disorders. Scores of pubs displayed a notice recalling the earlier words of Queen Victoria following a reversal in the South African war: 'We are not interested in the possibilities of defeat because they do not exist.' There was suddenly a new belief in a common purpose, a shifting of ambition from the self towards others, a live-for-today philosophy in which new tolerances were born.

From a passive acceptance of discomfort and disrupted routine, Londoners were swiftly changing to a stubborn refusal to be subjugated. Evening concerts belonged to the past, but lunchtime concerts at the National Gallery, with artistes like the pianist Myra Hess, had become the daily norm. By mid-October, too, the city was witnessing a phenomenon unique in contemporary history: lunchtime Shakespeare.

The concept was the brainchild of a 38-year-old classical actor, Donald (later Sir Donald) Wolfit, who hit upon the idea of renting London's Strand Theatre for a nugatory £10 a week. Assembling a company of twelve stalwarts, who were paid three guineas a week expenses, among them the now veteran actress Cathleen Nesbitt, Wolfit's repertoire was an hour long (1 p.m.–2 p.m.) symposium of Shakespearean excerpts – the sleep-walking scene from *Macbeth*, the casket scene from *The Merchant of Venice* and what Wolfit called 'potted versions' of *Othello* and *Richard III*. Only the theatre's stalls were used, and the audience paid one shilling a head admission.

On the first day – 13 October – they played to an audience of sixty-one. On the next day, following a direct hit by a bomb on the rear of the theatre, they arrived to find the dressing-rooms in ruins and the stage ankle-deep in dust and soot. But as troupers they were not deterred; they changed on the stage before curtain-up and the show went on.

By October's end, Wolfit's company was playing to audiences of 1,000 a week, and the *Daily Express*'s appropriate headline was: SHAKESPEARE BEATS HITLER. Ever ingenious, Wolfit had even been prompted to add the graveyard scene from *Hamlet* to the repertoire; the stage door, which had been blown clean into the street, would make a perfect bier for Ophelia.

The Minister of Food, Lord Woolton, was a seasoned enough politician to record a shrewd insight in his diary as the winter drew on: 'It isn't the Government of this country that's going to win the war – it's the people!'

Outside the Axis camp, one man remained resolutely disenchanted with the British: Eire's Eamon de Valera.

On 5 November, speaking in the House of Commons, Churchill had harked back to the vital treaty ports of Queenstown, Berehaven and Lough Swilly, which Chamberlain had handed back to Eire in 1938. Now that the U-Boats had intensified their war on British shipping, Churchill said, the deprivation of those ports was 'a grievous burden'.

Now Roosevelt's Envoy Extraordinary and Minister-Plenipotentiary in Eire, David Gray, entered the picture. Over lunch outside Dublin with de Valera's Permanent Secretary for External Affairs, Joseph P. Walshe, Gray put the U.S. case plainly: many Americans would view Churchill's complaints with sympathy. There was likely to be impatience with de Valera for withholding those bases.

Walshe was equally blunt. If the Irish ever leased those ports to the British, the devious British would never hand them back.

Gray looked further ahead. Supposing at a later stage, America was attacked by Japan, and needed those ports – what then? As far back as April, de Valera had told Gray: 'If you [America] should become involved in the war, of course that would change matters for us overnight.'

Walshe agreed. Whether or not Ireland entered the war, there would be little difficulty in arranging to lease the Americans ports and airfields. But even if the Americans stood in as guarantors, he doubted if the British would be granted such a lease.

'As we see it here,' Gray summed up in his dispatch to the State Department, 'any attempt by Churchill to negotiate for the ports would be hopeless. He has the choice between seizing them and paying the price in possible bloodshed and certain hostility, or doing without.

'De Valera's whole power,' he pointed out shrewdly, 'is based on his genius for engendering and utilizing anti-British sentiment ... He is probably the most adroit politician in Europe and he honestly believes all he does is for the good of his country. He has the qualities of martyr, fanatic and Machiavelli. No one can outwit him, frighten or blandish him. Remember that he is not pro-German or personally anti-British but only pro-de Valera ...'

In contrast with Churchill's buoyant demeanour, Adolf Hitler knew only frustration. In the last week of October, his potential allies were one by one proving bent or broken reeds.

As far back as 6 September, alarmed by Roosevelt's destroyer deal, Hitler had set the seal on Operation Felix – the seizure of Gibraltar, designed to give Germany control over the Mediterranean before any further American intervention. In this he counted confidently on Spain's readiness to enter the war. One week later, Ribbentrop, in Berlin, began applying the first pressures to General Francisco Franco's Foreign-Minister-designate, Ramon Serrano Sûner. Sûner temporized. If Spain were to be involved, he pointed out, she would need 38-centimetre guns – which he knew Germany could not supply – to say nothing of up to 700,000 tons of grain to feed her people, food and equipment for her army, aircraft and artillery. Then, too,

Spain had territorial rights in Morocco, which she would call on Germany to support.

Thus, on 22 October, as his armoured nine-coach train rolled into the sunny little French town of Hendaye, hard by the Spanish border, Hitler had two objectives in his first-ever meeting with Franco: to bring Spain into the Axis alliance and to gain Franco's assent for the attack on Gibraltar. Franco, by contrast, had but one objective: to avoid precise commitments of any kind.

The *Caudillo*'s motives were unimpeachable. Fifteen days earlier, he had informed Roosevelt that it was now in his power to affect the whole course of the war: if the United States provided Spain with wheat, Spain would stay neutral. The British Cabinet, sounded out by the State Department, had approved, provided always that American agents handled the distribution, and that none was re-exported. Franco was on the point of clinching a better deal than the Führer could hope to offer, one that would fill his country's granaries.

In the panelled saloon of Hitler's train, there now ensued some of the most frustrating hours of the Führer's life – 'rather than go through it again,' he told Mussolini later, 'I would prefer to have three or four teeth taken out'. For the most part, Franco sat huddled impassively on his chair, saying nothing, as Hitler launched into flights of strategic fancy. In the New Year, he urged, Spain could declare war on England, and the crack assault troops who on 10 May had stormed the Belgian fort of Eben Emael would seize Gibraltar. Then it would be restored to Spain.

When Hitler finally subsided, Franco began to speak in a high quiet voice which reminded the interpreter, Paul Schmidt, 'of a muezzin calling the faithful to prayer'. Spain, Franco said, was hungry and needed several thousand tons of wheat immediately. Could Hitler undertake to fill her granaries? Then it was unthinkable to offend Spanish national pride by using foreign troops against Gibraltar. Spanish troops must be used, and they would need modern equipment.

In growing irritation, Hitler began to drum his fingers on the side of his chair, but Franco had by no means finished. It was very premature, he opined, to say, as Hitler had said, that the

274

British had been defeated, for they would fight to the last man on their own soil, and behind them stood the enormous power of the United States.

When Hitler countered this with hints of an anti-British alliance with France, Franco was scornful. This was pure delusion on the Führer's part, for France would never ally herself to fight with Germany.

At one point, Hitler sprang to his feet, exclaiming that there was no point in going on, but although he controlled his temper within minutes, he won no ground from the canny Galician. That evening, after an expansive dinner, Hitler sought to pressure Franco further, but in vain. After nine hours of fruitless parley, he left Hendaye with no more than a protocol providing for Spain's entry into the war, on a date unspecified, subject to prior deliveries of food and arms.

From the frustrations of meeting with 'that Jesuit swine', Hitler journeyed on for a galling encounter, on 24 October, at Montoire, near Tours, with 'that dirty democratic cheapjack politician', Pierre Laval, Vice-Premier of France, who had persuaded the reluctant Marshal Henri-Philippe Pétain to accompany him. Once more the Führer was irked by the French statesmen's evident awe of the United States – 'the thought of an American landing on the Continent is militarily speaking a pure illusion', he told Pétain irritably – and by their palpable desire to stay on the sidelines. Pétain was ready to accept the principle of collaboration, he agreed, but he could not define the limits. 'Don't press us to make war on Britain,' Laval interjected; 'it will be necessary to prepare public opinion.' Pétain, he added, could not declare war without a vote from the Chamber of Deputies, which the Chamber would probably refuse.

The one man thirsting for action, Benito Mussolini, had already embarked on the precise commitment from which Hitler had sought to avert him. 'This is downright madness,' the Führer had raged. 'How can he do such a thing?' For at 9 a.m. on 28 October, passing through Bologna en route to Florence, Hitler and his party had learned from the railway telegraph office that they were two hours too late to halt Mussolini in a reckless invasion of Greece.

'The Italians will never get anywhere against the Greeks in

autumn rains and winter snow,' Ribbentrop had explained to his entourage before the blow fell. 'The Führer intends at all cost to hold up this crazy scheme.'

No man among the Germans could divine the real reason for Mussolini's action: the Italian's lifelong persecution-phobia. On 4 October, when the two dictators had met on the Brenner Pass, dividing Austria from Italy, Hitler had made no mention of the fact that he was sending troops to occupy oil-rich areas of Romania. The news of this coup on 12 October reduced Mussolini to trembling fury.

'Hitler always faces me with a *fait accompli*,' he exploded to Count Ciano. 'This time I am going to pay him back in his own coin. He will find out in the papers that I have occupied Greece. In this way the equilibrium will be re-established.'

Hitler, knowing nothing of this, was not only angry but perplexed besides. 'If he wanted to pick a fight,' he asked *Feldmarschall* Keitel rhetorically, 'why didn't he attack in Malta or Crete? It would at least make some sense in the context of war with Britain in the Mediterranean.'

Nor was his humour improved by Mussolini's greeting as his train reached Florence. As Hitler's face, smiling strainedly, appeared at his compartment window, Mussolini hailed him from the platform in the high-flown style of a Fascist war communiqué: 'Führer, we are on the march! Victorious Italian troops crossed the Greco–Albanian border at dawn today!'

'The whole outcome will be military catastrophe,' were Hitler's first words as the two men entered the privacy of a waiting-room, but neither man could then foresee that with this foolhardy gesture Mussolini had ultimately doomed both the Third Reich and his own Fascist régime.

Within weeks, the Duce's ill-equipped troops were in headlong retreat, surrounded at the ports of Durazzo and Valona, their backs to the sea. To rescue them, and to maintain German supremacy in the Balkans, Hitler had to divert 680,000 troops to strike at Greece through Romania and Bulgaria. But to achieve this, in April 1941, called for a ruinous change of priorities; Operation Barbarossa, Hitler's long-awaited assault on Russia, had to be delayed four weeks, until 22 June – time enough to bog down the German armies in the sub-zero nightmare of a

Russian winter. Nor did the Führer's efforts to redeem his ally save the 20,000 Italians who died on Greek battlefields, the 40,000 wounded, the 26,000 taken prisoner, the 18,000 crippled with frost-bite.

Mirroring the Führer's mood of black futility as October ended, an editorial in that day's *Le Temps* of Paris confessed: 'There are days when it is difficult to write anything at all on any subject whatsoever.'

Around 5.30 p.m. on Thursday, 14 November, Dr R. V. Jones was once again in a quandary. In his London office by St James's Park, the young scientist was listening with growing disquiet to Wing Commander Edward Addison, of No. 80 Signals Wing, which handled the jamming of the German detector beams. A Luftwaffe raid was scheduled for that night, and Addison needed a snap decision.

In the weeks since the dockland raid of 7 September, Jones, with the help of 'Enigma' cryptographers at Bletchley Park, had at last plumbed the long-standing mystery of the X-Gerät. An intricate device involving up to six intersecting beams, code-named after German rivers – 'Weser', 'Spree', 'Rhein', 'Elbe', 'Isar' and 'Oder' – the X-Gerät ensured the German bomber pilots using it an aiming accuracy of around ten yards at 200 miles. The first aircraft to have been equipped, the Heinkels of *Hauptmann* Friedrich Karol Aschenbrenner's Bomber Group 100, could thus find their target even under blind bombing conditions – and start up fires which the bombers in their wake could not fail to see.

Since 3 p.m., Addison now explained to Jones, the beams had been intersecting over the industrial Midlands. So on what frequency should the jammers be set tonight?

Jones had known for days now that an all-out German air attack, called 'Operation Moonlight Sonata', was imminent. This much 'Enigma' traffic had established, although predicted targets had included Greater or Central London, the Farnborough–Reading area, and the Isle of Sheppey. To compound confusion, Coventry and Birmingham had been mentioned, too – with the raids timed for any night between 15 November and 20 November.

Thus Jones could offer little more than an inspired guess. The filter of a salvaged Heinkel 111, which had crashed at Bridport, Dorset, on 6 November, had been tuned to 2,000 cycles per second – a high-pitched note, corresponding to a piano's top 'C'. Feasibly, he told Addison, 2,000 cycles would be the frequency in use that night.

Few men had any inkling that Coventry was the target, and none less so than Winston Churchill. At this hour, the Premier was departing for a working week-end in the country, along with his duty private secretary, John Martin. At the last moment, a top secret message arrived, which he tucked inside the yellow box reserved for 'Enigma' messages. But barely had his car reached Kensington Gardens than Churchill was instructing chauffeur Joseph Bullock: 'Back – back to Downing Street!' The beams, he explained to Martin, indicated a mammoth raid – 'and I am not going to spend a night peaceably in the country while the metropolis is under heavy attack.'

Later the legend was to arise that Churchill, following days of anguish, had abandoned Coventry to its fate rather than compromise the 'Enigma' secret, but the truth was more prosaic. Aside from indicating a large-scale raid on a variety of targets, 'Enigma' had made no more positive contribution, and Churchill's night of anguish was passed on the Air Ministry roof, along with General Ismay, awaiting bombers that never came.

Even the duty cypher watch, at Hut No. 6, Bletchley Park, were sure of only one thing: tonight's target had never yet been attacked in strength. All of them by now knew *Liebe* as Liverpool, and *Mülkasten* (dustbin) was Hull, but tonight's target bore a codename never previously encountered: *Korn*.

Coventry was indeed a prime industrial target. To its 238,000 citizens it was much more than the medieval 'City of Three Spires', with its crooked timbered back streets, and its legend of Lady Godiva and Peeping Tom. Scattered across its thirty square miles were scores of shadow factories given over to vital war production: the Vickers Armstrong and Hawker Siddeley works, turning out engines for Blenheim and Whitley bombers, a Rolls-Royce plant, whose Merlin engines powered the Spitfire, the Daimler factory, producing scout cars, Courtauld's, devoted to nylon parachutes, and the Dunlop tyre company.

By now, after seventeen tip-and-run raids, the citizens had grown wary. Trekking – by bus, train or bicycle – to country chalets or 'safe' towns like Kenilworth or Warwick, had become a way of life; up to half the population slept away from the city each night. Hundreds of garden gates bore a laconic chalkmark, 'S.O.' (Sleeps Out), to save rescue parties needless digging if the house was hit.

On 14 November, few had premonitions. At 62 Tennyson Road, Mrs Dorothy Prideaux was baffled by the strange antics of her Aberdeen terrier, Susan, recently the proud mother of seven puppies. As early as 5.30 p.m. Susan became uneasy – whining and tugging her mistress's skirts, urging her towards the outdoor Anderson shelter. In vain, Dorothy Prideaux protested, 'Go on, you fidgety Phil!'; finally, past patience, she flung open the shelter door. At once the terrier carried all seven pups to their boxes beneath Mrs Prideaux's bunk, then returned to the kitchen door, yelping a warning.

At The Bell Inn, Keresley, the landlord, Harry Ward, was uneasy, too. On an impulse, not knowing why, he phoned his staff of three, bidding them not to come on duty.

Thousands left in the city had no choice; almost every factory was working at full pitch now, a 12-hour 7-day week. At the main Daimler works, on Sandy Lane, due north of the city centre, 400 workers were just then punching the time clock for the night shift. It was the same all over Coventry.

At a score of airfields in Northern France and Holland – Vendeville, near Lille, Castle Roland, by Versailles, Eindhoven – the German bomber pilots had assembled for their pre-flight briefing as early as 5 p.m. *Oberfeldwebel* Werner Handorf was one of many who heard the official reason for the sortie: a reprisal raid for an attack on Munich, Hitler's cherished city, on 6 November. The truth would have been less reassuring: the need to stage a knock-out blow before American industrial output gave Britain the edge over Germany. But there seemed every chance of success. Between them, over an 11-hour period, 500 HE 111s and JU 88s were to drop an unprecedented 503 tons of high explosives, including fifty parachute (or land) mines on the city known as Target 53, a city already ablaze with incendiaries dropped by Aschenbrenner's spearhead force.

Nothing was left to chance. At 6.17 p.m., local time, as the first HE 111s of Bomber group 100 crossed the English coastline at Lulworth, Dorset, riding the tone zone of the Director beam 'Weser', every man was flying in unwavering Indian file, as if the pilots walked a kind of aerial tightrope, until the main cross signal beam indicated Coventry five kilometres ahead. In the bluish light of the instrument panels, the plane commanders examined their pocket street-maps of the city, the key objectives clearly circled in red: the Hill Street gasholders, the Alvis aero-engine works, the British Piston-Ring Company.

At 7.11 p.m., the cold high voice of the siren wavered and cried for one long minute over Coventry's rooftops. Then the first of 30,000 incendiary bombs came whistling from the sky.

To those watching, the scene was indescribable. The bombs were falling on tenement gutters, and on warehouse roofs; lodging in drain-pipes and window ledges; on pavements and in doorways; on the chancel roof of the thirteenth-century St Michael's Cathedral. They burned with a sizzling blue-white glare; above them, chandelier flares came dripping beautifully down, like Chinese lanterns, bathing the streets, the factories, the slate roofs in a purer whiter glow than moonlight.

Even trained observers were aghast, as if they sensed already this was bigger than anything a British city had ever known. At the thirteenth-century Church of Holy Trinity, in the city centre, the Reverend G. W. Clitheroe remarked to his curate, Kenneth Thornton: 'Strangely persistent, this raid tonight, Kenneth.' At Gulson Road Hospital, Student Nurse Kathleen Colwill, heading for the Emergency Operating Theatre, clutched a precautionary plate of baked beans on toast; who knew when she would get to eat again?

The unearthly beauty of the fires mesmerized all who saw them. To City Chamberlain John Bayley Shelton, in Little Park Street, the leaping flames seemed to drift 'like the sparks from a blacksmith's forge'. For hairdresser Megan Ryan, watching from her flat, atop a wooden table, 'it was like a transformation scene in a pantomime'. Deputy Chief Fire Officer John Watkin, on duty at the Rootes plant, saw the yellow licking flames as 'like a row of beautiful crocuses in early Spring'.

Now the high explosives followed – a whining shuddering roar like an express train flashing from a tunnel. Between each shockwave of sound, eerie noises became audible: distant bombs, 'as if a truck was unloading a consignment of bricks'; the sinister 'adder-like hissing' of burning incendiaries; very far away, a fire-engine tolling like a passing-bell. Bargee William Prue, sheltering with a crowd under a railway arch at Longford, heard one woman voice the awestruck feeling: 'He means it tonight.'

As the blind fury of the raid struck home, one single thought outraged the citizens: the bombers were having it all their own way. For Dr R. V. Jones, 100 miles south in Richmond, Surrey, his sense of guilt was at first overwhelming: because he had guessed the wrong frequency, hundreds were doomed to die. Yet by tragic irony, Jones had been right: every bomber airborne this night was operating on the carrier frequency that he had forecast.

Later a post-mortem revealed that a careless – or tone-deaf – jamming technician had identified an audible frequency of 1,500 cycles per second – a note equivalent to the 'G' below top 'C'. Thus with the jammers operating on the wrong frequency Aschenbrenner's spearhead force could home in on their targets unopposed – with only twenty-four 3.7-inch anti-aircraft guns and twelve quick-firing 40-mm Bofors guns to defend the stricken city.

By 8 p.m., the Central Fire Station had charted 240 fires, many of them out of control – and thirty minutes later, volunteer firemen drafted in from Rugby found the city centre's water mains fractured. By 9.30 p.m., the telephones were out; Coventry was cut off from the outside world. Slowly the defenders were acknowledging defeat; at 11 p.m. Provost Richard Howard and his firewatchers abandoned the battle to save St Michael's Cathedral. From the doorway of St Mary's Police Station they listened, sick at heart, to the steady drip-drip of molten lead, until the great steel girders spanning the nave, glowing white-hot, 'tugged the walls and pillars from their foundations like so many Samsons'.

It was a night of horror that none would ever forget. Gunner William Davies, on ten days' leave, stumbled over a prostrate body in Hertford Street and recoiled aghast – then realized it was one of the city's three statues of Peeping Tom. Along with a colleague, Daimler's Labour Manager, Leslie Wale, tussled for minutes on end to free a signalman on the railway embankment near by; telephone wires had fallen to enmesh the man from head to foot like an escapologist. Ambulance Driver Wilfred Bevan recovered one torso so maimed that only the absence of genitals told him that this had been a woman; bomb blast had concertinaed both stomach and breasts. At Courtauld's, Fire Officer Bert Bucknall and his mate Cecil Heward were buried by blast astride the main steam duct to the nylon factory, the scalding steam playing like a geyser's jet on Bucknall's legs and Heward's head.

Both men were to survive – though Bucknall was to endure twenty-six plastic surgery operations, and Heward, for whom surgeons fashioned a new face, a new ear and new thumbs, double that number.

Everywhere there were alien sights ... drifting barrage balloons bobbing like giant whales at roof-top level ... a kitten patting absorbedly at charred scraps of paper floating across the gardens ... a length of streetcar track sailing twenty clear yards like a monstrous rocket, clean over a three-storey house. Landlord Harry Ward emerged from his pub cellar, where he had taken shelter, then ran for his life; a knee-high river of boiling butter from a dairy near by was coursing down the street.

At 167 Beechwood Avenue, William Heynes, a liaison officer with Short's Aircraft, was fascinated by what seemed like a large tree felled across the road – a trunk almost twelve feet long, two feet in diameter. 'Come and see this tree,' he called to Dorothy, his wife, then a second later, 'Get *back* – there's a mine outside!' At that moment, in a thunderclap of sound, 1,560 lb of high explosive went sky-high, bursting Heynes's eardrum, burying him upside down in blue clay, showering Dorothy with broken glass, and killing outright their 4-year-old son, Simon, who was crouched beneath the stairs.

For every civil defence worker, it was the most frustrating

night they ever knew. Ambulance Driver Katie Fensom never got within sight of the city's two hospitals – the Coventry and Warwickshire and Gulson Road – all evening; high explosives had cratered the roads like a lunar landscape, cutting off all access. Auxiliary Fireman John Bowles, who brought a fire-engine eighteen miles from Birmingham, was checked by a policeman who counselled, 'You may as well go back, mate; you can't even get in.'

By midnight, many men were as resigned to die as Rescue Worker Albert Fearn. He told himself: 'This is the end – we'll be dead lucky if we see the sun again.'

A few found relief in action. In the sixteenth-century court-yard of Bond's Hospital, a home for aged men, old Edwin Walsh was up all night smothering incendiaries with sand. Told to lie down, he demurred stoutly; he had lain down for no man all his life, and he didn't aim to break the habit at 90 years of age. It was the same with Dr Harry Winter, a young Canadian, at the Coventry and Warwickshire Hospital. Amid carnage which reminded one doctor of 'the wounded in *Gone With The Wind*', Winter carried out fifteen emergency operations this night – most of them by the light of an automobile headlamp rigged to a battery set.

Blitz philosophers had an old adage – 'A bomb never falls in the same place twice' – but tonight even this comforting fiction failed. Soon after midnight, word came to St Mary's Street Police Station: a shelter under Smith's Furnishing Store had been hit and fourteen people were trapped. Police Constable Wilfred Burchett was one of eight men making up a volunteer party to rescue them – but at length, after an hour's digging, he and two others were dispatched to enlist more help.

The errand saved their lives. Minutes later, a hurtling bomb wiped out the five men who had remained.

Even miles from the target, Coventry's agony was a terrible and palpable force. At 6,000 feet above the city, in JU 88 'Bruno', *Oberfeldwebel* Werner Handorf felt his nostrils prickle; the smell of burning buildings had penetrated even the bomber's cockpit. Nine miles away, in Leamington Spa, Station Officer John Barnes, of the Auxiliary Fire Service, watched stupefied as shockwaves of blast lifted slates from the rooftops in a prickly mass like a hedgehog's spine.

Six weeks before 1940 ended, a new word had entered the language of war: to lay waste a city by aerial attack was now to *koventrieren*, to 'coventrate'.

An unwilling eyewitness of this 'coventration' was Assistant Divisional Officer Geoffrey Blackstone. On 13 November, following sixty-six consecutive nights on duty, Blackstone was the first London Fire Brigade Officer to be granted a rare privilege: twenty-four hours' leave. Even so, Major Frank Jackson had added two provisos: Blackstone must travel in a fire car with a driver and leave a telephone number. Almost too weary for jubilation, Blackstone headed ninety miles north for his sister's home near Stamford, Lincolnshire.

At 4 a.m. on 15 November, Jackson awoke him groaning from sleep: 'There's been a heavy raid on Coventry. Get over there – they want 200 London firemen.' One hour later, after a hasty breakfast, Blackstone set off at top speed. But in a village some miles from the city centre he stopped short. A huntsman in pink coat and black cap had loomed like a ghost rider from the early morning mist, peremptorily signalling him to halt. As Blackstone watched incredulously, a pack of thirty foxhounds ambled slowly across the road, then vanished from sight. With mingled anger and disbelief, Blackstone thought: Coventry may burn to the ground, but England's still going on.

He drove into a city that had been gutted almost beyond recognition. At 6.16 a.m. as the last wave of bombers receded towards the coast, fully 60,000 out of 75,000 buildings had been destroyed or badly damaged – among them twenty-seven vital war plants, whose production was checked for weeks. At least 568 men, women and children had died, and more than 1,200 had been injured – and of those fatalities 420, never identified, were buried in a communal grave.

Few of the survivors even knew the raid had ended; with the electricity cables torn apart, the sirens stayed silent that day. Only the wardens' shouts of 'It's all over,' echoing into basements and Anderson shelters, brought the people forth into drizzling rain to view a terrible devastation.

For more than a square mile, the city's centre lay in ruins –

grotesque piles of rubble and masonry, twisted steel girders and looped telegraph wires, wastes of open space pock-marked by gutted shells. 'The streets are plastered with thick red mud,' noted Daimler's Leslie Wale in his diary. 'Everywhere destruction.'

All over Coventry the scene was the same – the silent staring crowds grouped before ruined landmarks, before fires that would smoulder on even until Christmas morning. In hundreds of gardens, dogs and cats waited patiently for their owners to return, outside homes that had vanished forever. Ironically, the smell of the city that morning was the smell of affluence: burning cigars in gutted tobacconists, 300 tons of Sunday joints roasting in the Government Meat Store.

Even a veteran war correspondent, Hilde Marchant of the *Daily Express*, could scarcely take in this year's oft-repeated lesson: nothing and no one was immune. 'It was a familiar sight,' she wrote, as thousands thronged from the city, pushing handcarts and prams piled with belongings, 'one I had seen in Spain and Finland. Yet this was worse . . . These people moved against a background of suburban villas, had English faces, used the English tongue, wore English clothes. They were our own kind . . .'

Many more of them were staying – deeply thankful to be alive, striving to carry on somehow. Gunner William Davies spent his entire ten days' leave at his rented home in Dartmouth Road, cleaning up the mess of plaster dust. Mrs Jessie Pykett set out from Hinckley, thirteen miles away, incongruously clutching a steak-and-kidney pie; the detours, when she reached Coventry's outskirts, took her almost ten miles through cratered streets, and the gravy was running down her skirt, but somehow her fireman husband was going to be fed. In Cox Street, one shopkeeper seemed to those who saw him a symbol of the will to carry on. Sitting stolidly before his ruined premises, he was trying to boil a kettle on a still-smouldering incendiary bomb.

For weeks yet, most citizens would lack the bare essentials of life – gas, running water, electricity – yet the Englishman's sense of business-as-usual still prevailed. Master confectioner Herbert Moore, finding his twelve shops and his bakery miraculously intact, set his staff to work and produced £1,000 worth of eat-

285

ables by the Saturday. At one branch of Barclay's Bank, the cashiers paid out money next day standing on bricks, to dodge the water lapping round them. A department store took press space to announce: 'Messrs Marks and Spencer of Smithford Street are playing their part in defying the activities of the Hun by opening up in Whitefriars Street.'

All through this Friday, the hours ticked away, and Blackstone kicked his heels in black frustration. With the water mains fractured, there was nothing he or any fireman could do. Towards 7 p.m., however, an emergency telephone link was established with London, and one of the first calls was for Blackstone. It was from Major Jackson: 'The X-beam is on London. Come back at once.'

His twenty-four hours' leave was over.

10

'For Me
You Shall Always be Greatheart'

15 November–31 December 1940

On Tuesday, 3 December, quite suddenly, Roosevelt dropped from the sight of official Washington. On the face of it, it seemed a curious decision, as if the President, following his electoral triumph, had grown indifferent to Europe's plight. Even so, at Miami, Florida, on this day, he went purposefully aboard the navy cruiser, *Tuscaloosa*, which had been tied up at Pier 3 since dawn. Thousands gathered to cheer him at 2 p.m. as Roosevelt, standing on the quarterdeck, lifted his hat at arm's length to wave them good-bye.

There was mystery in the air. Reporters aboard the presidential train which had brought him hither had heard more esoteric talk of fishing tackle than of global strategy. The President 'expected' to be absent from Washington 'for about fifteen days'; rumour – unconfirmed – had it that he would 'combine rest with a tour of inspection of defences in the vicinity of Puerto Rico'. Accompanying him were only his close aide, Harry L. Hopkins, and his personal physician and Navy Surgeon General Admiral Ross T. McIntire. There thus seemed no prospect that earth-moving decisions would be reached aboard *Tuscaloosa*.

The President was thinking. 'I didn't know for quite a while what he was thinking about, if anything,' Hopkins said later. 'But then – I began to get the idea that he was refuelling, the way he so often does when he seems to be resting and carefree. So didn't ask him any questions.'

There was much for the President to think about. As far south of the Caribbean as Ecuador, hemisphere defence rested largely on U.S. shoulders, since both the Caribbean and the

Panama Canal were vital to the defence of the continental United States. True, Argentina, Brazil and Chile were arming fast, promising a strong southern half of the hemisphere to balance the strong northern half that American and Canada were building. What loans could do to shore up the hemisphere, the U.S. was doing: $60,000,000 was slated for Argentina, $7,500,000 to Uruguay. Already the United States was becoming banker to the world, a role she would assume increasingly from this time on.

America was giving its all, but could its all ever be enough? China was begging for old trainer planes, for almost anything that would fly. Concerned citizens were urging whole fleets of planes, to aid the Greeks and knock Italy out of the war.

Meanwhile, the last vestige of British influence had been banished from the continent of Europe. Hungary, Romania and Czechoslovakia had all joined the Axis. King Boris of Bulgaria, the last of the Balkan monarchs, was manoeuvring for his life. Only Yugoslavia stayed – until March 1941 – outside the Axis enclave.

If the President was inwardly concerned, it was his particular pride not to show it. On the surface, this was no more than a placid tropical cruise to banish post-election traumas. Following a radio signal from that intrepid fisherman Ernest Hemingway, Roosevelt trawled for marlin between the Dominican Republic and Puerto Rico. He used pork rind on a feathered hook, as Hemingway advised, and caught nothing. He gave lunch aboard ship to the Duke of Windsor, now Governor and C.-in-C. of the Bahamas, and his Duchess. In the evening he played poker, watched boxing matches between crew members, and motion pictures: Alice Faye and Betty Grable in *Tin Pan Alley*, Jean Arthur and William Holden in *Arizona*.

But all along the Chief Executive seemed to be waiting.

On the morning of Monday, 9 December, his vigil was rewarded. In the bright sunlight off Antigua, two Navy seaplanes came roaring out of a cobalt sky, gliding to rest beside the *Tuscaloosa*. Harry Hopkins, who watched them come, felt a perceptible quickening of interest. One of the mail pouches aboard those planes, he thought, might contain a long-awaited letter from Churchill, who had signalled its composition back on 16 November. It would be, the Premier had promised, 'a very long letter on the outlook for 1941'.

It was indeed a long report that Roosevelt read and re-read, reclining in his deck-chair: 4,000 words of it, its tenor universally bleak. The year's escalating losses of over one million tons of British merchant shipping were beginning to make themselves felt. Not less than three million tons of additional merchant shipbuilding capacity would be required for 1941 – a need which only the United States could supply.

But, Churchill warned,

the more rapid and abundant the flow of munitions and ships which you are able to send us, the sooner will our dollar credits be exhausted . . . The moment approaches when we shall no longer be able to pay cash for shipping and other supplies. While we will do our utmost and shrink from no proper sacrifice to make payments across the exchange, I believe that you will agree that it would be wrong in principle and mutually disadvantageous to us if, at the height of this struggle, Great Britain were to be divested of all saleable assets so that after victory was won with our blood, civilization saved and time gained for the United States to be fully armed against all eventualities, we should stand stripped to the bone.

The letter bore out much that Roosevelt had gleaned back in late October from Lord Lothian. 'You must let me know when the red light goes up,' the President had impressed on the ambassador, meaning 'when the British cupboard was bare'. Lothian, who harboured a suspicion that America's bill for the sinews of war might entail selling British holdings in South American railways and Malayan rubber, had replied with a covert warning: if Britain lost her foreign investments and the war's end brought a sharp fall in her living standards, this might precipitate a British revolution. Roosevelt had taken due heed of this.

Although Churchill was not specific in terms of hard cash, Britain was nearing rock-bottom. On the economic battlefield, the country's adverse balance had risen from £27,000,000 (then $108,000,000) to £49,000,000 ($196,000,000). On the home front, she was close to the breadline. In three weeks' time, a gloomy Lord Woolton would report to the Cabinet wheat stocks for fifteen weeks, meat supplies for no more than two weeks, eight weeks' butter supply, three weeks' margarine, twenty-seven weeks' bacon. A stringent cut in the meat ration – to one shillingsworth per head per week – was imminent. Due to tonnage losses, imported fruits – grapes, apricots, bananas – were now a thing of the past. For lack of imported feeds, milk, pork and eggs were running short.

The sole crumb of consolation came from Egypt, where a task force of 80,000 Italians who had rashly invaded from Libya in September found themselves hopelessly routed following a surprise attack launched by the Commander-in-Chief, Middle East, General Sir Archibald Wavell. By 12 December, 39,000 Italians had been taken prisoner, but even this triumph was short-lived when Hitler in February 1941 dispatched *Generalleutnant* Erwin Rommel, whose 7th Panzer Division had harassed the British all the way to Dunkirk, to succour the Italians.

Roosevelt fell to brooding. He recalled not only the 'destroyers for bases' deal but a more recent proposal to build merchant ships in the United States and then lease them for a stated period to Britain. Then, too, there was the 1892 statute, unearthed in the summer by a Treasury lawyer, Oscar S. Cox, empowering the Secretary of War to lease Army property 'not required for public use' for not more than five years 'when in his discretion it will be for the public good'. So, if ships could be leased, why not guns? Why not other munitions?

'One evening he suddenly came out with it,' Hopkins recalled excitedly later. 'The whole programme. He didn't seem to have any clear idea how it could be done legally. But there wasn't a doubt in his mind that he'd find a way to do it.'

'The whole programme' – the answer to Britain's impasse, the weapon that was ultimately to destroy Hitler – was to be known as Lend-Lease, or, appropriately, House Bill 1776, embodying the notion that the United States could supply Britain with munitions for free, to be repaid not in dollars but in kind once the war was over.

On a chill and drizzly afternoon, Roosevelt returned to Washington to share his 'brand new thought' with the White House press corps. It was Tuesday, 17 December, and observers noted that he was tanned and jovial, deceptively off-hand in his manner. 'Of course,' he began, 'there is no doubt in the minds of a very overwhelming number of Americans that the best immediate defence of the United States is the success of Great Britain in defending itself – and that, therefore . . . we should do everything to help the British Empire defend itself . . .'

Then, for forty-five unbroken minutes, Roosevelt held forth in monologue. 'What I am trying to do,' he explained, by way of preliminary, 'is eliminate the dollar sign . . . get rid of that silly, foolish old dollar sign.'

He amplified. Henceforth, he proposed, the United States Government should place *all* the contracts for munitions manufactured by U.S. factories – using some of the products themselves but leasing or selling others if they could prove of greater use in Britain.

Noting the puzzled frowns, he hit upon a homely aphorism. Supposing, he suggested, his neighbour's house caught fire, and he, the President, had a length of garden hose four or five hundred yards long. By taking that hose and connecting it with his neighbour's hydrant he might help quench the fire.

'Now what do I do?' the President asked. 'I don't say to him before that operation, "Neighbour, my garden hose cost me $15; you have to pay me $15 for it." What is the transaction that goes on? I don't want $15 – I want my garden hose back after the fire is over.'

In the question period that followed, the reporters were pressing, but all through Roosevelt contrived to reassure them. No, convoys would not be involved – nor would the Neutrality Act need to be amended. Yes, the United States would pay for all British arms under a 'gentleman's agreement'; the British could pay in kind after the war. Right now, the British were being told to go ahead and order all they needed, up to $3,000,000,000 worth, regardless of ability to pay. No, such steps would not mean a greater danger of getting into war. Yes, a great speed-up of defence production *was* needed – 'to keep all the machines that will run seven days a week in operation seven days a weeks'.

Such speed would be necessary to meet a grim short-term deadline: the spring of 1941, when Hitler might invade Britain.

With their own deadlines in mind, the reporters took his point. The conference ended; they scrambled from the room.

Roosevelt had acted in all good faith, but the danger to the British mainland was receding with each passing day. True, the long night of the bombing was to endure for six months more, and now the fury of the Luftwaffe was extended to the provincial ports, as the bombers smote Southampton, Bristol, Liverpool, Plymouth and Hull. But on 17 December, the same day that Roosevelt had taken the press into his confidence, Hitler set the seal on what he saw as his life's mission: the destruction of Bolshevism.

Twelve days earlier, on 5 December, the Führer had conferred with Brauchitsch and Halder on their basic plan of attack against Russia. To their dismay, he took exception to a move that both men saw as of supreme importance: a blitzkrieg drive for Moscow, in line with Napoleon's initiative in 1812. Not only was Moscow the key to the Soviet communications centre, Brauchitsch protested, but an important armaments centre besides. Hitler would have none of it. 'Only completely ossified brains, absorbed in the ideas of past centuries, could see any worthwhile objective in taking the capital,' was his insulting retort. Now Leningrad and Stalingrad – *there* were the seedbeds of Bolshevism. Wipe out these and Bolshevism would be dead.

On 17 December, the revised plan was laid before Hitler. Once more he made amendments: any advance on Moscow must be delayed until the Baltic States were cleared and Leningrad captured. The operation's title became Barbarossa (Red Beard), after Frederick I, the Holy Roman Emperor, whose legions had marched east in 1190 towards the Holy Land. Its final objective became 'to erect a barrier against Asiatic Russia on the general line Volga–Archangel'.

Next day, 18 December, these decisions were codified in Directive No. 21, the most consequential and far-reaching of all Hitler's directives:

The German Armed Forces must be prepared, even before the conclusion of the war against England, *to crush Soviet Russia in a rapid campaign.*
The Army will have to employ all available formations to this end, with the reservations that occupied territories must be insured against surprise attacks.

The Air Force will have to make available for this Eastern campaign supporting forces of such strength that the Army will be able to bring land operations to a speedy conclusion . . .
The main efforts of the navy will continue to be directed against England . . .

The secret was well-kept. Only in the villages of East Prussia, around Lötzen and Rastenburg, were the farmers and field-workers bewildered: an official circular from the local branch offices of the Nazi Party had forbidden them to prepare their fields for spring planting. At the same time every man was told to submit a return of all his available draught horses. By degrees, it seemed, the area was being transformed into a vast military operations zone.

This was the year when the Christmas message of peace on earth and goodwill to men could mean everything or nothing at all. For much of occupied Europe, in this second year of war, it meant nothing. Few would have heat, fewer still enough to eat, not one in a thousand could travel where he pleased or hear uncensored news. Comfortable clothing would be a luxury, and the old killer diseases were stalking the land: influenza and pneumonia, typhus, tuberculosis and cholera.

Nor was this bleak outlook confined to the occupied nations. Italians in the hills of Greece passed Christmas chewing on raw mule flesh, and the average German civilian's Christmas fare would have been unacceptable in any American gaol.

Many lessons had been learned, and many of them were negative. Twelve months of anguish had trespassed on human hope. Young men had been struck down, boundaries had been swept aside, loyalties had faltered. The whole world from the Arctic to the Southern Pacific, had learned to fear, to suspect, and to hate. Everywhere there had been symptoms of insanity. Saxons had fought against Anglo-Saxons and destroyed their monuments; ally had turned against ally; Oriental had fought against Oriental in China. Nations had made alliances to destroy other nations, preparing to turn on one another when the task was complete.

Many lucky enough to celebrate Christmas at all celebrated in alien surroundings. Count René de Chambrun and his wife

Josée passed Christmas not in their Paris flat, but in a suite in New York's Ritz Hotel. Ex-Mayor Theodor Broch, whose wife and daughter would not arrive until February, saw out Christmas far from Narvik, in Minneapolis, Minnesota.

Werner Mölders, promoted *Oberstleutnant* at twenty-seven, had eleven months to live before a flying accident ended his life in 1941. But already, as 1940 ended, his disillusionment went deep. The R.A.F. had not been beaten, the Royal Navy had not been destroyed; so many brave and good men from Fighter Group 51 had died in vain. At last he acknowledged the truth; from the first Göring had been a crass egotist, who had lost all interest in the war. It was out of this anguish that Mölders cried to his friend Fritz von Forell: 'A world is breaking up under my feet.'

Kapitänleutnant Otto Kretschmer was disillusioned, too, for different reasons. Christmas with his crew at Krummheubel, a Silesian ski resort, had been unwarrantably interrupted by a publisher from Berlin, pestering him to write his memoirs and refusing to take no for an answer. 'The answer is still no!' Kretschmer retorted, pale with rage, on the second occasion. It was days before his anger subsided; he and his men were fighting a private war, a combat only they and perhaps those who hunted them could comprehend. On 16 March 1941 the destroyer H.M.S. *Walker* put an end to that war, sinking U-99 and taking Kretschmer prisoner, but until that time he kept faith. Neither he nor any of his men ever jumped through hoops for Dr Göbbels's three-ring propaganda circus.

Polly Peabody finally got air passage from Lisbon to England on Christmas Eve and passed a subdued Christmas in Bristol's Royal Hotel. A handful of people with paper hats perched on their heads sat in the hotel's dining-room, silently eating the traditional plum pudding. Suddenly a poker-faced man alone in a corner picked up a cardboard trumpet lying beside his plate and blew a defiant toot. Fired by the challenge, a middle-aged woman tripped across the floor and blew a whistle in somebody's ear. A mild frenzy took hold; wads of pink cotton wool splashed in Polly's soup and eddying confetti spangled her hair. Just as suddenly, the gaiety petered out; the room relapsed into silence.

The year was dying as it had dawned – 'not with a bang but a whimper'.

At the White House, Washington, D.C., it had been a quieter Christmas than usual for the Roosevelts. For the first time the family were scattered; only Franklin Roosevelt III, aged two-and-a-half, and Harry Hopkins's small daughter, Diana, were in the right age bracket to hang their stockings on the President's bedroom mantelpiece. One tradition, though, remained unbroken; on Christmas Eve, following the family dinner, Roosevelt, as always with dramatic relish, read from Dickens's *Christmas Carol,* winding up with Christmas dinner at the Cratchits' and the jubilation of Tiny Tim.

This year, too, he had set his speechwriters Sam Rosenman and Robert E. Sherwood a harder task than usual. The last Fireside Chat of 1940 was scheduled for 29 December, and Roosevelt was determined to make an end of the euphemisms that, aside from his famous 'stab in the back' reference, had peppered his speeches all through 1940. For the first time he was going to mention the Nazis by name and lash out against the isolationists. 'We cannot escape danger or the fear of danger,' he would warn them, 'by crawling into bed and pulling the covers over our heads.'

As late as the afternoon of 29 December, Hopkins raised a final point. 'Mr President,' he ventured, 'do you feel that you could include in this speech some kind of optimistic statement that will hearten the people who are doing the fighting – the British, the Greeks, the Chinese?' Roosevelt pondered this, tilting his head, puffing his cheeks, until finally he dictated: 'I believe that the Axis powers are not going to win this war. I base this belief on the latest and best information.'

Both Sherwood and Rosenman were intrigued; what, they wondered, could that 'latest and best information' be? Only later did they learn that it was no more than Roosevelt's unquenchable optimism that the Lend-Lease Bill would pass through Congress and make an Axis victory impossible.

That night saw the climax of all that Roosevelt had worked for in the months since he had sat in the silent Oval Office drafting his eighth State of the Union message. Wearing pince-nez and a bow tie, he was wheeled into the stuffy little diplomatic reception room where a plain desk housed a battery of network microphones. A small, intensely partisan, group surrounded him: his mother, Sara Roosevelt, Cordell Hull and sundry Cabinet members, Clark Gable and his wife, Carole Lombard, both militant New Dealers.

It was a speech to echo like a clarion-call across the free world. Within minutes of its culmination, telegrams from all over America were streaming into the White House, and their keynote was set by a letter from Secretary of the Navy Frank Knox: 'For me you shall always be "Great-Heart" after that speech of last night.'

'Never before since Jamestown and Plymouth Rock,' Roosevelt told his listeners, 'has our American civilization been in such danger as now ... The Nazi masters of Germany have made it clear that they intend not only to dominate all life and thought in their own country, but also to enslave the whole of Europe and then to use the resources of Europe to dominate the rest of the world.'

Appeasers in high places, he charged, were in most cases unwittingly aiding foreign agents. 'The experience of the past two years has proven beyond doubt that no nation can appease the Nazis. No man can tame a tiger into a kitten by stroking it ...'

Renewing his pledge to keep America out of the war, the President still rallied his fellow Americans. 'There is far less chance of the United States getting into war if we do all we can now to support the nations defending themselves against attack ...'

That support, he made clear, would be unstinted. 'There will be no "bottlenecks" in our determination to aid Great Britain. No dictator, no combination of dictators, will weaken that determination by threats of how they will construe that determination.'

In a phrase that went down to history, Roosevelt charted the course that Americans must follow for all the days ahead: '*We must be the great arsenal of democracy. For us this is an emergency as serious as war itself ...*'

Even as Roosevelt was on the air, democracy was again

under fire. Promptly at 6.15 p.m., the 'Fire Raisers' of *Hauptmann* Friedrich Karol Aschenbrenner's Bomber Group 100 zeroed in on the vulnerable square mile of the old walled City of London. The recipe for disaster was total: a Sunday night in Christmas holiday week, shops and office blocks closed, churches locked, most fire-watchers off duty. Incredibly, after four months, the Minister of Security, Herbert Morrison, had still fought shy of introducing a compulsory fire-watching service.

By 8 p.m., the situation that Geoffrey Blackstone had all along predicted was reality. A strong westerly wind sprang up to fan the billowing flames; the Thames was at low tide and fifty feet of sticky black mud in which the firemen floundered and struggled, trying to get fireboat hose ashore, lay between the river and the bankside wharves.

Again, emergency water supplies could have proved the answer, and again the Home Office and the London County Council had left it too late.

Huge fires were started, stretching from Moorgate to Aldersgate, from Old Street to Cannon Street. In the wake of 600 incendiary canisters came a hail of high-explosive bombs, to fracture no less than twelve of the City's largest water mains, among them the dirty water main laid to cope with fire-fighting emergencies between the Thames and the Grand Junction Canal by Regent's Park.

It was typical of Polly Peabody to contrive to be in the thick of it. On arriving in London and checking in at a hotel, she had made a bee-line for Fire Brigade Headquarters, intent on hitching herself a ride before the raid had even started. Her father, she explained, had been an active Honorary Member of the New York Fire Department, with two sets of fire-alarms in his front hall and boots and raincoat always at the ready. Her plum reward for being good as a child was always to be taken to a fire.

Jackson, Fordham and Blackstone heard out this breathless stranger in open-mouthed amazement, until Lieutenant-Commander Newcome Hoare, Blackstone's opposite number for the Northern Division, saved the day. Convulsed with laughter, he assured Polly, 'Come on, America, you shall ride in my fire-car as a mascot.' Now, helmeted, booted and in outsize trousers, Polly watched the City burn.

Near by, a bank had caught fire, and cheques and letters of credit were eddying past, performing a frenzied flamenco in hot whirling air. A charred fragment of a cheque fluttered at her feet – 'Pay Bearer, £10,000' – and Polly grabbed for it as a souvenir. Then it spiralled out of reach, caught in the updraft, and was gone.

The firemen's overall reaction was one of total frustration. At Guy's Hospital, south of the river, whose frontage was one wrapping mass of flame, Geoffrey Blackstone realized at length that there was nothing for it; though much of the hospital was ultimately saved, the patients would have to be evacuated. Suddenly Blackstone recalled that in The Ship and Shovel pub, blazing near by, was a mighty wooden table carved with the names of past generations of medical students. 'There's a table in there,' he yelled to two passing firemen. 'Get it out.' To the hospital's eternal gratitude, they did.

Few other achievements were as positive. Auxiliary Fireman Maurice Richardson, watching other firemen on a turntable ladder vainly seeking to save the City's fifteenth-century Guildhall, the home of the City Corporation, was reminded of 'little boys peeing on an enormous bonfire'. Another fuming fireman, Michael Wassey, found no water units, no control centres – two had already been bombed out and evacuated – and 'not one pennyworth of salvage effected or performed'.

By 9 p.m., as the last bombers droned southward, almost 1,500 fires were raging – so intensely that 2,600 pumps mobilized by London Region, and 300 brought in from outside, could achieve almost nothing. Dispatched north of the river in the small hours, Blackstone found the same familiar scene – 'lots of pumps, lots of men, no water'. As he watched, St Paul's Cathedral, ringed by fire, seemed on the point of being engulfed.

From the roof of the Air Ministry, west of the City boundary, the Deputy Chief of the Air Staff watched London burn with an emotion that he recalled as akin to anger. Eight Wren churches – among them, St Lawrence Jewry, St Bride's, St Andrew's – were flaring as brightly as birthday candles; the spectacle of the leaping livid light was so extraordinary that he went downstairs to fetch his chief, Air Chief Marshal Sir Charles Portal. 'Well,' he told Portal, as they watched, 'they are sowing the wind.'

The deadly precedent for Dresden and Cologne, for Berlin and Hamburg, had been established. The Deputy Chief of the Air Staff was Air Vice-Marshal Arthur Harris.

Hundreds of feet above the blazing City, on the roof of St Paul's Cathedral, the Dean, the Very Reverend William Matthews and his fire-watchers, saw disaster as imminent. One incendiary bomb had struck the mighty 148-foot dome, and Matthews and all of them realized the danger; between the outer dome, visible from the street, and the inner dome, floating above the nave, was a hollow space packed with old dry beams.

The incendiary that they watched was lodged upright, halfway through the dome's shell; the lead of the roof was melting and no man could reach it. Then, perhaps appropriately on such a night, in such a place, a miracle occurred. The bomb tilted sideways and fell harmlessly on the Stone Gallery, where a rush of fire-watchers extinguished it.

Though the Cathedral emerged from the inferno almost unscratched, the Chapter House, the Dean's Verger's House, and the Organist's House, all hard by, were gutted. 'Six pails of water,' the Dean noted bitterly later, 'could have saved any one of them.'

The bitterness was justified, for the British Government were still painfully slow to learn the lessons of total war. On New Year's Eve, Herbert Morrison, broadcasting over the B.B.C., threw all the blame on the public for 29 December. Over half the fires could have been avoided if compulsory watching had been in force, yet only now did Morrison announce that all males between sixteen and sixty would register for up to forty-eight hours of fire-watching each month. 'Now we are ready,' commented the Labour Mayor of Stepney, Frank Lewey, sardonically, 'after the event.'

Geoffrey Blackstone was too tired to know what to think. It was 11 a.m. on the Monday before he reached his quarters in Southwark Bridge Road for a bath and a change of uniform. Then it was the same routine as always: office paperwork, an afternoon of drugged and weary sleep, up once more at dusk to dress and await the siren.

It was Major-General Harold Alexander, G.O.C., Southern Command, who on New Year's Eve produced a suitably detached verdict. Over lunch with the Ministry of Information's Harold Nicolson, Alexander summed up the wry equation: 'Archie Wavell mops up 40,000 Italians and we claim a victory. In two hours the Germans destroy five hundred years of our history.'

On New Year's night, Hitler was at the Berghof, his white-painted chalet-style retreat perched on the Obersalzberg, high in the Bavarian Alps. Those present never forgot the Führer's air of calm confidence. It was in keeping with the Christmas card he had selected that year, received by a few intimates such as *Il Duce* and the Göbbels family: a photograph of the Winged Victory of Samothrace, which had been taken from the Louvre in Paris to stand in his Berlin office. The card showed a frieze of German bombers and fighters hovering above the statue, with the caption, 'Our Winged Victory'.

Because it was New Year's Eve and all his thoughts were focused on 1941, Hitler permitted himself a rare glass of champagne. On impulse he approached the huge picture window of the main salon. He signalled to a servant, and the window slid soundlessly from sight. For some time the Führer stood with glass raised, looking out into the night, staring eastward towards invisible sights: the snow-capped Carpathian mountains and the territory of the Ukraine. The most triumphant year of his life was behind him.

Beyond lay the unknown.

Acknowledgements

This narrative of 1940 derives in part from the recollections of several hundred eye-witnesses of events, and in part from records and archive repositories in the United States and six European countries. Those participants whose testimonies I have used are hereby gratefully acknowledged; the details of their individual contributions are listed in the appropriate sections of the source apparatus.

I have to thank Victor Gondos, Jr, Elmer O. Parker and John E. Taylor, of the National Archives and Records Services, Washington, D.C., for furnishing valuable microfilms, and, most particularly, Mrs Kathie Nicastro, of the Diplomatic Branch, National Archives, for help in tracing the dispatches of individual ambassadors and ministers. My thanks is also due to Lieut.-Col. Asbury H. Jackson, Lieut.-Col. Carl W. Ivins, and Major William A. Hintze, of the U.S. Army Historical Division, Karlsruhe, Germany, for the chance to study several unpublished monographs, and for a number of valuable introductions. Equally I owe a special debt to Professor Gordon Prange, of the University of Maryland, and to CWO Katherine V. Dillon for background guidance on the events preceding Pearl Harbor.

In Germany, Professor Dr Jürgen Rohwer, of the Bibliothek für Zeitgeschichte, Stuttgart, was of inestimable help in gaining fresh perspectives on the Battle of the Atlantic. I must also acknowledge the kindness of *Generalleutnant* Panitzki, *Briggadegeneral* Rudolph Jennett, *Oberstleutnant* Technau and Dr Lupke, for the long-standing loan of Luftwaffe records held by the former Führungsakademie, Hamburg, and of General a.D. Paul Deichmann, Werner Andres, Hans-Joachim Jabs, Robert Kowalewski and Hans Ring in providing both manuscripts and introductions. In France, similar help was most generously accorded by the late Professor Hervé Cras, of the Service Historique de La Marine, and M. Henri Michel, of the Comité d'Histoire de la Deuxième Guerre Mondiale. Both for the original material that they indicated and for useful interpretations of vexed questions, I am likewise indebted to archivists and officials in the following countries: *Denmark:* Colonel Prince Georg of Denmark, Dr Jørgen H. Barfods, of the Museet fur Danmarks Frihedskamp, Copenhagen, Dr Jørgen Haestrup, of the University of Odense and Bjarne Maurer. *Netherlands:* Dr Louis De Jong, of the Rijksinstituut voor Oorlogsdocumentatie, Amsterdam and Colonel W. Epke. *Norway:* Lieut.-Col. N. Borchgrevink, of Forsvarets Krigshistoriske Avdeling, Oslo and Lieut.-Col. Jørgen Mørtvedt.

British archives for this period proved singularly revealing, and for permission to study, and in some cases to quote from, records in their keeping, I am grateful to the following: Correlli Barnett and Mrs Patricia Bradford, Churchill College, Cambridge; Dr G. M. Bayliss, Keeper, Department of Printed Books, Imperial War Museum and Mr T. C. Charman; Dr B. S. Benedikz, Head of Special Collections, University Library, Birmingham; Maurice Bond, Clerk of the Records, House of Lords, and Dr A. J. P. Taylor; Sir Norman Chester, Nuffield College, Oxford; Dr Felix Holt, Kent County Archivist, Maidstone; the National Maritime Museum; the Public Record Office; Angela Raspin, British Library of Political and Economic Science (London School of Economics); Robert Shackleton, Bodley's Librarian, Oxford; the University of Sussex (Mass-Observation Archive), in particular Professor David Pocock and Dorothy Wainwright.

All writers in this field are well aware that the documentation and literature of 1940 have now grown beyond all possibility of total coverage. That I have been able to study even a fraction of it has been largely due to a loyal band of researchers and translators. Hildegard Anderson once again covered every phase of my American research meticulously, and in England her efforts were matched by the pioneer investigations of Pamela Colman in many university archives, the long hours spent by both Joan St George Saunders and Alexandra Lawrence in the Public Record Office, and by the valuable translations of Elly Beintema, Inga Forgan and Eva Travers. A special debt is here acknowledged to Margaret Duff, who tackled assignments as diverse as interviewing Coventry blitz survivors and synthesizing French secondary sources and whose final marathon typing stint enabled the manuscript to be delivered on time.

The whole daunting project was first broached by my American publisher, James O'Shea Wade, in the reassuring setting of the cocktail lounge in the Algonquin Hotel, New York, and I have to thank both him and my English publisher, Christopher Sinclair-Stevenson, for waiting so long and so patiently for the final draft, as well as Roger Machell for his invaluable editorial counsel. During that time, also, my agents in London and New York, Graham Watson and John Cushman, offered moral support and solid counsel; Joe and Christine Garner came up with secretarial help whenever it was needed, and Jill Beck, as always, oversaw an impeccable final typescript. In addition I must thank the staffs of the Library of Congress, the British Library, the London Library and the Wiener Library for their unfailing help and courtesy.

The heaviest burden fell on my wife, who not only researched, typed and collated as devotedly as she has always done in the twenty-five years leading up to our silver wedding, but miraculously contrived to nurse me back to health following a prolonged bout of sickness when the manuscript was almost due. Whatever is of value between these covers is in essence due to her inspiration.

Source Apparatus

Chapter One: 'A Shabby and Dangerous Place . . .'

Background on Roosevelt's 'State of the Nation' speech and American involvement is from Baruch, Burns, *Lion and the Fox* (hereafter Burns, *Lion*), Kenneth Davis, Langer and Gleason, *The Challenge of Isolation* (hereafter, Langer, *Challenge*), Long and Sherwood. The Miami scene is from *Time*, issues of 15 January and 19 February. Lothian's correspondence with Chatfield is in the Chatfield Papers, CHT/6/1–5.

The number from *Lights Out*, 'I didn't really never ought 'ave went' was written by Jack Warner and sung by Doris Hare.

For France, see Beaufre, Boothe, Fabre-Luce, Fonvielle-Alquier and Worth. For Germany, see Bayles, Shirer's Diary and Kirk's Telegram 1727 to the State Department, 24 January. For Britain, see Busch, Brittain, Calder, Kenneth Clark, Lampe's *Last Ditch* and Laurence Thompson. Britain's peace-wish is in Mass Observation Report No. 164, Morale. The peers' memorandum to Chamberlain is in NC 7/11/33/1–26D (Misc. Correspondence). The armaments allegation is File NC 8/29/1–8/31/19 (Armaments Scandal).

The Maginot Line mentality is based on an interview with Count René de Chambrun (who also contributed material to Chapters 3, 4, 5, 6, 8 and 10) and on books by Barlone, Chapman, Cot, de Bosmelet, Draper, Horne and Shirer, *Third Republic*. B.E.F. material (and in Chapters 3 and 4) is from interviews with Mr and Mrs William J. Hersey. The Reinberger incident is from Bartz, supported by Irving's *Luftwaffe*. For Finland (and in Chapter 2), see Auren, Cowles, Langdon-Davies, Luukkanen, Mannerheim, Paasikivi, Soloviev, Stowe, Tanner, Upton and Wuorinen. Mannerheim's declaration is from *Time*, 5 February.

The Kaiser is from *Time*, 12 February. Mussolini's advice is quoted by Payne. Roosevelt's brush with the AYC is in Lash, *Eleanor and Franklin*. U.S. waverings over Finland are from Langer, *Challenge*.

Altmark material is based on an interview with Cdr Bradwell Turner, R.N., A. V. Alexander's papers, Dalton's diary entries for 15 April and 2 May, and books by Foley, Jackson and Frischauer and Vian. The Göbbels comment is from Bölcke.

Chapter Two: 'The Position of Small Nations . . . is Clarified'

The finale of the Finnish war (and further material in Chapter 5) is based on an interview with Erik Seidenfaden. Roosevelt's letter to Chamberlain is from the Chamberlain Papers, NC 7/11/33/1–26D, 14 February. For 'Operation Wilfred', see Ash, Ironside and Kennedy. Lothian's reservations are CAB/65/WM 50(40); Daladier's from WM 80(40). The operational plan forms part of Chamberlain's file NC/8–35, Norway Debates. Edwards's objection is quoted by Roskill, *Churchill and the Admirals*.

Gandhi and Bose (and also in Chapter 6) derive from White's Telegrams to the State Department, Nos 1426, 1441, 1459 and 1488, and from books by Ayer, Bose, Kurti, Roy and Toye. Material on the Norwegian scene (and further details in Chapters 5, 6, 8, 9 and 10) is based on an interview with Mrs Polly (Peabody) Drysdale, and supplemented by her book. Denmark's fall is based on Gudme and Telford Taylor's *Conquest*; the invasion of Norway on accounts by Dik Lehmkuhl and Stowe. Narvik material comes from an interview by Theodor Broch, who further supplied information used in Chapters 5, 6, 9 and 10. For Quisling, see Hewins, Knudsen and Vogt. Hauge's trek is from his account, *Odds Against Norway*. For the British débâcle in Norway, see Ash, Connell, Derry and the appropriate regimental histories.

Chapter Three: 'This War is Sheer Madness'

The Chamberlain debate (and subsequent attempts to cement a deal between the parties) is based on information supplied to the author by Sir Martin Lindsay of Downhill, on Dalton's diary entries for 8, 9 and 16 May, Euan Wallace's diary for 8 May, and published accounts by Amery, Blythe, Channon, Donoughue, Duff Cooper, Macmillan, Mosley (*Backs To the Wall*), Nicolson, Spear, Tree and Francis Williams. Gilbert and Gott describe the ousting of Sir Horace Wilson.

Churchill's working methods were described in interviews with Det.-Supt. Walter Thompson and Mrs Mary (Shearburn) Thompson (who also supplied material for the conclusion of Chapter 4). Other sources were Dalton's diary entries for 29 August and 3 September, Wallace's diary for 11 May, and accounts by Cadogan, Colville, Kennedy, Mark and Reith. Churchill's letter to Chamberlain is in File NC 7/9/59–93 (Churchill Correspondence). Beaverbrook's methods emerge from the

Beaverbrook Papers (File D338, letter of 26 August) and from books by Farrer, Maisky, A. J. P. Taylor and Kenneth Young. Churchill's 'muddle and scandal' comment is from the Sinclair Papers (AIR 19/162/1a). The Beaverbrook midnight meeting is from Lockhart.

Accounts of the French campaign (and in Chapters 4 and 5) are based on works by Allard, Barber, Bardoux, Baudouin, Beaufre, Bell, Bertrand, Bloch, Bois, Chapman, de Chézal, Gamelin, Gontaut-Biron, Guderian, Horne, Janon, Jardin, Macksey, Reynaud, Ruby, Soubiran, Spears, Waterfield, Weygand and Williams (*Ides*). Gavoille's experiences are from Mason's *Luftwaffe*.

Dutch material, here and in Chapter 6, is in part based on an interview with Mrs Ida (Van de Criendt) Oxenaar, and on accounts in Boothe, *Dagboek*, De Jong, Douglas of Kirtleside, Maass, Strijdbos, Van Kleffens, Van Someren and Wheeler-Bennett's *George VI*. For Rotterdam, see Bekker.

Roosevelt's dilemma is outlined by Baruch, Berle, Blum, Davis and Lindley, Hull, Ickes, Langer, *Challenge*, and Sherwood. Pétain's farewell to Spain is from Crozier's *Franco*. Sikorski's meeting with Weygand is from Dalton's diary entry of 25 December. Hitler's euphoria is from Ansel. The British Cabinet's mooted deal with Mussolini is based on Chamberlain's diary entry for 25 May (NC 2/24a) and on CAB 65/13/WM 40, 142nd Conclusions, Confidential Annex.

Chapter Four: 'Are We Building Golden Bridges for the British?'

Based in part on interviews with Maj.-Gen. Sir Allan Adair, Lt.-Col. Geoffrey Anstee, Thomas Benstead, Herbert C. Bidle, Thomas Blackledge, Gen. Günther Blumentritt, Lord Bridgeman, Field-Marshal Lord Alanbrooke, Capt. Eric Bush, R.N., Percy Case, Cdr Harold Conway, R.N., Robert Copeman, Lt.-Cdr Ian Cox, R.N., Gen. Paul Deichmann, Victor de Mauny, M. Jean Domoy, *Oberst* Oscar Dinort, *Oberst* Gerhard Engel, Hugh Fisher, Sidney Garner, Amy Goodrich, Lt.-Gen. Sir George Gordon-Lennox, Capt. Renfrew Gotto, R.N., Sidney Grainger, *Generaloberst* Franz Halder, Capt. Harold Henderson, R.N., Cyril Huddlestone, Charles Jackson, Capitaine de Frégate François Kerneis, Bernard Lockey, Lt.-Col. Jack Lotinga, Haydn Mathias, Field-Marshal Lord Montgomery, the late Earl of Munster, Thomas Nicholls, M. Eugène Pauchot, Walter Perrior, Lt.-Gen. Henry Pownall, Fred Reynard, Brig. Eric Rippingille, Gen. Hans von Salmuth, Bill Searle, Gen. Hans Seidemann, Sidney Mason Springgay, Col. Stanton Starkey, Capt. James Stopford, R.N., *Oberst* Gustave Streve, Admiral Sir William Tennant, Admiral de Toulouse-Lautrec, Wilfred Pym Trotter, Lt.-Col. G. F. Turner, Cdr Harold Unwin, R.N., Wilfred Walters, Capt. Eric Wharton, R.N., Fred Williams and James Wilson.

Hitler's halting of the tanks is discussed at length in Speidel's un-published monograph. The Admiralty's reticence in respect of the French is from Mengin. Gort's failure to inform the Cabinet of the Belgian crack-up is Dalton's diary entry for 23 July. Gort's inquiry to Keyes is from Keyes's report in the Gort Papers.

Chapter Five: 'Thank God We're Now Alone'

Churchill's broadcast is from Agar; Kennedy's estimate is from *Foreign Relations Of the United States* (hereafter FRUS), Vol. III, p. 37. Eden's search for 'Storm Troopers' is in CAB/65/WM 170(40). Chamberlain's meeting with Dill is NC 2/21a, diary entry for 1 July. Eden's York conference is from Hudson's diary. The transfer of Britons to Canada is discussed in Longmate's *Fallen*.

Comments on British morale and incipient Hitler-worship are from the following Mass Observation Reports: Attitudes to Hitler; Science, Morale and Propaganda; Defeatism (dated 19 June); A New Attitude to the Problems of Civilian Morale (dated 12 June), and The New Leadership.

Material on Mölders (and in Chapters 6, 7, 8, 9 and 10) is drawn from Forell, and from interviews with Hans-Heinrich Brustellin, Hartmann Grasser, Erich Hohagen, Erich Kircheis, Gunther Matthes and Victor Mölders.

For the end in Norway, see Ash, Connell and Lapie. The flight from Paris follows accounts by Barber, Beaufre, Boothe, Chapman, Dorothy Clarke, de Bosmelet, Fontaine, Habe, Koestler, Mackworth, Paxton, Salesse and Vidalenc. Mussolini's declaration of war is based on inter-views with Gen. Giacomo Carboni, Count Dino Grandi, Count Luca Pietromarchi and the Marchesa Myriam Petacci, supplemented by the accounts of Badoglio and Favagrossa. Aosta's meeting with Lady Loraine is in CAB/65/WM 87(40). 'Duplicity' is Dalton's diary entry for 10 June. For growing U.S. involvement, see Burns, *Lion*, Chadwin and Compton. The German occupation of Paris is documented by Barber, Blumentritt, Corday and Langeron. The Queen's speech is from Litynski. The liquor-train incident is from Habe.

The text of Churchill's undelivered broadcast is in the Alexander Papers (AVAR 13/3). His comment to Morrison is from Morrison's Papers, letter of 5 July. Facets of Hitler at Compiègne and in Paris are from Andreas-Friedrich, Bopp and Huss. Ley's fantasy is from Orlow. German euphoria is from Moen, Prüller and Van Duren.

Ismay's invasion counter-measures are in CAB/65/WM 133(40). The inception of the Home Guard is from CAB/65/WM 130(40). The first invasion precautions are from Wallace's diary entry of 6 June, and accounts by Arnold, Horner and Reith. Initial approaches to de Valera are based on Pound's letter of 4 June to Alexander (Alexander Papers); Macdonald's mission is described in CAB/65/WM 168(40) and 173(40), as well as in Chamberlain's diary entries for 18 June and 25 June. The fate of the spy Goertz is in Stephan.

The exploits of Professor R. V. Jones (continued in Chapters 7 and 9) are taken from his book and supplemented by an interview which he kindly granted to the author. For British ground defences, see Wallace's diary for 2 July, CAB/65/WM 218(40) and works by Bryant, Connell and Horrocks. The Winchester spy is from Royde-Smith; alarm and despondency fines are from *Time*'s 29 June issue. Churchill's plea for a Foreign Legion is in CAB/65/WM 174(40). Conditions at Huyton are in the Monckton Papers (Reports of 13, 16 and 17 July). British xenophobia features in the following Mass Observation reports: Public Feeling About Aliens; German Bomber Down at Eype (dated 11 June); Refugees (dated 6 June). Dowding's remark is from Robert Wright.

Chapter Six: 'I am . . . the Victor Speaking in the Name of Reason'
The Cabinet thinking that prompted Mers-el-Kebir is contained in F.O. 371/24311(2), C 7301/65/17 of 17 June and F.O. 371/2438, C 7074/5/18 of 8 June. The best overall analysis is in Bell. The Churchill–Beaverbrook encounter is from A. J. P. Taylor's *Beaverbrook*. Events at Mers-el-Kebir are documented by Sicard and Tute. Lothian's footnote is from Lash's *Roosevelt and Churchill*.

For conditions in occupied Europe, see, for France: Bopp, Corday, Galtier-Boissière, Langer, *Gamble*, Murphy and Warner. For Holland: De Graaff, Engels and Maass. For Norway: see Alan S. Milward, *The Fascist Economy in Norway*, Clarendon Press, 1972. For Belgium, see Delandsheere, Duner and Moen. Peace-feelers are in Ansel, FRUS, III, 41 (the Duke of Windsor) and Laurence Thompson.

Grew's early warnings on Japanese intentions are from his lengthy Telegram No. 400 of 3 June to the State Department; further details (as in Chapter 9) are in Farago, Pelz and Prange. Halifax's attitude on the Burma Road is in Hoare's Papers (TEM XIII, 12, of 8 July). For Chiang's reactions, see Crozier/Chou and White/Jacoby. Swiss and Hungarian material derives from Kimche and Listowel respectively. Carol's Romania (as in Chapter 7) has been treated by Cretzianu, Hollingworth, St John and Waldeck. For Latin-American material, see Fernandez Artucio, Dulles, Hull, and issues of *Time* for 27 May, 24 June, 1 July and 12 August. For Vargas see, also, Caffery to the State Department, Telegram No. 14 of 14 June, and FRUS, V, 46, 49.

Material on the Battle of the Atlantic (and in Chapters 7, 9 and 10) owes much to information from Prof. Dr Jürgen Rohwer, *Flotillenadmiral* Otto Kretschmer, the definitive study by Robertson and private information from John Costello and Terry Hughes. Churchill's brushes with the Air Ministry begin with his memo to Kingsley Wood (AIR 19/26/1a, dated 27-3-39) and continues with his correspondence with Sinclair (AIR 19/162/1a of 3 June, 6a-6b of 5 June, 12a of 18 July and 18a of 9 August). Lindemann's memo is from the Cherwell Papers, dated 10 July. Churchill's letter to Woolton is from the latter's papers, dated 12 July; Woolton's reply is dated 13 July. For the changing face of London, see the Mass Observation Report on Fashion, and books by Bilainkin, Lee, Panter-Downes and Sansom. Hoare's complaint to Beaverbrook is from the Templewood Papers, dated 6 June. For the inception of Operation Barbarossa, see Ansel, Cecil, Leach, Lossberg, Speer and Warlimont.

Chapter Seven: 'The Whole Bloody World's on Fire'

Battle of Britain material, both British and German (and in Chapter 8) is based primarily on interviews with Michael Appleby, Vera Arlett, Patrick Barthropp, Victor Bauer, Hans-Ekkehard Bob, Bryan Considine, Michael Constable-Maxwell, Michael Cooper-Slipper, Roland Dibnah, G./Capt. Eric Douglas-Jones, Air Chief Marshal Lord Dowding, Johannes Fink, Ludwig Franzisket, Gen. Adolf Galland, G./Capt. Denys Gillam, Marshal of the R.A.F. Sir John Grandy, Hans 'Assi' Hahn, Peter Hairs, Gen. Martin Harlinghausen, Hans-Joachim Helbig, Gen. Max Ibel, Hans-Joachim Jabs, Bryan Kingcome, G./Capt. Thomas Lang, G./Capt. James McComb, Eduard Neumann, Gen. Theo Osterkamp, G./Capt. Robert Oxspring, Air Chief Marshal Sir Keith Park, Dietrich Peltz, G./Capt. Norman Ryder, Raymond Sellers, Eva Smithers, Gen. Johannes Steinhoff, Paddy Stephenson, Henning Strümpell, Mrs Johanna Thompson, Air Cdr John Thompson, Gen. Hannes Trautloft, W/Cdr Robert Stanford Tuck, Dudley Williams, Air Vice Marshal John Worrall and W/Cdr Robert Wright. Peenemunde details are from David Irving's *The Mare's Nest*, William Kimber, 1964. Otto Begus appears in Comer Clarke.

The onset of the London Blitz (and further details in Chapters 8, 9 and 10) is based on interviews with Chief Fire Officer Geoffrey Vaughan Blackstone, and accounts by Bryher, Calder, Harrisson, Lambert, Lewey, Matthews, Barbara Nixon, Robb and Sansom.

Chapter Eight: 'The Way Across the Channel Will Soon be Clear'

Details of Britain's petroleum warfare capability are from the Lindemann Papers. Eyewitness accounts of the night of 7 September came from interviews with Alfred Brind, W/Cdr D. H. Clarke, Reg Cooke, Mrs Barbara (Hornsey) Cunningham, Chief Fire Officer Thomas Goodman, Mrs Lillian Ivory and Alfred Neill. Churchill's

letter to Anne Chamberlain is dated 20 September (File NC 7/9/59–93).
Britain's underground fighters are described in Lampe's *Last Ditch*.

City of Benares details are based on information supplied by Derek
Bech, Mrs Bess (Walder) Cummings, Phyllis and Digby Morton, Mrs
Barbara (Bech) Partridge, Paul Shearing, Mrs Lillian Towns, Louis
Walder, Mrs Beth (Cummings) Williams and Mrs Sonia (Bech)
Williams. Further valuable documentation was supplied by CPO
Arthur Bartle of H.M.S. *Sussex*. Mary Cornish's story is in Huxley.

The birth of resistance in Europe comes from background supplied
by Dr Jørgen H. Barfods, Dr Louis De Jong, Dr Jørgen Haestrup, Bjarne
Maurer, M. Henri Michel and Mrs Ida Oxenaar and on published
works by De Graaff, Delandsheere, Engels, Foot, Gudme, Gunderssen,
Hendrikse, Michel, Myklebost and Riess.

Chapter Nine: 'Dead Lucky if We See the Sun Again'

Churchill's letter to Chamberlain is in File NC 7/9/59–93, dated 24
September. His comment to Ismay is recorded by Lee. Woolton's diary
entries for 11 October and 30 November record his impressions of
Queen Elizabeth the Queen Mother and the British will to resist. Gray's
interviews with Walshe and de Valera are summarized in his Annexure
No. 1, Despatch No. 96 to the State Department, dated 7 November.
Franco's approach to Roosevelt is Dalton's diary entry for 7 October.
The section on the Coventry blitz is based mainly on interviews with
John Barnes, Wilfred Bevan, Bert Bucknall, Kathleen Burrell, Mrs
Emily (Caskie) Fairclough, William H. Davies, Albert Fearn, Mrs
Kathleen Fensom, Dr Henry Gregg, Ernest Hazlewood, Evelyn and
William Heynes, Alfred Holt, Herbert Moore, John Poole, Mrs Dorothy
Prideaux, Mrs Jessie Pykett, Josephine Salond, Leslie Sidwell, Mrs
Mollie Simpson, Sydney Taylor, Dr Charles Turner, Leslie Wale and
John Watkin. The hitherto anonymous account held by the Imperial
War Museum (reference K. 6. 066) was written, vide the *Coventry
Evening Telegraph* of 14 November 1950, by Police Constable W. G.
Lambert. The controversy as to whether Churchill had prior warning
of the raid is well summarized in Longmate's *Air Raid*.

Chapter Ten: 'For Me You Shall Always be Greatheart'

Roosevelt's cruise and his speech of 29 December are amply detailed
by Burns, *Soldier*, Kenneth Davis, Langer, *Challenge*, and Sherwood.
Knox's tribute is from Lash, *Roosevelt and Churchill*. Roosevelt's
confidential talk with Lothian is Dalton's diary entry for 24 October.
(For Britain's parlous food situation, see the Beaverbrook Papers, File
D 337, Correspondence with Woolton, letter of 30 December.)

Hitler's New Year's Eve is recorded by Schirach. His Christmas card
featured in *Time*'s issue of 30 December.

Bibliography

Acart, Captain, *On s'est battu dans le ciel*, Algiers: Arthaud, 1942.

Acevedo, C. de, *A notre corps défendant*, Paris: Dupont, 1945.

Addison, Paul, *The Road to 1945*, London: Jonathan Cape, 1975.

Agar, Herbert, *Britain Alone*, London: The Bodley Head, 1972.

Ailesbury, Marquis of, *I Walked Alone*, London: Routledge & Kegan Paul, 1950.

Albert-Sorel, Jean, *Le Calvaire*, Paris: Juilliard, 1944.

Aleramo, Sibilla, *Dal Mio Diario*, Rome: Tumminelli, 1945.

Alfieri, Dino, *Dictators Face To Face* (trans. David Moore), London: Elek Books, 1954.

Allan, James, *No Citation*, London: Angus & Robertson, 1955.

Allard, Paul, *La Verité sur l'affaire Corap*, Paris: Les Éditions de Frappe, 1941.

Allen, F. L. (with Agnes Rogers), *I Remember Distinctly*, New York: Harper, 1947.

Allingham, Margery, *The Oaken Heart*, London: Michael Joseph, 1941.

Amery, Leopold, *The Unforgiving Years*, London: Hutchinson, 1955.

Amouroux, Henri, *La Vie des Français sous l'Occupation*, Paris: Fayard, 1977.

Andenaes, Johannes, *Svek Och motstånd under Norges ockupationsår*, Stockholm: Bonnier, 1950.

Andersson, Ingvar, *A History of Sweden*, London: Weidenfeld & Nicolson, 1956.

Andreas-Friedrich, Ruth, *Berlin Underground* (trans. Barrows Mussey), London: Latimer House, 1948.

Ansel, Walter, *Hitler Confronts England*, Durham, N.C.: Duke University Press, 1960.

Archer, Laird, *Balkan Journal*, New York: W. W. Norton, 1944.

Arenstam, Arved, *Tapestry of a Debacle*, London: Constable, 1942.

Armstrong, Warren, *The Red Duster at War*, London: Victor Gollancz, 1942.

Arnold, Ralph, *A Very Quiet War*, London: Rupert Hart-Davis, 1962.

Aron, Robert, *Le Piège où nous a pris l'Histoire*, Paris: Michel, 1950.

Ash, Bernard, *Norway 1940*, London: Cassell, 1964.

Astley, Joan Bright, *The Inner Circle*, London: Hutchinson, 1971.

Auren, Sven, *Signature Tune: Conditions in Europe* (trans. Evelyn Ramsden), London: Hammond & Hammond, 1943.

Ayer, S. A., *Unto Him a Witness: The Subhas Chandra Bose Story*, Bombay: Thacker, 1951.

Badoglio, Marshal Pietro, *Italy in the Second World War* (trans. Muriel Currey), London: O.U.P., 1948.

Baldwin, Hanson W., *The Crucial Years, 1939–41*, London: Weidenfeld, 1977.

Ba Maw, *Break Through in Burma: Memoirs of a Revolution, 1939–46*, New Haven: Yale University Press, 1968.

Banks, Sir Donald, *Flame Over Britain*, London: Sampson Low, 1948.

Barber, Noel, *The Week France Fell*, London: Macmillan, 1976.

Bardoux, Jean, *Journal d'un Témoin de la Troisième . . . 1940*, Paris: Fayard, 1957.

Barlone, D., *A French Officer's Diary*, Cambridge: Cambridge University Press, 1942.

Bartz, Karl, *Swastika in the Air* (trans. Edward Fitzgerald), London: William Kimber, 1956.

Baruch, Bernard, *The Public Years*, London: Odhams Press, 1960.

Baudouin, Paul, *Private Diaries* (trans. Sir Charles Petrie), London: Eyre & Spottiswoode, 1948.

Bauer, Eddy, *Der Panzerkrieg*, Bonn: Bodo Zimmermann, 1965.

Bayles, William, *Postmarked Berlin*, London: Jarrolds, 1942; *Wartime Germany*, in *Life*, New York, 7 January 1940; *Hitler's Salesman*, in *Life*, New York, 11 March 1940; *Raeder The Raider*, in *Life*, New York, 29 April 1940.

Beard, Charles A., *President Roosevelt and the Coming of War*, New Haven: Yale University Press, 1948.

Beaton, Cecil, *The Years Between*, London: Weidenfeld & Nicolson, 1965.

Beaufre, General André, *1940: The Fall of France* (trans. Desmond Flower), London: Cassell, 1967.

Beesly, Patrick, *Very Special Intelligence*, London: Hamish Hamilton, 1977.

Bekker, Caius, *The Luftwaffe War Diaries* (trans. Frank Ziegler), London: Macdonald, 1966.

Bell, P. M. H., *A Certain Eventuality*, London: Saxon House, 1974.

Belloc-Lowndes, Marie, *Diaries and Letters* (ed. Susan Lowndes), London: Chatto & Windus, 1971.

Bénoist-Mechin, J., *Sixty Days That Shook the World* (trans. Peter Wiles), London: Jonathan Cape, 1963.

Bentwich, Norman, *A Wanderer in War*, London: Victor Gollancz, 1946.

Berle, Adolf A., *Navigating the Rapids* (ed. Beatrice Bishop Berle & Travis Beal Jacobs), New York: Harcourt Brace Jovanovich, 1973.

Bernanos, Georges, *Les Enfants Humiliés*, Paris: Gallimard, 1949.

Bertrand, Gustave, *Enigma*, Paris: Plon, 1972.

Bethouart, General Émile, *Cinq années d'espérance*, Paris: Plon, 1968.

Bidou, Henri, *Une Bataille de 45 Jours*, Pointe-à-Pitre: Imprimerie d'Entr'aide, 1941; *La Bataille de France*, Geneva: Éditions du Milieu du Monde, 1941.

Bielenberg, Christabel, *The Past is Myself*, London: Chatto & Windus 1968.

Bigham, Hon. Clive (Viscount Mersey), *Journal and Memoirs*, London: John Murray, 1952.

Bilainkin, George, *Diary of a Diplomatic Correspondent*, London: Allen & Unwin, 1942.

Billingham, Mrs Anthony, *America's First Two Years*, London: John Murray/The Pilot Press, 1942.

Birkenhead, Earl of, *Halifax: The Life of Lord Halifax*, London: Hamish Hamilton, 1965; *Walter Monckton*, London: Weidenfeld & Nicolson, 1969.

Blackstone, Geoffrey, *A History of the British Fire Service*, London: Routledge & Kegan Paul, 1957.

Bloch, Marc, *The Strange Defeat* (trans. Gerard Hopkins), London: O.U.P., 1949.

Bloch-Michel, Jean, *Les Grandes Circonstances*, Paris: Gallimard, 1949.

Blum, John Morton, *Years of Urgency, 1939–41: From the Morgenthau Diaries*, Boston: Houghton Mifflin, 1965.

Blum, Léon, *Mémoires*, Paris: Michel, 1955.

Blumentritt, General Günther, *Rundstedt, the Soldier and the Man* (trans. Cuthbert Reavely), London: Odhams Press, 1952.

Blythe, Ronald, *The Age of Illusion*, London: Hamish Hamilton, 1963.

Boas, J. H., *Religious Resistance in Holland*, London: George Allen & Unwin, 1945.

Bodley, Ronald, *Flight into Portugal*, London: Jarrolds, 1941.

Bois, Élie J., *Truth on the Tragedy of France* (trans. W. Scarlyn Wilson), London: Hodder & Stoughton, 1941.

Bölcke, Willi, *The Secret Conferences of Dr Goebbels, 1939–43* (trans. E. Osers), London: Weidenfeld & Nicolson, 1970.

Bolitho, Hector, *War in the Strand*, London: Eyre & Spottiswoode, 1942.

315

Bond, Brian, *Liddell Hart: A Study of his Military Thought*, London: Cassell, 1977.

Bonnet, Georges, *Dans la Tourmente*, Paris: Fayard, 1971.

Boothe, Clare, *European Spring*, London: Hamish Hamilton, 1941; '*Der Tag*' *in Brussels*, in *Life*, New York, 19 May 1940; *Europe in the Spring*, in *Life*, New York, 29 July 1940.

Boothby, Lord, *My Yesterday, Your Tomorrow*, London: Hutchinson, 1962.

Bopp, Marie-Joseph, *L'Alsace sous l'Occupation allemande*, Le Puy: Éditions Xavier Mappus, 1945.

Bose, Subhas Chandra, *An Indian Pilgrim*, London: Asia Publishing House, 1965; *The Indian Struggle*, London: Asia Publishing House, 1964; *Crossroads*, London: Asia Publishing House, 1962.

Bourdan, Pierre, *Carnets des Jours d'Attente*, Paris: Trémois, 1945; *Carnet de Retour avec la Division Leclerc*, Paris: Trémois, 1945.

Bourget, Pierre, *Histoires secrètes de l'Occupation de Paris*, Vol. I, Paris: Hachette, 1970.

Bourne, Richard, *Getulio Vargas of Brazil*, Maidstone, Kent: C. Knight, 1975.

Bouthillier, Yves, *Le Drame de Vichy*, Vol. I, Paris: Plon, 1950.

Brasillach, Robert, *Journal d'un Homme Occupé, 1940–41*, Paris: Au Club de l'Honnête Homme, 1963.

Briggs, Susan, *Keep Smiling Through*, London: Weidenfeld & Nicolson, 1975.

Brittain, Vera, *England's Hour*, London: Macmillan, 1941.

Broch, Theodor, *The Mountains Wait*, London: Michael Joseph, 1943.

Brusselmans, Anna, *Rendezvous 127* (trans. Denis Hornsey), London: Ernest Benn, 1954.

Bryans, John Lonsdale, *Blind Victory*, London: Skeffington, 1951.

Bryant, Sir Arthur, *The Turn of the Tide: the Alanbrooke Diaries*, London: William Collins, 1957.

Bryant, Rear-Admiral Ben, *One Man Band*, London: William Kimber, 1958.

Bryher, Winifred, *The Days of Mars*, London: Calder & Boyars, 1972.

Brzeska, Maria, *Through a Woman's Eyes*, London: Max Love, 1944.

Bullitt, William C., *For the President: Personal and Secret* (ed. Orville H. Bullitt), London: André Deutsch, 1973.

Bullock, Alan, *The Life and Times of Ernest Bevin*, Vol. I, London: Heinemann, 1967; *Hitler*, London: Odhams Books, Edn of 1965.

Burns, James McGregor, *Roosevelt: The Lion and the Fox*, London: Secker & Warburg, 1957; *Roosevelt: The Soldier of Freedom, 1940–46*, London: Weidenfeld & Nicolson, 1971.

Busch, Noel, *England at War*, in *Life*, New York, 1 January 1940;

Little Lord Beaverbrook, in *Life*, New York, 5 August 1940.

Butler, Ewan, *Amateur Agent*, London: George Harrap, 1962.

Butler, Lord, *The Art of the Possible*, London: Hamish Hamilton, 1971.

Byrnes, James F., *All in One Lifetime*, London: Museum Press, 1958.

Cabanis, José, *Les Profondes Années*, Paris: Gallimard, 1976.

Cadogan, Sir Alexander, *Diaries, 1938–48* (ed. David Dilks), London: Cassell, 1971.

Calder, Angus, *The People's War*, London: Jonathan Cape, 1969.

Calvocoressi, Peter, *The Ultra Secrets of Station X*, in the *Sunday Times Weekly Review*, London: 24 November, 1974.

Calvocoressi, Peter and Wint, Guy, *Total War*, London: Allen Lane, 1972.

Cammaerts, Emile, *The Prisoner at Laeken*, London: The Cresset Press, 1941.

Carcopino, Jerome, *Souvenirs de Sept Ans*, Paris: Flammarion, 1953.

Carroll, Joseph T., *Ireland in the War Years*, New York: Crane Russak, 1975.

Cartwright, Reginald, *Mercy and Murder*, London: Iliffe, 1941.

Casey, Lord, *Personal Experience*, London: Constable, 1962.

Cecil, Robert, *Hitler's Decision to Invade Russia*, London: Davis-Poynter, 1975.

Cervi, Mario, *The Hollow Legions* (trans. Eric Mosbacher), London: Chatto & Windus, 1971.

Chadwin, Mark, *The Hawks of World War II*, Chapel Hill, N.C.: University of North Carolina Press, 1968.

Chamberlin, Eric, *Life in Wartime Britain*, London: Batsford, 1972.

Chambrun, René de, *I Saw France Fall*, London: Jarrolds, 1941.

Chandos, Lord, *Memoirs*, London: The Bodley Head, 1962.

Channon, Sir Henry, *Chips, The Diaries of Sir Henry Channon* (ed. Robert Rhodes James), London: Weidenfeld & Nicolson, 1967.

Channon, Howard, *Mid-Ocean Massacre: The Sinking of the City of Benares*, in the *Liverpool Echo and Evening Express*, 13–21 September 1965.

Chapman, Guy, *Why France Collapsed*, London: Cassell, 1968.

Charles-Roux, F., *Cinq Mois tragiques*, Paris: Plon, 1949.

Chatterton, E. Keble, *The Royal Navy*, Vol. I, London: Hutchinson, 1941.

Chézal, Guy de, *En Auto-Mitrailleuse à travers les Batailles de Mai, 1940*, Paris: Plon, 1941.

Christophersen, Major-General Bjorn, *Krigen i Norge 1940*, Oslo: Forsvarets krigshistoriske avedling, 1965.

Churchill, Sir Winston S., *The Second World War*, Vol. I, *The Gathering Storm*, Vol. II, *Their Finest Hour*, London: Cassell, 1948–9.

Ciano, Galeazzo, *The Ciano Diaries, 1939–43* (ed. Hugh Gibson), New York: Doubleday, 1946.

Ciano-Mussolini, Edda, *My Truth* (trans. Eileen Finletter), London: Weidenfeld & Nicolson, 1977.

Citrine, Sir Walter, *My American Diary*, London: George Routledge, 1941.

City We Loved, The, Coventry: Three Spires Publications, 1942.

Claire (pseud.), *Escape From France*, London: Robert Hale, 1941.

Clark, Douglas, *Three Days to Catastrophe*, London: Hammond & Hammond, 1966.

Clark, Kenneth, *The Other Half*, London: John Murray, 1978.

Clarke, Comer, *If The Nazis had Come*, London: World Distributors, 1962.

Clarke, Dorothy, *No Time To Weep*, London: Robert Hale, 1942.

Clegg, Howard, *A Canuck in England*, London: George Harrap, 1942.

Clitheroe, Rev. G. W., *Coventry Under Fire*, Gloucester: British Publishing Co., 1942.

Clonmore, William (The Earl of Wicklow), *Fireside Fusilier*, London: Hollis & Carter, 1958.

Cole, Hubert, *Laval*, London: Heinemann, 1963.

Cole, J. A., *Lord Haw-Haw – and William Joyce*, London: Faber & Faber, 1964.

Collier, Basil, *The Defence of the United Kingdom*, London: H.M.S.O., 1957.

Collier, Richard, *The Sands of Dunkirk*, London: Collins, 1961; *Eagle Day*, London: Hodder & Stoughton, 1966; *Duce!*, London: Collins, 1971.

Collins, Sarah, *The Alien Years*, London: Hodder & Stoughton, 1949.

Colville, Sir John, *Footprints in Time*, London: William Collins, 1976.

Colvin, Ian, *The Chamberlain Cabinet*, London: Victor Gollancz, 1971.

Compton, James V., *The Swastika and the Eagle*, London: The Bodley Head, 1968.

Connell, John, *Auchinleck*, London: Cassell, 1959.

Constable, Trevor and Toliver, Raymond, *Horrido!*, London: Arthur Barker, 1968.

Cooper, Alfred Duff, *Old Men Forget*, London: Rupert Hart-Davis, 1953.

Cooper, Diana, *Trumpets from the Steep*, London: Rupert Hart-Davis, 1960.

Corday, Pauline, *J'ai vécu dans Paris occupé*, Montreal: Éditions de l'Arbre, 1943.

Cortvriend, V. V., *Isolated Island*, Guernsey, C.I.: Guernsey Star and Gazette, 1947.

Cosgrave, Patrick, *Churchill At War*, Vol. I, London: Collins, 1974.

Costello, John and Hughes, Terry, *The Battle of the Atlantic*, London: William Collins, 1977.

Cot, Pierre, *Triumph of Treason* (trans. Sybille and Milton Crane), Chicago: Ziff-Davis, 1944.

Cowles, Virginia, *Looking for Trouble*, London: Hamish Hamilton, 1941.

Craigie, Sir Robert, *Behind the Japanese Mask*, London: Hutchinson, 1946.

Crawley, Aidan, *De Gaulle*, London: Collins, 1969.

Cretzianu, Alexandre, *The Lost Opportunity*, London: Jonathan Cape, 1957.

Cross, J. A., *Sir Samuel Hoare: A Political Biography*, London: Jonathan Cape, 1977.

Crozier, Brian, *Franco*, London: Eyre & Spottiswoode, 1967; (with Eric Chou), *The Man Who Lost China*, London: Angus & Robertson, 1977.

Crozier, William, *Off The Record* (ed. A. J. P. Taylor), London: Hutchinson, 1973.

Cruikshank, Charles, *The German Occupation of the Channel Islands*, London: Oxford University Press, 1975.

Cudahy, John, *Belgium's Leopold*, in *Life*, New York, 25 November 1940.

Curtis, Monica, *Norway and the War*, London: Oxford University Press, 1941.

Dagboek fragmenten, 1940–45, Gravenhage: Martinus Nijhoff, 1954.

Dahl, Colonel Arne, *Med Alta Bataljon mot tyskerne*, Stockholm: Bokförlaget Natur och Kultur, 1945.

Darling, Donald, *Secret Sunday*, London: William Kimber, 1975.

Dawidowicz, Lucy S., *The War Against the Jews, 1939–45*, London: Weidenfeld & Nicolson, 1975.

Davis, Forrest and Lindley, Ernest K., *How War came to America*, London: George Allen & Unwin, 1943.

Davis, Kenneth S., *The American Experience of War*, London: Secker & Warburg, 1967.

De Bosmelet, Diana, *In Golden Spurs*, London: Frederick Muller, 1945.

De Graaff, F. A., *Op Leven en Dood*, Rotterdam: Brusse, 1946.

Deighton, Len, *Fighter*, London: Jonathan Cape, 1977.

De Jong, Louis, *Holland Fights the Nazis*, London: Lindsay Drummond, 1941; *The German Fifth Column in The Second World War* (trans. C. M. Geyl), London: Routledge, 1956.

Dekobra, Maurice, *Sept ans chez les Hommes libres*, Paris: Sfelt, 1946.

Delandsheere, Paul and Ooms, Alphonse, *La Belgique sous les Nazis* (4 vols), Brussels: L'Édition Universelle, 1946.

De Monchy, Salomon, *Twee Ambtsketens*, Arnhem: Van Loghum Slaterus, 1946; *Bezetting en bevrijding*, Den Helder: Van Stockum & Zoon, 1953.

De Polnay, Peter, *The Germans Came to Paris*, New York: Duell, Sloan & Pearce, 1943.

Derry, Thomas, *The Campaign in Norway*, London: H.M.S.O., 1952.

Deutsch, Harold C., *The Conspiracy against Hitler in the Twilight War*, Minneapolis: University of Minnesota Press, 1968.

Diary of a Staff Officer at Advance HQ, North BAFF, The, London: Methuen, 1941.

Documents on British Foreign Policy, London: H.M.S.O., 1946.

Documents on German Foreign Policy, London: H.M.S.O., 1948.

I Documenti Diplomatici Italiani, Rome: Ministero degli Esteri, 1952.

Dönitz, Admiral Karl, *Memoirs: Ten Years and Twenty Days* (trans. R. H. Stevens and David Woodward), London: Weidenfeld & Nicolson, 1951.

Donoughue, Bernard, *Herbert Morrison: Portrait of a Politician*, London: Weidenfeld & Nicolson, 1973.

Doorman, P. L. G., *Military Operations in the Netherlands*, London: George Allen & Unwin, 1944.

Douglas of Kirtleside, Lord, Marshal of the R.A.F. (with Robert Wright), *Combat and Command*, New York: Simon & Schuster, 1966.

Downing, Rupert, *If I Laugh*, London: George Harrap, 1940.

Draper, Theodore, *The Six Weeks' War*, London: Methuen, 1946.

Drawbell, James Wedgwood, *The Long Year*, London: Allan Wingate, 1958.

Drees, Dr Willem, *Van mei tot mei*, Assen: Van Gorcum, 1958.

Dubois, Edmond, *Paris sans lumière*, Lausanne: Librairie Payot, 1946.

Duhamel, Georges, *Lieu d'asile*, Paris: Mercure de France, 1945; *Chronique des Saisons Amères*, Paris: Hartmann, 1946.

Dulles, John W. F., *Vargas of Brazil*, Austin, Texas: University of Texas Press, 1967.

Duner, Paul, *A Year and a Day*, London: Lindsay Drummond, 1942.

Dunning, George, *Where Bleed the Many*, London: Elek Books, 1955.

Durand, Ralph, *Guernsey under German Rule*, London: The Guernsey Society, 1946.

Dybwad, Ejnar, *I saw the Invader*, London: The Pilot Press, 1940.

Eden, Rt Hon. Anthony (Lord Avon), *Memoirs, Vol II: The Reckoning*, London: Cassell, 1965.

Ehrlich, Blake, *The French Resistance*, London: Chapman & Hall, 1966.

Einzig, Paul, *In the Centre of Things*, London: Hutchinson, 1960.

Ekpenyon, E. I., *Experiences of an African Air Raid Warden*, London: The Sheldon Press, 1942.

Eliot, Major George Fielding, *France's Weygand*, in *Life*, New York, 20 May 1940.

Ellis, Major L. F., *The War in France and Flanders, 1939–40*, London: H.M.S.O., 1953.

Eloy, Victor, *The Fight in the Forest* (trans. N. C. Hunter), London: Robert Hale, 1949.

Engels, Adriani, *Nacht over Nederland*, Utrecht: privately printed, 1946.

Fabre-Luce, Alfred, *Journal de la France* (2 vols), Geneva: Bourquin, 1946.

Farago, Ladislas, *The Game of the Foxes*, London: Hodder & Stoughton, 1972; *The Broken Seal*, London: Arthur Barker, 1967.

Farrer, David, *The Sky's the Limit*, London: Hutchinson, 1942; *G for God Almighty*, London: Weidenfeld & Nicolson, 1969.

Favagrossa, General Carlo, *Perchè perdemmo la guerra: Mussolini e la produzione bellica*, Milan: Rizzoli, 1946.

Fernandez Artucio, Hugo, *The Nazi Underground in South America*, New York: Farrer & Rinehart, 1942.

Fernet, Vice-Admiral Jean, *Aux Côtés du Maréchal Pétain*, Paris: Plon, 1953.

Fest, Joachim, *Hitler* (trans. Richard & Clara Winston), London: Weidenfeld & Nicolson, 1974.

Feuchtwanger, Lion, *The Devil in France* (trans. Phyllis Blewitt), London: Hutchinson, 1942.

Fitzgibbon, Constantine, *The Blitz*, London: Allan Wingate, 1957.

Flannery, Harry, *Assignment to Berlin*, London: Michael Joseph, 1942.

Fleming, Peter, *Invasion 1940*, London: Rupert Hart-Davis, 1957.

Foley, Thomas, *I was an Altmark Prisoner*, London: Francis Aldor, 1940.

Fontaine, Peter, *Last to Leave Paris*, London: Chaterson, 1941.

Fontes, L. and Carneiro, G., *A Face Final de Vargas*, Rio de Janeiro: O Cruzeiro, 1966.

Fonvieille-Alquier, François, *The French and the Phoney War* (trans. Edward Ashcroft), London: Tom Stacey, 1973.

Foot, M. R. D., *Resistance*, London: Eyre Methuen, 1976.

Ford, Corey, *Donovan of O.S.S.*, London: Robert Hale, 1971.

Foreign Relations of the United States (5 vols), Washington, D.C.: U.S. Government Printing Office, 1959–61.

Forell, Fritz von, *Mölders*, Salzburg: Sirius, 1951.

Foster, Reginald, *Dover Front*, London: Secker & Warburg, 1941.

Fourcade, Marie-Madeleine, *Noah's Ark* (trans. Kenneth Morgan), London: George Allen & Unwin, 1973.

321

François-Poncet, André, *Au Palais Farnese, 1938–40*, Paris: Fayard, 1961.

Frank, Wolfgang, *The Sea Wolves* (trans. Lt.-Cdr R. D. B. Long), London: Weidenfeld & Nicolson, 1955.

Franzero, C. M., *Cinquantanni a Londra*, Turin: S.E.I., 1975.

Führer Conferences on Naval Affairs (Vol. II), Admiralty mimeograph, Official Publications Library, British Museum.

Galland, General Adolf, *The First and the Last* (trans. Mervyn Savill), London: Methuen, 1953.

Galtier-Boissière, Jean, *Mon Journal pendant l'Occupation*, Garas: La Jeune Parque, 1944.

Gamelin, General Maurice, *Servir* (3 vols), Paris: Plon, 1946–7.

Gaulle, General Charles de, *The Call to Honour, 1940–42* (trans. Jonathan Griffin), London: William Collins, 1955.

Gérard-Libois, J. and Gotovich, J., *L'An 1940*, Brussels: Crisp, 1971.

Gex Le Verrier, Madeleine, *France in Torment* (trans. Eden & Cedar Paul), London: Hamish Hamilton, 1942.

Gibson, Guy, *Enemy Coast Ahead*, London: Michael Joseph, 1946.

Gide, André, *Journal, Vol. IV* (trans. Justin O'Brien), London: Secker & Warburg, 1951.

Gilbert, Martin and Gott, Richard, *The Appeasers*, London: Weidenfeld & Nicolson, ed. of 1967.

Girier, René, *Chienne de Vie*, Paris: André Martel, 1952.

Gladwyn, Cynthia, *The Paris Embassy*, London: William Collins, 1976.

Goffin, Robert, *Was Leopold a Traitor?* (trans. Marjorie Shaw), London: Hamish Hamilton, 1941.

Gontaut-Biron, C. A. de, *Les Dragons de Combat*, Paris: Maillet, 1954.

Gow, Alexander, *Letters from Cambridge*, London: Jonathan Cape, 1945.

Graebner, Walter, *One Year of War in Britain*, in *Life*, New York, 30 September 1940.

Graves, Charles, *Off the Record*, London: Hutchinson, 1942; *The Home Guard of Great Britain*, London: Hutchinson, 1943.

Grazzi, Emanuele, *Il Principio della Fine*, Rome: Faro, 1945.

Grew, Joseph C., *Turbulent Era* (Vol. II), London: Hammond & Hammond, 1953.

Guastalla, Pierre-André, *Journal, 1940–44*, Paris: Plon, 1951.

Guderian, General Heinz, *Panzer Leader* (trans. Constantine Fitzgibbon), London: Michael Joseph, 1952.

Gudme, Sten, *Denmark: Hitler's Model Protectorate* (trans. Jan Nolle), London: Victor Gollancz, 1942.

Guéhenno, Jean, *Journal des Années noires*, Paris: Gallimard, 1947.

Guerlain, Robert, *A Prisoner in Germany*, London: Macmillan, 1944.

Gunderssen, Karl, *Ordforerens dagbok*, Drammen: privately printed, 1946.

Habe, Hans, *A Thousand Shall Fall* (trans. Norbert Guterdan), London: George Harrap, 1942.

Halder, General Franz, *Hitler as War Lord* (trans. Paul Findlay), London; Putnam, 1950; *War Diaries, Vols III, IV, V*, Washington, D.C.: Infantry Journal Press, 1950.

Hambro, Carl J., *I Saw it Happen in Norway*, New York: D. Appleton-Century Co., 1940.

Hanselaar, Bert., *De Zwarte Duivels van Rotterdam*, Rotterdam:Wijt, 1954.

Harriman, Florence, *Mission to the North*, London: George Harrap, 1941.

Harrisson, Tom, *Living Through the Blitz*, London: William Collins, 1976; and Madge, Charles, *War Begins at Home*, London: Chatto & Windus, 1940.

Hart, B. H. Liddell, *The Other Side of the Hill*, London: Cassell, 1948.

Harvey, Oliver, *Diplomatic Diaries, 1937–40*, London: William Collins, 1970.

Harwood, Ronald, *Sir Donald Wolfit*, London: Secker & Warburg, 1971.

Hassell, Ulrich von, *The Von Hassell Diaries, 1938–44* (ed. Hugh Gibson), London: Hamish Hamilton, 1948.

Hauge, Eiliv, *Odds Against Norway* (trans. V. Firsoff), London: Lindsay Drummond, 1941; *Salt Water Thief* (trans. Malcolm Munthe), London: Gerald Duckworth, 1958.

Hauser, Ernest, *Konoye of Japan*, in *Life*, New York, 9 December 1940.

Hautecloque, Françoise de, *La Guerre chez nous en Normandie*, Paris: Colbert, 1945.

Heckstall-Smith, Anthony, *The Fleet that faced both Ways*, London: Anthony Blond, 1963.

Hedin, Sven, *German Diary* (trans. Joan Bulman), Dublin: Euphorion Books, 1951.

Heide, Dik Van Der, *My Sister and I* (trans. Mrs Anton Deventer) London: Faber & Faber, 1941.

Hendrikse, Dick, *De Dag waarop mijn vader huilde*, Haarlem:Drukkerij de Spaarnestad, 1960.

Herriot, Edouard, *Épisodes 1940–44*, Paris: Flammarion, 1950.

Hewins, Ralph, *Quisling: Prophet without Honour*, London: W. H. Allen, 1965.

Higgins, Trumbull, *Winston Churchill and the Second Front*, New York: Oxford University Press, 1957.

Higgs, Dorothy Packard, *Guernsey Diary*, London: Linden Lewis Ltd, 1942.

Hitler e Mussolini: Lettere e documenti, Rome: Rizzoli, 1946.

Hoare, Sir Samuel, *Ambassador on Special Mission*, London: William Collins, 1946.

Hobson, Harold, *The First Three Years of the War*, London: Hutchinson, 1942.

Hodgkinson, George, *Sent to Coventry*, Bletchley: Robert Maxwell, 1970.

Hodgson, Vere, *Few Eggs and No Oranges*, London: Dennis Dobson, 1976.

Hoehling, A. A., *America's Road to War*, London: Abelard-Schuman, 1970.

Hoemberg, Elisabeth, *Thy People, My People*, London: J. M. Dent, 1950.

Hoffmann, Peter, *The History of the German Resistance, 1939–45*, London: Macdonald & Janes, 1977.

Hollingworth, Clare, *There's a German just behind me*, London: The Right Book Club, 1943.

Homa, Corporal, *Onze 80 urige Oorlog*, Amsterdam: De Uil, 1961.

Horne, Alastair, *To Lose a Battle*, London: Macmillan, 1969.

Horner, Arthur, *Incorrigible Rebel*, London: MacGibbon & Kee, 1960.

Horrocks, Lieut.-Gen. Sir Brian, *A Full Life*, London: Collins, 1960.

Horsley, Terence, *Find, Fix and Strike*, London: Eyre & Spottiswoode, 1943.

Howard, Provost Richard, *Ruined and Rebuilt*, Gloucester: British Publishing Co., no date.

Hull, Cordell, *Memoirs, Vol. I*, London: Hodder & Stoughton, 1948.

Humble, Richard, *Hitler's Generals*, London: Arthur Barker, 1973.

Huskinson, Air Commodore Patrick, *Visions Ahead*, London: Werner Laurie, 1949.

Huss, Pierre J., *Heil! And Farewell*, London: Herbert Jenkins, 1943.

Huxley, Elspeth, *Atlantic Ordeal*, London: Chatto & Windus, 1941.

Hyde, H. Montgomery, *British Air Policy between the Wars*, London: William Heinemann, 1977; *The Quiet Canadian*, London: Hamish Hamilton, 1962.

Ickes, Harold, *The Secret Diaries, Vol. III: The Lowering Clouds, 1939–41*, London: Weidenfeld & Nicolson, 1955.

Idle, E. Doreen, *War over West Ham*, London: Faber & Faber, 1943.

Ingham, H. S. (ed.), *Fire and Water: An Anthology of The National Fire Service*, London: Lindsay Drummond, 1942.

Ironside, General Sir Edmund, *Diaries, 1937–40* (ed. R. Macleod and D. Kelly), London: Constable, 1962.

Irving, David, *The Rise and Fall of the Luftwaffe*, London: Weidenfeld & Nicolson, 1973.

Ismay, Hastings Lionel, Baron Ismay, *Memoirs*, London: William Heinemann, 1960.

Jackson, Robert and Frischauer, Willi, *The Navy's Here*, London: Victor Gollancz, 1955.

Jacobsen, Hans-Adolf and Rohwer, Jürgen, *Decisive Battles of World War Two* (trans. Edward Fitzgerald), London: André Deutsch, 1965.

Jakobsen, Max, *The Diplomacy of the Winter War*, Cambridge, Mass.: Harvard University Press, 1961.

James, Admiral William, *The Portsmouth Letters*, London: Macmillan, 1941.

Jamet, Claude, *Carnets de déroute*, Paris: Sorlot, 1942.

Janeway, Eliot, *Struggle for Survival*, New Haven: Yale University Press, 1951.

Janon, René, *J'avais un sabre*, Algiers: Charlot, 1945.

Jardin, Pascal, *Vichy Boyhood* (trans. Jean Stewart), London: Faber & Faber, 1975.

Jasper, Marcel, *Souvenirs sans retouche*, Paris: Fayard, 1968.

Joesten, Joachim, *Stalwart Sweden*, New York: Doubleday, 1943.

Johnen, Wilhelm, *Duel under the Stars* (trans. Mervyn Savill), London: William Kimber, 1957.

Johnson, Brian, *The Secret War*, London: B.B.C. Publications, 1978.

Johnson, Bryan, *The Evacuees*, London: Victor Gollancz, 1968.

Jones, Professor R. V., *Most Secret War*, London: Hamish Hamilton, 1978.

Jones, Thomas, *A Diary with Letters, 1939–50*, London: Oxford University Press, 1954.

Jourdain, Francis, *Jours d'Alarme*, Paris: Correa, 1954.

Jucker, Ninette, *Curfew in Paris*, London: The Hogarth Press, 1960.

Junger, Ernst, *Gärten und Strassen*, Berlin: Mittler, 1942.

Kammerer, Albert, *La verité sur l'Armistice*, Paris: Éditions Médicis, 1944.

Kankrud, Johan, *1940, Krigshendinger i Gausdal-bygdene*, Ostre Gausdal: Mariendals Boktrykkeri, 1956.

Keitel, Field-Marshal Wilhelm, *Memoirs* (trans. David Irving), London: William Kimber, 1965.

Kennan, George, *Memoirs, 1925–50*, London: Hutchinson, 1968.

Kennedy, Major-General Sir John, *The Business of War*, London: Hutchinson, 1957.

Kenney, Rowland, *Northern Tangle*, London: J. M. Dent, 1946.

Kerkmeijer-De Regt, C., *Hoorn in de verdrukking*, Hoorn: West Friesland, 1953.

Kernan, Thomas, *Report on France*, London: John Lane, 1941.

Kesselring, Field-Marshal Albert, *Memoirs* (trans. Lynton Hudson), London: William Kimber, 1953.

Keun, Odette, *And Hell Followed*, London: Constable, 1942.

Kimche, Jon, *Spying for Peace*, London: Weidenfeld & Nicolson, 1961.

King, Cecil, *With Malice Toward None*, London: Sidgwick & Jackson, 1970.

Kleczowski, Stefan, *Poland's First 100,000*, London: Hutchinson, 1945.

Kleffens, Eelco Van, *The Rape of the Netherlands*, London: Hodder & Stoughton, 1940.

Klein, Catherine, *Escape from Berlin* (trans. Livia Laurent), London: Victor Gollancz, 1944.

Knowles, Bernard, *Southampton, The English Gateway*, London: Hutchinson, 1951.

Knudsen, Harald Franklin, *Jeg var Quislings Sekretaer*, Copenhagen: privately printed, 1951.

Koestler, Arthur, *Scum of the Earth*, London: Collins with Hamish Hamilton, 1955.

Koht, Halvdan, *Norway Neutral and Invaded*, London: Hutchinson, 1941; *For fred og fridom i krigstid 1939–40*, Oslo: Tiden, 1957.

Kops, Bernard, *The World is a Wedding*, London: MacGibbon & Kee, 1963.

Kramer, G. and Ballintijn, G., *De Meidagen van 1940*, Enschede: M. J. Van Der Loeff, 1945.

Krier, Pierre, *Luxembourg under German Occupation*, New York: Western Newspaper Union, 1941.

Krock, Arthur, *Memoirs*, London: Cassell, 1970.

Kruk, Zofia, *The Taste of Fear*, London: Hutchinson, 1973.

Kurti, Kitty, *Subhas Chandra Bose as I knew him*, Calcutta: Mukhopadhyay, 1965.

Lambert, Derek, *The Sheltered Days*, London: André Deutsch, 1965.

Lampe, David, *The Savage Canary*, London: Cassell, 1957; *The Last Ditch*, London: Cassell, 1968.

Langdon-Davies, John, *Finland: The First Total War*, London: George Routledge, 1940.

Langer, William L., *Our Vichy Gamble*, New York: Knopf, 1947; and Gleason, S. E., *The Challenge to Isolation*, New York: Harper, 1952; *The Undeclared War*, New York: Harper, 1953.

Langeron, Roger, *Paris Juin 1940*, Paris: Flammarion, 1946.

Lapie, Captain Pierre O., *With the Foreign Legion at Narvik* (trans. Anthony Merryn), London: John Murray, 1941.

LaRuche, P., *La Neutralité de la Suède*, Paris: Nouvelles Éditions Latines, 1953.

Lash, Joseph P., *Eleanor and Franklin*, London: André Deutsch, 1972; *Roosevelt and Churchill, 1939–41*, London: André Deutsch, 1977.

Launay, Jacques De, *Secrètes Diplomatiques*, Brussels: Brepols, 1963.

Laval, Pierre, *Unpublished Diary*, London: The Falcon Press, 1948.

Lazareff, Pierre, *The Fall of France*, in *Life*, New York, 26 August 1940.

Leach, Barry, *German Strategy Against Russia, 1939–41*, Oxford: The Clarendon Press, 1973.

Lean, E. Tangye, *Voices in the Dark*, London: Secker & Warburg, 1943.

Lee, General Raymond E., *The London Observer*, London: Hutchinson, 1972.

Lehmkuhl, Dik, *Journey to London*, London: Hutchinson, 1946.

Lehmkuhl, Herman, *Hitler Attacks Norway*, London: Hodder & Stoughton, 1943.

Leitch, Michael, *Great Songs of World War II*, London: Wise Publications, 1975.

Lemkin, Raphael, *Axis Rule in Occupied Europe*, Washington, D.C.: Carnegie Endowment for International Peace, 1944.

Leske, Gottfried, *I was a Nazi Flier*, New York: The Dial Press, 1941.

Lespes, Henri, *Corps à Corps avec Les Blindés*, Paris: Plon, 1944.

Leuchtenberg, William E., *FDR and the New Deal*, New York: Harper & Row, 1963.

Lewey, Frank, *Cockney Campaign*, London: Stanley Paul, 1947.

Liebling, A. J., *The Road back to Paris*, London: Michael Joseph, 1944.

Lina, H., *Dagboek van een motor-ordonnans*, Amsterdam: Scheltens & Giltay, no date.

Lind, Jakov, *Counting my Steps*, London: Jonathan Cape, 1970.

Listowel, Judith, *This I have Seen*, London: Faber & Faber, 1943.

Littlejohn, David, *The Patriotic Traitors*, London: William Heinemann, 1972.

Litynski, Zygmunt, *I Was One of Them* (trans. Anna Maclaren), London: Jonathan Cape, 1941.

Lloyd, Alan, *Franco*, London: Longman, 1970.

Lochner, Louis P., *Germans Marched into a Dead Paris*, in *Life*, New York, 8 July 1940.

Lockhart, Robert Bruce, *Comes the Reckoning*, London: Putnam, 1942.

Loewenheim, Francis L., Langley, Harold D., and Jonas, Manfred, *Roosevelt and Churchill: Their Secret Wartime Correspondence*, London: Barrie & Jenkins, 1975.

Lomnitz, Alfred, *Never Mind, Mr Lom!*, London: Macmillan, 1941.

London Children In Wartime Oxford, London: Oxford Uinversity Press, 1947.

Long, Breckinridge, *The War Diary* (ed. Fred L. Israel), Lincoln, Neb.: University of Nebraska Press, 1966.

Longmate, Norman, *If Britain Had Fallen*, London: Hutchinson, 1972; *How We Lived Then*, London: Hutchinson, 1971; *Air Raid*, London: Hutchinson, 1976.

Lossberg, Bernhard von, *Im Wehrmachtführungsstab*, Hamburg: H. H. Noelke, 1950.

Lothian, Lord, *The American Speeches of Lord Lothian*, London: Oxford University Press, 1941.

Lu, David J., *From the Marco Polo Bridge to Pearl Harbor*, Washington, D.C.: Public Affairs Press, 1961.

Lukacs, John, *The Last European War, September 1939–December 1941*, London: Routledge, 1977.

Lundin, C. Leonard, *Finland in the Second World War*, Bloomington, Ind.: Indiana University Press, 1957.

Luukkanen, Eino, *Fighter over Finland* (trans. M. A. Salo), London: Macdonald, 1963.

Lyall, Gavin (ed.), *The War in the Air, 1939–45*, London: Hutchinson, 1968.

Lytton, Neville, *Life in Unoccupied France*, London: Macmillan, 1942.

Maass, Walter, *The Netherlands at War*, New York: Abelard-Schuman, 1970.

Macdonald, Rt Hon. Malcolm, *People and Places: Random Reminiscences*, London: William Collins, 1965.

Macintyre, Donald, *Narvik*, London: Evans Bros., 1952.

Macksey, Kenneth, *Guderian, Panzer Leader*, London: Macdonald & Janes, 1975.

Mackworth, Cecily, *I Came Out of France*, London: Routledge, 1941.

Macleod, Ian, *Neville Chamberlain*, London: Frederick Muller, 1961.

Macmillan, Harold, *The Blast of War*, London: Macmillan, 1967.

Maisky, Ivan, *Memoirs of a Russian Ambassador, 1939–43*, London: Hutchinson, 1967.

Maitland, Patrick, *European Dateline*, London: The Quality Press, 1946.

Makucewicz, Peter, *I Escaped from Germany*, London: Max Love, 1944.

Manchester, William, *The Glory and the Dream*, London: Michael Joseph, 1975.

Mangan, Sherry, *Paris under the Swastika*, in *Life*, New York, 16 September 1940.

Mannerheim, Marshal Gustav, *The Memoirs* (trans. Count Eric Lewenhardt), London: Cassell, 1953.

Manstein, Field-Marshal Erich von, *Lost Victories*, London: Methuen, 1958.

Marder, Arthur, *Operation Menace*, London: Oxford University Press, 1976.

Mark, Jeffrey, *Mr Churchill runs the War*, in *Life*, New York, 9 December 1940.

Martienssen, Anthony, *Hitler and his Admirals*, London: Secker & Warburg, 1941.

Martin, Joe (with Robert J. Donovan), *My First 50 Years in Politics*, New York: McGraw-Hill, 1960.

Marwick, Arthur, *The Home Front*, London: Thames & Hudson, 1976.

Mason, Henry C., *The Purge of Dutch Quislings*, The Hague: Martinus Nijhoff, 1952.

Mason, Herbert Molloy, *The Rise of the Luftwaffe, 1918–40*, London: Cassell, 1975.

Mastny, Vojtech, *The Czechs under Nazi Rule*, New York: Columbia University Press, 1971.

Matthews, Very Rev. W. R., *St Paul's Cathedral in Wartime*, London: Hutchinson, 1946.

Maugham, R. C. F., *Jersey under the Jackboot*, London: W. H. Allen, 1946.

Maugham, W. Somerset, *Strictly Personal*, London: William Heinemann, 1942.

McKee, Alexander, *The Coalscuttle Brigade*, London: Souvenir Press, 1957.

Meerloo, Major A. M., *Total War and the Human Mind*, London: Allen & Unwin, 1944.

Mees, Dr H., *Mijn Oorlogsdagboek*, Rotterdam: Van De Rhee, 1945.

Mengin, Robert, *No Laurels for De Gaulle* (trans. Jay Allen), London: Michael Joseph, 1960.

Menu, General Charles, *Lumière sur les ruines*, Paris: Plon, 1953.

Mercer, Asja (with Robert Jackson), *One Woman's War*, London: Allan Wingate, 1958.

Merchant Shipping, U.K., lost by enemy action, London: H.M.S.O., 1947.

Merseyside, Bombers Over, Liverpool: Daily Post & Echo Ltd, 1943.

Metternich, Princess Tatiana, *Tatiana*, London: Heinemann, 1976.

Michel, Henri, *The Shadow War* (trans. Richard Barry), London: André Deutsch, 1972.

Michie, Allan, *Ernie Bevin, Britain's Labour Boss*, in *Life*, New York, 11 November 1940.

Minart, Colonel Jacques P. C., *Vincennes Secteur 4* (2 vols), Éditions Berger-Leyrault, 1945.

Minney, R. J. (ed.), *The Private Papers of Hore-Belisha*, London: William Collins, 1960.

Moen, Lars, *Under the Iron Heel*, London: Robert Hale, 1941.

Mollett, Ralph, *Jersey under the Swastika*, London: The Hyperion Press, 1945.

Mosley, Leonard, *Backs to the Wall*, London: Weidenfeld & Nicolson, 1971; *Lindbergh*, London: Hodder & Stoughton, 1976; *The Reich Marshal*, London: Weidenfeld & Nicolson, 1974.

Mouchotte, René, *The Mouchotte Diaries* (trans. Philip John Stead), London: Staples Press, 1956.

Muggeridge, Malcolm, *Chronicles of Wasted Time, Vol. II: The Infernal Grove*, London: Collins, 1973.

Muir, Peter, *War Without Music*, New York: Charles Scribner's, 1940.

Murphy, Robert, *Diplomat among Warriors*, London: Collins, 1964.

Murrow, Edward R., *This is London*, London: Cassell, 1961.

Myklebost, Tor, *They came as Friends* (trans. Trygve M. Ager), London: Victor Gollancz, 1943.

Nicolson, Sir Harold, *Diaries and Letters, 1939–45*, London: William Collins, 1967.

Nixon, Barbara, *Raiders Overhead*, London: Lindsay Drummond, 1943.

Nixon, St John C., *Daimler, 1896–1946*, London: Foulis, 1946.

Norris, Frank, *Free France, Poor and Paralysed, waits for Germany to Finish War*, in *Life*, New York, 16 September 1940.

O'Brien, T. H., *Civil Defence*, London: H.M.S.O./Longmans, 1955.

Oliphant, Sir Lancelot, *An Ambassador in Bonds*, London: Putnam, 1946.

Olsen, Olaf, *Two Eggs on my Plate*, London: George Allen & Unwin, 1952.

Orlow, Dietrich, *The History of the Nazi Party*, Vol. II, Newton Abbot: David & Charles, 1973.

Overstraeten, General Raoul Van, *À la Service de la Belgique*, Vol. I, Paris: Plon, 1960.

Paasikivi, Juho, *Toimintani Moskovassa ja Suomessa, 1939–41*, Porvoo: Werner Söderstrom, 1959.

Paine, Jr, Ralph Delaye, *France Collapsed from Internal Decay*, in *Life*, New York, 8 July 1940.

Palmer, Paul, *Denmark in Nazi Chains*, London: Lindsay Drummond, 1942.

Panter-Downes, Molly, *London War Notes*, London: Longman, 1972.

Parker, Robert, *HQ Budapest*, New York: Farrar & Rinehart, 1944.

Parkinson, Roger, *Peace for our Time*, London: Rupert Hart-Davis, 1971; *Blood, Toil, Tears and Sweat*, London: Rupert Hart-Davis, Macgibbon, 1973.

Parrott, Sir Cecil, *The Tightrope*, London: Faber & Faber, 1975.

Passy, Colonel, *10, Duke Street, Londres*, Monte Carlo: Raoul Solar, 1947.

Paul, Oscar D., *Farewell France!*, London: Victor Gollancz, 1941.

Pawle, Gerald, *The Secret War*, London: George Harrap, 1956; *The War and Colonel Warden*, London: George Harrap, 1963.

Paxton, Robert, *Vichy France*, London: Barrie & Jenkins, 1972.

Payne, Robert, *The Life and Death of Adolf Hitler*, London: Jonathan Cape, 1973.

Peabody, Polly, *Occupied Territory*, London: Cresset Press, 1941.

Pelz, Stephen E., *Race to Pearl Harbor*, Cambridge, Mass.: Harvard University Press, 1974.

Perau, J., *Priester im Heere Hitlers*, Essen: Ludgerus, 1952.

Perry, Colin, *Boy in the Blitz*, London: Leo Cooper, 1972.

Petrow, Richard, *The Bitter Years*, London: Hodder & Stoughton, 1974.

Picht, Werner, *The Campaign in Norway*, Prague, Orbis, 1940.

Porter, Roy P., *Uncensored France*, New York: Dial Press, 1942.

Pratt, John (ed.), *The War at Sea, 1939–45*, London: Hutchinson, 1967.

Price, Alfred, *Instruments of Darkness*, London: William Kimber, 1967.

Prüller, Wilhelm, *Diary of a German Soldier* (ed. H. C. Robbins Landon & Sebastian Leitner), London: Faber & Faber, 1963.

Pruszynski, Ksawery, *Poland Fights Back*, London: Hodder & Stoughton, 1941.

Puttkamer, Karl Jesko von, *Die Unheimliche See*, Munich: Kuehne, 1952.

Raczynski, Count Edward, *In Allied London*, London: Weidenfeld & Nicolson, 1962.

Reith, Lord, *Diaries*, London: Collins, 1975.

Reitlinger, Gerald, *The Final Solution*, London: Vallentine Mitchell, edn of 1968.

Reynaud, Paul, *In the Thick of the Fight* (trans. James D. Lambert), London: Cassell, 1955.

Richards, Denis, *The Royal Air Force, Vol. I, The Fight at Odds*, London: H.M.S.O., 1953.

Rieckhoff, H. J., *Trumpf oder Bluff*, Genf: Interavia, 1945.

Riess, Curt, *Underground Europe*, London: John Long, 1943.

Rigby, Françoise, *In Defiance*, London: Elek Books, 1960.

Ritchie, Charles, *The Siren Years*, London: Macmillan, 1974.

Robb, Nesca, *An Ulsterwoman in England*, Cambridge: The University Press, 1942.

Robertson, Terence, *The Golden Horseshoe*, London: Evans Bros., 1955.

Rohwer, Jürgen (and Hümmelchen, G.), *Chronik des Seekrieges, 1939–45*, Oldenburg: Stalling, 1968.

Rommel Papers, The (ed. B. H. Liddell Hart, trans. Paul Findlay), London: William Collins, 1953.

Roon, Ger Van, *German Resistance to Hitler* (trans. Peter Ludlow), New York: Van Nostrand Reinhold, 1971.

Roosevelt, Franklin D., *Wartime Correspondence with Pope Pius XII*, New York: Macmillan, 1947.

Roskill, Stephen, *Churchill and the Admirals*, London: William Collins, 1977; *British Naval Policy between the Wars*, London: William Heinemann, 1976.

Ross, Alan, *The Forties*, London: Weidenfeld & Nicolson, 1950.

Rothberg, Abraham, *Eyewitness History of World War II*, New York: Bantam Books, 1966.

Rothenstein, Sir John, *Brave Day, Hideous Night*, London: Hamish Hamilton, 1966.

Rouchaud, Martine, *Journal d'une Petite Fille*, Paris: Gallimard, 1945.

Rowe, Vivian, *The Great Wall of France*, London: Putnam, 1959.

Roy, Dilip Kumar, *Netaji – The Man*, Bombay: Chaupatti, 1966.

Roy, Jules, *The Trial of Marshal Pétain* (trans. Robert Baldick), London: Faber & Faber, 1968.

Roy, Pravash Chandra, *Subhas Chandra*, Rajshahi: Mitra Bros., 1929.

Royde-Smith, Naomi, *Outside Information*, London: Macmillan, 1941.

Ruby, General Edmond, *Sedan, Terre d'Épreuve*, Paris: Flammarion, 1948.

Ruge, Vice-Admiral Friedrich, *Sea Warfare* (trans. Cmdr M. G. Saunders, R.N.), London: Cassell, 1957.

Russell, William, *Berlin Embassy*, London: Michael Joseph, 1942.

Saint-Exupéry, Antoine de, *Flight to Arms* (trans. Lewis Galantière), London: William Heinemann, edn of 1955.

Salesse, Simone, *I Was a Refugee in France*, Cape Town: Galvin & Sales Ltd, 1942.

Sansom, William, *Westminster in War*, London: Faber & Faber, 1947.

Sarkar, Sudhira, *Subhas Chandra*, Calcutta: J. C. Bannerjee, 1939.

Saunders, Hilary St George, *Left Handshake*, London: William Collins, 1949.

Schellenberg, Walter, *The Schellenberg Memoirs* (ed. and trans. Louis Hagen), London: André Deutsch, 1956.

Schirach, Henriette von, *The Price of Glory* (trans. Willi Frischauer), London: Frederick Muller, 1960.

Schlabrendorff, Fabian von, *The Secret War against Hitler* (trans. Hilda Simon), London: Hodder & Stoughton, 1966.

Schmidt, Paul, *Hitler's Interpreter* (ed. R. H. C. Steel), London: William Heinemann, 1951.

Scobbie, Irene, *Sweden*, London: Ernest Benn, 1972.

Scott, Sir Harold, *Your Obedient Servant*, London: André Deutsch, 1959.

Shakespeare, Sir Geoffrey, *Let Candles Be Brought In*, London: Macdonald, 1949.

Shelton, John, *A Night in Little Park Street*, London: Britannicus Liber, 1950.

Sherwood, Robert, *The White House Papers of Harry Hopkins, Vol. I*, London: Eyre & Spottiswoode, 1948.

Shipley, Rev. S. Paul, *Bristol Siren Nights*, Bristol: Rankin Bros. Ltd, 1943.

Shirer, William, *Berlin Diary*, London: Hamish Hamilton, 1941; *The Rise and Fall of the Third Reich*, New York: Simon & Schuster, 1959; *The Collapse of the Third Republic*, London: William Heinemann, Secker & Warburg, 1970.

Sicard, Étienne, *The Battle of Mers-el-Kebir*, in *Life*, New York, 4 November 1940.

Simon, Paul, *One Enemy Only* (trans. W. G. Corp), London: Hodder & Stoughton, 1943.

Simoni, Leonardo, *Berlino, Ambasciata d'Italia*, Rome: Migliaresi, 1946.

Singh, Durlab, *The Rebel President*, Lahore: Hero Publications, 1941.

Smuts, Field-Marshal Jan C., *Selections from the Smuts Papers, Vol. VI* (ed. Jean Van Der Poel), London: Cambridge University Press, 1973.

Smyth, Brigadier, The Rt Hon. Sir John, *Leadership in War*, Newton Abbot: David & Charles, 1974.

Soloviev, Mikhail, *My Nine Lives in the Red Army* (trans. Henry C. Stevens), New York: David McKay, 1955.

Snoep, J., *Nederland in de Branding*, Dordrecht: De Longte, 1945.

Someren, Liesje Van, *Escape from Holland*, London: Herbert Jenkins, 1942.

Soubiran, André, *J'étais Médecin, avec les Chars*, Paris: Didier, 1943.

Soustelle, Jacques, *Envers et Contre Tout* (2 vols), Paris: Robert Laffont, 1950.

Spanier, Ginette, *The Long Road to Freedom*, London: Robert Hale, 1976.

Spears, Major-General Sir Edward, *Assignment to Catastrophe* (2 vols), London: William Heinemann, 1954.

Speer, Albert, *Inside the Third Reich* (trans. Richard and Clara Winston), London: Weidenfeld & Nicolson, 1976.

Stam, Wim, *Kruit en Bloesem*, Amsterdam: Bigot & Van Rossum, no date.

Stein, George, *The Waffen S.S., 1939–45*, Ithaca, N.Y.: Cornell University Press, 1966.

Stephan, Enno, *Spies in Ireland* (trans. Arthur Davidson), London: Macdonald, 1963.

Stimson, Henry C., and Bundy, McGeorge, *On Active Service in Peace and War*, New York: Harper, 1948.

St-John, Robert, *Foreign Correspondent*, London: Hutchinson, 1960.

Stout, Rex, *The Illustrious Dunderheads*, New York: Alfred Knopf, 1942.

Stowe, Leland, *A Few Thousand Nazis Seized Norway*, in *Life*, New York, 10 May 1940; *No Other Road to Freedom*, London: Faber & Faber, 1942.

Strijdbos, Jan Pieter, *De Noordvaarders*, Amsterdam: L. J. Veen, 1946.

Tanner, Väinö, *The Winter War*, Stanford, Cal.: Stanford University Press, 1957.

Taylor, A. J. P., *The Second World War*, London: Hamish Hamilton, 1975; (ed.), *Churchill – Four Faces and the Man*, London: Pelican Books, 1973; *The Origins of The Second World War*, London: Hamish Hamilton, 1961; *Beaverbrook*, London: Hamish Hamilton, 1972; *English History, 1914–45*, London: Oxford University Press, 1965.

Taylor, Telford, *The March of Conquest*, London: Edward Hulton, 1959; *The Breaking Wave*, London: Weidenfeld & Nicolson, 1967.

Teissier Du Cros, Janet, *Divided Loyalties*, London: Hamish Hamilton, 1962.

Ter Weele, Carl Frits, *Inside Holland*, in *Life*, New York, 14 October 1940.

Thiry, N., *La Belgique pendant la guerre*, Paris: Hachette, 1947.

Thomas, John Oram, *The Giant Killers*, London: Michael Joseph, 1975.

Thompson, Rear-Admiral George, *Blue Pencil Admiral*, London: Sampson Low, Marston, 1947.

Thompson, Laurence, *1940: Year of Legend, Year of History*, London: William Collins, 1966.

Tissier, Lt.-Col. Pierre, *I Worked with Laval*, London: George Harrap, 1942.

Toland, John, *Adolf Hitler*, New York: Doubleday, 1976.

Tony-Revillon, M., *Mes Carnets*, Paris: Lieutier, 1945.

Torris, J. M., *Narvik*, New York: Brentanos, 1943.

Toye, Hugh, *The Springing Tiger*, London: Cassell, 1959.

Tree, Ronald, *When the Moon was High*, London: Macmillan, 1975.

Trial of the major war criminals before the International Military

Tribunal, Nuremberg, 1947–49 (42 vols), Washington, D.C.: U.S. Government Printing Office, 1949–51.

True Story of Pearl Harbor, The, in *U.S. News and World Report*, Washington, D.C.: 11 December 1961.

True to Type: A Selection of Letters and Diaries from German Soldiers and Civilians, London: Hutchinson, 1945.

Turner, E. S., *The Phoney War on the Home Front*, London: Michael Joseph, 1961.

Tute, Warren, *The Deadly Stroke*, London: William Collins, 1973.

Twyford, Henry, *It Came to our Door*, Plymouth: Underhill, 1946.

Undset, Sigrid, *Return to the Future* (trans. Henriette C. K. Naeseth), New York: Alfred Knopf, 1942; *My Escape from Norway*, in *Life*, New York, 10 June 1940.

Upton, Anthony F., *Finland in Crisis, 1940–41*, London: Faber & Faber, 1964; *Finland, 1939–40*, London: Davis-Poynter, 1976.

Van Creveld, Martin, *Hitler's Strategy, 1940–41: The Balkan Clue*, London: Cambridge University Press, 1973.

Van Duren, Theo, *Orange Above*, London: Staples Press, 1956.

Van Heerde, H., *Tusschen Vuur en Ijzer*, Meppel: Boom & Zoon, no date.

Van Kempen, Bep, *Te Mogen Helpen*, Assen: Born, no date.

Van Paassen, Pierre, *That Day Alone*, London: Michael Joseph, 1943.

Vian, Admiral of the Fleet Sir Philip, *Action This Day*, London: Frederick Muller, 1960.

Vidalenc, Jean, *L'Exode de mai-juin, 1940*, Paris: Presses Universitaires de France, 1957.

Vogt, Benjamin, *Mennesket Vidkun och Forraederen Quisling*, Oslo: Aschehoug, 1965.

Vomécourt, Philippe de, *Who Lived to See the Day*, London: Hutchinson, 1961.

Waldeck, Countess Rosa Von, *Athénée Palace, Bucharest*, London: Constable, 1943.

Walker, David, *Death at my Heels*, London: Chapman & Hall, 1942.

Warlimont, General Walter, *Inside Hitler's Headquarters* (trans. R. H. Barry), London: Weidenfeld & Nicolson, 1964.

Warmbrunn, Werner, *The Dutch under German Occupation*, Stanford, Cal.: Stanford University Press, 1963.

Warner, Geoffrey, *Pierre Laval and the Eclipse of France*, London: Eyre & Spottiswoode, 1968.

Wassey, Michael, *Ordeal by Fire*, London: Secker & Warburg, 1941.

Waterfield, Gordon, *What Happened to France*, London: John Murray, 1940.

Watney, John, *He Also Served*, London: Hamish Hamilton, 1971.

Watson-Watt, Sir Robert, *Three Steps to Victory*, London: Odhams Press, 1958.

Watt, Donald Cameron, *Too Serious a Business*, London: Temple Smith, 1975.

Welles, Sumner, *A Time for Decision*, New York: Harpers, 1944.

Werth, Alexander, *The Last Days of Paris*, London: Hamish Hamilton, 1940.

Westphal, General Siegfried, *The German Army in the West*, London: Cassell, 1951.

Weygand, General Maxime, *Recalled To Service* (trans. E. W. Dickes), London: William Heinemann, 1952.

Wheatley, Ronald, *Operation Sealion*, Oxford: The Clarendon Press, 1958.

Wheeler-Bennett, Sir John, *Special Relationships: America in Peace and War*, London: Macmillan, 1975; *John Anderson, Viscount Waverley*, London: Macmillan, 1962; (ed.), *Action This Day*, London: Macmillan, 1968; *The Nemesis of Power*, London: Macmillan, 1953; *King George VI*, London: Macmillan, 1958.

While, Jack, *Fire! Fire!* London: Frederick Muller, 1944.

White, Theodore H. (with Annalee Jacoby), *Thunder Out of China*, London: Victor Gollancz, 1947.

White, William L., *Atlantic Crossing on U.S. Destroyer*, in *Life*, New York, 2 December 1940.

Whittington-Egan, Richard, *Liverpool Roundabout*, Liverpool: Philip, Son & Nephew, 1957.

Wilhelmina, H.R.H., Princess of the Netherlands, *Lonely but not Alone* (trans. John Peereboon), London: Hutchinson, 1964.

Williams, Francis, *A Prime Minister Remembers*, London: Heinemann, 1961.

Williams, John, *The Ides of May*, London: Constable, 1968; *The Guns of Dakar*, London: William Heinemann, 1976.

Wilson, Louis Abbott, *London Firefighter*, in *Life*, New York, 21 October 1940.

Winter, Dr Harry, *Coventry*, in *Life*, New York, 20 January 1941.

Winterbotham, Group Captain F. W., *The Ultra Secret*, London: Weidenfeld & Nicolson, 1974.

Wolfit, Sir Donald, *First Interval*, London: Odhams Press, 1954.

Woodman, Dorothy, *Europe Rises*, London: Victor Gollancz, 1943.

Woodward, David, *Front Line and Front Page*, London: Eyre & Spottiswoode, 1943.

Wrench, John Evelyn, *Immortal Years*, London: Hutchinson, 1945.

Wright, Myrtle, *Norwegian Diary*, London: Friendspeace International Relations Committee, 1974.

Wright, Robert, *Dowding and the Battle of Britain*, London: Macdonald, 1969.

Wuorinen, John, *Finland and World War II*, New York: The Ronald Press, 1948.

Young, A. P., *The 'X' Documents*, London: André Deutsch, 1974.

Young, Brigadier Desmond, *Rommel*, London: Collins, 1950.

Young, Gordon, *Outposts of War*, London: Hodder & Stoughton, 1941.

Young, Kenneth, *Churchill and Beaverbrook*, London: Eyre & Spottiswoode, 1966.

Youth at War, London: Batsford, 1944.

Zbszewski, Karl, *The Fight for Narvik*, London: Lindsay Drummond, 1940.

Zimmerman-Wolf, R. S., *Het woord als wapen*, Gravenhage: Martinus-Nijhoff, 1945.

Zoller, Albert, *Hitler Privat*, Dusseldorf: Droste, 1949.

Zuckermann, Professor Solly, *From Apes to Warlords*, London: Hamish Hamilton, 1978.

Manuscript Sources

Aitken, Sir William Maxwell, 1st Bt, 1st Baron Beaverbrook, Ministry of Aircraft Production Papers, May–Dec. 1940 (*House of Lords Record Office, London*).

Alexander, Albert Victor, Earl Alexander of Hillsborough, 1st Lord of the Admiralty, Memos and Correspondence, Feb.–Dec. 1940 (*Churchill College, Cambridge*).

Bliss, Don C., Groth, Edward M., White, J. C., & Wilson, Thomas M., Reports from the American Consulate-General, Calcutta, India, Feb.–Nov. 1940 (*U.S. National Archives, Washington, D.C.*).

Blumentritt, General Günther, Dunkirk, 1940: an unpublished study (*Author's Collection*).

Bullitt, William C., U.S. Ambassador to France, Telegrams to State Department (*U.S. National Archives, Washington, D.C.*).

Caffery, Jefferson, U.S. Ambassador to Brazil, Telegrams to State Department (*U.S. National Archives*).

Chamberlain, (Arthur) Neville, Prime Minister, 1937–May 1940, Lord President of the Council, May–Nov. 1940; Diary and Correspondence (*University of Birmingham, Warwickshire, Special Collections, and University Library, Cambridge*).

Chatfield, Sir (Alfred) Ernle Montacute, 1st Baron Chatfield, Minister for the Co-ordination of Defence, January 1939–April 1940: Miscellaneous correspondence (*National Maritime Museum, Greenwich, South London*).

Crookshank, Captain Harry Frederick Comfort, Financial Secretary to the Treasury, May–Dec. 1940: Miscellaneous Papers (*Bodleian Library, Oxford*).

Dalton, (Edward) Hugh (John Neale), Baron Dalton, Minister of Economic Warfare, May 1940–1942: Diary (*British Library of Political and Economic Science, London*).

Deichmann, General Paul, *Actions of No. II Flying Corps in the Battle of Britain. German Attacks on R.A.F. Ground Targets, 13-8-40–6-9-40: a study. Mass Day attacks on London: a monograph. Some Reasons* for the Switch to Night Bombing: an appreciation. *The Struggle for Air Superiority During Phase I of the Battle of Britain.*

First Flying Corps, Luftwaffe, Operational Orders for Attacks 'Sea of Light' and 'Loge'.

Gefechtskalendar, Air Fleets Two and Three, 1-8-40–15-9-40 (*All studies from the Luftwaffe Karlsruhe Collection, Freiberg, Germany, translated for the author by Nadia Radowitz.*)

Goering, Reichsmarschall Hermann, Conference Decisions of July 21, August 1, 3, 15 and 19 (*Luftwaffe Karlsruhe Collection, Freiburg*).

Gordon, George A., U.S. Envoy-Extraordinary and Minister Plenipotentiary to The Netherlands, Telegrams to State Department (*U.S. National Archives*).

Gort, General The Viscount, *War Diary and Official Correspondence* (*Courtesy of the late Earl of Munster*).

Grabmann, General Walter, The Fighter's Role in The Battle of Britain: a study (*Luftwaffe Karlsruhe Collection, Freiburg*).

Gray, David S., U.S. Envoy-Extraordinary and Minister Plenipotentiary to Eire, Telegrams to State Department (*U.S. National Archives*).

Greiner, Helmuth, The Battle of Britain, 4-9-40–7-9-40 (*Luftwaffe Karlsruhe Collection, Freiburg*).

Grew, Joseph C., U.S. Ambassador to Japan, Telegrams to State Department (*U.S. National Archives*).

Hoare, Sir Samuel John Gurney, 2nd Bt, Viscount Templewood, Lord Privy Seal and Member of the War Cabinet, Sept. 1939–April 1940; Ambassador to Spain from June 1940: Diary and Correspondence (*University Library, Cambridge*).

Hudson, Brigadier Charles, Diary (*Courtesy Mrs Gladys Hudson*).

Ibel, General Max, The 27th Fighter Group, Luftwaffe: a private diary (*Courtesy General Ibel*).

Kennedy, Joseph P., U.S. Ambassador to Great Britain, Telegrams to State Department (*U.S. National Archives*).

Kirk, Alexander C., U.S. Chargé d'Affaires in Germany, Telegrams to State Department (*U.S. National Archives*).

Lindemann, Professor Frederick (Lord Cherwell), The Cherwell Papers (*Nuffield College, Oxford*).

McVeagh, Lincoln, U.S. Envoy-Extraordinary and Minister Plenipotentiary to Greece, Telegrams to State Department (*U.S. National Archives*).

Margesson, (Henry) David (Reginald) Margesson, 1st Viscount Margesson, Secretary of State for War, 1940–42: Miscellaneous Papers (*Churchill College, Cambridge*).

Marquis, Sir Frederick James, 1st Earl of Woolton, Minister of Food, 1940–43: Diary and Memoranda (*Bodleian Library, Oxford*).

Mass-Observation Archive, The, File Reports, 1940 (*University of Sussex*).

Milch, Generalfeldmarschall Erhard, Report of the Inspector-General of the Luftwaffe, 25-8-40 (*Luftwaffe Karlsruhe Collection, Freiburg*).

Monckton, Sir Walter Turner, Deputy Director General, Ministry of Information, Memoranda and Reports on Internees (*Bodleian Library, Oxford*).

Morrison, Herbert Stanley, Baron Morrison of Lambeth, Minister of Supply, May–Oct. 1940; Secretary of State for Home Affairs and Home Security, 1940–45, Miscellaneous Memoranda (*Nuffield College, Oxford*).

Osterkamp, General Theo, Experiences as Fighter Leader 2 on The Channel (*Luftwaffe Karlsruhe Collection, Freiburg*).

Page, Wing-Cdr Geoffrey, Autobiography: unpublished MSS. (*Courtesy W/Cdr Page*).

Phillips, William, U.S. Ambassador Extraordinary and Plenipotentiary to Italy, Telegrams to State Department (*U.S. National Archives*).

Public Record Office, Kew, Surrey – Series CAB: Cabinet Papers – F.O.: Foreign Office Papers – H.O.: Home Office Papers – PREM: Prime Minister's Papers.

Richthofen, General The Baron von, Private Diary (*Luftwaffe Karlsruhe Collection, Freiburg*).

Salmuth, General Hans von, Private Diary (*Courtesy General von Salmuth*).

Seidemann, General Hans, Actions of No. VIII Flying Corps on the Channel Coast (*Luftwaffe Karlsruhe Collection, Freiburg*).

Sinclair, Sir Archibald Henry Macdonald, 4th Bt, 1st Viscount Thurso, Secretary of State for Air, 1940–45; Air Ministry Papers (*Public Record Office, Kew, Surrey*).

Speidel, General Wilhelm, The Western Campaign: a study (*U.S. Historical Division, Karlsruhe, Germany*).

Stanhope, James Richard, 7th Earl Stanhope, 13th Earl of Chesterfield, Lord President of the Council, 1939–May 1940: Miscellaneous Correspondence (*Kent County Archives, Maidstone, Kent*).

Steinhardt, Laurence A., U.S. Ambassador in the Soviet Union, Telegrams to State Department (*U.S. National Archives*).

United States Strategic Bombing Survey Records: including Record Group 243: interrogations of General Karl Koller, Professor Messerschmitt, Dr Albert Speer, General Werner Junck, Dr Kurt Tank, Generalfeldmarschall Hugo Sperrle, General Werner Kreipe,

General Halder, Generalfeldmarschall Albert Kesselring, Feld-marschall Wilhelm Keitel, General Adolf Galland (*U.S. National Archives*).

Wallace, Captain (David) Euan, Ministry of Transport, 1939–May 1940: Private Diary (*Bodleian Library, Oxford*).

Weddell, Alexander W., U.S. Ambassador in Spain, Telegrams to State Department (*U.S. National Archives*).

Weir, Sir William Douglas, 1st Viscount Weir, Director-General of Explosives, Ministry of Supply, 1939–41: Official Correspondence (*Churchill College, Cambridge*).

Wood, Sir (Howard) Kingsley, Secretary of State for Air, 1938–April 1940: private correspondence with Winston Churchill (*Public Record Office, Kew, Surrey*).

Index

343

344